Light My Fire

by Ian Chillcott

Light My Fire is a limited edition book.
Published in 2008 by Freebird Publishing
☎ 01293 405781 or 07941 637336
©Ian Chillcott 2008

Edited & proofed by Keith Jenkins and Lynn Chillcott
Illustrations by Sue Lane
Layout and Design by Cathy Card
Print Management by Linda Jenkins
All photography supplied by the Author unless marked.

Printed in Great Britain by
Butler, Tanner & Dennis
Caxton Road, Frome, Somerset BA11 1NF

CONTENTS

DEDICATION

For my Mum and Dad, Penny and John, thanks for putting up with me. It cannot have been easy for you at times, but I think your little boy got there in the end.

ACKNOWLEDGEMENTS

I owe them a heck of a lot more than a mere thank you, but for now that is all I can really do. A book is so much more than the name on the cover, and without a great deal of help this tome would simply not have been written.

Freebird Publishing is in its infancy, and I was there at its inception. I, however, got the easy part, all I had to do was write! Putting it all together was a task totally beyond me, so a huge thank you to my wife Lynn, Linda Jenkins, Keith Jenkins and last, but by no means least, Cathy Card. I cannot adequately express in words my gratitude.

My great friends, Adam Penning, Dave Lane, Richard Howell (aka Reg) and Chrissie Pearson. "Tis the company, not the carp, that maketh the feast!"

My 'little sister' Ruth Lockwood, for always being there when I needed guidance, and constantly reminding me of my mortality!

Tim Paisley and Jim Foster, who between them conspired to make me the writer I am today.

Steve Morgan and Kev Knight at Mainline Baits, neither of you will ever fully understand what your friendship and support have meant to me.

Cliff Fox, for giving me the opportunity I have always sought in carp fishing. Here's to the future fella.

Marc Coulson and Richard Stewart, your words of encouragement have kept me sane these past few months.

Mick Barnes and CEMEX Angling. Mick for simply being my friend, and to CEMEX for giving me the chance to chase my dreams.

Phil Jackson, Micky Foot, Richard Spencer, Captain Mike Tomkins, Terry Hearn, Steve Mogford, Chris Ball and Micky Gray, your words of encouragement and help have been greatly received.

To everyone that I have met along this incredible journey, and the part they played in the fun that has transpired.

FOREWORD

It was at Oxford Manor in early '97 when Chilly and I first shared bankspace, although he won't remember the occasion I am sure. It was one of those wonderful spring days that hinted at the glory of summer to come and he was busying himself setting up on the river bank side of the lake. We didn't know each other and I stood on the periphery of a small crowd that had gathered around this vest wearing, crew cutted and moustachioed carper who seemed about 7½ foot tall but in reality must have been a little less. I listened as he was congratulated on the surface capture of Jack and then looked on as he proceeded to blast 3 rigs into the middle of the lake, further than I had ever been able to put a bait. Well, I am a margin angler...

We next crossed paths, again at Manor, a while later; I was doing a feature with Jim Foster for what was then Catchmore Carp magazine, and Chilly was down, set up just along from us on the road bank. Jack Daniels was also in attendance and before long the stories were flowing. As anyone who has shared company with Chilly will know, he is a formidable raconteur and before long the three of us were in uncontrollable fits of laughter which echoed across the dark lake. I don't recall the 'fun police' being on shift that night, but the evening was a precursor for countless riotous bank side jollies over the next decade. For all those who lost sleep as they shared water with us I apologise – it wasn't big, and it wasn't clever, but it sure was fun!!

The evening in question culminated in something that, unbeknown to me, was to become a common theme over the years – Chilly retiring to bed early in a bit of a state! He was awoken sometime in the middle of the night as I introduced a double figure common to his sleeping face. They touched noses, Chilly yelled and it was really quite a sweet moment.

At around this time I had taken a job at Drennan, in Oxford, and was busy developing what was to become the ESP range. At the company's disposal is a truly beautiful estate lake and, as it seemed we shared the same sense of humour, I offered him a guest trip. It was September, the lake was clear and weedy and we caught a couple of fish – Chill bagging a stunning old prehistoric mirror that I had never seen before or since, and a lovely dark common. What I remember most about the trip though, was a rerun of the Manor drinking. You see I thought that somebody of Chilly's' size and experience would be more than a little accomplished at drinking. How wrong could I be – barely had we finished the second bottle of Rioja than he was mumbling and slurring and not long after that, he retired to his pit. We were awoken a few hours later as one of his rods roared off in the pitch darkness. I got to the rod a tad before he did (!) and shouted friendly words of encouragement, while dutifully manning the net. The next thing I knew was that Chilly was doing very well controlling one rod, while totally neglecting the other – bladder fit to burst and unable to wait until the fish was landed, he chose to unleash himself where he stood and the first I knew of it was when a hot jet of pee sprayed over my bare feet!!

Chilly is one of those anglers who it seems to me, is part of an ever decreasing breed. Here is a guy who gets so insanely excited about a carp that, whether he has caught it or not, seems fit to burst into flames just thinking about it. Indeed, one of my all time favourite carp fishing images is of him racing up the bank like a coked up break-dancer who has been electrocuted after catching his dream, Horton's Shoulders. To me, that is what it is all about – for Chilly, the other guys in this book, and to many of you reading this, carp play a hugely important part in our lives and you will never see him sullenly staring at the camera across the broad back of a carp, you will never find him seemingly nonchalant after a capture, and you would never find him reluctant to share in another anglers celebration of victory. Chilly is one of those anglers to whom the capture of a carp means everything. In these days where passion seems in short supply, his never-ending enthusiasm and boyish excitement are wonderful to behold.

It is perhaps not surprising that when I finally summitted a particularly arduous piscatorial mountain, the first person I dialled was Chilly. He had shared every drop of pain and sweat along the way, and had promised that he would be there to witness the moment I held my obsession aloft. Not only that, he is one of few who, like me, could spontaneously combust at the sight of an ancient, long and dark carp.

He waited and waited through a near three year period, offering unfaltering words of encouragement, at times having far more faith in my ability than I did. When it finally happened, my phone emitted something I didn't expect – a foreign ring tone. Alas, after all that time, at the moment of triumph, Chilly was in France, angling at Rainbow so it was never possible to share the relief and ecstasy of a long overdue final whistle.

Not wishing to state the obvious, Chill is clearly a very talented carp angler who is capable of catching from any type of venue using just about any tactic, but I think one of his greatest strengths is his endurance – a man who will never give up the pursuit of his most desired, and if that carp is a cunning fox, then Chilly is the entire pack of hounds.

And then there is ECHO. Don't worry I won't get all political - as we know, sadly too many anglers simply couldn't care less. However, since forming the organisation, countless carp have been saved from death and suffering. For services to carp fishing there could be few more weighty donors than Chillcott and the legacy of ECHO will be around for a very long time to come. Indeed, I believe the entire sport owes him a sincere debt of gratitude for what he has achieved.

Throughout the course of this book, you will get to meet the wonderful Lynn, although how often I am not quite sure. I say this because Chill does like to keep his private life, well, private. And why shouldn't he? The obstacles that they have overcome together are nothing short of incredible, and although these are private matters, it is the mark of the man that they are so devoted to each other and stand strong in the face of all that is put in front of them.

To those looking in, it could perhaps paint a less caring image – a man who is constantly in pursuit of his obsession while his wife is too rarely firing on all cylinders. What most of you won't realise is that this remarkable woman demands that he goes angling and is so stubborn in her love for her man that she refuses to let anything get in the way of them leading 'normal lives'. Believe me, there have been times when Chilly wanted to stay at home, but was virtually pushed out of the door and sent on his next mission. When he is successful Lynn weeps tears of joy (as does Chill) and when he isn't, she shares in his frustrations. To me, they are in so many ways the ultimate partnership.

If you are ever lucky enough to meet this amazing woman, a lady of such extraordinary strength and stature, then prepare yourself because, and I don't say this lightly, she permanently changed my outlook on life for the better. Never was it truer to say that behind every great man....

Throughout all the laughs we have shared, we have also had a few fallouts along the way and I think that is one of the great strengths of our friendship. No grudges or resentment are ever harboured and before long we are roaring with laughter once again. I have no doubt that Chilly will describe just what an unbearable arse I can be at times, and there have been occasions when things have become rather fraught between us! One of the main reasons is that I am one of those guys that just has to get his sleep while Chilly is the opposite extreme in every way. Not only can he do without sleep for long periods, but to my eternal annoyance and frustration he is able to sleep soundly either on a bed of nails or on a razorblade – he really isn't bothered which. The problem is once he has quickly slipped into the deepest slumber imaginable, he begins to make this sound. Now I think this could (by a half deaf person who had no mastery of description) be very loosely described as snoring, but believe me it is unlike anything you will have ever experienced before. I have heard it from well over 100 yards on a stormy night, so you can imagine what it is like when we share a swim. Well, it would cause a married couple to fight, let alone a pair of rough old carp anglers!

On those occasions when Chilly has lost his temper and threatened to physically deactivate me, my reaction is always the same. I tell him that if he does that (and the outcome would indeed be boringly predictable), not only would he lose a source of amusement, but also one of his ears and the ability to pleasure his wife. That usually stops him in his tracks...

Of course it isn't just me that the occasionally mildly opinionated (!) Chilly has fallen out with, and I know Laney has shared the ring for an evening or two of raised hackles and voices. Talking of Laney, one of my favourite Chilly memories was the result of us joining forces one wine soaked night at Chilham. It was the social get together the night before one of those 'Fish with the Idiots' events (us lot being the Idiots obviously), and as none of us were fishing until the next day, we were able to indulge freely. The evening culminated in one of the most unexpected and amazing things I had ever witnessed – by the time dawn arrived Chilly was the last man standing, having consumed an epic quantity of hops, malt and barley. For once, he truly was unstoppable.

In fact, that last bit was a total lie. Not surprisingly, normal service was resumed and Chilly had sloped off to bed rather early, stumbling off into the darkness something like a zombie flesh eater with both Achilles severed.

His destination was the Chilham signing in shed which he rather foolishly told us earlier was going to be his hotel room for the night.

Laney and I carried on gargling export when suddenly I hatched an idea. 'Have you got any bulk spools of line in your truck mate?' What would have once been the most stupid question on earth now seemed a realistic enough enquiry to the new found tackle mogul, and Laney didn't disappoint. 'Penners I have got EVERYTHING in my truck!' So off we trotted, keen to torture the man who claimed to be a para, but which I had come to realise was actually short for paralytic and not paratrooper.

Pushing nettles aside we peered through the cobwebbed window, and before us he lay, SnoreZilla, flat on his back and totally out for the count. Laney was clasping a 1000m spool of 15lb line and so we began to execute a plan so clever, so cunning, and so devilish, that Diablo himself would have been proud.

By doing half a lap of the shed each and then passing the spool over like a relay runner's baton, we began to slowly cocoon the shed from top to bottom in line. Considering the state we were in, it really was a work of art. Only Chilly could have slept through our uncontrollable fits of giggles and the occasional stumble off course into the nettles, as dizziness, combined with the poison we had consumed, left our sense of direction spinning like a roulette wheel. I have not worked out how many times you need to run around an 8 x 6 shed to empty a 1000m spool of line, but I can assure you it is not a feat I would be keen to repeat! The end result was a prison from which it would be impossible to enter or leave without either a blow torch or a chainsaw, and we sat back on the gravel, bathed in sweat, admiring our handiwork. It was at this point that Chilly awoke to respond to one of very few things indeed, that could have roused him – a call of nature! He banged and shook the door with the strength and fury of a semi sedated Miss Marple, and weakly muttering 'what have you done? Let me out you bastards', over and over again.

Eventually, deafened by our roars of laughter as we rolled around listening to his predicament, he eventually found a small gap at the bottom of the door to relieve himself. We took pictures of the puddle as it quickly increased in size, before retiring to our bedchairs – he would be fine where he was until the morning or maybe later if we felt inclined!

There are many other stories I could tell; our plans for maggot domination at Frimley that resulted in nearly three gallons escaping into my car, the wild bears in the forests of darkest France, and laughing until we cried in America. Maybe one or two of those will be told later in this book; what great memories the last decade of friendship have given me, and I feel fortunate to be able to call Chill my mate.

I guess you can tell by the theme of this introduction that our main objective is always to enjoy ourselves, and while this book will no doubt capture many emotions, I know that Chilly's greatest satisfaction will come from the reader putting the book down and thinking 'Man, that was FUN'!

Adam Penning
August 2008

INTRODUCTION

I could never have envisaged that one day I would write a book about my carp fishing exploits, but here I am finishing off the last part. I could also not have imagined how hard some sections would be to re-live, it has been a very emotional roller coaster ride. You see, I never wanted carp fishing to take over my life, but at times I have let it, and that has only ended in disaster. My pursuit of carp has always been about fun, a pastime that allowed me to escape from the real world, and come to terms with the trials and tribulations that that creates. The real world, now there's a thought. I have no doubt that I have carried a lot of emotional baggage around with me, and much of that has to do with the Army. I wasn't sure that those particular issues belonged in the pages of a carp fishing book. Losing many good friends along the way has been a very difficult thing to live with, but I don't believe that glorifying this tome with stories of their passing would be the right thing to do. These demons, have at times, turned me into a bit of a monster, and in some respects my angling allowed me to become something I hated. Carp fishing, by its very nature, gives me plenty of time to think, and at times the only way I could deal with my gremlins was to look at the world through the bottom of a bottle. That said, and although I lived through those horrible periods, my fishing has also given me a chance to take stock of my life and make the necessary adjustments to turn me into the (hopefully) better person I am today. For much of my existence I settled everything with my fists, but over the course of time I have realised the futility of that, which all means that I have arrived at a very tranquil and contented period in my life. Just what I have always wanted. What you are about to read is not all about big carp, and neither is it solely about carp fishing, it is a blood and guts look at reality, my reality, and the part that my obsession has played in it over the years.

There is also the not insignificant part that my friends have played. Without their support and company, the journey would have been very boring. I have not included guest chapters as such, within these pages, but there can be no better person to tell some of the stories than those that the tale revolves around. Keith's remarkable twelve months at Horton and Wrasbury are, for the first time, visited in considerable detail, as is Reg's tale of an Oxfordshire monster. I would dearly have loved something from Laney and Adam, but Dave is writing his own story and Adam, as always, didn't want to give the game away for the anglers fishing the water I wanted him to write about. A very magnanimous gesture indeed!

And the rest of the book? Well, it's about me of course, and the incredible highs and lows that I have experienced along the way. It's been hard, too damn hard at times, but most of all it has been fun. So, may I suggest you tighten your seat belt another notch, and hold on tight. It's been one hell of a ride!!

Section 1

The Road to Hell

Chapter 1

Please Allow Me to Introduce Myself

The plane heaved itself from the tarmac, and began to bank steeply as it drew away from Aldergrove airport. I was leaving a week early from a six month tour of Northern Ireland. The trip itself had been the quietest of the nine I had done previously, but that does nothing to lessen the impact that such tours have on your nerves. It is hard to describe just how relieved I was to be leaving. Unbeknown to me, however, this would be the last time I would ever make this journey. Life was just about to take a serious change of direction. As I sat and watched the land quickly disappearing from view, I caught a glimpse of Lock Kneagh, a huge expanse of water that dominates the province and I couldn't help smiling when I thought what it would be like to carp fish such a place. There are no carp in there of course, but isn't it strange how we all look at any piece of water and dream? Northern Ireland had taken up much of my army life through the 1980's and the first half of the 90's, and as I strained to watch the last of its beautiful countryside slip from view, I realised how stunning it was. A place filled with the most amazing and friendly people, who had been living in terror for years because of the actions of a mindless and evil minority. I had given my pound of flesh, as it were, and in some small way I hope I have contributed to its peaceful future, but as we disappeared into the clouds I rested my head on the back of my seat and thought of the many friends who had not made this journey home. What a terrible price to pay. Although these soldiers are never far from my mind, I have always been the kind of guy that looks to the future. That said, whenever I am on my way home I tend to think back on my life, and reflect just how lucky I have been.

I had married my wife Lynn in the March of 1994 - a marriage that came about because, for the first time in my life, I believed I had a relationship that could last. But it didn't start off too well. Up until our first meeting I was probably the most horrible human being you could ever have met. Let me explain. I passed my parachute course in 1978 and from that point on I believed I was the baddest and meanest son of a bitch that ever walked the face of the planet, which is exactly what the instructors had wanted me to think. Like most things in life though, I took things a little too far! I had always worked hard, as I think anyone who knew me then would testify, but I had a penchant for playing just as enthusiastically. It was during one of my 'play hard' sessions that Lynn first clapped eyes on her future husband, although at the time I would think that nothing could have been further from her mind. I had ended up, as I normally did, in a very famous Airborne watering hole called Fives Wine Bar. It was like something out of the old wild west, a real spit and sawdust kind of place. No chairs to sit on, not much paint on the walls and generally full of drunken Para's. Hell, even the DJ was set up in the roof behind bullet proof glass!! The nights would inevitably end up in a fight, and it was whilst I was engaged in one of my favourite off duty delights, that our first meeting took place. Battered and thoroughly bruised, I ended up in the gutter outside the infamous pub, at which point several ladies tried to step over me. Most of them I knew, but one I did not. Lynn said something, and the others tried desperately to lead her away from the prostrate Para. I really wanted to say something profound, but was in no position to do so, and off they went. It didn't get any better on our next meeting either, which was in one of the local Indian restaurants. This time I was asleep in my curry! Over the course of time, and for reasons I cannot fully fathom, we got to know each other and the courting began. I could tell things were getting serious because I stopped my hell raising, and most surprisingly of all, started

Lynn and I just as the courting began

to give my carp fishing a whole lot more thought. It wasn't long before we were sharing a flat in the town centre together. Life was good, and it was about to get a whole lot better when she allowed me to move my fishing gear in. Now that was handy. What wasn't so handy, and it took me a little time to find out, was that Lynn was not well. Infact for several years she had been suffering from cancer; breast cancer to be precise. But even then neither of us realised just how much this would shape our future. I took Lynn fishing as often as possible, but after a while it became obvious that she could no longer cope

I started to give my carp fishing a whole lot more thought

with nights on the bank. Through it all, though, she encouraged me to go, and to this day has never complained about a husband that is as about as obsessive as it is possible to be. Everything came to a head six days after we were married in Plymouth. It had been the best day of my life, surrounded by family and friends, however, on our return to Aldershot we were summoned to a meeting with her breast surgeon. To cut a very long story short, he informed us that unless he carried out a double mastectomy then Lynn, in all probability, would be dead within six months. "Talk about it", he said, "and let me know". He left us together in the

Now that was handy!

room and waited outside. It was a hammer blow. Lynn said she would understand if I wanted a divorce. Oh really! What ever was going to happen, all I wanted was for her to live through this, and so the decision was made. How I managed to keep it all together, I will never know, but it probably has more to do with her strength than mine. Six weeks later and I was saying my goodbyes as they were about to carry out the operation. Lynn has always looked after herself, and even ran a gymnasium in Aldershot for many years. To that end the surgeons have always pushed the boat out as far as her well being is concerned. Instead of leaving her with only scars to reflect on, they had agreed to carry out reconstructive surgery, and in that way no one would know what had happened, and that suited Lynn perfectly. She has never wanted anyone to know just how ill she is, and will go to any lengths to hide the truth. I have always said that I need not look any further than her for inspiration! From that moment on, it was obvious that everything else would have to take a back seat, and that included my army career. As keen as both Lynn and I were to keep on going, I could simply no longer function as I had once done. Promotion went by the way side, as did my chances for more trips away. Thinking back, I was probably aware of this on my flight home from NI, but I wasn't quite ready to accept that just yet. For all of my adulthood I had lived the military life. I had achieved just about everything I wanted to, and visited a whole host of countries around the world. All the major jungles and deserts had seen me stomping through them, as had many of the flash spots from time to time. To say it had been exciting would grossly understate it all.

For all of my adulthood I had lived the military life

Malaysia, and another year away

And what of that time away? Well, as you can imagine, it had the most dramatic effect on the amount of time I could go fishing, but you will hear no complaint from me. I am a great believer that life throws you a set of chips, and it is up to us to deal with them. So often I hear people complaining that they have little time to fish. I can think of several occasions, certainly in the 80's, when I was sent away to some far flung corner of the globe at the beginning of June, not returning until December of that year. A whole seasons angling gone. Military life is certainly not

for the carp angler, I can tell you! In saying that though, I have been fortunate to fish all over the place, and for a whole host of exotic species. Marlin, sailfish, grouper, snappers and barracuda are just some of the many fish I have caught, and it was great fun. The problem I have is that I have a love of carp, and everything I seemed to do always led me back down that path. How bloody marvellous!

I have caught a whole host of exotic species

Aldershot is ideally placed for the would-be carp fisherman. Yateley is only ten minutes up the road and Horton and Wrasbury a twenty minute drive, but for now these places were the stuff of dreams. Thankfully, the area close to my barracks was, and still is, blessed with an abundance of carp lakes. Indeed, Aldershot Garrison runs its own fishing club. The reasons for this hark back to one of the most fundamental military philosophies, which is to dominate the ground that you are occupying. The garrison itself has been in existence for a few hundred years and, in order to control the area, the military had bought most of the land that surrounds it. Think of it rather like a moat that surrounds a castle. By doing so, security can be somewhat assured, and on this land we had some lakes. One that will be the focus of our attention for a while was dug in 1962, the reason for this was to cap a rubbish tip, and this now forms the high ground around a third of the lake. Chalk Farm was to play a major role in my development as a carp fisher, and if I am anything of a carp angler then it is because of the things I learnt at this lake and one other. Just up the road at Farnborough are a series of pits, very imaginatively named, Pit One to Pit Five. Don't let the dull names detract from the impact that they have had, not only on my fishing, but on carp fishing as a whole. For the purposes of this story I will be concentrating on Pit Five, truly the most special lake I have ever fished.

I first became aware of Chalk Farm when I went to Aldershot in 1978. At the time it was match fished quite heavily, the main quarry being bream, but the lake held a few stunning Crucians, and it was these that I spent much of my down time chasing around. It really was the centre of my angling universe, and I angled nowhere else for a couple of years. At the time it looked as if the lake was miles from anywhere, and you could really get a sense of isolation. Slowly, however, this would change drastically, and so would its inhabitants. Bear in mind here that I hadn't really ever set my stall out for carp. Indeed, I had caught so few I could hardly be considered a carp angler. Now, without delving into a rather murky past and, rather predictably, telling you that when I was fishing as a boy I saw a carp, and a carp angler was born, I think it best to say that the first picture that I ever saw of a carp was Richard Walker and his

Chalk Farm

record 44lb common carp. That picture was indelibly imprinted in my brain, but it would be many years before I would realise a lifetime's ambition.

During the early part of 1980, I decided to sever my contact with my familiar world, and set out on a life changing adventure that would take up the next six years of my life. That story however, is for another time maybe, but doesn't belong in the pages of

Walker and Clarissa – A dream that was to last many years

a carp fishing book, and I would suggest that one of the main reasons for that is that I did not land or angle for a single carp during that time, so it will remain untold for now. On my return to Aldershot in 1986 things had changed somewhat. In 1981 and 1982 the lake had received its two stockings of carp, and what stunners they were. Their appearance, though, brought up an interesting story, and one that shows how the army operated in those days. I'll not mention any names here for fear of embarrassing those involved. At the time the lake was open to both military and civilians, a situation that did not sit well with the predominantly army members (of which I was one). The lake was there for their recreation, and returning from a trip and not being able to even get a swim made for some bad feelings. One civilian member, however, was breeding carp and he was approached about providing some for the lake. This he did, and they turned out to be some of the best looking Galician strain of carp I, or anyone else, had ever set eyes on. Shortly after the second lot went in, the then committee decided that it would close its doors to civilians and the fish supplier was never allowed to fish for his own carp. Charming! That said, it did mean that the military had the lake to themselves, just the way it was always intended to be. Moving back to Aldershot was a major upheaval, but I was keen

The start of a life changing adventure

to reacquaint myself with the lake. Not before, of course, sampling the delights of fighting and drinking my way around the town centre pubs! At least that side of things hadn't changed, only the cast of characters. Life was hectic, but I did spend a lot of my free time trying to do some angling. The Basingstoke Canal saw me creeping along its banks from time to time, mainly with a spinning rod, but it was obvious that there were plenty of carp to angle for. That stretch of water had changed dramatically from the time I arrived as a young squaddie. It was so much cleaner. I remember very well on our early morning runs, swimming across it dodging shopping trolleys, dead dogs and any number of turds! Eventually, though, I started to get a little direction to my fishing. I had obviously joined the Garrison Club, but I had also bought myself a Redlands ticket that allowed me access to Pit 3 at Farnborough. As keen as I was to start chasing the Crucians once again in Chalk Farm, I had been a little disappointed to find out that they had been massively affected by the introduction of the Galician carp. Although at the time they were not that big, I did have some fun on my light gear. The battles,

The Basingstoke Canal saw me creeping along its banks from time to time

unfortunately, often ended with a broken line flapping in the wind (a similar fate experienced by the match anglers). Indeed it wasn't too long before they stopped fishing competitions there; they just couldn't land the fish they were hooking. What I did find of interest was that when a match was being fished the best place to do my own angling was in the peg that had received the most bait on a Sunday morning. It was where the carp ended up. One other interesting carp location device came courtesy of the RAF. Being a Paratrooper meant that I had to do a certain number of jumps a year to maintain my parachute pay. To that end, for many years the RAF had been using an old barrage balloon with a cage fitted below it to enable us to keep our hand in, as it were. This was sent up 750 feet into the air with four jumpers on each lift. Basically, when the cage came to rest a dispatcher would oversee your descent back to earth. They could never understand why I insisted on doing more jumps than anyone else and that I always wanted to be the last to jump. The reason made perfect sense to me. You see, Queens Avenue (where the jumps took place) was only a stones throw from Chalk Farm, and a vantage point of 750 feet was just about the best observation post a carp angler could imagine. Believe it or not I lost count of the amount of times I was on the fish simply because I could see them from the balloon. Mad or what? That said, I did spend a fair amount of time fishing Pit 3, simply because it had bigger fish in it. Not many, I might add, five commons and two mirrors (I guess I have always been a sucker for punishment!). Although the story of my fishing there is somewhat uninteresting, there was one particularly painful story.

A post match carp and quite possibly Chalk Farms first twenty pounder

For some strange reason, I had decided to get myself married. Don't ask me why, because I have absolutely no idea. It just seemed like a good thing to do at the time. It was all over within a year anyway, and carp angling had everything to do with the relationships' demise. That, along with the fact that the said female grew more heads than a Hydra! Anyway, for company I had bought myself a dog, a Rottweiler. Living only a short walk from the lake in married quarters meant that I could spend all my free time at the pond. I had been doing so for a couple of months, but every time I did I had to take the dog home before I could settle down for the night. I had plenty of company there, because the place was normally rammed out with pike anglers (there were some big pike in there at the time). On this particular day I was fishing along side a couple of guys who have since become good mates, Micky Foot and his mate Sym. It was getting towards doggy home time, and I had asked Mick to look after my rods, which he kindly agreed to do. Bear in mind here that I had yet to catch one of the few carp in the lake, but I think they were quite impressed with my determination actually. So off I went, dog through the door, quick argument, and I was soon making my way back to my swim. On arrival I was met by one concerned looking Mick. "How hard do you hit", were his first words. My heart sank, and I was tempted just to smack him there and then. No sooner than my back was turned, I got a take. He had landed the smaller of the two mirrors that lived in the lake. I was gutted as you can imagine, but could not bring myself to have

The Pit 3 Piking Crew, Mick Foot is second on the left

a picture with the fish. I had not landed it so it would have to go back. They insisted, and I eventually had a very grumpy picture taken. I still wish I had not. A salutary lesson about leaving your rods in the hands of others, perhaps?

Fishing Pit 3, I soon got to know some of the guys on the fabled Pit 5, as they would pop in for a chat on their way further up the lane. Their stories of carp that were almost impossible to catch had me fired up, but it was unlikely that I would get a ticket. That was until a few months later when one became available, and they asked would I like it? Would I ever! I had to make a call to the member who was going to give up his ticket. His name was Chris Sandford, and some of you may recognise the name. I have no idea if he was involved in it then, but he now deals a lot in antique fishing tackle, and has done a fair amount of TV work. Although he had caught a few fish from the lake, he felt that the sightings of big uncaught monsters were the result of someones' day dreaming. I wasn't bothered about the size of the fish, just that they were hard to catch and the mystery that surrounded them, something that still fires me up to this day. The ticket was paid for, and I looked forward to casting a line. At the time I had little idea just how much the lake would influence the future, but one thing for sure, though, I immediately fell in love with the place. Picture, if you will, a miniature Savay. The lake was about 14 acres with lots of long islands that created intimate channels in which you had to be as stealthy as possible. It taught me so much. Couple all of that with many stunning lily beds and features galore, and it was little wonder I was under its spell.

I really didn't want to have my picture taken

My first session there just happened to coincide with Bonfire Night 1988. I was excited and couldn't wait to get started. There was access to one of the many islands, and this is where I set up. And then the most shocking thing happened only five hours after I had made my first cast...I got a bite! It will be hard for some of you to imagine just how heart stopping a moment that was, as we now live in an age where carp fishing can appear so easy, but I was now playing a carp from an impossible lake. The 19lb mirror finally succumbed to my feeble efforts, and rolled into the outstretched net. It was a definitive moment in my carp fishing life, and as the fireworks lit up the night sky, I had a couple of quick pictures taken before slipping her gently back into her home. I didn't know it at the time, but the lake was going to help me rid myself of a huge burden, namely the afore mentioned Hydra. At the start of 1989, I was to be tied to a job that would keep me in the barracks for the foreseeable future. This in turn would allow me a lot more fishing time. The marriage was doomed already, but I could find no way to get rid of the damn woman. I had not lived in a house for more than ten years and, to be frank, I was never really designed to do so. Couple that with the fact that she could not understand my passion for fishing, and you start to get the picture. As the weather warmed up through the

At 19lb it was a definitive moment in my carp fishing life

My first surface caught 20lb carp at 20.12

spring, I practically lived on the lake. I would do my days work and then change into my fishing clothes. I could then cycle to the lake and get myself onto an island where my fishing gear was stashed. It was rather pleasant to fish the nights and weekends away from the constant nagging (remember, we didn't have mobile phones in those days). I could then reel in in the mornings, and cycle back to the barracks. After a quick shower, a shave and a change into my uniform, I could then do another days work. Heaven!! It was around this time that I caught my first twenty pound carp off the surface, a moment I shared with a fellow by the name of Richard Cracknell. Richard had been fishing the lake for a while, and it was great to have someone around who understood what that meant to me. Try as I might, the Hydra still refused to leave and this way of life lasted for several months - then the army offered me a life line. My boss called me into his office one day and asked if I would like to go to Kenya for a while? Oh yes please! I immediately drove to my house and told her that I would be away for some time, and wouldn't it be great if she wasn't around when I got back? All I could hope for was that she would eventually get the message. I busied myself grafting hard for a few months, until it was time to fly home. I had, mercifully, heard nothing for a while, and it was with some trepidation that I eventually arrived at the married quarters. As I pushed the key into the door there was that marvellous echoing sound of an empty house. Hoorah! The trouble was, the Hydra had taken everything. All that was left was a portable TV and my fishing tackle piled up in the living room. I was ecstatic, but the woman had left me

Buffalo hunting in Kenya

one last, very sad surprise. On the floor was a big pile of ripped up pictures and no negatives. All of my fishing memories had been wiped out in one nasty gesture. As much as I couldn't understand why she didn't like me fishing, she sure knew how much it meant to me. I probably only have myself to blame, but for now all I wanted to do was get back to the lake...like you do!

The ensuing years drifted by in a blur of military and fishing activity, but I still had time to find myself involved with one more disastrous relationship. Now, I am as red blooded as the next man, and as much as I love my fishing, there are other aspects of life that need to be explored just as thoroughly. I simply couldn't imagine going through life without contact with the opposite sex. In those days, though, it was not for any intellectual reasons, or a need to be with someone, oh no. It was all about a little bit of how's your father! And this time around that is exactly what I got, trouble was she was as mad as a bag of frogs. Fishing was a complete enigma to her, and the more I went the madder she got. I eventually ended up moving in with her, and that was probably the worst thing I could have done. It didn't help matters too much that the military side of things was fairly unstable too. The Airborne Brigade had been on standby so many times for the Gulf War, no one knew if they were coming or going...literally! This mad situation lasted more than a year, by which time things had really come to a head. I needed to get away from the crazy cow, and I also needed a change in my army career. Both of which I subsequently got in 1992. The army thing improved greatly when I changed my job, but once again my fishing tackle was going to take another beating. I had been away for a few weeks and during that time I had informed the mad one that things were now well and truly over. On my return, however, I was greeted with the sight of not only my pictures having been destroyed, but all my fishing tackle as well. Now I was in a bit of a pickle. I moved back into the Sergeants Mess, and set about re-newing all of my gear. Once again carp fishing was about to come to the rescue of my sanity, but not before I had got my fill of the single life in down town Aldershot of course. So, situation normal, drinking, fighting, females and fishing. And not necessarily in that order.

Once again carp fishing rescued my sanity

Now, you would think that fishing would be an ideal pastime for a soldier, but you will be surprised at how few anglers there were around me at the time. No one could really understand my obsession, and I was constantly having the mickey taken out of me. That's not to mention getting myself into trouble when the angling kind of took over from time to time. It was probably quite a strange excuse to many officers that I simply had to take a picture of a big fish I had caught in the night. It didn't go down too well I can tell you! In saying that, though, there have been occasions when it has stood me in good stead. In the early nineties I was seconded to work with the Welsh Guards on their six month trip to Belize, along with six other guys from Aldershot. It was a bit of a culture shock, as the Guards operated somewhat differently to what I had been used to. My only saving grace was that 29 Royal Marine Commando's were also there providing artillery support. You may not be aware that there is a lot of friction between Marines and Para's and, to be honest with you, I did nothing on that trip to make matters any better. On the particular day in question the six of us had initiated an impromptu Airborne Forces Day, something the Para's celebrate every year. It looked quite like the film The Great Escape where Steve McQueen and his American colleagues celebrate Independence Day. We finished it all off with a free fall demonstration from the toilet block roof. That didn't go down too well either, however, that evening we

No one in the army could really understand my obsession

were invited to the Marines bar for a quiz night. They really did have entertainment sorted, including a band, lead guitarist and all. The quiz was to be contested between the two warring factions, and eventually came down to the last question. Things had been heated up to this point, and it was about to get a whole lot worse. We needed to get this one right to take the trophy but, as they pulled the question from the box, they briefly looked at it and all burst into fits of laughter. We were worried. The quiz-master started to read. "What is the Latin name for the fresh water fish the pike?" I jumped into the air and roared. This made the atmosphere even tenser. When things had settled down a little, an expectant silence fell on the place. I replied with all the dignity I could muster (not much to be honest), Esox Lucius! There was a moment's hush, before all merry hell broke loose. Bloody hell what a scrap that was! Sadly out numbered, we took a bit of a beating, but fishing had once again saved the day.

By now I had been splitting my time between Chalk Farm and Pit 5. I had fished occasionally at other lakes, but it seemed best, with my hideously limited time, to concentrate on the places I knew best. I even got talked into fishing on the Car Park Lake at Yateley for a week by my old mate Jeff Pink. Why, I shall never know, but I did and had never felt so out of my depth in all my life. The miracle of it all, was that I actually hooked a fish. In all probability it was one of two, either Heather or Chunky. I had found them both grazing on the works bank bar and had hurriedly positioned a bait there. Fifteen minutes later I was playing a carp, but it came adrift in the weed some time later. I ran for home later that day. The only other thing of note is a very painful memory. Jeff had arrived one evening after work and had set about leading around to find a clear spot in the incredibly weedy lake. I stood behind him, watching as he got more and more frustrated. Just as I was taking the piss for the hundredth time, the lead he was desperately trying to pull from the weed came loose. Under incredible tension the lead had shot from the water like a bullet. It missed his hip by an inch, and caught me full-square in the bollocks! I dropped like a stone; I really cannot remember ever being in so much pain. At first Jeff was concerned, but that soon changed to hysterical laughter when he realised I wasn't going to die! My most prized possession swelled to three times its normal size (I only wish it had stayed that way), and was unusable for weeks. At every tackle shop I visited for a good while after, I was presented with a cricket box with 'Chilly's 4oz lead protector' written on it. Sympathy has always been in short supply in carp fishing! I promised myself I would return when I was able, to give it a little more of my attention. And so it was, whilst Lynn and I were courting, I spent some quality time fishing two remarkable lakes...and having fun!

During my stints at Chalk Farm I had seen the lake produce its first double and then its first twenty pounder. With so many carp in the lake it seemed as if they would surely get no bigger. They did of course, and at every turn the fish gave me more reason to wonder at their fortitude. Civilians had by now been allowed back into the club, and to be honest I could see nothing wrong with the situation. Until, of course, they started to actually run the place. The army was a predominately match orientated club, and as soon as the carp became too big to match fish for, they lost all interest in the lake. Indeed, they even began to add to its problems. At the back of the lake used to be a small, shallow bay. It was no more than two feet in depth and was a brilliant place to do some stalking. At some stage the club decided that they would block this off and dig it out. The intention was to create a small lake on which to hold matches. What happened in the end was that they created an abomination to the word angling. They stuffed it full of small carp, and there they spent their time dying because of over stocking. Some grew, of course, and these were then chucked into the main lake. It was already heavily stocked, and it was this constant influx of fish that stopped Chalky from reaching its true potential. Most of those responsible still walk around to this day unaware of the travesty they have caused. Dick heads!! I even had a go at running the place myself,

I spent some quality time fishing two remarkable lakes

which proved to be a big mistake. I have spent my life sticking it to the man, and for a while I was the man. I don't think I could ever run a water again. God, the whinging nearly drove me mad, but fair play to all of those that do. It wasn't long before I had somewhat hurriedly passed on that poisoned chalice.

What this did mean was that from 1993 I could simply concentrate on my fishing. This was something that, until now, I had never been able to do. The blessing, of course, came with a price. Don't they always? Lynn was becoming increasingly unwell; the cancer had taken hold in other areas. This in turn had an even more dramatic effect on my army career, but once again events conspired to make things a little easier. Having spent my entire adult life serving with the Airborne Forces meant that I had acquired something of a good relationship with everyone. My friends came to the rescue. Having already been passed over for promotion I watched as others made their way to the top. I have picked out two people that understood; one, what I had given to the Brigade over the years; and two, just how poorly Lynn actually was. Capt Steve Morgan and Regimental Sergeant Major Dave Catchpole called me into a meeting one day. The bottom line was that my role would be scaled down to absolutely nothing so that I could concentrate on caring for Lynn. I must admit that I was surprised when Steve said that if she was okay,

The Torpedo at a little over ten pounds, it went on to be a thirty

Blimey, if you insist!

I should ensure I did a bit of fishing. Blimey, if you insist! I don't think either of them will ever fully understand what that gesture meant to Lynn and I, but we shall be eternally grateful. The army can be, and had been for me, a very harsh environment. I am proud of the things I achieved, and the things that I was part of, but it seemed that that was now over. I could now concentrate on the two things that had brought some sanity to my life. My wife and my fishing.

The Airborne Brigade is like one big happy family. I must be honest here, and tell you that at times I used this to my advantage. Living in married quarters meant that Lynn was surrounded by her friends, and it was these that I left in charge of Lynn when I deemed it necessary to go fishing, which was quite a lot actually! Because of my inability to live in a house and do normal things, I think Lynn was pleased to see the back of me anyway. Remember, she was used to me not being around most of the time. It was also around this time that Lynn and I had to come to some sort of agreement. You see, I would feel unbelievably guilty about leaving her, and by the same token she would feel guilty about me not being able to do the things I wanted. Some people, even to this day, cannot understand why she lets me do what I do. If I have a sick wife then I should be at home to care for her. Well yes, but Lynn doesn't want her illness to stop normal service being continued. It is a very delicate juggling act, but it suits us. At the end of the day it really is no one else's business.

Which, in a round about way, brings me back to that last flight from Northern Ireland. All those thoughts had been running around my head during the trip, but it was time to get my 'game face' on because there was still plenty of Admin to do before I could get the leave that was due to me. The next couple of days were spent sorting out the paper work and generally ironing things out. It was now that my friends had told me of the decision they had made. I was sad that it was over, but happy that I could start to look to the future for Lynn and myself. And do you know what one of the first things she said to me when I got home? "When you going fishing then?" Soon, I assured her...very soon. Any operational tour will have a massive effect on anybody, but it is not until you have time to rest that the full impact comes home to roost. In many respects this is where fishing, and more importantly carp fishing, has come to my aid. Disappearing for a couple of days gave me time to reflect, a time to come to terms with the things that had happened. I was now in serious need of some down time, and planned a trip to Chalk Farm four days after my return. This would be my first trip as a semi retired soldier and the last time I would have to take stock of the crazy life that had ensued. Personally and professionally, life was getting more and more difficult, and I was unaware of the nightmares to come. In saying that, you may even feel a little sorry for me at times, but I can assure you, you shouldn't feel any sympathy for this old devil. At that moment I had no idea just how pivotal this session would be. Life was just about to change once again.

Normal service was continued. A Willow Park twenty

Chapter 2

Chalk and Cheese

With everything taken care of in the barracks, I could start to think about some time at the lake. Having missed most of the season, (a situation that I was not unfamiliar with), I had no idea what had been going on there. Chalk Farm was one of those lakes, however, that seem to pop up in our lives every now and again where we can do no wrong. It wouldn't have surprised me if I had turned up one day to find the carp waiting to carry my kit to the swim! To say it had been good to me in the past would be an understatement. Of course there were plenty of carp in there, and the competition which that created for food always ensured that if I got it right, then a bite wouldn't be too far away. I had first visited the lake back in 1978, and on and off it had played a big part in my education as a carp angler. Because of my Army commitments, although I had been a member for a long time, I had not actually fished it that much. I had seen it go through massive changes though. For many

I could start to think about some time at the lake

years, although the lake was only five minutes from my barracks, it seemed so isolated. Once through the little wooden gate, it was as if you were in the middle of nowhere. That peace and tranquillity was lost forever when the MOD decided to build some married quarters right on the banks of the pond. The nearest one was only twenty yards from one of the most productive swims on the lake. First of all came the construction, and what a complete pain in the arse that was. Builders coming and going, and of course, taking rather noisy dinner breaks. It was also the ideal place to clean their tools at the end of the day. All in all it did nothing to endear me to them and it came to a head one day, when I am afraid I snapped. I had set up in a small swim that allowed me to fish just off the end of some marginal reeds. By Friday afternoon the traps were set and I was settling down, when to my utter amazement several of the workforce decided to have a wash up just around the corner. With spades, trowels and buckets clanking away in the margin I had just about had enough, so, like you would, I stormed around the corner. I was so angry that I didn't fully take in the fact that there were four of them, and only

one of me. The first guy I came to had his shovel launched into the lake, and subjected to some serious abuse. It wasn't until I was making my way to the next bloke that I realised I was in a spot of trouble. With the red mist well and truly down over my eyes I wasn't actually that bothered, then two of the chaps grabbed me and at that point all merry hell broke out!! Now, it was very obvious that I was going to come second here, but if that was the case then I was going to be the best second they ever saw. During the melee I managed to grab another shovel, and this seemed to bring things to an end.

To say the lake had been good to me would be an understatement

They cleared off, and I was left to nurse my wounds back in my plot. Strangely enough, they never came back, and I was one spade to the good!! We never did get into round two, but there were some pretty fierce staring over the works fence when ever I was in the area. Once the construction was complete the silence was great, the trouble was that this heralded the start of an even worse nightmare. Army families and their children. As most of you will be aware, water holds a great fascination for kids, and those kids have little respect for the poor old angler. For a long time we had to suffer all kinds of things being chucked into our swims, along with all kinds of crazy behaviour. Mummys and Daddies didn't help the situation much either. They were just happy that little Johnny and Jill were occupied and out from under their feet. It wasn't until several of them decided to go afloat, and nearly drown, that some kind of order was restored. Then there was the dog walker. Everyone seemed to own one and it was their greatest joy to let them wander around the lake and crap everywhere. I lost count of the arguments I had with them, but amazingly my harassment did

have some effect. In any case, I had my own secret weapon, and he came in the shape of an eleven and a half stone Great Dane, that went by the name of Max. I really need to tell you about this fellow. Shortly after Lynn and I were married we were walking in the town centre when we spotted a rather leggy, but huge, puppy. We had talked about getting a dog and a Dane was what we wanted, so we stopped the chap and enquired where he had got the dog. It turned out the puppy belonged to his 'soon to be – but its never going to happen' son-in-law. Basically, the guy had bought it and just left it in

I had my own secret weapon . . .   meet Max!

his flat all day. If we wanted him he would sort it out. Which he did. For a couple of days we excitedly talked about the new addition to the family, and then the time arrived when we would take charge of the 'little' fellow. The guy was a dick head and as soon as I could, got him out of the house. From that day on, Max ruled our lives. Everything seemed to revolve around him, and I am sure he would not have had it any other way! At that time Lynn was able to walk him, so I could pretty much carry on as I had before. The problem was that he loved his creature comforts, so much so that he even had his own two seater settee in the living room. He also had one other nasty habit, and it was this that I could use to my advantage. Implementing my plan, however, was not quite as simple as I thought. If he wanted to tear it up with dogs, then I had the very place in which he would be spoiled for choice, Chalk Farm! I sorted everything out so we could do a nights fishing, no easy thing when you are talking about a dog of that size. Four massive tins of dog food, a bag full of tit-bits and a bed the size of your average living room. With everything packed we set off. To begin with this was all a bit of a hoot to the big fellow. Even better was the fact that he was two brown Labradors and a Springer Spaniel to the good as evening set in. All the commotion meant that the doggy walkers were leaving my area of the lake alone. My plan was coming together nicely. That was until it came to bed time. Max sat and looked at me as if I was some kind of alien, you could just see it on his face, "if you think I am sleeping on the floor, then you can just think again". I got out of the bag and tried to drag him onto his bed, at which point he

If you think I am sleeping on the floor, then you can think again!

out manoeuvred me and dived onto the bed chair. His head went straight into the sleeping bag, and there he stayed until first light. I, on the other hand, had to be content with curling up on his rather large bean bag with just a coat thrown over me. I actually caught two fish in the night, events that didn't even elicit the slightest movement from his Royal Highness. I literally had to drag him out of bed and point him in the direction of some nasty dog walking types. That did the trick, and I supped my tea as the fur flew. He had wreaked so much havoc by nine in the morning that I almost forgave him for nicking my bed. One thing for sure though, the dog walkers had got the message. A few more trips like this and I would be rid of them...or so I thought. I arranged another night a few days later and once again I ended up on the floor. We fished a different area of the lake, just to see if we could get some more victims, which we did, several of them in fact. It was whilst he was into his third mongrel that I got a visit. The Chairman of the club had received numerous calls about Max and his acts of terrorism, and he had had enough. And so it was that Max got himself banned. You would have thought, if you listen to the sad rumour mill around this area that it would have been me, but I only ever got banned once. More of that in a while, and it wasn't even my fault! Max and I packed away and with his head hanging in shame (not!) we left the lake. He had served his purpose though, and very soon the dog walkers had to do so under strict rules. There was at long last some order brought to the proceedings, and we lived with an uneasy, but lasting, truce. Having every comfort, I knew Max was pleased he didn't

have to go off on those rather unpleasant trips any more. Indeed, every time I packed my fishing gear he made an absolute meal of getting on to his settee and going to sleep.

And so it was, with Max snoring his head off, Lynn sorted and the Northern Ireland trip starting to fade from memory, I packed the car. I am just like every other man really, in that I want to make life as easy for myself as possible. As luck would have it, one of my mates had moved into the closest married

His Royal Highness slept on oblivious to all the fun

quarter to the lake, which meant that I only had to carry my gear twenty yards to one of the best swims on the pond. I pulled up on his drive way and unloaded. On arrival in the plot I was pleasantly surprised to see no one else on the lake, it was Friday afternoon after all. First thing, as always, get the rods out, and just as I was doing so I heard someone ask if I would like a cup of tea. Thinking I had no neighbours, I swivelled round and glared at the intruder. I glared even harder when I was confronted with the loudest dressed bloke I had ever seen. God there were some colours involved. And his hair, well it was half way down his back. I didn't know whether to laugh or tell him to bugger off, but he was offering tea and that's just about as important as catching a carp! Now Keith will tell you that I was suffering from a cold and snivelling away, but I simply don't remember that. What I do remember, along with his very eye catching attire, was a guy who had with him everything but the kitchen sink. You see, I had spent my life living in camouflage, doing everything as silently as possible and surviving on the bare minimum. And so, there we were, Captain Camouflage and, for want of a better description, Coco the Clown! For all the outrageous apparel it was obvious that he was a really nice bloke, and the more we talked, the more I liked him. I needed to get the rods out, so once the tea was finished I disappeared to sort things out. Our swims were only a few yards apart, but separated by a large bed of reeds so at least I wouldn't have to look at him once I was in my swim!

Captain Camouflage …

Do you know what? I can't even remember if we caught any fish that night. It really didn't matter. Once I was happy with everything, I went round for a bit more of a chat. We introduced ourselves properly, and I found out his name was Keith Jenkins. Things didn't look like they were getting off to a good start really. As it was dark, Keith had at least three candles burning in his Aqua one man bivvy, and I was horrified. Remember, I was your ultra stealth bomber; I didn't even have isotopes in my bobbins because I hated light of any sort. If you looked inside my sleeping bag you would have also found any number of cigarette and lighter burns, because I refused to show any light at all. The phrase chalk and cheese sprang immediately to mind. That said we chatted for a while. He was so obviously a complete football fanatic, which I didn't hold against him. Apart from those differences, it would be harder to find two fellows who held such similar beliefs. I spotted lots of food and wine in the darker corners of his bivvy and although I did not sample those delights that weekend, the food and wine would become the stuff of legend.

. . . meets Coco The Clown

As I made my way back to my bivvy I couldn't help chuckling to myself. Coco the Clown had turned out to be anything but. Most interesting of all, though, was that he had mentioned Horton Church Lake. He, and a few of his mates, had been fishing there for a couple of years. Now, you would have had to have been living on another planet if you had not heard of this lake, and the fish it held. The transfer of fish had taken place in 1990, when RMC Angling had moved, practically the whole stock, into their new home at Horton. I had read so much about the place, and had promised myself that I would try and get a ticket once the army was out of the way. He also informed me that Dave Lane was his best mate. Bloody hell! Dave's successes had been well documented, and in all likelihood I would be meeting him some time soon. He had a ticket for Chalk Farm too! And then there were the other anglers that he was fishing along side. Sir Pete Springate and Ritchie MacDonald to name but two. Heady stuff indeed. Eventually we got around to the fish. I had heard their names of course, and even seen some pictures. Just speaking to someone who actually fished for them was putting my head in a bit of a spin. But then that's what dreams are all about, aren't they? There was one, of course, that would hold me spell bound for many, many years and that was Shoulders. You could have knocked me down with a feather when Keith told me he had actually caught him. WOW!! All I could think of at the time was that I needed to plug this guy into a mains socket and extract every last bit of information he possessed. I had no idea, then, that not only had my fishing just started to take on a whole different meaning, but my alcohol consumption was just about to go through the roof. I settled down for the night and woke at dawn. Lynn rang a few minutes later, she really wasn't well. This wasn't the first time this had happened and it most certainly wasn't going to be the last. I love my carp fishing, but my wife is infinitely more important, so as soon as I could, I had all the gear packed away and was heading for home. Once I was happy that she didn't need a hospital visit, I decided to tell her about my new found buddy, and how much I was looking forward to our next meeting. As it happens it was to be the following week.

With winter setting in I was looking forward to some great company

It's a very difficult thing to describe to those that don't know about such things, but leaving the army is just about as big a jolt to your system as anything could be. When you are not used to dealing with anything remotely civilian, the culture shock is enormous. Indeed it has been the downfall of a great many ex-soldiers. It is hard to adjust, and if I forget I will thank them now. Keith, Dave and Reg (aka Richard Howell) will never really know how much they did to soften that blow, and although I could hardly call it a gentle progression, I became a civilian a long time before I left the services. Thanks guys, I owe you...but not that much!! I can't have any of them thinking that I am getting generous in my old age, now can I? With the rest of the winter pretty much free from any long term military commitments, I was looking forward to the fishing more so than I had for a very long time. I had always fished on my own, experimented for myself and was never really bothered about anyone else. Indeed, I had only ever sent one picture off to the press. That was my first twenty pound common, and it had come from Chalk Farm. Even this situation would change, although I was unaware of it, and to be honest I wasn't in the least bit bothered about getting my ugly mug in the papers. It sounded like I was in for some good company, and there is nothing better than that to while away the long winter nights.

My first twenty pound common, and it had come from Chalk Farm

Chapter 3

Hope Springs Eternal

It was now December 1994, and I had not been so excited about my fishing for a very long time. The whole week had been spent thinking about the conversation I had had with Keith. I still had some responsibilities in the army, although that role had by now become almost non existent. Caring for someone is a very arduous thing to be involved with, but yet again I was lucky. The Airborne family came to my rescue as often as I needed it to because many of Lynn's friends lived close to us in the married quarters, and most of them understood my dilemma. To that end, Lynn would have a house full of volunteers when it came to seeing she was safe. That suited me just fine, I can think of nothing worse than sitting around in a house full of women who are intent on gossiping. In any case, all I would do is get in the way, wouldn't I? There was only one thing to do at times like these, and that was to go fishing. So, a week after my first meeting with Keith, I set off again for a session at Chalky.

The lake, as usual, was free of anglers on my Friday morning arrival, so as always I set out for a look around. I was, by now, very familiar with the venue and its inhabitants, but they sometimes threw a bit of a curve ball into the proceedings so it was always best to see what the carp were up to first. I eventually came upon an absolute cart load of them in front of an area known rather imaginatively as the Snags. As hard as it is to imagine, there were a load of snags out in front of the swim at about 60 yards. The snags themselves marked the edge of a plateau that extended some 15 yards out from the only island on the lake. What that meant was there was a clear stretch of water behind them, and a bait cast as far past the end of them as your bottle allowed, would invariably result in a bite or two. To be honest, the plateau that surrounded the island was a blinding place to get a bite anyway, it was just that a bit of 'derring do' made the whole thing more exciting. I sorted myself out and waited for Jenkins to arrive.

It may surprise a lot of people, but Keith is, and always has been, a nine to five

A swim rather imaginatively known as the snags

worker, five days a week. Couple that with the fact that he is the ultimate family man, and you will understand why he has so little time for fishing. This only makes some of the fish that he has caught all the more remarkable, as you will see a little later in this tome. Himself arrived as darkness was spreading across the sky, and once again I was left speechless at the amount of gear he had with him. What I did not realise at the time, was that a lot of that gear revolved around food. He doesn't just eat on the bank, he indulges in gourmet cooking, and I was just about to discover the delights. For me, food has always been fuel. Doing the things I had done in the army meant that all I ever wanted was for my belly to be full; I was never really bothered about what it tasted like. Even with my fishing, I carried around army rations, the boil in the bag type. As bland as they were, they hit the spot, and that is all that mattered. I also never carried a water bottle around, simply drinking water from the lake. That situation soon changed when someone discovered Weils Disease! We had one thing to do before he could get sorted, and that was to photograph a carp for me. The 18lb mirror was the first one Keith had seen from the lake, and as I knew he would be, he was impressed. They may not have been the biggest fish in the world, but they more than made up for that in good looks. With rods out, Keith decided that it was now time to eat. As an appetiser we popped the cork on a nice bottle of Nuits St George. At that point neither of us could have realised just how many times we would be doing that over the coming years. Jeez, we have probably kept the French economy buoyant for most of that time! I sat and looked in total fascination as he prepared the evening's banquet. There were even knifes, forks, spoons and plates. His accoutrements far out shadowed my meagre frying pan and spoon. Most amusing of all was a matching pair of salt and pepper dispensers, innocent items you may think, but the following year they were to nearly end my army career. Sounds strange doesn't it, but the green eyed monsters soon started to show their true colours. We'll get to that in a while. The culture shock continued apace when he read out the menu for the evening. Chicken in white wine sauce with some kind of faffy rice stuff, followed by steamed pudding and custard all washed down with a bottle of the finest red, and finished off with liqueur coffees. Being used to army rations (they are designed to bung you up), I was beginning to think that maybe I hadn't brought enough toilet paper with me.

And so we dined, and the conversation flowed just as readily as the wine. I was keen of course, to get him talking about his experiences at Horton. The thing with Keith is that he very rarely talks about fishing, a situation that normally I am more than happy with. I can think of nothing more boring than listening to someone prattling on about the latest jingly rig, and how they prefer to fish it. Yawn!! In the short term, though, because I had led such a sheltered carp fishing

life, I needed him to focus on the information in question. I succeeded to some extent, but the more the wine took a beating, so the conversation turned to total bullshit. Things haven't changed much to this day really!

Remarkably, carp were caught. I managed a couple more, and Keith landed his first Chalky fish. We were a bit here and there in the morning, and I was just firing his cooker up for the second time when all of a sudden one of his Neville's let out a shrill series of bleeps. He was on it in a flash and, to this day I am not sure who was more excited. I clucked around generally getting in the way, but eventually he won the day, and there in the bottom of his net lay the most perfect little linear. It was a fine way to open

Keith landed his first Chalky fish

his account. I think he was surprised how excited I was for him, but it is something that I simply can't help doing. I get nearly as much satisfaction from seeing others catch carp as I do myself. With a fish under his belt, I managed to swing the conversation round to bait.

For as long as I can remember, bait has always been the key for me. Its quality and how you use the stuff are so much more important than using the latest rigs. All they need is good mechanics and a sharp hook. I made my own for a long time, and not a lot of it was done in a conventional way. I started out using all the high tech mumbo jumbo, and for some I suppose it worked. I caught a few that way, but boillie making detracted from my fishing time, and there wasn't a lot of that to spare. Anyway, the whole thing gave me a head ache. I would rather spend my time finding a good place to introduce the bait, than putting it all together. It is sometimes difficult for younger anglers to realise just what went on in those days. But hey, thems the breaks, I used to use a slide rule at school to work out equations when ever I could be bothered to go, now it's just a case of clicking away at a calculator! Things move on, and nowadays it's a simple case of ordering or buying your bait ready rolled. Having spent a fortune on ingredients over a number of years, I stumbled across something that made life easier and a whole lot cheaper. When I was working with 2Para, I came across another angler. Now there's a surprise. He was into match fishing, which actually interested me as much as pulling my teeth out with pliers. What he had, though, was a ground bait that he got from a farming friend of his. You could see it had a whole host of ingredients in it, and I couldn't help thinking that it would make a good base mix for a boillie. Trouble was I wanted a sweet flavour, and all I could come up with was custard powder. Now, I wasn't too fussed about measurements and all that stuff, so I used an ice cream scoop. Eight helpings of groundbait, six of custard powder, and all added to four eggs. I had to add a little of each to get the required consistency. This is the bit that I actually think made all the difference - I had managed to get a good supply of Jeff Kemps Maple flavour. The stuff has now gone down in history as one of the greats. This dough was then rolled into

I really did make them eat their words

little balls boiled for a couple of minutes, and then fed to the expectant carp. Cheap as chips and the best bait I had used to date. When I eventually got to fish Pit 5 at Farnborough I took that bait with me. All the experienced anglers there constantly took the piss. As much as it was never my intention, I really did make them eat their words. I used that bait up until 1990 when, by chance, I met a guy who could get ready rolled bait by the cart load, so I started to get bait from him. Although it was commercially available, and everyone said it was the business, I never did have the same results as I did on my Paupers bait, as it had become known. This was the bait I was using when I happened across Mr Jenkins. During that time I had also experimented with particles, hemp being the most used, along with various nuts including almonds, hazelnuts and Brazils. None of which really floated my boat apart from the hemp. There was also the trout pellet revolution, which I contrived to let slip right on by. Everyone was doing it, and I wanted to be just a little different. I still maintain to this day, if your time is limited then use it to find the best place to put it, the carp will sort out the rest for you.

It turned out that Keith and his mates were using a bait from Mainline called the Grange. I had heard of it, of course, who hadn't at the time? It had even been referred to as the next best invention since the hair rig, so great was its impact. It turned out that Laney had rung Mainline to sort out some kind of deal, and as a consequence he had caught everything that moved in Horton. Now I may be a little slow on the uptake from time to time, but today I was as sharp as a razor, and of course there is nothing like being a little forward. Can you get me some, I said? He would see what he could do. I still don't know if he is aware, but I went home after that trip having nicked a couple of kilos. Mighty fine angling in my book! Speaking to Keith in the week, he said he had twenty kilos of bait for me, and would deliver it on his next visit.

This left me in a bit of a dilemma. You see, I had about fifty kilos of the old stuff in my freezer at home, and I needed to make some room for it so I hatched a plan, and decided that if I could blag a couple of days off, I would really let them Chalky fish have it. I have always been a lover of lots of bait, and will employ this tactic whenever I think I can get away with it. It was now that I was to learn that all I had read about carp shutting up shop for winter and not feeding was a croc of shit! With no Jenkins for a week or two, I got the days I needed to instigate my plan. I arrived on a Wednesday evening and was still sticking baits out as darkness fell. To this day I don't think those fish had ever seen anything like it, and neither had my right arm, bloody hell I had sweated less on many of the long runs I used to take daily. With two rods nicely positioned at the bottom of the plateau,

I sat down to wait. By one in the morning I had had not so much as a line bite, and was starting to think that I had probably killed the action not only for this session, but the rest of the season. The carp, as they always do, had other ideas. Ten kilos of bait was a lot and I wondered how long it would take them to get through it - I reckon about an hour and a half. Because at three in the morning just as the frost was settling, the bites began. I had seven in all, and then the action stopped completely. In my infinite wisdom I decided that the problem was that they had eaten all the bait. So I reeled in and got myself another ten kilos from the house, I only lived five minutes away, so it was no bother. Once back at the lake, I started all over again; the carp didn't take too long to respond. Bite after bite after bite, it was all getting a bit ridiculous, and I was getting some very disparaging looks from around the lake. Now I am never one to let one off results influence my decisions, so this theory needed to be tested as much as possible. Twenty one bites at a time when I was, according to the guru's, not supposed to catch anything! Although Chalky had a fair head of fish, it could never have been considered a push over, and most of the fish were good un's. I made the decision that as long as I had enough money, then I was going to ladle it into the lake as often as possible. Shit or bust time!

The next time I shared the lake with Keith, I was the proud owner of twenty kilos of Grange and, as soon as I had snatched it from his hand, I told him I would need more, in fact as much as he could get his hands on. Again I enjoyed a fantastic weekend, the nice thing now was that with all the information I needed extracted from Keith, we had little need to talk about fishing. He even brought a TV along

Twenty one bites on two very cold nights

from time to time, so that we could watch the five nation's rugby. It may surprise a lot of people, but we have never found the need to search out the holy grails that don't actually exist in carp fishing. There is also the not insignificant fact that there are an infinite number of things in life that are far more important; sport in all its various forms, music, families and of course, in my case, a wife that was far from well. As yet, carp fishing had not dominated my life, and I have striven for that to be the case ever since. That said, there have been one or two times when nothing else mattered. To my eternal shame this obsession only hurt the one person I was desperate to keep alive, Lynn.

As much as I wanted to keep throwing hundreds of pounds worth of bait into the lake, things had been getting progressively worse for her. She had been in so much pain that the doctors had been steadily increasing her medication. When they had carried out the mastectomy all Lynn wanted was not to be able to see her feet once the operation was finished. To that end the consultant had agreed to put implants in place. I held out for a set of 36FF, but practicality won the day...unfortunately!! The problem with this kind of operation is that they remove every single bit of

muscle and flesh away from the area. This in turn meant that the implants had no support what so ever. Slowly, over the course of time, her body started to reject them. She has never been one to complain about the pain she is in, in fact she will go to great lengths to disguise that she is even ill at all. The increase in medication might well have been dulling the pain, but it was also having a massive effect on her ability to do anything normal. God, how I hated those drugs, and in many respects the experiences I have had with this, leaves me with absolutely no sympathy with anyone that uses the stuff for 'recreational' purposes. And in these caring, sharing, vegetarian times, we are supposed to feel sorry for them! What a load of bollocks. Lock 'em up in a cell and feed them bread and water, until it

I enjoyed a fantastic weekend

is out of their system. Then, maybe give 'em a good kicking once a day, whether they need it or not. It isn't society's fault, it is theirs and I don't see why I, or any one else for that matter, should have to suffer the consequence of their addiction. Wankers!! Phew, I feel a little better for that. Being so fit and not ever having taken so much as an aspirin, Lynn's body was acting badly to the stuff and, as the winter was coming to a close, I took the decision to do something about it. Very quickly the consultant saw us at the Royal Surrey Hospital, Guilford. He was very concerned, and rightly so, and immediately he came up with a plan. It involved two massive operations, and he could only operate on one side at a time. I think at this point I realised how much carp fishing had taken over my life. To my eternal chagrin, for a fleeting moment, I thought how much this would affect my fishing. Very sad! I had to make a conscious effort to force those thoughts to the back of my

Chrissie and his first Chalky carp ... I do have my uses at times

mind. The operations themselves sounded horrific. Basically they would bring muscles around from her back, splay them out, and encompass the implants. The more detail he went into, the more my angling slipped from my mind. This was serious stuff, and would require my full attention. Dates were set, and they weren't hanging around. A few weeks later I was at her bed side. Although the operations weren't life threatening, we both knew how long and painful the recovery would be. It was two weeks before I was able to pick Lynn up from the hospital, two weeks in which Max and I had had to cohabitate for the first time. Now that was an interesting experience in itself. I spent as much time at the lake walking him and trying to keep a low profile (he was still not welcome) but the problem was feeding him. All he ever wanted to do was eat the food I was having, and I was not about to disappoint the lad. Trouble is, when you have a dog that big the turds tend to be on the rather large size anyway. Feeding him 'take away' food from just about every delivery service in the area, meant that said turds had increased so much in size, I needed a crane to get them out of the garden! He had also noticeably put on weight, the first thing Lynn commented on when she got home. We were in trouble, and he spent the next few weeks on a diet, which didn't go down a bundle, I can tell you. Once again our friends and neighbours came to my rescue. They were all as keen as you like to look after Lynn, and this gave me the opportunity to escape for a night or two. It was whilst I was preparing for a night that I had the pleasure to bump into a couple of Keith's friends from Horton. Robby Stoddard and Chrissie Pearson had set themselves up in two swims that went by the name of the Big Beech and the Little Beech. As it happens these two guys would become close friends, but at this time all I wanted was for them to catch a carp or two. It had been my intention to have a look see where I should be angling in a few days time, but as normal I got sidetracked talking to them. They had not caught anything in the short while they had been there, so I suggested Chrissie put a bait at the bottom of the plateau some fifty yards in front of him. This he did and whilst we chatted that rod ripped off. Rather pleasingly he played and landed a stunning little fully scaled carp. As always, that was two more anglers that had fallen in love with the carp here. I do have my uses at times, not very often I might add, just every now and then. Both Robby and Chrissie would be somewhat infrequent visitors, but they were great company and I always looked forward to their arrival. There were now only two more chaps that I had to meet before the little group would be complete. Meeting Laney had to wait a while, but my next trip to Chalky coincided with Reg's first visit. As much as it grieves me, Reg was a fair bit younger than the rest of us. What he lacked in years, though, he more than made up for in humour. As much as I was always threatening him with physical violence, he rather annoyingly had the ability to cut you down to size with the sharp side of his tongue. Clever little git! He came from the Swindon area, but we never held that against him, of course. Most things seemed to involve a little drama; even his nick name involves a rather complicated story, so I won't bore you with that. And so it was that Richard Howell, aka Reg, started to enjoy the delights of fishing the Army lake. Looking back on those times, it felt as if we had fished together for years, so well did we get on. Having several fellows to talk to now about Horton just made me more determined than ever to actually fish the place. It was during a particularly cold, but wine fuelled session in February '95 that the seeds of my future angling were sown. The world had become an infinitely better place because Keith, Reg and I had put it all to rights. At which point Keith asked why I didn't put my name down for a Horton ticket? I was speechless. For a kick off, I did not know whether I was ready for that sort of thing, and secondly, I may have to wait years for the privilege. Waiting has never been one of my strong points, if I have something I want to do then I want to get on with it there and then. Both of them assured me that it wasn't necessarily what you know, but who you know. Once on the list I intended to spend as much time there as I could and get to know the anglers. I reasoned that it would be better for them to choose the devil they knew, and I had one other ace up my sleeve, but whether it made a difference I am not entirely sure. Ian Welch, the then head of RMC, was a member of the Garrison Club, and therefore spent as much time as he could fishing Chalk Farm. Now that was handy! I remember well the first time

Reg started to enjoy the delights of fishing Chalk Farm

we met. He had no idea that I was snivelling around trying to get in his good books. I gave him a detailed account of what I thought he ought to do on his arrival, and he promptly ignored it all, and fished somewhere completely different. When he bagged himself a 28lb mirror shortly after setting up, I could see my Horton ticket slipping from my grasp. I would have to try a little harder in future. Still, we got on okay and I made sure that he knew I had applied for the said ticket. All I could do now was to hope...and hope some more!

Reg the clever little git!

Chapter 4

Brothers in Arms

By the end of February 95, Keith was once again back on the banks of Horton, as were Reg, Robbie and Chrissie. Although I missed their companionship greatly, it gave me some time to think, and I needed it, I can tell you. Lynn still had the other operation to endure, I really wasn't sure what the army had in store for me, and would I even have the time to fish somewhere like Horton, should my name come up on the wheel of fortune? I had spoken to Lynn at great length and, as normal, she said if that was what I wanted, then I should simply go for it. Trouble is, I am not the kind of guy that can mess around with things, its all or nothing in my book. That way I will know if I am good enough, and not have to give out any lame excuses for my lack of success. It was a few weeks later that my mind was totally made up. And once again, it was Keith that brought some sense to it all.

I had been fishing at Chalky over the weekend in late March. It was cold, horrible and I had slowly been losing the will to live since five in the morning. I decided to pack everything away and go and visit Keith. I knew he had been at Horton for the weekend, so as soon as I was able I set off. It took me five minutes to scrape the ice from the windows of the car, it was that cold. You will understand, therefore, that the last thing on my mind was that a carp may have been caught. I parked in the Five Bells pub, and made my way down to the lake. Everything was white with frost, and looked quite beautiful. I was heading towards the Ski Slope swim, and was unsurprised to see several frosty and very empty bottles of wine around Keith's bivvy. What did surprise me was evidence that a carp had been caught. The fumes (as they would over the next year or so) from nearby Heathrow, had obviously made the lads a little unwell. Shaking him to life, a rather pale, but extremely happy Jenkins informed me that he had landed the Lady. As the kettle boiled he brought me up to date with events. A gaggle of tuffties had landed on the lake at first light, and one had broken from the pack. Swimming across the lake it had dived. How the hell they do this sort of thing we will never know, but it found his 12mm pop-up. As it hit the surface, he launched a marker float at it, and smiled as it scuttled away. Just as he was laying his aching head back on the pillow, the same rod let out a short series of bleeps. Up and at it as fast as he could, he discovered that a carp was responsible. And not just any carp. The Lady was just about the best looking carp in the world. Eventually the crowds gathered to 'do the do' with the cameras, as Keith and his prize posed in the frost. At first the significance of the capture didn't dawn on me. Infact I was bombing down the M25 on my way home, when I really gave it some thought. The ultimate weekend warrior had succeeded where many had failed. Many who had much more time than him. If he could catch them then so could I. It was at that moment when Horton became the land of my dreams, I would fish there come what may. I also intended to spend as much time as I could there. The more I knew about the place if eventually I did get a ticket, the better I would be prepared. Chalk Farm had a regular closed season as did Horton, and once again there was that marvellous period of anticipation to endure. How we ever did without going insane, I will never know. I really do miss it.

There was one lake, however, that was to open its doors to all year round fishing, and that was Wrasbury. It was here that Keith and I were heading shortly after the season had closed. What we were trying to do was find Dave Lane, and hopefully his fishing buddy at the time, Phil Thompson. Easier said than done! We knew roughly where they were, and started off in that direction. Eventually Phil hove into view, and he was clearly on the move. Dave was somewhere behind him

according to Phil. We chatted to him for a few minutes, before the bushes behind us literally exploded. Out of the broken twigs and dust appeared, to me at any rate, the wild man of Borneo!! Kin hell, I had seen healthier looking specimens sleeping rough on the streets. At which point it seemed very obvious we were only going to get in the way. The other mistake I had made was to bring Max along, as he set about trying to eat Dave's dog, Fat Sam. All I

The Lady was just about the best looking carp in the world

Phil had also fished the big pit at Chertsey

could think about was that my only claim to fame would be that my dog had killed his. I need not have worried, this was Sam's turf, and she let him know in no uncertain terms! With a tenuous truce established we followed the intrepid pair all the way round Sunnymeads Bay until they eventually stopped at the rear of the North Lake off-licence, now there's a surprise! Whilst Dave sorted himself out, I chatted to Phil, and it appeared that we had fished a couple of waters, but at different times. One was a rather large lake near to Chertsey, and at 90 acres had been the largest I had fished by some margin. I had got my ticket through being a soldier and as part of the civil service I had my membership at a vastly reduced price. I am hopeless with names, but I do remember fishing along side two guys that went by the name of Gary and Stewart. Phil knew all of them, including that most colourful of characters, Micky Gray. Large, windswept and often bereft of anglers, the little time I spent there was most enjoyable. I had a modicum of success, nothing massive, but they weren't in there at that time. We talked about the fish for a while, and it seemed we had even caught the same fish occasionally. The lake itself has gone on to produce carp to over 50lb in recent years, but they were special fish even then.

At which point Laney arrived on the scene armed with ice creams. Now that was nice. What surprised me was how well I got on with Dave. After all, we were probably as far removed from each other as it was possible to get. In fact,

I had a modicum of success

They were special fish even then

I christened him the 'ultimate hippy'. It was all love and peace kind of stuff, and it looked as if he wouldn't say boo to a goose. Thankfully, that situation has changed of late, and we have a more normal 'putting the world to rights' conversation now a days. Most pleasing of all was, yes, he did have a Chalk Farm ticket, and he would be joining us come the winter. I couldn't wait, although my kidneys would rue the day!

I spoke earlier about another lake that I was involved with at this time, and that was Pit 5 at Farnborough. As much as I was still heavily involved there, I had not cast a line in it for some time. And there was a very good reason for this. In 1991 the lake suffered a massive fish kill. It is hard to imagine what impact that had on me, and several others. It really was the most special place, filled with some of the oldest and finest Leney strain carp. It was far from easy, and in many respects made me into the fisherman I am today. We have all seen dead carp, its something that happens from time to time. This situation was different, as 80% of the population was dead, and the reason for their demise was the introduction of seventy two foreign carp. Well it was seventy into Pit 5 and two into the neighbouring lake, Pit 4. That lake faired even worse, where I think only one of the originals survived. Whether these fish were legal or not, I have never been able to find out. What I do know is that they came from Holland, and brought with them an unidentified disease, something the original fish had no immunity to. We did everything we could to save the situation, but it soon became clear that our efforts were in vain. The lake was all but finished. I was heartbroken, but the seeds of something that would all but take over my life had been sown. I could not shout and vent my frustrations because who was going to take any notice of someone the angling world had never heard of? As the years went by I witnessed more and more of this madness, as mans greed and ignorance began to shape the world of carp fishing for ever. We dug a grave and buried the fish that we found, I even had the Army divers in from Gibraltar Barracks to see if they could find any more, which they did, but thankfully not that many. The lake was left alone until the following spring, when we set out to restore the venue as best we could. The re-stocking would take a while, but at least we could

The pit five crew trying our hardest to save the lake

start to make the water a better place for carp to live in. The first thing was to get a few hundred tons of chalk into the water. As far as we knew this contained all the goodies that helped to restore the food chain. Anyway, it was left to a couple of us to get this chalk into the lake...by hand! I toiled away for days and days, using an old aluminium boat to transport the damn stuff to all the bars and shallow features. As fit as I was, I ended up in hospital for my troubles. Evidently, exhaustion was to blame, but what ever the reason, I was done in. After I had recovered we then started on tidying up the surrounding area, and generally sorting the swims out. It was ball busting, but was eventually ready to receive its new stock. Redlands had allowed a certain individual to take over the lease on both Pit 4 and 5. A situation that worked for a while, that was until it was time for the restocking. Pit 4 received the lion's share of the carp, and all the big ones too. It was 'his' water and we got the shitty end of the stick. I never saw anything stocked into Pit 5 over 12 to 14lb. It really did make me angry, and for a long time I thought about getting some of his fish, and redistributing the wealth. The problem with that was two fold; firstly, I would be breaking the law, and secondly, I could quite possibly re-inflame the disease problem. I had to put that to the back of my mind, but it took a huge amount of self discipline to do so.

By June 95, the lake was once again ready to be fished. We needed to know if there were any of the originals left, and also see how the stockies had fared. We had to photograph everything we caught, and for a while I had plenty of fun finding out. Unfortunately, it was obvious that most of the bigger fish had died, but what remained was healthy and we could ask for no more than that. They hadn't been fished for, for a while, so the angling was slightly easier than normal. Although still devastated by the fish kill, things for the first time in a while, were looking up. What I had no idea about then is that I would have to stop fishing there at the end of the season. For reasons I could never really fathom, they never let me fish there again. With the passage of time I have now got a good idea, and much of that has to do with the old green eyed monster once more.

For now, I was just content to be fishing the pond that meant so much to me again. It really was like pulling on a favourite pair of comfy slippers. When I had first fished there it held such mystery, and none of it had faded in the least over the years. Any carp I caught from there was treated much the same way as if I had won the lottery. Thankfully, I learnt not to take things for granted, and still don't to this day. And so for the summer of 95, I had two lakes to fish. Still unsure as to what the future held in terms of my wife, the army and my fishing, I carried on as before. Chalk Farm continued to be good to me, but Pit 5 refused to give up that easily.

This one went on to be one of the biggest in pit 5

You would have thought that with a whole load of new fish to angle for then the old rollers would have been rattling, but no. I believe the ghosts of the previous occupier's lived on, and I don't think that anyone who has fished there would have it any other way. The stockies that we did catch had put on a phenomenal amount of weight though. The year before I had caught one of them on a little test mission, and he had weighed 12.14. Exactly one year later I landed the same fish at 21.10. All the hard work had paid off. As far as I am aware that fish went on to become one of the biggest in the lake...little wonder eh?

I have difficulty concentrating on more than one thing at a time, like most blokes, it just doesn't seem to happen. To that end the whole of that summer was spent day dreaming about Horton. I had also been keeping up to date with Dave and Phil at Wrasbury. It was all so exciting, and so far removed from the fishing I had been doing up to that point. Don't get me wrong here, I had caught some good fish, and was more than happy with that considering the unbelievable limitations I had on my time. There were simply no other carp anglers in the army that I knew of, which meant that I was rubbing shoulders with anglers that were, how shall I put this,

not as motivated as my army buddies. The mind set is, and has to be, different. That said, over the summer I did discover a couple of army carpers, and they have become great friends over the years. One was Mark Denton from 1 Para, and the other, Mark Brown from 3 Para. Working, as we did, in different areas of the Brigade we had not met before. Thankfully that situation changed, and we enjoyed some great

I was more than happy considering the severe limitation on my time

times together at Chalky. Mark Denton was more infamous for his incredible personal life, a situation that has changed little to this day, and I truly believe he should write a book about that, but I suspect some woman would come along and ruin the whole

Mark Denton caught a few when women weren't getting involved

thing! Still, at least I had a couple of guys that I could relate to. Even more pleasing was the fact that we all caught our first 30lb carp from the lake that year. The lake would have done so, so much earlier if the stupid match anglers hadn't insisted on putting everything over 5lb from their horrible little match lake, into the big pond. The day my thirty came along will live long in my memory. I was having to do some night time work, and instead of heading off to my bed, I went to the lake instead. I put a marker float out along side the snags, and positioned a hookbait either side of it. I had come into possession of 20k of Grange in 10mm, something once again the carp had never seen. I spodded some out, and whilst in the process I hooked and landed a fine twenty pound mirror. Followed by another, and another, the biggest of which was 26lb. Through it all the marker rod stayed in position. The problem, if I can call it that, was there were fish a little way round the corner looking for all the world like they wanted some Chum Mixers. After putting another couple of pounds of 10mm er's out and reeling the rods in, I went around the corner armed with my floater rod and a bag of bait. As soon as I sent some biscuits into the bay they started taking them with so much gusto I wondered if I had enough with me. Within the hour I had landed four more fish, topped by a lovely linear of 27lb, aptly named, Bar Code. Eventually they drifted away, so it was back to the marker float swim. I was tired, and reasoned that I would put the rods back out, and get a couple of hours kip. Fat chance of that. I landed four more twenty plus mirrors, before I had to pack up and head off for work. And one of those was probably the best looking carp in the lake. I had caught him once before, he was a very infrequent visitor to the bank, and went by the name of Big Joe. At 30.10 he meant so much to me. I was to catch him twice more during my time there, and both were significant moments. Oddly enough, the night's activities seemed less of a chore. Although completely knackered I spent the night bollocking recruits with a huge smile on my face.

Mark Brown and I shared some great times together

The lake furbished me with so many results like this, it was little wonder that I was totally in love with the place. I knew though, that it would soon be time to move on. My association with Chalky had lasted on and off, for over fifteen years. It is easy to get the impression that I was fishing here all the time, but take into account that I had a six year sabbatical, a few occasions where I did not fish for a whole year, and that I was fishing several other waters. One of those was also on army land in Gibraltar Barracks. Hawley Lake was home to some stunning old Leney carp. The problem was that I had caught most, if not all, the fish in Chalk Farm at one time or another. I still reflect in wonderment when I see people angling the same old lake for the same old fish, year after year. I can think of nothing more boring. You will not learn anything, and most frustrating of all is that you are robbing others of their dreams. I can think of a couple of examples that border on crass exploitation. It's each to his

A 27lb linear, aptly named Bar Code

own of course, but by fishing different waters, you are expanding your horizons and learning. It's a big world out there, and the voyage of discovery is what makes carp fishing such a fascinating place for me.

The summer marched on, and with it came the second of Lynn's big operations. The first of which had been a nightmare for me, so goodness only knows what it was like for her! The pain and the drugs had taken their toll, so much so, that the second op had been postponed a few times. With her strength returning, we were once again making our way to the hospital. This time though, it was with a lot more trepidation...we knew what was coming, and I drove home to sort out my life with the Hound from Hell. Yet again we would be living closely together, and I was a little nervous about that. You see, when daddy was at home it was play time. I was simply

not allowed to go to sleep. The duvet was ripped off me continuously, and the pillow was taken from under my head on more occasions than I care to remember. And don't get me talking about food, I was never allowed to eat either. Not until he had sampled everything first. To some extent he took my mind off all the things going on at the hospital. You would also think that I would be able to do a little fishing, but I have

The shockingly handsome Big Joe at 30.10

Hawley Lake was home to some stunning leney strain carp

never done that when Lynn has been laid up. I just can't seem to concentrate, and with Max still being banned from the lake, I really didn't have much choice. That said, I was able to have a couple of visits to Horton. Slowly, over the course of time, I was getting to know everyone at the lake. No one had told me to bugger off, so I guess I was making the right impression. Leaving Max to digest yet another of my meals, I set off for a visit. It was a lovely hot day, and I slowly made my way to Keith's bivvy. He was set-up in the Mouth of the Bay swim, and a little further round to his left was little Robbie, in a swim that no longer exists, called Lenny's. We went round to see him, and set about his brew kit. I was spellbound, as I gazed at the area of his hookbaits. There for all to see were several of the Horton monsters. I was speechless. Keith tried everything in his powers to get Robbie to move, but that was never going to happen. The only option he had was to move to the other side of the bay, into the Church Bay Steps. And as you would, he got me to help him make the move. Even his wife Linda was loaded up, and off we went. I helped Keith get a couple of hookbaits in position, before wandering off to see if I could find some more fish. Five minutes later I was back in his plot gibbering incoherently. I had just reached Springates Point when I spotted an absolute monster finning its way elegantly through the weed. I didn't know the fish that well, but thought it maybe either Shoulders or Moonscale. Who ever he was it was the biggest carp I had ever seen. I went and told Keith, who had the devil of a job stopping me nicking one of his rods and having a go! He had to remind me, that as yet, I didn't have a ticket. I left them to it a little later, but vowed to return in the morning. Someone was having one, of that I was sure, and as if by magic I got a call late the following morning. Robbie had landed Shoulders! We got on with the pictures once I arrived. I cannot easily express my feelings when he revealed his prize from within the folds of the sack. Here was a fish I had first seen in print in 1988, and now I was seeing him in the flesh. It was an incredible day; it was great to see everyone so happy for the little man. And do you know what? I can't even remember the weight, which only adds to the memory. Days like this are so not about the pounds and ounces, its about the fish. He was well in excess of forty pounds, that much I do remember, and my resolve to catch him strengthened greatly on the drive home.

Back at the hospital everything went as well as we could have expected, but as always, it was the aftermath that was to wreak its vengeance. When I went to pick up Lynn, she was shocked at how poorly I looked; life with Max had that affect on me. To top it all, when we got back to the house, there was Mr Innocent sitting on his sofa, acting like butter wouldn't melt in his mouth. Cunning little git! My wife now looked as if she had been bitten in half by a great white shark. I was actually shocked at the extent of the injuries, and these of course take time to heal. Once we had got the drugs at the right level, things moved on quite quickly. It may sound strange to put it this way, but Lynn was so fit that her body was able to recover remarkably well. Which only made her more determined that I should get out fishing. Her efforts not to let her illness get in the way of what I wanted to do have to be resisted from time to time, so I would be the one to decide when the time was right. With friends

Robbie had landed Shoulders

It was great to see everyone so happy for the little man

and neighbours in the house at all hours, I decided a little sooner than expected, that the time was now well and truly right!

During this period of inactivity I had been saving up all my allowances of Grange. To that end, I had about eighty kilos of the stuff stored in the freezers. There was only one place that lot was going. And as I packed twenty kilos into the car, I couldn't help thinking how fat those Chalky fish were going to get. It was now late August, and I had hatched a plan to fish, what was at the time, one of the less popular swims on the lake. At least for a while if I could keep my results quiet and the fish responded of course, I would have the swim to myself. It was called the Little Oak, and covered some of the deeper water on the lake. The plan kicked off in fine style, as basically, the more bait I put in the more I caught. To that end I spent all my time baiting up. The area I was concentrating on was nothing special, just that the carp had been spending a great deal of their time there.

Come September, my conversations with Keith were revolving more and more around the lack of action he was getting at Horton. It sounded so hard, and I couldn't help thinking that if I ever did get a ticket, would I be good enough to catch anything? In truth though, it was just what I needed from my fishing. A challenge, and a very big one at that! I had arrived for a weekend session, and was once again installed in the Little Oak. Interestingly, I had been joined by another Horton angler, Frimley Mark (Mark Davies). He was the head bailiff at Frimley at the time, and had spent three rather fruitless years at Horton. At least I had another unsuspecting victim from whom I could extract information. I had settled down for the night after first having a little chat with Keith, and unbeknown to me he would also be the next person I would speak to again. My phone chirped into life shortly after first light. All I could hear was some gibbering fool shouting at the top of his voice. What I did manage to make out was the word Jack, and that could only mean one thing. I didn't even give him time to tell me that Robbie had caught Heart Tail, because I was packing up and running for the car. On my way I informed Mark, and he joined me in the race up the M3. The first thing that struck me as I arrived, was that every man and his dog had reeled in to come and see the spectacle. And what a spectacle it was! I stood in awe, as they posed in one of the most impressive brace shots I have ever seen. Jack at 46lb and Heart Tail weighing 37lb. It's not often you will find Keith lost for words, but that is exactly what he was. In fact none of us really knew what to say or think, so as you do, we drank tea...and giggled...and giggled some more. I had to get away fairly quickly, so bade them farewell. As I drove home, I wondered when I would get a ticket. Nothing had been said, and I took that as a sign I wasn't going to be hearing good news any time soon. It was not until October that the clan started to gather at Chalk Farm. At the very least, if I wasn't angling for them, I would be able to talk about all the great carp my new found friends were fishing for. And apart from actually angling for them, there is nothing like that to get the old juices flowing. This was shaping up to be a good winter, and I really couldn't wait to get started. To say the lake had been pre-baited for their arrival, would be a bit of an understatement. Little Robbie kind of lost his way after his capture of Heart Tail, and we saw very little of him, only doing

the odd day. However, the rest of us merrily set about testing every wine the French ever made, and of course catching a few carp. And do you know, one of the worst things you can do in carp fishing is to actually catch carp? It's a very strange thing, but the more successful you are, the more likely it is that someone will want to have a pop. Over the years I had seen many anglers come and go, but this year, for some reason, there seemed so many more new faces. The thing that upset them was that only a few were catching the majority of the carp. Having Dave Lane and Keith Jenkins along only seemed to

The plan kicked off in fine style

enhance the problem further. One particular individual became a real pain in the arse. He had taken to lying about what he caught in an effort, as he saw it, to gain some notoriety. When that failed, as it was always going to, he turned his attentions to making life as difficult as possible. This culminated in the wretched person making accusations about Keith and myself. I told you earlier about Keith's cooking accoutrements, and that he had the most spellbinding set of salt and pepper pots. Well, at some stage Mr Cowardly Arse Wipe had informed the military authorities that Keith had drug taking paraphernalia in his bivvy. Now that is not too big a thing when you are talking about a civilian, but for an army man it can be a career ending event. I was called into my boss's office the Monday after the spineless little toad had done his worst, and informed that I was to be interviewed by the SIB. They are like the special branch of the Royal Military Police. I did have one thing in my favour though, I had never heard of them solving a single case in all my time in the army. With the allegations being untrue, I had even less reason to fear, but for four days I was grilled. It wasn't until the results of a blood test indicating that I had not so much as taken an aspirin for most of my life, that the situation cleared itself. But what could have been? It could have ruined eighteen years of my life, just because of someone's pitiful jealousy. It wasn't this guys only act of cowardness either, he was responsible for soaping up several areas of the lake a year or so later. Unbelievably, he got away with that too. And if you are thinking, is this guy still walking without a limp? Yes he is, but I have always maintained that vengeance is a dish best served cold.

It is still one of the most impressive brace shots I have ever seen

With Dave now well and truly on the case, and my wine intake increasing on a weekly basis, we had plenty of chance to talk. I was fascinated that he was a consultant for Fox and also for Mainline Baits. Indeed, he was the first such angler that I had ever got to know. Far from slagging him off and generally behaving like some jealous twit, as seems to be the way these days, I was keen to find out what the score was. At the time I had no idea where my carp fishing would take me, not to those dizzy heights, of that I was convinced. He got all his gear for free, plus the bait! The better I got to know him, the less guilty I felt about liberating some of it from his tackle box. I, on the other hand, had to pay for everything, a situation that I was not unhappy with. I could never envisage the day when I would only use one companies gear. What the situation did mean, however, was that I had a never ending supply of bait as long as I had the money to pay for it. We all caught some cracking fish that winter, and the friendships were set in stone. So much so that Keith even added me to his Christmas card list. And the first one he ever sent me was by far the best. Working as he did, in a packaging firm, he had used some of their resources to fashion a card for me. He had taken a picture of myself and cut out a picture of Jack, which he'd stuck together and glued onto the card. He wrote on the front, Just Dreaming. Well yes I was, but I would show him! The more I talked to Keith and Dave, the more I knew I needed to get away from the Garrison club and its waters. It had all become too familiar, I had proved to myself that I could catch carp, and lots of them. What was needed now, was a challenge. But where the bloody hell was that Horton ticket?

Although Lynn was still desperately ill, the army was going to call on my services for one last final hurrah. As the year ended and 1996 began, I was asked if I would be able to take part in a big exercise in the United States. I am not suggesting for a second that I was the best at what I did, but when you are going to be showcased

on the world stage, it is a sound idea to have your most experienced troops available. I could have said no, but in truth I wanted to be part of it. This was to be the largest airborne assault in history, and I rather liked the idea of having that on my CV. We would be leaving in March, but for the foreseeable future there was much planning to be done. None more so than in Lynn's case. I had to ensure that I had all the bases covered, and that she would be adequately looked after. The angling once again took a back seat.

I have always had fond memories of America, and had spent many pleasant weeks and months training and serving with their army. Mind you, they still need plenty of training

This was shaping up to be a good winter

when it comes to the subject of fire support. They have the most marvellous military doctrine, and this basically revolves around "Death by superior fire power"! The more ordinance you can lay down on the enemy, the more likely you are to kill him. Simple! The problem is that when you are chucking that much exploding crap around, the more likely you are to incur friendly casualties. I know for a fact that Lynn has had more sleepless nights over this issue than with any enemy I have faced! One of the more crazy things I had to do during my time in the mob, was to test parachutes. It really is the ultimate test of ones bottle, but in a perverse sort of way, it is the most exciting thing I have ever done. You will never know how alive you really are, until you put that life at risk. Okay, so I am completely bonkers, but these trips were spent in South Carolina, one of my favourite places on earth. Much of the desert like terrain here is below water level, and there aren't that many people that can say they have parachuted from that height.

With my fishing time once again limited beyond belief, the Brigade prepared for the trip. During those preparations I learnt that I may be in line for that much craved Horton ticket. I am never one to believe anything unless I can see or touch it, but I must admit I nearly burst into flames when I heard. I tried desperately to push that to the back of my mind. This wasn't so easy to do! With all the preparations made, we were a week away from departure. I had been out for my customary early morning run, and had just arrived back at the house. As I was boiling the kettle, the

Testing parachutes... How crazy is that!!

postman dropped the mail through the door. I hadn't been expecting it, but in amongst it was a letter from RMC. I hardly dared open the damn thing, but eventually I did. I have no idea what the neighbours, or indeed Lynn, thought when I roared at the top of my voice. My Horton application had been accepted, and I was going to be fishing there come June 1st. I think it fair to say that this one single thing occupied more of my thinking time than anything else over the next couple of months. First though, I had to survive the trip to the States.

It is very hard for the un-initiated to comprehend what actually goes into this sort of operation. The simple logistics of looking after tens of thousands of troops is quite mind-blowing. Getting them on to hundreds of C130 Hercules aircraft, and disgorging them onto several drop zones is nothing short of a miracle of Biblical proportions! It may also surprise you how much the thought of fishing Horton was distracting me. I found it very hard to concentrate on anything, but I had to. My small band of merry men would be looking to me to get our part of the mission right. Although we only constituted a tiny fraction of the numbers involved, the planning was intense and complicated. It was a few days after our arrival that I eventually got my head in the ball game. Soon enough, the day arrived and this massive parachute operation was just about to begin. We turned up at one of the three airfields that were being used for the night's airborne activities. It is very difficult to describe the sight that greeted us. Literally hundreds of aircraft lined the

Disgorging this lot onto several drop zones was nothing short of a miracle of Biblical proportions

runways. It was a very humbling experience and, if I was honest, kind of frightening. All of my troops, as had everyone else's, had been tactically loaded onto the planes. This meant that should one of them be shot down or disabled, there were still troops in the air that could carry out the tasks required. What it also meant was that all I could do was to hope the planning was okay, because there was absolutely no way to change things now. It was at this point that I realised what a grip carp fishing had taken on my life. All I could think about was that ticket lying on my desk at home, and as the lumbering aircraft heaved its huge frame into the night air I was trawling through my memory banks to recall the carp I would be fishing for in a month's time. We had a three hour, low level flight to contend with first. Following the contours of the land at a hundred feet is guaranteed to have a few people reaching for the sick bag. That, coupled with a load of smelly soldiers farting away, adds up to a rather horrible environment to spend any amount of time in. That said, and just as the interior red lights came on, I was merrily day dreaming. Forty minutes out and it was time to prepare for the jump, not an easy task with 90 men and all their equipment wedged onboard. As uncomfortable as that was, the only thing on my mind was Johnny Allen landing Jack from Longfield off the top, and using a candle as a controller! The green light came on and it was time to exit the aircraft into the cool desert air. I hardly noticed the thousands of other paratroopers I was sharing the night sky with, although you must have your wits about you at a time like this. Having to carry a Bergen that probably weighed in excess of 130lb, and was suspended by a fifteen foot rope below me, my landing could hardly be described as delicate. My main canopy landed on some great big thorny bush and as I lay in the sand I started laughing. No one, or so I thought, could see me so I took my time. The whole while, I was chuckling away to myself. I had just got my weapon prepared, when a hulking great American Master Sergeant loomed over me. "And what is so god damn funny soldier?" he boomed. I simply laughed even louder, as there was little point in explaining; I hardly think he would have understood if I had told him about the Horton 'A' team, do you? The whole trip was a complete success, as I was still alive, and after much back slapping and a little slice of R and R, it was time to return to the UK. I had been talking to my bosses about the situation at home, it was very hard to disguise anything that went on, as we all lived and worked so closely together. The long and the short of it all was, by the time we got on the aircraft, my military career was at a complete and utter standstill. And yet again they said that if I had time in between caring for Lynn, then I should try and find some time to go fishing. I would only do that if they twisted my arm, you understand!

I explained everything to Lynn when I got home. As always, she blamed herself for what was happening. And as always, I suggested that she should do if she had made this dreadful disease take hold of her as it had done! There was nothing to be sorry about, and in any case, I could now concentrate on her well being (and to a slightly lesser extent) the search for my dreams. And what dreams they were. I could hardly have imagined what was about to happen, but that is the great thing about this game we play. Oh the thrill of it all! The phone lines between myself and Jenkins went into meltdown. It was now the middle of May and I really couldn't wait to get on with the draw the week before the off.

You have to have your wits about you at moments like these

Section 2

Hell Ain't a Bad Place To Be . . .

Horton, land of my dreams

Chapter 5

The Magic of Your Dreams

Thinking back on all the things that I had done in my life, it surprised me at how nervous I was about the draw at Horton. You could say that my existence in the army was sheltered from every day life in Civvy Street. I had always found it hard to make friends with anyone outside of the mob, unless of course they were female (and most of those never ended up as friends). In that respect, Keith was my first civilian mate and, preparing to set off for the draw, I wondered what the hell I was in for. Carp fishing, up until this point, had always been about escapism, it had always been fun. I had caught some good fish, and also managed to keep things in perspective. Instead of getting insanely jealous and bad-mouthing those who had more time than myself, I let the stories they told inspire me. This, contrary to popular opinion, is why many carp anglers write about their exploits. Sure, there are plenty of egos that need to be regularly massaged, but they are easily spotted and ignored and, having already met some of the members, I was a little more prepared than if I was going into this blind. In saying that, Horton was, at the time, the pinnacle of carp fishing and I would be rubbing shoulders (excuse the pun) with some of the most dedicated carp anglers in the land. As I sped up the M3 these thoughts were spinning round my brain. There would have to be sacrifices, of that I was sure, and I really didn't know if I was capable of sacrificing a good night on the town, just so I could be at the lake. By the time I was on the M25, I had made the decision; if I wanted to catch them I would have to overlook some of the finer things in life. Trouble was, most of those things were much more fun than sitting by the side of a lake! Setting those thoughts to the back of my mind, as I raced over the River Colne I was once again dreaming of monster carp.

I pulled up in the car park and was astounded by the amount of people that were there. Although it was a fifty-man syndicate, it seemed that every man and many of his dogs had turned out just for the spectacle. Hell, even Laney and Phil Thomson had turned up from their Wraysbury exploits, although I suspect that had more to do with free beer than any entertainment that was on offer. What struck me most, as I made my way around the gathered masses, was that there were clearly two groups of anglers - one was the more serious, talking about bait and their rig collections, and the other was, well, less serious I suppose. They generally took the piss out of each other and wanted to know about how cold they could keep their lager. There was no doubt which group appealed to me, and as I sat with a couple of the lads, I couldn't help thinking how much one group could potentially annoy the other. Oh, this was going to be fun, of that I had little doubt!

Once our small clan, consisting of Reg, Robbie, Chrissie, Dave, Phil and myself, had sorted the world out, it was time to get on with the draw. Dragging himself away from his bar-b-que duties, Ian Welch began the proceedings. This was all a bit serious for my liking. Ranting and raving about rules and the like did nothing to make me feel comfortable, and it felt as if we were getting a bollocking before we had done anything wrong. Man management played a big part in my life, and as far as I could see, this guy couldn't even spell it! Once all the fun had been taken out of the affair, Del Smith rather somberly got on with the draw but I have very little memory of that, other than that I came out last. Humph! I do remember, however, that Harry Haskell, who angled at the pits I was fishing at Farnborough, came out in the first two or three. There was a huge cheer for the old boy, and rightfully so, as he put his name on the Plateau swim. He didn't realise it at the time, but the wheel of fortune was definitely starting to turn in his favour. I, on the other hand, would be fishing a corner of the Dog Bay at the far end of the lake and eventually,

Dreaming of monster carp

after a couple more pre-emptive bollockings, we managed to get around the water to see what was what. I can't say I was too delighted at the thought of fishing my selected swim, but at least I was going to be there for the start. The only thing I could think of as we made our way back to the lodge was that things, from this point on, could only get better! With a week to go, it was time to put my game face on.

I cannot ever remember a time when I had spoken so much on the phone, certainly about carp fishing, I also don't think that I had ever been so excited. The most important things were sorted out first. What we were going to eat, and what the wine menu consisted of. I do vaguely remember talking bait and other such mundane things, but that just bored me, as it always does. In saying that, I ensured that I had a huge supply of the Grange, a bait that I knew the carp would readily accept. Always handy, because I could simply concentrate on finding the best place to put it. In the week leading up to the off I made sure to read up on all the information I could get my hands on about the fish I was going to be angling for, which did me no good at all. I just kept going back to Johnny Allen and his capture of Jack off the top, maybe that was a way of sorting one of these carp out? It was all I had to go on, and soon enough the time came for me to set off for my first session. To say the lake was going to be busy, would not quite sum it up. I had never fished in such a claustrophobic environment. Every swim was taken and all I could think was how the hell was anyone ever going to catch a carp from here? The centre of the lake looked more like a slalom course on a ski lake than a fishing pond - there were leads, markers and spods flying all over the place; I had visions of the fish running around with crash helmets on! My tiny corner of the lake looked even smaller and the carp even further out of my reach than ever. Now, there is only one thing for it in a situation like this...arrange a carp party!! So that is exactly what we did.

Once again Phil and Dave arrived from Wraysbury, the lure of cold, and in the main, free beer was too much to resist. Things kicked off

The lure of free beer was too much to resist

around seven and I was desperately trying to pace myself. Being able to cast out at nine in the evening was nice; being slightly wobbly on my feet was not! As with any plan, it never survives first contact with the enemy, and this one was no different. Come the appointed hour I was a little worse for wear, the rods were baited and waiting patiently for the off, and as I made my way to them, the gathered revellers offered some fine words of encouragement. This, as far as I could tell, was going to be at best a little embarrassing. Not to let them down I swang the first lead into position. The problem was, that happened to be up a tree!! My how the throng cheered, bless 'em. The obvious answer was to drop them at my feet in the deep margins and reach for a cold lager...so that is exactly what I did. Most seemed to think that was mighty fine angling, and the party continued apace but, with some of the party goers having obviously gone back to their swims, that just left the hard core. I didn't realise it at the time, but this would be a familiar situation over the coming months. By ten in the evening I was on my own and, not quite sure what planet I was on, fell into the sack.

My fine angling of the evening before had not been enough to induce a bite, but I was delighted to hear that Harry Haskell had bagged himself a brace of Horton carp. CP's at over 45lb and Heart Tail, a mid thirty mirror but, unfortunately, we were too late for the pictures; I would dearly have loved to see them. What it did mean was that Harry had bagged a carp bigger than Walkers record and, to a man, everyone was delighted for him. My only bit of excitement was when one of my rods let out a series of bleeps, and all of a sudden I was attached to a tench. My heart was in my mouth for a second or two but, although a little disappointed, at least I had caught something. I packed up later that day and vowed to return as soon as I could.

Which just happened to be the next day! Trouble was, I was now in the company of another hard core drinking posse. Oh well, if they really insisted then I would

Kent leg-end, Rob Tough

help them with their burden and, as frowned on as this is now, it was simply what happened back then. In any case, it was a great way to get to know some of the other members on the lake. As much as I like to think that my drinking prowess is good, nothing could be farther from the truth. Being in the company of lager monster Steve Mogford, Horton lothario Richard

Stangroom, and Kent leg-end Rob Tough, only compounded the problem further. Lordy, there was some beer drunk, which only left everyone vowing, once again, to never touch another drop. All I could think of was that this was getting me no closer to catching a Horton carp. The next time out, I was determined to put that situation right - little did I know what was about to happen.

I went home on the Wednesday morning feeling a bit the worse for wear, those fumes from the planes were obviously doing me no good at all! Checking that Lynn was fine and had everything she needed, I got ready to return on the Thursday. I didn't arrive until late afternoon, but thankfully the lake was much quieter than earlier in the week. This gave me a little time to have a look around but, as there was nothing much to go on, I dragged my gear round to the weedy bay area. The weed was horrendous, but after a while I eventually found a couple of spots to place my hook baits, then, with around a hundred baits following them into the lake, I settled down for the night. For the first time I felt as if I was in with a shout, although the carp had given me no indication, things just sort of felt right, and if all else failed I would have Keith for company the following evening. It was my birthday on June 8th, so at least we could celebrate that. We have no way of knowing these things, but the wheel of fortune was just about to start turning in my favour. Friday arrived without so much as a bleep and I spent much of the day simply walking around and climbing trees. I spotted a load of fish, and many of them were the monsters I so desired, and although it really is hard to drag yourself away sometimes, I needed to get the rods back in position. A lot of the fish I was seeing were making their way into my area of the lake so, with Jenks inbound, I crept around the margins of the weedy bay and found some fish, one of which was the Lady. The others I could not identify but I managed to get some bait on the spots they were visiting, and bugger me if one or two of them didn't pick a few up. The area was so out of the way, I decided to give them some more bait and get back to my swim, a few yards away, and was just thinking about what to do next when Keith turned up. After filling him in on events he set up to my left in the Dug Out, in the meantime the bait was rapidly disappearing from the spot, and I had hatched a plan - I would leave them with a free meal and set a trap at first light. We shared a lovely meal and a fine bottle of wine and retired early and, as I drifted off to sleep, I couldn't help thinking about the fish I had seen, maybe I should have angled for them there and then. Surely they would come back?

My internal alarm clock had me up shortly before first light, my favourite time of the day, and I quickly made a brew for us whilst we went over the plan one more time. I would creep into position and check that there were fish present, once that was done, Keith would climb a rather spindly tree and tell me when it was okay to lower a hookbait into position. Remarkably, the plan went without a hitch. Armed with a few boillies I crept into the bushes and there, under my feet, were three of the carp I saw the evening before. I decided not to put any bait in and informed Keith that he needed to get into position. With a little huffing and puffing he shimmied up the tree, and I prepared a rod. The rig, armed with a 14mm bottom bait, was hovering over the water as I waited for Jenks to give me the nod. A few minutes later I heard him hiss that all was clear so, silently, the lead donked down on a small clear patch. Although I couldn't see it, I was sure all was as good as it could be. The bait had been in position for only a minute or so when it became obvious I wasn't comfortable, so, to save twitching around, I decided to carefully move back a little, and as I did, the rod tip moved slightly. Convinced I had hit the thing I stopped and checked my feet, at which point the rod hooped round and the spool became a blur - bloody hell, I had only gone and hooked a Horton carp!!

Being so damn weedy, the bay offered the fish a whole host of places to get his cunning little nose into and, as much as I didn't want to, I had to give it a little more stick than I would have liked. Having been dreaming of this moment for a very long time, you may well understand how terribly nervous I was. Feeling almost physically sick and with my knees knocking lumps out of each other, the battle raged for a while and I was in a world of my own. That was until Keith passed the landing net to me and, as soon as I had sunk the mesh, the fish was ready to slide right on in. The feeling was indescribable, and the pair of us probably made a little bit of noise in our celebrations, then all that was left to do was to have a good look at my prize. It was a stunning mirror and at that moment size was completely immaterial. Keith seemed to think it was a carp called Polly but I was not in the least bit bothered, I had landed one from this incredible lake. I was shaking so much that Jenks had to do most of the sorting out. Obviously, this involved weighing her and at 20.12 we posed in the early morning sunshine. Oh baby...sweet dreams are made of this!

Interestingly, more than ten years after the event, I eventually came to know which carp this was. I had written an article in which the fish appeared, and on the day it was released my phone went into melt down. When the fish had been moved from Longfield, with them was an unidentified mirror of around twenty pounds. It was universally accepted that the fish was first landed from Horton at the beginning of the new century, and got the name of the Missing Mirror but, whilst not wishing to take anything away from that capture, it was I who had first landed that fish from his new home four or five years earlier. It's hard to think of anything that could make my capture of this fish anymore special, but knowing that this was that particular fish has really been the icing on the cake.

With the pictures done, the pair of us set about making a cup of tea. There really wasn't a lot to say, but as is our wont, we discovered that a load of bullshit normally suffices. The day, however, was moving on and I was in carp catching mode so by eight in the morning we had both sorted out some stalking gear and set off on our travels. We headed toward the lodge end first (having a toilet block made that essential), and just as we were getting there we bumped into Pete Springate, who was angling in the Plateau swim. He had been there for the last four days and was heading home later that morning. Unfortunately, nothing had occurred for him, but as we sat and talked I couldn't help noticing how many fish had turned up. They were sunning themselves on top of the plateau from which the swim gets its name so I asked if anyone had wanted to move in after him, to which he, somewhat

Sweet dreams are made of this

surprisingly, said no. Not being too slow on the uptake I asked if I could leave some gear there, thus saving it for me once he had gone. I scuttled back to my swim and moved some stuff round, the rest of it would have to wait until we had been around the lake, then I thanked Pete and off we went. We bumped into a few more anglers who very kindly passed on their congratulations, until eventually we came to the Church Bay. There was one angler set up in the mouth of the bay but he was not in residence, and we could see no one else fishing it, which was pretty handy really as the bay was stuffed full of very big carp. We made our way through the recently installed gate and arrived in the Heart Tail swim. All the fish were cruising on the surface, so the first thing was to get some mixers in and drifting toward them. Keith was further to my left, but we both noticed that the carp were showing a modicum of interest. I probably should have waited a while longer, but when Jack materialised from the main lake, I could resist no longer. The small controller with a six-foot hooklink came to rest, and no sooner had the small ripples died away than the mighty fish swam confidently up to the hookbait. I was sure she would take it, but no, she just followed it for fully fifteen yards with her nose no more than an inch from the bait. Eventually she turned and headed into Phil's corner and I legged it past Keith, who was still messing around with his tackle, until I had got just past the last place I had seen her. Unbelievably, she was grubbing about on the marginal shelf, if I could get a rig in there I had every chance of catching her. Eventually, I super glued a couple of pellets to a hook, the intention being to free line them in the edge, and I watched her swim back and forth until, at last, I had an opportunity. What she had been doing was to waft up the few pellets I had introduced, then turn sharply and devour the ones that were suspended off the bottom. Clever girl, but along with the super glued pellets I had also included a sliver of cork. Off she moved and in went the hookbait, then a minute later she was back and with one sweep of her huge tail all the bait was washed off the bottom. All I could think of was here comes carp number two, but I should not have been so confident. Just as she swam back into the cloud, I nearly jumped out of my skin as a rather large lead landed almost on her head. In the blink of an eye she was gone and so was my chance. Thank god for locked gates and barbed wire fences because, without them, I know I would have committed murder. The angler was fully aware of what I was up to, he just thought, as most pitiful weasels do, that it was better to muck up my chances, even at the risk of messing up his own. I was spitting fire by the time I got back to Keith, and as he has always done, he slowly calmed me down. In any case, it was now time for us to move to the lodge end of the lake where, unbeknown to me, the wheel of fortune had slowed just a little more.

The move from the Weedy Bay only involved bundling the gear seventy-five yards to the Plateau swim, so in no time at all we were sorted. Keith was in Two Up, which meant I had Del Smith for company immediately to my left. Whilst I waited for Sir Pete to vacate the swim, I must admit, at that point, I did feel sorry for him. You see, he had spent most of the opening week here and it was only in the last couple of hours that the fish had turned up in front of him. As he departed, that left Keith and I, somewhat excitedly, looking out at just about every carp in the lake. There were glistening backs everywhere, and for a few minutes there seemed to be some sort of control, as we were discussing just how I was going to get a surface bait to the fish. But then things started to get a little more disorganised. Laney and Phil turned up, once again armed with a stack of very cold lager beers and as nice as it was to see them, Dave is about the last person you need in your plot when there is a stack of fish in front of you. He went into absolute melt down, and at one point I was sure he was going to burst into flames, however, the difference in their two characters came shining through that day. Dave 'the gibbon' Lane was fifty foot above me in a very tall tree, giving a running commentary about what fish were out there, and what they were up to. Phil, in the mean time, was cool as you like, offering me a cold beer and quiet advice. The ale I could do without, but when he said an anchored floater might be my best choice, I had to agree. Maybe I should have accepted the drink, because tying up the hooklink was a fraught business as my fingers simply refused to work, it was more like trying to control ten Cumberland sausages. At ground zero, things eventually settled down, but up there in the treetops, Laney was getting himself into a right state. I begged him to calm down, but all he would say was, get a friggin' bait out...get a friggin' bait out...your gunna have one son!!! Eventually, but I have no idea how, I had attached the eight foot nylon hooklink to the swivel on my lead core leader. To this I attached two chum mixers; normally I only like to use a single in these situations, but hoped the extra one would give the whole set up a bit more buoyancy. I vaguely remember a few more people turning up, but I just wanted to be on my own, as an audience is a sure fire recipe for disaster. The next problem was casting the monstrosity out but, ever cool, Keith grabbed hold of a cup and stood behind me.

Once the goose was removed, we used the cup

We coiled the hooklink into it and I got in position and remarkably, at the first time of asking, the rig sailed out and landed on target. I mended the line and placed it on the rests, buzzer on and at last I could relax...or so I thought. The addition of a bait into the equation only spurred Dave into even more of a frenzy. I just wanted him to shut up; whatever was going to happen (or not) would do so with out his help now.

"They're using the bait as a roundabout, and there's Shoulders, oh, and that's got to be the Lady". On and on he went, until eventually there was such a substantial swirl in the area of the bait, that I had lost sight of it. I called up to Dave and asked if something had taken it, after all there had been no indication at the rod. He wasn't sure, but all became clear when the buzzer let out a single bleep, and I saw the line pick up from the surface.

I was on the rod in a flash, and will never forget the cheer from the crowd as the rod settled into a healthy bend. Once again I was attached to a Horton carp. The fish moved steadily left away from the plateau, at which point I turned to Keith and said that it was only a grass carp. He gave me one of his best withering looks, I think he knew, and I wish he hadn't because all of a sudden I was more frightened than I had ever been in my life (and I must tell you that at times I have been in some pretty hairy situations)! An expectant hush settled over the gathered crowd, and I tried desperately to get the unseen monster heading in my direction. Eventually, it was moving my way, and more normal service was resumed, that was until thirty yards out when a huge flank, and a distinctive patch of scales, rolled on the surface. In one voice the on lookers roared – 'Jack!!'

For the third time that day, I was eyeball to eyeball with the biggest carp in the lake but the problem, this time, was that she was attached to the end of my line! With sphincter muscles being challenged above and beyond the call of duty, I tried to stay in control and, after what seemed an eternity, she was in the deep, clear margins, and all I could see was her trying to shed the hook by burying her head into the silt. Steady pressure got her up in the water, and Keith made his way to the front of the swim to take up arms. The long hooklink meant that I had to walk backwards, and as I did so the crowd started to move in front of me. I could hear Keith telling me to keep her moving and, as I did so, the crowd burst into rapturous applause, by which I could only assume that my prize was in the net. The rod was unceremoniously dispatched to the bushes, and I went into my now customary headless chicken routine and eventually, by the time I had settled down, we were ready to get her onto the bank. You have to realise here, I had never seen a carp of this magnitude on the bank, the sheer size simply blew me away, and there in her bottom lip, held in position by the tiniest sliver of skin, was my little size 8 hook. I was glad I hadn't noticed that whilst the fight raged on. Everything was on auto pilot by now, so for the first time I was glad there were so many people around. I hadn't given the weight any thought at all, but when Dave called out 49.04 I fell silent for the first time. Speechless, I agreed to sack her for a few minutes so the photographers could sort themselves out, but most importantly, so could I.

She came to rest in the shadow of the pontoon, and for a few moments I watched as she settled down. Bloody hell, I had caught her, was all I could think, and then it was time to do the pictures. Gary Bond very kindly said he would get the fish,

Speechless, I agreed to sack her for a few minutes

She was massive

I just didn't think I could do it. Once on the mat, Laney helped me take my first close up view; she was massive, and as she was revealed, the crowd made all the right noises. We posed as best we could as the cameras and videos worked away then, eventually, Dave and I carried her back to the water, and it was time to say goodbye. After a few returner shots, she did a lap of honour, even swimming through my legs. Somehow I managed to get an early bath along with Phil, and as I made my way out of the water I remember Keith shouting something about the state my liver was going to get in. This comment only spurred Dave back into action and people were dispatched to all four corners of Berkshire to collect the necessary supplies for a carp party. I tried to find a little space to be on my own, I needed to ring Lynn, who just couldn't believe what had happened. A few close friends were informed and at last I could grab one of Phil's cold lagers...I needed it!

An early bath

It was time to say goodbye

Furniture was brought from the lodge and we got down to doing what we did best, namely eating and drinking! It was sad that Reg, Robbie and Chrissie weren't there, but I could not think of better company than Keith, Phil and Dave to share the moment with, plus some other worthies. It wasn't too long into the proceedings that I realised I hadn't even set anything up in my swim, so I took a few minutes to get sorted and, with the lake, at this time, being an absolute sea of weed, I simply tied up some four foot hooklinks to which I attached a couple of pop ups. Let me tell you, two pub chucks never felt so good and, at the very least I was angling, but in truth I really didn't give a shit!

The night was filled with cries of 'angler down' as the merriment continued and, as a huge thunderstorm rolled in and the drink took its toll, we all tottered off to find our beds. I was too wired to sleep immediately, and simply sat in the darkness trying desperately to get a handle on the situation. Sleep, as it

Carp party!!

does, overcame me in the end and the next thing I remember was waking to a howling buzzer at seven the next morning. Somewhat unsteadily, I joined battle with a very angry carp which ran from one weed choked area to another, scary stuff, but it really is one of the best hangover cures known to man. That said, once I had the fish in the margins I still needed some assistance because the weed had gathered horribly on the line and at one point I could not retrieve any more line. Del trotted down from his plot and grabbed the net and actually had to net it several yards down to my left, then, after a little messing around, there was a stunning looking mirror, plus a fair bit of weed, lying in the bottom of the net and I let out the familiar battle cry, one that surely would wake the dead. Indeed it had the desired effect as, seconds later, Keith and Laney stumbled into my swim. We quickly sorted the fish out on the mat, which was identified as the Long One, a beautifully proportioned and elegant mirror that weighed 28.12. At that point Keith warmly shook my hand and wished me a happy birthday. I had forgotten all about that, but indeed it was a great day. In fact, I could think of no better birthday present.

A beautifully proportioned and elegant mirror

We got the pictures done as quickly as we could, and soon enough she was back in the lake. I didn't know what to say, so I sat in silence as the three of us supped some tea, then, with the celebratory cuppa out of the way, Dave grabbed Phil from the lodge and they headed back to Wraysbury. Keith and myself whiled away the day but nothing further happened (I don't think I could have handled it if it had) and the following morning I was making my way out of the creaky old gates. Surely it could never get better than that! Three Horton carp to my name, and the biggest one in the pond to boot. 'Kin hell!!

Oh yes!

Chapter 6

Where Do You Go From Here

think the only way I can describe how I felt in the aftermath of my birthday session, is that I was suffering a Jack hangover. It really was a case of where the hell do I go from here? I doubt there is a carp angler alive that doesn't sit and daydream of a veritable monster most of his waking hours. The problem now was that I had fulfilled that dream, and for a while I felt, for all the world, like a lonely turd floating down the River Thames. Drifting aimlessly, I decided that the best thing to do was go and do some more angling, like you would. There were, however, two things, which were going to conspire to make that just a little bit difficult - Lynn's illness, and the army. Cancer really is the most evil of diseases and no sooner than we thought Lynn was in the clear, it reared its ugly head once again. This time it had made its way to her bowel, and we had plenty of hospital visits to attend. The concern, here, is that you never know the extent and severity of the situation until they have gone in for a look-see. That simple sentence, however, does little to sum up how desperate the condition was, and the impact it would have for many years to come. There was also the fact that some officious bastard in the army decided that I should be doing a bit more work although, as much as the man was an unfeeling imbecile, he did have a very good point. I was being paid by the army, and he was well within his rights to expect a little pay back from me. I think he understood the wife situation, but I suspect my pleading about carp fishing would have fallen on deaf ears! The job had something to do with recruiting and, as far as I could tell, sounded most boring. Still, I would pretty much be my own boss, and looking after Lynn would take priority. That left finding some time to go fishing, and the more I thought about it, the more unlikely that seemed to be. I remember this guy actually ringing Lynn to find out where I was, one day. Well, I was at Horton, and she had rung Del's dungeon to try and get a message to me. We stood by the phone for a while wondering what I could say, and how we could stop him finding out the number I was ringing from - all pretty drastic stuff. The excuses were made, and Del even had a way of hiding the telephone number, but the long and the short of it was that I postponed the inevitable for only a few more days. The following week I would be given my job description, which just happened to be as flexible as a fine length of braid, now that was handy. However, Lynn was getting worse and I knew, sooner rather than later, that my fishing would have to stop. In the meantime, both of us agreed that I should do as much angling as I could. So I did! I cannot remember why, but for some reason Keith and I had decided that we wanted to put loads of bait into Horton. Boillies were the obvious choice as they were fairly easy to get hold of but we also had some of the new Response Pellets to mess around with. Both of us, though, wanted some particles in the mix as well and Parti Blend, hemp, maples, and tigers all figured in our discussions, and eventually we decided we should put them all in the mix - we were going to invite everything to the party, and see what would happen. It was also quite handy that Reg lived in Swindon, because he could get hold of all the stuff we needed through Brian Jarrett at Hinders, the trouble was, Reg couldn't resist getting hold of all the mixes that Brian had available, and that only confused both Keith and I. Bored rigid, and starting to dribble down our chins with his waffling, we decided to just chuck the lot into one bucket and go along for the ride. It didn't half look the bollocks, but there was only one way to find out how good it was, and that was to get it into the pond so, with fingers crossed, we set out to introduce as much of this crazy mix as we could. Much of the fishing here had been done with boillies in the past, and whilst still proving highly effective, I have always felt that in weedy waters they lacked one vital function, and that would be to clear weed. Particles, by their very nature, tend to hang up in the weed and encourage the fish to forage in it, which in turn has the carp ripping the weed up, thus creating lovely clean areas. For two weeks the spod rods were sent into meltdown, but apart from giving me arm ache and the carp a headache, nothing really happened for a while. The first sign that we may be on to something occurred in the middle of June. Not being the greatest football fan in the world, I cannot quite remember why England were playing Spain that particular weekend, probably the European Championships, but who cares? What it did mean was that we would have a good reason to have a little party; well quite a big one actually, but it was only supposed to be small, honest! I had got myself set up in the Ski Slope on the Friday afternoon and settled down waiting for Jenks to arrive. There was a fellow from up North in the Sick Swim next door to my right, so Keith would have to fish in the Church Bay until the chap upped sticks on the Saturday morning. In accordance with our plan, I had spodded out a fair bit of the mix onto the only two relatively clear areas I could find. I think our bodies must have been aware of what was to come on the Saturday, so the first night was relatively quiet. In the morning, though, coupled with trying to get matey boy out of the Sick Swim, Keith got his television sorted out and arrangements were made to get supplies to the lake. Someone was dispatched to the deli, whilst I visited Bosses, just up the road, for as much cold lager as he had in stock and by one in the afternoon we were ready for kick off. Jenks was still unable to move into his new swim, so he busied himself with the seating arrangements in front of his profile brolly that housed the TV. Then the crowd arrived. Sir Pete, Reg, Rob Tough, Laney, Phil Thompson, Keith and myself started to feed on the impressive spread laid out on a couple of trolleys, then the football match started. Even Laney got a little interested and the bottom line was that it ended in a draw and would go to penalties. My overriding memory was not, as you would suspect, Stuart Pearce's reaction to scoring his penalty, but the reaction of Rob Tough. Every time England converted a spot kick he thought that we had won the match, so set off roaring in triumph down the track, at which point someone would have to go and get him back and explain what was going on. Which made no difference at all, because as the next one went in, off he went again. Mad! Once the game was over (England won, I believe, because Toughie went bonkers!), and the swim Keith wanted was empty, we set about getting him set up in there. And this is where Jenkins showed what he does best in carp fishing...poaching!! With plenty of cold beer still on offer, he could see my attention was focused in another area and this gave him a chance to do his angling in my bit of water. Having already been baited, I suppose it made sense, well to him anyway. I half suspected that his two hookbaits were loitering with intent in my swim, but let it pass.

England playing football was a good reason to party

The rest of the rather sweltering day was spent trying to quench our thirsts, but as darkness fell I think we had all had enough - and then I got a bite! I wasn't sure that a carp was responsible at first, expecting a tench to be the culprit, but as I started to gain line, so the fish decided to wake up a little. Keith made a very good effort at acting like a butterfly collector with the net, but eventually a rather small carp lay in the folds of it. The fishing had slowed dramatically since the first week of the season, and it was just nice to see a Horton carp on my mat. At 12lb you may be surprised at how happy I was, but this little fish had come across from Longfield with his larger brethren and this, as far as we were aware, was his first capture from his new home. Indeed, I later found out he had only been caught once or twice

It was just nice to have a Horton carp on my mat

from his old abode. Sometimes it's just not about the weight of the carp we catch, more what they represent. By the time we had done a couple of happy snaps and he was back in the water, I was knackered, and fell onto the bedchair. The next thing I remember, at around six in the morning, was the sound of Keith's tonsils getting some early morning exercise. Evidently, he had been shouting at me for some time but I had heard nothing, must have been those aviation fumes playing havoc with me again! Anyway, in the bottom of his net lay one of the most magnificently ugly carp on the planet, the Parrot. I was truly happy for the old boy, even though, as I constantly reminded him, she had come from my bit of water. It was the start of something truly incredible for him; the Weekend Warrior was just about to set the world on fire!

The following week I managed to get myself in an area the carp obviously wanted to be in. They had spawned for a couple of days whilst I had been away, and I was hoping that they might just be a little hungry. This was also the weekend that Dave was taking part in the Masters competition at Great Linford fisheries and Keith, Reg and I had promised to go up and lend him a bit of moral support. So, on the Saturday morning, we set off and I had somewhat naively asked those fishing

I was truly happy for the old boy

around me if they wouldn't mind leaving the area alone, as I would only be gone for a few hours. Unfortunately, as soon as my back was turned, one of them was in there like a rat out of an aqueduct. When we returned a few hours later, I was confronted with news that the chap had landed the Koi from my carefully prepared spot. I didn't know whether to laugh, cry or punch him in the face, and he looked a little worried as I strode towards him, however the deed had been done and there was nothing I could do to change that, so I simply shook his hand. His name, however, was quickly removed from my Christmas card list!

The following week, as August began, I set myself up in the same area. Once the bait had been introduced, at distance from the Salt Circle swim, I was encouraged when an absolute monster crashed out over the baited area. A couple of liners a little while later had me on the edge of my seat so it really shouldn't have taken me by surprise, but it did, when I got a take a couple of hours after casting. The fish found all the necessary weed to make things very tense but, once free, I started to make some headway. Then it started to kite quickly into the weedy bay and, believe me, that swim was really living up to its name this year. Convinced the monster I had seen earlier was responsible, I probably didn't give it as much stick as I should but then things came to a grinding halt and I did all the normal tricks to try and get him on the move again. Eventually, something gave and I was winding in a dead weight and a few minutes later I was left with that gut wrenching feeling of a lost fish as a large ball of weed, minus a carp, lay in the margin. The loss of any carp is hard to take, but from Horton it was shattering and it started one of the most disaster-strewn periods of my life. Keith arrived rather late that evening and, as normal, had the greatest panacea for this kind of situation...red wine! Whilst we supped, he had to endure my pain countless times, like you do, but by morning, although still somewhat pissed off, I had started to get my head back in the ball game, that was until Del informed me that Lynn was trying to get hold of me. I reeled in immediately and ran to the lodge to ring her. She could hardly speak, so much pain was she in so I told her to stay exactly where she was and I would be home as soon as I was able. Running back to my swim I had the gear stowed in record time, with Keith's help, and I didn't realise it at the time, but I would not be able to return for a couple of months. By the time I got home, the ambulance had been and gone, so I had to quickly get myself out to Frimley Park Hospital. This was looking increasingly more serious as the hours passed and, not being allowed at her bedside, I wasted my time getting in the way of everyone. Until, that was, the bowel consultant arrived. First of all he went to see Lynn and, with his assessment of the situation made, he called me over to tell me what the score was. Now forgive me here, this was dire stuff, but when he introduced himself as Mr Gudgeon I nearly swallowed my tongue. As the snot flew from my nose I couldn't help remarking that he was a bowel surgeon, and was named after a bottom dwelling fish! It was priceless, but did nothing to endear me to him or his staff. We had got off on the wrong foot, and I could never understand why his grovelling hoards didn't find it at all amusing. I have had other name related giggles during my time with Lynn at all the various hospitals, most famously of all was when we were going to get her eyes checked (she is registered blind). As we waited to be called, a nurse entered the waiting room and asked if Mr Onion was there. Well, it was irresistible really. I commented, rather loudly, that there was not shallot they could do for him, and that he was obviously in a bit of a pickle. Packed with mostly old people, the room reverberated with their laughter, and Lynn kicking me in the shins just added to the chaos. It got no better when we were eventually called in and this chap introduced himself as Doctor Bladder- I asked, as straight faced as possible, if he was taking the piss, at which point I was asked to leave and wait outside. Really, some people have absolutely no sense of humour!

Sorry, I digress. Leaving Keith sorting himself out, I disappeared toward my car. I wished him luck, and told him to bag himself a whacker. So he did.

The weedy bay

Chapter 7

A Year of Living Dangerously

watched thoughtfully as Chilly promptly packed away and, with a quick 'good luck', was off along the causeway, not to return for a couple of months. I have nothing but admiration for guys like Chilly and Tony Badham who, at the drop of a hat, will pack away and leave to attend their ailing wives, with never a negative word or thought. It certainly hammers home what the important things really are in life, and little did I know that, a few years hence, that would be forcefully hammered home to me.

But this was now, and with Chilly's departure I felt quite sullen. We'd spent the previous day in a sense of heightened excitement as the carp, present in quite large numbers, casually ignored Chilly's hookbait in the Weedy bay, and, expecting similar today, had been disappointed on every one of our dozen or so ascents of the tree that overlooked the bay. My mood, not helped by the continuing high pressure, was less than confident, and as I sat there pondering my next move, I couldn't help but think back a couple of months, and the contrasting feelings I was experiencing.

"June the first! What d'you mean, June the first? They can't be serious!"

This outburst was elicited by the news that Horton, along with many other waters, was to take advantage of the recent abolition of the Close Season and start on June 1st (ending on March 31st). I, like many thousands around the country, was less than pleased about this.

"It's like making Christmas Eve, December the first, it's just not the same!"

But my cries of anguish were much too late, and as much as we complained and bemoaned the loss of June 16th, the vast majority gave into the old 'if you can't beat 'em, join 'em' philosophy and prepared for an earlier start.

There was one other slight problem for me, and that was what had been an annual, close season jaunt to France. Lin and I had taken the kids and had been joined by Mick Dickens and Graham Jarman and, over the previous couple of years, had enjoyed some great sport. This year was to be no exception but there was one small problem – the ferry docked at Dover on…June 1st. I was going to miss the start of the season for the first time in decades and wasn't bleeding happy about it. Such was my unhappiness, however, that we did a bit of jiggery-pokery and managed to bring the ferry forward to 4.00pm on May 31st. This helped a bit, but I would still miss the draw on the preceding weekend so would be highly unlikely to get a swim, but what the heck. Lin was up for a couple of nights on her favourite lake, just to unwind from the French trip, so away we went.

As the White Cliffs hove into view I took Lin's phone and called Del at the lake.

"A couple haven't turned up yet so you might even get a swim if you get here on time."

Ah, what a tantalising thought, but on leaving Dover we would have 90 miles to go at 5.00 pm on a Friday afternoon, and a good wedge of that would be around the M25. If we reached there by midnight I'd be happy! But, the Gods of the road were really looking down on me and it was a little after six that we were bumping down the track to the lake (little did I realise, but the Gods of the road would never look down on me in such a way again!). The look on the Para's face was worth the effort alone, even if I didn't get a swim, and as I poured myself out of the car he gave me a huge bear hug – especially as the car was also laden with copious containers of liquid refreshment! One way or another it was going to be a weekend to remember. Amazingly, one of the two free swims was at the top of the Dog Bay, about three swims away from Chilly – now, that would do nicely. I wasn't overly confident of any action on the busiest weekend of the year, and was quite content to just drop 'em in the edge for a couple of days. Chilly, however, was fit to burst. In fact I was amazed that, during the preceding couple of months, after his ticket had been confirmed, he hadn't actually burst into flames. I was sure that he had smouldered a few times, and the thought that he was actually going to cast into one of the most famous lakes in England in the next few hours meant that we had to regularly douse him down with the liquid from France. By casting out time, which was 9.00pm (not even midnight!), Chilly's swim had become the hub, and we'd been joined by Phil Thompson and Dave Lane, amongst others, to welcome in the new season. If memory serves me right, Chilly's first cast didn't actually find water, just a passing Oak tree, and I'm sure you can work out for yourselves what the reaction was from the gathered throng. From there, it was downhill all the way, and the night was rent with the bellows of a beleaguered Para as he continually reminded us that he was 'fishing the bloody margins' - he really should learn to keep the noise down when he's fishing the margins.

By midnight most of the revellers had disappeared, leaving just a couple of us to drunkenly wish each other the best of luck for the coming campaign. Then news reached us that the wonderful Harry Haskell had bagged the first one of the season, and what a carp. Fishing the Plateau swim, near to the Lodge, he'd bagged the glorious CP's at 46+ and smashed his personal best in the process. Elated with this news, I wound in the rods and tottered round to congratulate him, which I'm sure he was most bemused by. I left soon after, promising to witness the photographs in the morning, but who was I kidding? Morning arrived accompanied by a brass band and hallelujah chorus, and the only thing I witnessed was someone who looked worse than me, and I was married to her! Chilly was equally battered and bruised and it was long after CP's return that we eventually made it to Harry's swim to congratulate him once more, just a little more sedately this time. But as we stood there he had another take and, in front of an expectant crowd, landed Heart Tail at 37lb – what a session! We loved him even more after that! Breakfast in the lodge soon followed and the day took on a brighter hue. We had a nice stroll round the lake and the nearer we got to our swims, the less welcoming the reception – can't imagine why, it was only the first day of the season, there was plenty more where that came from. Later that afternoon, Chilly had a belter of a run and I have never before seen diarrhea stacked so high! It turned out to be a seven-pound tench and, after it's return, it only took a few minutes to resuscitate the big fella! Oh, how I laughed!

The evening followed a similar, but less raucous, pattern as the first and we were much less tottery when we went to bed. Nothing had come to our rods, unsurprisingly, and Lin and I were away by mid-morning. It was grand to be back, and highly enjoyable, but the season would really begin next week – I couldn't wait. The next weekend proved to be one of the most enjoyable I have spent carp fishing.

Chilly's capture of the twenty pound mirror was excitement enough, but nothing could have prepared us for what was to come and the capture of Jack, in the circumstances that it happened, and with the people present, was truly one of the days – one that none of us will ever forget. The capture of the Long One, the following day, was not greeted with the glee that it should have been due to the excess inhalation of aircraft fumes the previous night, but that would be rectified at a later date.

Start of the season, in the Dog Bay

I didn't feel that I'd even started fishing yet and, with Euro 1996 starting the following week, I could see that lethargy continuing for a few weeks. When I arrived, the following Friday, Chilly was in the Captors and as the Weedy Bay swim was free next door, it seemed a logical place to start. Reg arrived later that evening so we had a post-Jack drink, but nothing too serious, and by 5 the next morning I was aloft in the tree that I had watched Chilly get his first fish from beneath. The weed looked to have doubled during the week, and with no visible clear spots I opted for a pop-up 12" off the lead. The football was due to start at 3'oclock in the afternoon, and with my telly set up behind Chilly's swim, that was where the crowds began to gather. However, another trip up the tree, a few hours before kick off, revealed six or seven carp milling around the weed beds in front of my swim and although they didn't exactly look in a feeding frenzy, at least they were in the bloody swim, and suddenly I got a little serious. I still thought that an 'off the lead' approach was safest because there was no way I wanted to be casting around to find clear spots, so that was how it went. Both baits were fished about 12" high, and I flicked them out to what appeared to be the thinnest areas of weed, about 15 yards out to right and left. The fish, although initially disturbed, soon returned and spent the next hour or so lazily sunning themselves ten feet above my hookbaits – bastards! This caused me to miss the kick off, and most of the first half, but I eventually adhered to the old 'a watched pot never boils' adage, and joined the small, but increasingly well lubricated crowd to watch England defeat the Scots 2-0, and to witness that stunning goal by Paul Gascoigne that had me and Reg dancing around like a couple of school kids! This, obviously, initiated a bit of a celebration, although not on the level of the previous weekends, and the sun was just setting when we heard a buzzer scream for about ten seconds, then nothing. The problem with fishing at Horton is that, from dawn to dusk, there is a plane going over every two minutes and although it's something you get used to quite quickly, there's always that twenty-second window when you can only hear the plane. So was it a buzzer or not? Chilly, Reg and I all strolled back to our respective swims, which were all in close proximity to the beer and food, and it was me who was soon calling for assistance. The line was out of the clip, indicator tight to the rod, and line guitar string tight. As soon as I picked up the rod, the line cut off to the left and was immediately solid in the weed and, so, after about ten minutes of pulling, angle changes, slack lining and all the other ploys we could think of, it was eventually decided to get the boat. Reg went to get it and soon he and I were out in the dark, carefully and patiently removing weed, gaining line, removing weed, gaining line until, after what seemed an eternity, I just simply reeled the lead and rig to the surface – fishless. The lead had moved about fifteen yards and although I tried to convince myself and everyone else that it was probably a tench, I was pretty damn sure it wasn't.

Bad angling was the bottom line and, on my way home the following morning, I berated myself every mile of the way. You can't afford to do that sort of thing on lakes like Horton, a lesson painfully learnt.

Now, I mentioned our displeasure at the start of the season changing to June 1st, but we weren't strong enough to stick by our 'June 16th forever' convictions, and all fished from the off. All, that is, bar Frogger, who did stick by his guns and turned up at the lake as I was leaving for home, on June 16th – and, boy did he get his just reward. He moved into the Captors after Chilly had moved out and, the following morning, landed the much sought after Lumpy at 41.12lb, a brilliant result, and the first of many for him that season.

One really scary thing happened on that morning, as we were packing away. We were sitting in my swim, having a final brew before leaving, when Chilly pointed to something floating about a hundred or so yards out into the lake. We couldn't tell if it was a log, a fish or what, but if it was a fish it was pretty big, and suddenly the thought of the previous weeks capture of Jack was suddenly uppermost in all of our minds. Binoculars revealed a scaly flank, but that was all, however that was enough for Chilly to go into the depths of despair and so, pretty quickly, we shot up to the Lodge jetty and broke out the boat. Reg and I rowed and, the nearer we got to the fish, the further down into the depths Chilly plummeted. Then, from ten yards or so, one of us said 'It's a pike!'

Immediately, we could all see the truth of that, but it was a bloody big pike nonetheless, and could only be one fish – Thicky. We didn't know how long Thicky had been in Horton, long before the carp were introduced, that's for sure, and living on a fine diet of trout for all of those years had catapulted him to beyond thirty pounds in weight. The name, obviously, gives away the ease at which he was captured, and once a few hardy souls had dusted off the lures and deadbaits for the winter, he would normally make a visit to the bank every couple of weeks until the end of the season. Laney had caught him a couple

Thicky, not Jack. Relief mixed with sadness

of years previously at 32lb, and I had seen him only a few months earlier than our boat trip, when Barry the catfish man had caught him at a similar weight. He was a huge fish, with a massive head, but now that head was lolling around, on the verge of death. Chilly got hold of him and we quickly made our way back to the Lodge steps, where Del was waiting. On inspection, it looked like the fish had a bloody great tench lodged in its throat and, try as they might, Del and Barry were unable to extract it and the great fish was gone. Although there was huge relief when we realised that the ailing fish wasn't Jack, it was still tremendously sad to see such a magnificent fish die, and it put a bit of a damper on the whole weekend, especially for me (strangely, Jack was seen a couple of days later, in the arms of Weedbed Willy, when he caught the great fish from the Spindley Tree, still at 49lb). The following weekend was a huge problem for me because my car had blown something essential and mechanical, and was now as useful as an ashtray on a motorbike! Without any obvious means of transport there was only one option – the train! Laney was fishing at Wraysbury during the week, so I got him to drop my gear at the lake, and then arranged with Del for a lift from Wraysbury station. Even getting away early, the journey was horrendous and after nearly three hours of sweaty, frustrating commuting, I was heading towards the lake in Del's van. He'd informed me that the lake was really busy, with more than twenty people there, so it seemed like another fruitless weekend was in store – when would my bloody season actually start!?

Chilly was in the Ski Slope, some twonk from Bury (or Borry, as he kept calling it all night and day) was next to him in the Sick Swim, and his mate was in the Mouth of the Bay swim. We'd arranged for another football afternoon on Saturday, and the area behind these swims was the obvious place for it so, having learnt that the twonk and his mate were off in the morning, I decided to set up in the corner of the Church Bay, more from a convenience point of view rather than with any illusion of catching a carp. By the time the match started I would be in the Sick and we could seriously get on with some fishing. Unfortunately, it didn't quite pan out like that as the Bury lads, having learnt of the feast and football planned for the afternoon, decided they'd stay until early evening – brilliant!

It truly was a feast; tons of food and drink, seven or eight of us watching the football, and

Food, drink - and that Stuart Pearce penalty!

England winning on penalties – and of course, that Stuart Pearce penalty. As much as he says that wasn't his abiding memory of the game, Chilly hasn't stopped talking about it from that day to this (maybe a slight exaggeration, but you get the drift). Just as we were gathering, pre-match, Mainline's main man, Steve Morgan popped over to see us. It's very rare that Steve gets out to those parts so it was really nice to see him, but what about the bloke with him. Glen, a sixteen foot fourteen inch black guy, lovely as you like, was sort of Steve's 'minder'. I got chatting to him and he was well into his carp fishing, doing quite a bit of time on Steve's lake at Averley, then he told me he did a bit of work on the door at a few clubs in Essex and London. I commented that he probably only had to stand there and look mean, but he laughed a big, Frank Bruno laugh, then lifted his shirt to reveal a massive scar above his stomach.

'Someone pulled a shotgun. Pretty lucky really, a few inches higher and it could have been real bad!'

We all agreed, and then started calling him 'Sir'!

Steve had brought some dip over for us to try, we told him we already had the Garlic and Herb and Barbeque dips (ho, ho) but then he gave me a pot of a lovely, thick pineapple dip and I vowed that I would use it later that day.

After the football had finished, and the revelling had calmed down, the Bury boys eventually buggered off and I swiftly moved into the Sick swim. I'd left one of the baits soaking in the dip for a few hours and it was that one that was launched out to the left. In mid air, it was caught by a freak summer zephyr, which edged it a little further left than I'd intended, but it landed at the right distance, and I was sure that Chilly wouldn't mind sharing a weedbed with me. The right hand rod was nowhere near to Chilly's, or anyone else's swim, which was a little disappointing, but once the brolly was up and a few baits fired out, I at last thought I was fishing, and cracked a cold ale to celebrate.

The margins in front of these swims are remarkably deep, almost twenty feet deep in front of the Ski Slope, and it was because of this that Chilly was a little perturbed. He was using back leads to keep the line down as much as possible, but because of the deep margins, the line angle was very acute. How to overcome this? We pondered it over a couple of ales, and then the Flying Backleads circus troupe was formed! We decided we needed to fling a back lead down the line as far as possible and, for that, we required height, and we had it in the shape of Rob Tough. Although not in the same stratosphere as Glen, Rob is well over six feet tall, and with me on his shoulders we would be able to fling the lead from well over twelve feet above the ground. Amazingly, with the myriad possibilities for disaster available to us, we achieved the whole thing without a hitch, just the odd wobble. Chilly cast to the seventy-yard mark, then held his rod high into the air and walked behind us. Already aloft on Rob's shoulders, I attached the back lead, then flung it with all my might, the three of us whooping with delight as it entered the water fifty yards out – surely it could not fail?

And, bizarrely, it didn't. An hour after we'd retired to bed, I was standing beside Chilly as he played a tench to the net, but when it went into the net it became a fully scaled tench! At 12lb, it is probably one of the smallest carp in the lake, but just as prized as its larger brethren, and Chilly was suitably chuffed, especially having lost a carp from there a couple of days earlier.

I felt like I'd been back in bed a couple of minutes when, suddenly, I was wrenched from my dreams about clowns and acrobats by a screaming buzzer – and it was mine. The sun was dazzling, having risen an hour or so earlier, and I had to scrabble, one handed, to find my sunglasses, whilst something on the other end was really getting to dislike the taste of pineapple! I played the fish for about ten minutes, all the time shouting Chilly's name, but it appeared that he was the only one on the lake who couldn't hear me. Eventually, the fish was rolling in front of me and, just as it slipped over the net cord, I noticed a distinct lack of lips and knew exactly what fish it was – The Parrot. Chilly certainly heard the next sounds that issued from my lips, as I screamed my lungs raw. Over on the Plateau bank Reg was wandering down to Laney with a cup of tea, 'Jenks has had one then,' he said. 'Yup,

Beautifully ugly – and so was the fish!

certainly sounds like it,' was Laney's pained reply.

The throng gathered and photos were taken. At 44lb it was a big weight for the Parrot, and it was obvious they hadn't really spawned yet but, as is always the way at these times, the weight was really immaterial. Chilly claimed that it should have been his fish, but I laughed that off and told him that this was a really special carp and not many could catch it – how true that proved. This was a real history fish and I was ecstatic – now my season had started and I couldn't wait to get back next week.

Deep, deep JOY!

My car problems continued, and the following weekend I had to utilise Chrissie Pearson's services to get me from the station to the lake. It wasn't as busy as the previous weekend, but there were still a dozen or so on, with the main swims being occupied (well, the main ones I wanted to fish). Reg was in the Reeds, so I fished to his left in the Waiting Swim (I think it's called the Scooter or something, now). I'd brought the cooking equipment, as usual, so Reg joined me in my swim then, as the evening wore on, Robbie popped over for a chat, and we sat there enjoying the fine summer evening, with Virgin radio playing in the background. Then, the first chords of 'Shine on you Crazy Diamond' drifted across the swim and we all sat back and smiled. As the vocals began, we all joined in –

'Remember when you were young, you shone like the sun,'

'Shine –BEEP!

The left hand rod tip nodded and I was immediately beside it but, as the lyrics continued, unaccompanied, the indicator remained still and the buzzer silent, as it did for the rest of the night. Aah, what might have been, and that was the event that inspired me to write about the Crazy Diamond incident in 'the Myth', although the final fictional outcome was much more exciting than fact.

The next morning I was awoken by a fast take to the same rod but, on striking, felt no resistance and wound in the lead and rig. I felt up for a move, and had seen a few fish in front of the Ski Slope and Sick swim so, when Nick announced that he was moving out of the Ski Slope that afternoon, I was in like Flynn. Curly Bob was fishing in the Sick swim, and it's always a joy to fish with him, he's so bloody amusing, and we spent a humorous but fishless night with Rob Tough in attendance as well – bloody good company, all.

The next morning saw me, same time, same place as the week before, only this time it was Curly Bob that was wielding the rod and I soon netted a fine 27lb common, which he was delighted about because it was his first of the season. He followed that up the next morning with a 28lb grass carp, then moved out to let Kodak move in and, within 2 hours, Kodak had caught the Thorpe Park common at 35lb – that certainly was the swim to be in at the moment. Some sad news came out of that weekend, though, because the glorious Moonscale was found dead, heavily spawnbound. Tony Badham had seen it a week earlier in the Weedy Bay and said it looked huge but a bit distressed, and thus it proved. A sad day.

I couldn't put up with the train anymore so, whilst I was busy trying to get some dough together to buy myself a new car, I managed to badger Lin into lending me her car for the weekend (dunno how I managed that, it certainly wouldn't happen now), and when I arrived at the lake, was pleasantly surprised to see the Dog Bay free of anglers. I loved the Dog Bay, especially the Shoulders swim, which had been very good to me over the years, and it was there that I moved into that evening. The weed was quite thick in there, but after plumbing for about an hour in the rain, I eventually found a little bit of clear at about thirty yards. I put out about 200 baits in the area and fished both baits in the vicinity, then settled down for a very rare evening on my own. The rain carried on, unabated, all evening and I got my head

down fairly early, only to be awoken at two in the morning by the para. In fact I'd been awake a few minutes, having been woken by a big fish crashing to my right, in front of the Lookout, so it was there that Chilly headed, and I back to sleep. I was up and out fairly early in the morning, in search of a new motor but returned, unsuccessful, an hour or so later. After despatching the baits to their previous spots, I got the kettle on and was joined by Chilly and Frimley Mark for tea and toast, and it was whilst we

The wonderful Curly Bob, with 27lb common and party novelty.

were just into our second round that my right hand rod just ripped! There was toast and teeth flying everywhere, then there was me holding on as the carp moved steadily to the right, hitting the surface and sending up an impressive bow wave. I managed to slow it, turning it back towards me – then the hook pulled!

There is no substitute for that sickening feeling, and it never gets any better, no matter the size of fish you're fishing for, but here you never knew what it may have been, and I was not happy. That was the last of any action to me and Chilly, but Frimley Mark ended a frustrating 3 years by bagging a 19lb linear from the opposite corner of the bay and we were chuffed to buggery for him.

A couple of days later, our old mate C.P. had a brilliant session when, in the space of a couple of days, he caught the Lady, the Long One and the Koi, losing a fish as well! All were a little down in weight due to spawning, but that matters not in those situations and Chrissie was suitably over the moon. He was good at these little bursts of quality fish, and a few years hence he would have the session to end all sessions. So, with the knowledge that they had spawned and were a bit peckish, we all looked forward to the next session. That weekend was mine and Lin's anniversary and, as she has done before, she decided to come to the lake with me. She absolutely loved Horton, and would spend as much time as possible at the lake, so we booked a day off work and arrived on Thursday evening. I was, obviously,

keen on getting back into the Dog Bay, but with Kodak in the Shoulders swim and Chilly in the Lookout, we moved into the Gate for the night, ready to move in after Kodak in the morning. Another nice evening spent in good company, but with only a 6lb tench to show for my efforts by daybreak, I was happy to move into the Shoulders by mid morning. Nothing seemed evident in front of me, so I spent a fair part of the afternoon up the tree in the Lookout, watching the parade of the monsters. It was a truly stunning sight, seeing eight or nine fish well in excess of thirty, and some almost fifty pounds, meandering lazily through the weedbeds not five yards from Chilly's rod tips. Although

Perfect hangover cure – 19lb Anniversary common

frustrating for him, it was wonderful to watch from above and I could have stayed there all weekend, just watching. But there were Parrot's to be celebrated, and when Reg and Phil Thompson arrived in the early evening we all commenced on our quest to feel as sick as one!

Morning brought the fact that most of us had, in fact, succeeded, and we sat there moaning quietly whilst the kettle boiled for the umpteenth time, and the toast got buttered. Then, like Groundhog Day, the right hand buzzer screamed and the toast flew. The fish, this time, just continued on its right hand course and I had to take to the water and wade along the margins to the Lookout where Chilly soon netted a nice little 19lb common. Although nowhere near the size of what I thought I'd lost the previous week, at least it had stayed on and I was pleased as punch for that. That afternoon, the next morning, and the next couple of sessions, were spent just watching the carp cruising around in the weed, and it became more and more frustrating. At times there would be almost two dozen fish in view from the Lookout tree, or the Weedy Bay tree but, apart from the odd capture here and there, the lake was shutting up shop. The weather was very oppressive and muggy, and we seemed to have been stuck in this high-pressure system for ages and, with little sign of it moving, we braced ourselves for a hot, sultry and frustrating summer.

So, there I was, an hour after Chilly's departure and aloft in the Weedy bay tree yet again, but all in vain. The sun was high and the fish were nowhere to be seen – apart from that one! A hundred or so yards out into the lake, a carp rolled in between the Captors on the south bank and the Ski Slope on the north bank, dead centre. The Captors was occupied but I was sure that the Ski Slope had recently been vacated, and it was one of my favourite swims. Grabbing a bucket, I took a steady stroll around the lake but, just as I walked into the swim, I spied a water bottle – bollocks! Minutes later the water bottle was joined by a grinning Chrissie Pearson. 'Ha ha, beat you to it fella!' he crowed. Oh well, better CP than anyone else, he deserved a carp as much as any of us, and being one of the 'good old boys' there was no way I would begrudge him the swim.

I bade him 'good luck' and moped back to the Salt Circle. I'd taken Monday off of work, so Sunday afternoon was foreign territory for me and I was interested to see who else would be leaving soon. With that in mind I returned to my swim to cook in the early afternoon sun, but after ten minutes I felt stifled and had to pour a bucket of water over my head to revive myself. Oh well, just one more look won't hurt. So, up the tree I went again, but even before I reached the top I could see that this time it was different.

There be carp in them there weed beds! And bigguns at that.

Four or five fish were meandering around in a similar area to yesterday, no more than a dozen yards out, and it took all of my will power not to jump down the tree and cast right on top of them. I watched, transfixed, for about five minutes and could see that they kept coming back to the same silty strip in amongst a couple of big weed beds, huge clouds of the stuff being stirred up in classic fashion, so that would be my area of attack and just to confirm that, one of them slid out of the water up to the wrist of the tail, and slid back down just as gracefully – it was Shoulders, and I was suddenly in motion. As quietly as a ballet-dancing hippo I descended the tree and did the classic carp anglers 'fast tiptoe' ten yards back to the swim. I wound in one of the rods – 3 ounce lead and a balanced hookbait, yep, perfect stalking fare! But somehow I managed to slow myself down enough to change the lead for a 2 ounce one. I then grabbed a couple of handfuls of bait and some maples and snuck back to the swim where, with amazing restraint and self control, I lay the rod on the ground and climbed the tree to check the situation out. The fish were still there but the silty strip was no longer their area of occupation. Now they were a few yards further out and, although still casually feeding, I was not sure on what. After a few minutes I could make out a deep hole in the weed, probably only a couple of feet across, but this seemed to have their attention. Waiting for them to move away for a moment, I very carefully flicked some broken boilies and a few maples into the hole, then awaited events. Pretty soon a couple of fish returned, dropped into the hole, then came back out with their mouths obviously working around some food inside. That'll do for me. From floor level it wasn't so easy to see the hole, and it's always amazing how close it is from the ground, but I was pretty sure I had it pinpointed so, once it was carp-free, flicked the bait underarm to drop beautifully into the hole. I slackened the baitrunner, lay the rod on the floor, and then ascended the tree again. My heart was going like a steam hammer, and not just from the constant tree climbing – this was the most exciting angling I'd done for years and even if I didn't catch anything, I wouldn't forget it in a hurry.

As I was atop the tree, Del appeared below, but remained very quiet having quickly and correctly assessed the situation without the need for questions – good angling. I'd seen one or two fish a little behind the weedy hole, then a procession of four moved steadily towards it, led by Shoulders. There was a general milling around, then three left in one direction, to the right, and another went the opposite way – fast! Del was just saying 'Keith, you've got a run' as I heard the baitrunner squeal and, being quick on the uptake, I reckoned that fish might have picked up my hookbait! What transpired over the next hour was epic, really.

The fish tore away towards the open water at the back of the Weedy Bay, but I managed to stop it and guide it back into the bay where there was only ever going to be one outcome, and that was the launching of the boat once the carp became firmly embedded in the thick, twelve foot deep weed jungle. By now, Big Ollie and Richard Stangroom had arrived to offer advice and assistance, and I took both. Del, Ollie and I took to the boat whilst Stan took some great photos from the tree and, within five minutes, it seemed that we had won. I'd been guided over the top of the fish and the pressure and change in angle had freed her from the weed so that I had direct control. But, just as I was about to request a netsman, she made a last bid for freedom and found an even more impenetrable weed bed. Over the next ten minutes or so we tried all manner of angles and tactics, but my mind went back a couple of years to when Laney was in exactly the same spot, with the same problems, and eventually landed Shoulders. The solution that day had been the use of a pole, but he'd long since returned to his homeland, so we opted for the use of a really long stick instead! And long it was, probably fifteen foot long and remarkably unwieldy. Ollie did his level best to lever up the weed, but it took ages for us to get anywhere and I really couldn't see a good conclusion to this battle, but then an inch was gained, and another. Then a foot, and suddenly something was kicking on the end, and as we looked into the depths, there was the huge bulk of Jack floating towards us, mouth first. I could see the boilie in the side of her mouth, and the hook, and I really didn't want to look at that for too much longer. But I didn't have to, because with one deft sweep of the net she was netted and I went absolutely ballistic!

What a moment. What a battle. What a brilliant piece of angling, if I say so myself!

We got some great photos and, even though I'd caught her a year earlier a little larger, it detracted not at all from the capture. I was absolutely elated; my second forty in as many

After an epic battle – JACK!

months and nobody to celebrate with! It was mid-afternoon on Sunday and I had the next day off so.... I packed up and went home! Back then I shunned mobile phones so I had no way of letting anybody know, besides, I knew my chances of another from the bay were totally gone and I sure didn't feel confident where I was, so home it was, with a bloody great big smile on my face!

Three fish in a couple of months was more than I could have wished for, and suddenly my attitude changed. Yeah, we were still going to enjoy ourselves as much as we could, but I felt that there were a few more opportunities for all of us. The fish were definitely on the bait, the rigs were fine, and I had my big carp hooks – how on earth could we fail?

The next couple of weeks saw no let up in the weather, and although the bulk of the British public were lapping it up, most anglers were bemoaning the bloody sunshine and praying for some refreshing rainfall. The middle weekend in August saw me setting up in the Ski Slope, next to Frogger, and despite seeing a few fish in front of me on Friday evening, by Saturday evening I was still fishless. A hot and thirsty walk around the lake had revealed few fish, so another night in the Ski Slope it was, but that was brightened by the fact that Robbie had turned up to do a couple of hours fishing, and had set up in the Sick Swim, to my right. I stood with him whilst he plumbed the swim for a little while, and when he found a significant clear area at about 50 yards, I made him mark the line so we could get some bait onto it in the morning. That we did, and were then happy to show Reg what we had found when he arrived on Sunday morning for a weeks holiday. Somehow, for reasons totally beyond us, Reg had been made a bailiff and, for that, he had the privilege

of using the boat – don't ask me why, it was a constant bone of contention that, not only did they not pay for tickets, but also that the bailiffs could use the boat for baiting up their swims. It didn't go unnoticed that, although Del was well on the way to being top rod on the lake, barely any of his fish were caught without the aid of the floating spod (something Frogger never needed, and he ended up with a cartload by the end).

It was Reg – with the Thorpe Park Common!

But this time we relented and told Reg that the two 25 kilo buckets of party mix he'd brought with him had to be tipped right next to Robbie's marker float! I'd barely left the lake before the first went over the side of the boat, followed by five kilos of boilies. Despite not having any action by Tuesday, he stuck by his guns and deposited the other bucket, and a similar amount of boilies, over the side of the boat that afternoon, then sat back to await events.

I was, as usual, cutting it rather fine on Wednesday morning, and was just finishing in the bathroom prior to leaving for work, when the phone rang. Strange, I thought, then Lin came in with the phone, handing it to me whilst saying 'It's Reg.'

I was almost prepared for what came next, but not quite – decibels are very big at that time of the morning, and when issued at such velocity can crack porcelain! From the volume, I deduced that Reg might have bagged himself a carp, and well he had – The Thorpe Park Common at 35.08, and with it a phrase that he was able to use for almost another decade when discussing our personal best commons – 'Oh, do they come that small then?!'

But, at the time I didn't give a shit, I was just absolutely made up for him, as we all were, and Chilly and Dave soon arrived to help him with the photos, but it would be left to me to help him with the celebrations at the weekend.

He'd obviously had the fish from the clear spot that Robbie had found, and it was getting clearer by the day, especially as he had cooked up some more mix and stuck it out there on Thursday. It was a lovely family affair on Friday, with Katie joining Reg and Lin coming along with me; and setting up next to him in the Mouth of the Bay meant we didn't have to wobble far to get back to our swim when the celebrating was done. After a heavy night, a screaming buzzer at six in the morning is bad, but when it's not yours it's bloody awful. Still, Reg looked like he might need propping up so I dragged myself along side him and watched as he nearly made the carbon flex, but even that miniscule amount of pressure wasn't enough to stop the fish finding a weedbed, so it was boat time again and, after ten minutes of spinning and

Feeling dodgy, but Reg had a battle on his hands . . .

Reg and Starburst – a fine combination

tugging, we eventually netted Starburst for the old boy. Although elated, we were a little subdued after the previous nights excesses, and it wasn't until long after the photos that a semblance of normality returned – Saturday night was destined to be much quieter! Another great session, despite the lack of action to my rods; this was turning into an unforgettable season, and we were only half way through.

The following weekend, Reg and Katie were once again in the Sick Swim, having arrived earlier on Friday, but were leaving Saturday morning to pick up a new Jack Russell puppy from Tony Badham, so I set up in the same swim as last week, with the intention of moving in after Reg. There was no repeat of the previous weeks excitement, although Reg did land a catfish of about three pounds (wonder how big it is now?), and by midday I was eyeing up the area in front of the Sick Swim. It wasn't a simple case to find the clear area, in fact it seemed to have a fine covering of silkweed, but I managed to put two baits in the vicinity on slow sinking pop ups (paratrooper rigs, as they became known), followed by 2 – 300 boilies over the whole area. Chilly and Lynn popped over with Max, early in the afternoon, and it was great to see how well Lynn was recovering, so much so that I was sure that Chilly would soon be back on the pond. The night was uneventful until just before dawn, when I had a bream to the right hand rod, but once recast I could see another blank looming. By 7.30 it was already stiflingly hot, and I began slowly packing away, when Laney arrived in the swim. He was on his way to Wraysbury, and had popped in for a quick cuppa and a chat, then once that was over he left and bade me farewell. With everything ready to go, I just had the

and with the use of the boat he was victorious.

rods left when, with Laney's car barely out of the gate, I had a couple of bleeps then an absolute screamer to the right hand rod. On picking up the rod, I could see the line cutting across the swim to the left, picking up strands of weed like washing on a line as it went. I spent the next five minutes walking steadily backwards, whilst keeping the pressure on, then quickly walking forwards, winding all the time. Somehow, I managed to avoid the need for a boat and soon had a mass of weed in front of the swim, with a great big carp stuck in the middle of it. I quickly got it in the net and as soon as I parted the weed I recognised the fish – SHOULDERS!

I screamed with delight and let all the world know one definitive fact – 'I am God!!' Wickedly, I called Reg first and he was not in the best of condition. He'd had a heavy night, followed by a morning of clearing up brand new puppy sick and poo! Then there was my phone call! Sorry, Reg, didn't realise how much that hurt for so long – otherwise I would really have rubbed it in ('do they come that small?' my arse)!

The great fish, one of my favourite carp ever, weighed 42.04 and looked magnificent, and I was on cloud nine. As I drove home (in my new car) I put a Lynyrd Skynrd CD on and as I came past Gatwick airport, on came 'Freebird'. At full blast I let it assault me, with the final ear-splitting chords fading away just as I drove onto my drive – the most memorable, smile-inducing drive of my life!

The mood could so nearly have been repeated the following weekend, but obviously

Shoulders and the Holy Man – sublime!

my ordainment hadn't been heard of in the necessary quarters, and the hook pulled! I was in the Sick Swim again, this time getting in there before Reg, and on Saturday afternoon, whilst sitting with Chrissie, Frimley Mark and the recently arrived Reg, I had a take to the same rod as the previous week. The fish followed the same route for about 20-30 seconds, then the hook just popped out and it was all over. I tried to remain cool, but that didn't last long, and after a week of walking on water, my feet were firmly back on the ground – ho hum!

A holiday intervened after that and on my return it was great to learn that I would be fishing with Chilly. Lynn had made a very good recovery, and he was told in no uncertain terms to get his arse over the lake, so he did. I arrived a few hours before dark on Friday evening, the nights drawing in sharply as October loomed, and found the old boy set up in the Flat Swim, so the swim next door – the Dug Out – obviously had my name on it. I was not unhappy with the choice because exactly a year earlier I had caught Jack from this very swim, and dropped a couple of baits in similar areas as on that session. We then got down to the really serious stuff that we had both missed out on – cracking a few bottles together – but, with barely half a glass supped the most ridiculous thing happened, Chilly got a bite! He played it gingerly, but within five minutes it was solidly weeded and we knew the boat would be required. Chilly's mate, Stuart had just arrived and volunteered his services as oarsman and pretty soon they were out in the darkness, doing battle. I remembered my own nighttime boat battle from here earlier in the year, and hoped this one would be more successful, and so it proved as Chilly slid the net under the Long One. Although a repeat capture, we were all over the moon after what Lynn and he had been through, and I later realised that the faint, screaming noise I'd heard was my liver, foreseeing the future! At 28.06 it was a similar weight to his previous capture of it, but that mattered little as I reminded him that we really hadn't celebrated its previous capture in the right manner, so now was the time to rectify that slight. By the early hours of the following morning, it was truly rectified, and was by no means slight anymore.

The following morning was remarkably subdued, but by early afternoon the copious cups of tea were beginning to clear the fog. Chilly, Chrissie and I were sitting outside my bivvy, supping another brew, when Frogger came bounding up from his swim, along the bank, and told us to put the radio on, and from it came the strains of Phil Lynott confirming that the boys were, indeed, back in town. We crooned along for a few bars when, from along the bank, came the shriek of a buzzer and Frogger was off like a scalded cat. I grabbed the radio and we all sang at the tops of our voices as Frogger did battle with the unseen foe, the song having long finished by the time he had coaxed the 34lb Black Tail into the net – was that a chorus of livers I could hear, quietly whining?

That night was as bad as it ever got. Stuart, being of Czechoslovakian descent, had brought a bottle of Slivovich with him and it seemed a fine idea that we should pass the evening playing spoof, with a shot of Slivovich to the loser. I'm normally quite good at spoof, but that night I was good at drinking Slivovich and, quite frankly, have no idea how I survived. Come the morning, it was evident from the look of him that Chilly had somehow bent the rules to his favour the previous evening, for he was the only one of us able to stand upright without chundering! A memorable weekend, in more ways than one.

Then, my world changed drastically when the company I worked for suddenly went into liquidation, and I was out of work. I'd worked ever since I'd left school, and really couldn't envisage going on the dole so, as a stopgap, I contacted someone I used to work for to see if he had a vacancy. Although he didn't really, he took me on as a rep in the short term, commission only, and said he'd see if there was anything else in the near future; I ended up working there for the next ten years – cheers Nic. But, for now, I had to get myself a mobile phone and manage the accounts I'd been able to bring with me, so my office was wherever I wanted it to be – hmmm, must think this through real hard!

The first couple of sessions in my new office were pretty fruitless, for all of us, and it seemed like the lake was slowly shutting down for the winter. Rather than follow the crowds into the deeper water, nearer the Lodge, Chilly and I decided to head west towards the Dog Bay, and that's where I found myself on Thursday afternoon – I liked this rep work! I set up in the Lookout and had just put a couple of baits fairly close when my new phone rang. It was my new employer telling me that one of my customers needed to see me urgently - yeah, great job! I managed to put the guy off

NOW we can celebrate the capture of the Long One.

until the following morning, which was why I was up so early to see the fish rolling to my left in the Shoulders swim. As I left the lake, I phoned Chilly and told him to get his arse in the Shoulders swim, and that's exactly where he was on my return, a couple of hours later. To complete the triangle, Reg arrived just before dark and moved in to the Pallet swim to my right. As darkness fell, we were all gathered in my swim for an evening of fine food and drink when Robbie popped in with his missus. We chatted away for a while when, shattering the calm lake, a big fish boomed out in Chilly's swim and, being the excitable type that he is, he had to trot back to his swim to see where it was in relation to his baits. No sooner had he left than we heard a buzzer scream, and we tore round to his swim to see him doing battle with something angry! He'd just got to his swim as the buzzer roared and the fish had taken 20 or 30 yards of line, but was now fairly solid in weed, then his right hand rod ripped into life as well and line flew from the spool. I tentatively picked it up and could feel something on the end, but couldn't be sure if it was the fish that Chilly was playing, so flicked the bail arm open and awaited events. The weed, once again, took control of the matter, and pretty soon Reg and Robbie went for the boat but, whilst they were in transit, Chilly picked up the left hand rod and applied a bit of pressure, and the hook pulled. Quickly switching to the right hand rod, he wound that in without lead, hook – or carp! The mood was pretty black, and we trudged back to my swim to let Chilly sort himself out, and when he joined us there appeared to be only one obvious answer – drink heavily, so we did.

Fish were still getting caught, and some good uns as well, but it was really slowing down, so when I arrived at the end of October, with the clocks having changed, I reckoned this would probably be my last session of the year. I was still doing the reping thing so was able to arrive before midday on Friday, finding Chilly in the

Shoulders swim once again, and therefore it was only logical that I dropped into the Lookout again. The wind was southwesterly, which meant that we were on the back of it, a situation I'd been more than happy with before on Horton. Nothing had been out for more than a week, the wind having blown in

The calm before the Slivovich storm

that direction for most of that time, and as most of the small band of anglers had been fishing on the wind, that reinforced my confidence. I put out quite a bit of the party blend into a couple of holes in the weed, topped up with a fair few boilies, and we sat through the evening with the wind freshening but barely ruffling the reeds in front of us. The next morning we popped over to the Church bay to photograph a twenty pound common for Frogger, which made us even happier to be on the back of the wind, but by the time the evening drew in, nothing had occurred in front of us and we were beginning to plan our winter campaign, away from Horton. We'd just popped the cork from the first bottle when we heard a fish roll in between me and the Shoulders swim, to my left. Chilly had moved out of there earlier in the day and was fishing to my right, in the Pallet, and informed me that the fish was on its way to his swim. I told him it would have to swim past my baits first, when the right hand rod bent round and the buzzer screamed! I struck into a good fish, which hit the surface pretty quickly, thirty yards out, then powered away into a weedbed where it became stuck fast. By this time Barrow Mac had wandered into the swim and, in his usual deadpan way, said 'You in, then?' Certainly felt that way, I gotta say!

The fish wasn't moving, so off went the para, in pursuit of a boat, however, he'd not been gone a minute when the fish surged again and I began to gain line, so told Mac to grab the net. I could tell it was a good fish and when it wallowed over the net cord, and Mac lifted the net, I roared in ecstasy.

'It's out again!' said Mr Deadpan, and I felt a surge on the line and knew he wasn't lying. What the hell was that about! I played it back again for a minute or so, then made fully sure it was in the net before I bellowed again. Chilly was just entering the swim at the second time of yelling and was remarkably confused, but that was soon dismissed when we looked in the net with the torch – it was Jack! Like most of us, I'm not a great one for recaptures, but this was something else. I'd angled for it, I'd hooked and I'd landed it (eventually) and it was my fourth forty of the year, and we

Frogger with one of many from that season

thought that might just be a bit special. At 47.08 it was also a personal best and Chilly convinced me to take a couple of photos of it, although I knew I'd never get better ones than I already had, then we released her back into the pond and just laughed out loud! An hour later, only a little tiddly, and still giggling, I heard a fish roll close in so walked to the end of the jetty and there, at my feet, was Jack. Unable to get through the thick weed in front of the swim, she'd just laid there at our feet whilst we toasted her. I slipped the net under her, then we carried her down to the Shoulders swim and made sure she swam away strongly – what a night, two forties in the space of an hour! Little did we know that that would be the last time she'd be seen alive and, in hindsight, we both feel remarkably privileged to have been there that night.

'Welcome to Gatwick, we hope you have enjoyed your flight.'

As the captains announcement finished, so did our Florida holiday, and Lin and I made our way outside to be met by our chauffeur for the day, Laney. No sooner had he dropped us at home, than he and I were loading my gear up and heading off to Horton.

It was the 2nd of March and was to be our first session back at the lake since November, coincidently about the time that the last fish was actually caught from there. The winter had been spent over at Chalk Farm, at a frozen Averley Lake for our post-Christmas get together, and getting used to being in full time work again (my brief sojourn 'on the road' was soon exchanged for a permanent desk job –

suited me). The week in Florida had been great but now I was gagging to get back to Horton to see if there was a chance of a last-gasp whacker, and the fact that Laney was joining Chilly, Reg and I made it all the sweeter.

On our arrival, on that Friday morning, Chilly was in the Captors, with Reg to his right in the Dug Out, so it seemed only logical that I go to Chilly's left, in the Pallet, and Dave to Reg's right, in the Flat swim. Once we'd sorted all that out, I unleashed the plumbing rod, but took quite a

Jack again – for the first time that evening

while to find anything half presentable and eventually put out a couple of 12"
pop-ups in the most acceptable areas. We were about to use a new bait that Mainline
had made for us which was birdfood based and incorporated the wonderful Milky
Toffee flavour, and first impressions were that the carp would surely love it.
Assuming that they'd been going hungry all winter, I decided to fatten them up a
little, so put a couple of kilos of 14mm baits in the general vicinity of the hookbaits,
then turned at a sound that filled me with dread – the 'clink clink' of beer bottles!
There was Phil Thompson, Chinese eyes smiling, and proffering me a cold Stella –
having been awake for the best part of twenty-four hours I could see where this
would inevitably lead but, hey, it was the first session of a new year, certainly worth
celebrating. And so, down hill it went from there. We spent the best part of the
afternoon in Chilly's swim, drinking and laughing and generally slaughtering
anyone who came within tongue shot – apart from Frogger, we loved Frogger. The
evening didn't get much of a chance to make an impression on me and Chilly, and
bed was soon beckoning, with the others mumbling 'lightweights' and adjourning
to Reg's swim.

Morning brought the usual wreckage, mainly physical, but a hearty breakfast soon
sorted that out and, suddenly, we were all taking it a bit seriously. News had reached
us that half a dozen or so double figure carp had been stocked into the lake a month
or so previously, and for the life of us we couldn't fathom why. We had no idea
where the fish had come from and were sure it was bit of a gamble, but earlier in
the year Ian Welch had caught a couple of upper twenties from Thorpe Park and
dropped them into Horton, and they seemed none the worse for it, so maybe it
was just us, over reacting. That night was much calmer, and we retired to bed
remarkably sober and early, but that didn't mean we were going to get much sleep.
During the night, a huge south westerly blew up and I just lay there waiting to see
sky above me, rather than bivvy, but eventually sleep overtook me and I assumed
that I'd soon be aware if I was de-bivvied.

My next thought, in fact, was 'WHAAAAAT!!!' as my buzzer screamed and line
flew from the spool. The sky was just lightening and, after the initial burst of energy,
the fish was too. I assumed it was a tench, as they did tend to wake up at about this
time, and there was always a chance of real biggun. As I drew it closer it woke up a
little and I revised my estimation, thinking it may well be a carp, and sure enough,
a minute or so later I was netting a low double-figure mirror. My bellow soon
brought the rest of the cavalry and we gazed down on a 12lb mirror that we'd never
seen before, it was obviously one of the stockies, but it was also the first carp of the
year, and we whooped and hollered to our hearts content.

Welcome back – first of the New Year in the shape of Pebbles

We thought that would be the start of it, as did everyone else in the syndicate because, the following weekend, there were a dozen or so cars in the car park when I arrived. The swim I'd been in was, obviously, surrounded so we set up a little further down the lake but, by the time we left, nothing had been caught. I was, therefore, very surprised to receive a call when I got home to tell me that Mac, fishing in the Plateau, had caught three fish in the time my journey home took! All were doubles, two of them stockies, but that must mean that the wake up call had been heard and, sure enough, by the time I got to the lake on Friday afternoon, a further four fish had been hooked with all but one being lost. Richard Stangroom had also landed a 10lb tench, so that really did mean they were on the move.

Chilly was in the Lookout, so I set up in the Pallet, to his right, surprisingly free after a weeks inactivity. By morning, however, we were carpless and, as Reg turned up for breakfast, we all watched as, across the lake in the Church bay, a couple of fish showed themselves. Reg had all of his gear ready to go, and it took Chilly and I little time to be in a similar state of readiness – but who was to fish where? There was only one obvious answer, and that was to spoof for it. So it was that, ten minutes later, I was in Springates, Reg in Hearttail and the loser in the Church bay steps. Oh, how the para whinged and whined and bemoaned his misfortune, that was until a bloody great carp slid out of the water in front of his swim, then we nearly had to nail his feet to the floor!

We blustered and chortled but, by mid-afternoon, we'd not seen a carp for hours and the confidence was visibly draining from us; then Lin arrived with her sleeping bag and a couple of crates of beer, and we were all smiles and deep joy! Chilly and I took a stroll back to the car to get the beers, and on our way back, Del stopped Chilly and told him that 'you'll never catch carp by just socialising, y'know.'

Wise words, indeed – bollocks!

We socialised ourselves silly but, by early morning, it seemed that the wise ones words were not so hollow. Then, as I peered out across the lake I could have sworn I saw someone who looked just like Chilly standing in the Ski Slope – surely not. But, on wandering down to find his swim empty, it was obviously true. I strolled round to berate him for not waking me, but he was too excited to hear my admonishment, and when I saw a carp slide out of the water fifty yards from the Sick Swim, I was quite excited too. He'd seen fish from the moment he'd woken, and had quickly packed up and moved swims – too much snoring coming from our direction, apparently – and had been there for about half an hour when I arrived. Pretty soon, I'd packed all of my gear away and joined him, explaining to Lin that I was probably going to stay that night. She was cool with that, and said she'd stay for a few hours before going home.

The previous afternoon, on my walk back from the Lodge, I'd plumbed the Sick Swim and put out about 100 of the new baits in the area in front of it, so I didn't need to worry about freebies, just a couple of paratrooper rigs to combat the thin layer of silk weed. The baits had been out about ten minutes when one of them ripped off and, after a spirited battle, Chilly was netting an 18lb mirror for me and we went loopy. It was another of the stockies (one that Mac had caught the previous week) but certainly got the juices flowing, and I wasted little time in getting the bait back out, but the lead had barely hit the lake bed when we heard a buzzer howl from Chilly's swim. The battle that ensued was much fiercer than mine and, from atop the high bank, looking into the deep clear water, Reg and I swore that we could see the Lady twisting and turning on Chilly's line. Ten minutes after the initial run, I slipped the net under a big mirror and the para went into orbit! It wasn't the Lady but a fish called the Boxer that Welchie had put in from Thorpe Park last year, and at 31lb it was one to whoop and holler about.

'You won't catch while socialising' I warned Chilly, to which we howled with laughter.

After that mad half hour, we tried to calm things down a little by putting the kettle on, whilst constantly

The beginning of a memorable couple of hours

We could see it twisting and turning in the deep margins

wandering over to the rods and looking accusingly at the lake. An hour or so later we were sitting in Chilly's swim ready to down yet another cup of tea, then disaster – no teabags! I strolled back to my swim to grab some but, as I looked down at the rods, I saw that the left hand indicator was tight to the buzzer and the line out of the clip. On closer inspection, that mad half hour had meant that I'd not turned the bloody buzzer on! Lifting the rod and feeling a solid weight on the end, I called to the others, who soon gathered around to assess matters. A lot of line was missing from the spool, and it was pointing way to the left and passing through many weed beds. Slowly I made headway, but it was just a solid weight on the end, no thumps or signs of life. For what seemed an eternity, but was probably only five minutes, I walked backwards ten yards then walked forwards whilst winding furiously, repeating the process a dozen times until, thirty yards away, we saw a huge weed bed slowly moving towards us. As it got closer, Chilly and Reg started stripping weed away in great big chunks until, all of a sudden, I felt something kick on the end – we were still in the game. Chilly slid the net as far as possible and I pulled the whole jungle over the net but, when he lifted it, we saw the line going out of the other side of the weed and back into the lake. After another minute of frantic weed ripping, I suddenly felt a surge on the line and realised I was in direct contact. As with Chilly's margin, mine was

'You won't catch while you're socialising.' Oh, really!

deep and clear and we could see a big fish twisting ten feet below the surface and as it neared the top I said out loud 'Please don't let it be Jack!'

'Oh, it ain't Jack, boy,' assured Reg, then I watched Chilly reach forward with the net, before hollerin' at the top of his voice 'It's CP's!'

I went ballistic! The rod flew in the air and I screamed myself stupid. Loads of stuff was being shouted, little of it made sense, but it all made perfect sense. I was here and Chilly was there and it was all a bit here and there and,

If it don't make you feel like this...

once we sacked it up for a bit of a breather I had to retire to the darkness of the bivvy for a few moments, just to gather my composure and try to get to grips with what had just happened. Five forties in a season. As far as we knew, no one had ever done that before, but that didn't really seem to matter at the moment.

CP's, that was what mattered. I had caught her a couple of summers ago at 34lb, when she was really spawned out, and hadn't recognised her until we'd studied the photos, but now there was no doubt. 45lb of stupendous carp that would surely

The stupendous CP's – God rest her.

crack the fifty-pound barrier in the next few years. We did the photos and smiled and remembered that we would never catch anything whilst we were enjoying ourselves, then Reg and Lin went and it was just me and Chilly. The capture was oh so much sweeter because they'd been there, especially Lin who, although having seen me catch a few carp over the years, had never seen one of that size. But what a season we'd had, and Chilly and I soaked it up and talked bollocks for a few hours, drinking just tea, until I sloped off to bed, ready for an early morning departure for work. But, five in the morning saw me and Chilly drinking another cup of tea and watching the odd carp roll over our baits. I was off pretty soon after, but what a lovely way to end the most memorable session of the most memorable year.

The season ended the following week with Reg entertaining the crowds on the lake, then all of us entertaining each other in the lodge at the end of season party – a fitting way to end a great season for all of us.

But then the epitaph, and how were Chilly and I to know, at the time, that we would be the last people ever to see Jack and CP's alive? The joy we felt on those occasions was shattered and crushed a few months later when wanton stupidity saw some of the most wonderful creatures destroyed by crass negligence. Whether you know the story or not, it matters little, what matters is that we still haven't learned by this grossest of human errors. In hindsight, it was the deaths at Horton, and the same flagrant dicing with death at Wraysbury, that was the seed that saw ECHO bloom into existence, a couple of years later. What is so galling is that the people who were so blatantly to blame for this slaughter remain stain free, Teflon-coated.

I had the most wonderful season, with wonderful friends, and caught wonderful carp, but I would have forfeited the latter if it meant that they were still swimming around today. I know that sounds rather glib and throw away, but that's how I feel, as do the rest of us, I just hope we keep trying to learn from these mistakes.

But let's not end on a low – I, for a brief moment in time, was indeed a God, and that was good enough for us because, by heck, we enjoyed ourselves and that's what it's all about, really.

In the end, we just enjoyed ourselves

A stunning Oxfordshire mirror

Chapter 8

Wraysbury Bound

No one could ever complain again about not having enough time to go fishing, when you read a story like that. We all sat around and marvelled at what Keith had achieved that season. I am married to the greatest inspiration I will ever need, but Keith's story should light every ones fire and even though I missed a lot of the action, it was just great to get the calls from him, and the tales of monsters only made me more determined to get out fishing. And as you have read, that is exactly what I did. For me, the over riding memory will always be his capture of CP's, a very special day, spent with a very special friend. Unbeknown to both of us at that time, things were about to change quite drastically once again and this was a period when we would lose a huge part of our angling heritage, my scenery would change, and Keith and I would bag a whacker or two from, what for me, is the Everest of carp fishing.

Somehow, I managed to wangle the last few days of the season off, this meant that I could fish hard, right up to the end. I really wanted to be there for the infamous Horton party, and drink a toast to one of the most remarkable years in my fishing so far. Thankfully, when I arrived, the Ski Slope was empty so that was where I set up camp. The lake was quiet considering what had been happening and although there were a few anglers down towards the lodge end, that left only Micky Gray up to my right in Springates Point. Much the same as the week before, I set my traps and, despite the weather being decidedly cold, unsurprisingly my confidence was high. The night was quiet, as was the morning, but I managed to have a chat with Micky around lunch time as he made his way to the Five Bells for a swift half...or two. A little while later I was sitting by the rods, bemoaning my lack of action, when one of them registered a jittery sort of take. I lifted into it, not for one moment thinking a carp was involved, then the rod was wrenched over and, to my utter surprise, line ripped from the spool, at which point I decided that it just maybe a carp! We had a bit of a stand off for a while until I managed to get it moving toward me. Nothing exciting happened until it neared the deep margin and rolled, and there, for all the world to see, were the bulging eyes, and the superb ugliness of the Parrot. Micky was returning from the pub and had just entered my swim when the fish dived for the over hanging branches of a tree to my left then, suddenly, it all came to a grinding halt. With Micky holding the rod, I stripped off and made my way down the line into the margins and as I dove under, I was confronted with a whacking great big carp wrapped around a tiny twig. For the briefest of moments two ugly buggers sized each other up but, unfortunately, he reacted first and with a flick of his tail he turned away from me, leaving the hook neatly embedded in the twig, and that was the last I was to see of him for the next few years. I felt totally gutted, so much so that I reeled the rods in and decided to call a halt to my season a day or two early. I sat there for a very long time and thought about the previous nine months. Sure, I had lost a few, and there was the Lynn situation that needed dealing with on an almost daily basis, but I had indeed lived a large slice of my dream. I really couldn't wait for the following season to arrive -then I was going to learn 'em good!

There was still the end of season party to attend to, and when Reg arrived and moved into the swim I had vacated, I set about collecting as much beer as I could. Whether he liked it or not, the celebrations were going to begin in his swim,

and so the crowds gathered and the beer flowed. It was just nice to be surrounded by some great people, when all of a sudden Reg got a bite and the crowd roared! Now Reg isn't one to put the varnish on his rods through any undue stresses and strains, and the more we encouraged him to put a bend in the damn thing, the more the carp tried to make good its escape until, eventually, it all came to a stop. Embedded in weed, there was only one thing for it, so Keith and I legged it round to Del's swim for the boat, where it always seemed to be residing. Nothing had occurred when we eventually arrived back at Reg's plot, apart from the fact that he was taking more flack than a world war two

Reg got a bite, and the crowd roared

bomber. We quickly got him on board and set sail, and as is the way of these things, once over the fish it came free quite quickly. All the way out he had been telling us it was a monster, but when a tiny little mirror hit the surface, I thought every rib in my body was going to break, I was laughing that much - poor fella. We managed to get safely back to his swim, and the only thing for it was a group shot with Reg holding his prize. It turned out to be the small mirror that Keith had caught a few weeks earlier and it kind of set the mood for the evening, and what an evening it was. The lodge was rocking that night, but my drinking prowess, which was never actually that good, found me in the back of my car relatively early, but time and again I was dragged out to drink some more, and who was I to argue? A brilliant end to an incredible season. Then the world decided that it wanted to go mad, and plans had to be changed once again.

All I could think about was getting the money together to pay for next years fishing, but it was hard to ignore the news. All over the globe flash points were making the headlines, and suddenly the whole of the Airborne Brigade was on standby for just about everything. Eventually, I was called into my boss's office and whilst they would do everything they possibly could to make sure Lynn was looked after, I would have to be included in any of the planning. As much as I love my fishing, doing what I had joined the army to do in the first place was a much more appealing prospect and, at the end of the day, I simply didn't want to let anyone down, so if I was needed, then I was going to be there come what may. For the next few weeks it was all about getting things ready, but for what, we had little idea. All the equipment needed servicing and sorting, and that took a bloody long time and, to that end, I could see another year in the carp fishing wilderness coming up. I was loathe to simply fish at Chalk Farm just because of life's restrictions, but eventually

I came up with a plan. I explained the situation to Ian Welch, and he said that if I dropped my Horton ticket, I would get it back whenever I wanted it, which was nice. Now, the next water on my list to fish was Wraysbury, and although it looked as if I would be short on time, I decided to buy a ticket and spend what little time I had looking for opportunities, and getting to know the place. Laney was the font of all knowledge about the place, so

Reg held his prize aloft

maybe I could get a little head start. I couldn't help thinking how crazy I was to do this, but I was happy once the ticket arrived. With so little time to go fishing, and once the army madness had settled down a tad, I really needed to go angling, not just fart around for a quick overnighter, but a proper session. Keith had a couple of mates that he had met down at Anglers Paradise in Devon, Mick Dickens and Graham Jarman, and it just

Graham and Mick, our secret weapons

so happened that they were both bailiffs on the Linear Complex in Oxfordshire, and it was this handy little snippet that was about to save my sanity. One water at the venue, Manor, held their only forty pound carp, so I decided I would like a little dabble on there. We found out as much as we could about the place, and from the sounds of it the fishing was normally done at mega range (well it was a long way in those days). I just thought it would be fun to blast a few single hookbaits all over the place for a few days. A week before Easter, a mate from Aldershot, Stu MacDermot and I, headed off for the wilds of Oxfordshire where we would fish for a couple of days until Keith arrived, toward the weekend. With everything packed into Stu's little car, we looked like a pair of refugees rather than carp anglers and off we went, Oxford bound. A few weeks before this, I had grabbed a couple of hours at a local lake and whilst I was there, read a magazine. In side the pages there was a word search competition and I completed it, so, later that day at work I sent it off and, never having won a thing in my life, I promptly forgot all about it. I was, therefore, amazed a couple of weeks later to hear that I had won, and a set of Leslies of Luton Insight rods would be winging their way to me shortly. Well, they had arrived just before our departure and looked like the 'blast 'em over the horizon, nutter bastard' kind of rods, so I was now looking forward to breaking them...if I could! On our arrival we made our way around the lake until we came to an area without carp anglers in it, and that would do just fine. Manor, in those days, had just under half of its banks out of bounds, so much of the fishing revolved around getting hookbaits as near to those banks as possible. To begin with, it was very uninspiring and the first night passed with just a double to Stu for our efforts.

Come the morning, though, I was to meet a fellow that would become a good friend, and is the greatest bailiff that ever walked the face of the planet. He would not thank me for revealing how we first met, safe to say a rather loud bang not far from my brolly had me diving for cover. Once over the shock, I got talking to Roy Parsons, the head man of Linear, and from that day on I have enjoyed every single moment spent in that neck of the woods. But, back to the fishing. It was crap basically, and nothing I could do seemed to make

Roy Parsons, probably the best bailiff in the world

a difference, even the age old 'whack 'em into someone else's swim' ploy, failed to bring the desired response. As far as I knew, all Oxfordshire carp were bastards, and I wanted to go home. Remembering that Jenks was inbound, however, brightened the mood and I even went and bagged a carp. Now, the first carp you catch from any new water is an absolute result, as it breaks the spell, but this one

First blood at Manor

meant a lot to me considering the severe limitation that the problems with Lynn, plus the army situation, had put on my time. He wasn't the prettiest carp in the lake, and by no means the biggest, but that 22lb mirror put a huge smile on my face, so much so that I was compelled to go to the off-licence for some supplies! So it was, the following day, Jenks arrived and I was feeling a little under the

He'd only been there five minutes!

weather. I wasn't as much help as I should have been, so he simply lobbed them out in the pond and put the kettle on, after which we sat down, and he got himself a bite. I couldn't help moaning about the fact he had only been there five minutes, but hey, thems the breaks. He roared in triumph as the 27lb mirror rolled into the outstretched net - that was a nice start. Sometime later he tested my patience to the limit by hooking another, and what a fish it turned out to be. It was a shockingly dark linear carp, and looked outrageous on the unhooking mat. At 28lb and a few ounces, we were quite blown away, and it turned out that this fish was called the Random Linear, and there and then I decided I needed to catch it, but I had no idea at the time how much of a nemesis it would turn out to be. Keen to even the score, I resorted to sinew busting tactics, and really went for it. Now, I can chuck a lead a long way, I've always been able to, the thing is, I keep hearing that distance has as much to do with technique than anything else. Well, I have no technique, and rely solely on brute force and ignorance, so when we saw a fish at silly range, I wound up my new toys and blasted a bait right into the rings it had left. I smiled at Keith, and he just shook his head. It was without doubt the longest cast I had made up to that point and one which, we both thought, deserved a carp, which was exactly what I got. An uninteresting battle resulted in me holding a lovely 24lb mirror up for the camera, and with that the action

Jenks and the Random Linear

stopped, and we all departed the following day full of the joys of spring. I vowed to return, but it would be a while before I did. I loved the place, and in the end it was very good to me. For now though, I had a mission. Wraysbury.

Poor old Laney must have felt like a sucked maggot as I tried to get every last bit of information from him. What good it was going to do me, I had no idea, but at every opportunity I went for a walk around the place. Having only been there once before, and just getting brief glimpses as I drove by, it is hard to imagine how frightening the prospect of fishing the place was. It's not until you actually view it from an angling point of view that the enormity of the task is revealed. I was afraid...very afraid! My first visit found me driving to the end of the peninsula and stopping for a while in the Drive in Dredger swim. It was fairly warm, and to my total amazement there were several carp swimming around on the surface, just short of Ten-Acre island. They were so far out that I couldn't possibly have identified them, but I watched, fascinated, for ages, whilst running through my head the fish that I would be angling for. The pick of the bunch was obviously Mary, but I tend to get very dizzy and have nose bleeds when I think about carp of that size. Instead, my mind was full of images of Mallin's, he was just my kind of carp. I'd probably seen a picture of him five years before, and at that time I added him to my list

as the last member of a triumvirate I most wanted to catch, Shoulders from Horton and Single Scale from the Car Park being the other two. As I turned back to my car, I had convinced myself that Mallin's would be the first one to chalk off my list. Let battle commence.

But, first and foremost, the army situation needed addressing. One minute we were on twenty-four hours notice to move, then that was cancelled, and this was going on almost daily. It was very hard on

I vowed to return

the troops, and not doing my fishing brain any good at all but thankfully, by April, the world decided to come to its senses and the mayhem seemed to subside. With not a lot else happening other than the normal army routine of 'on the bus off the bus' and hurry up and wait, I thought I might ask a very leading question. I spoke again to my boss, who was just as fed up as me with the situation.

"You might as well go fishing," he said. Tempted as I was to run out of the door, I played it cool. Well, surely there must be something I can do? No, he said, all that could have been done was done so, half an hour later, I was at home checking with Lynn, and trying to throw all of my gear into the car. Wraysbury here I come! I had not expected to be spending any great amount of time there, and fully expected to fish much as Phil Thompson had done and if I had a fraction of his success then I would be happy. That said, I had got myself a boat, not the best bit of kit in the world, but it would get me afloat and with a little bit of help I'd managed to make it sea worthy. In reality, it was about the most unstable and down right dangerous thing I could have used, but needs must and all that.

Having never fished from a boat before, I was a little unsure how to proceed. I figured the best way would be to throw everything in and see what happened but, from the very off, it was obvious that I needed some kind of baling device - Lordy, it had more holes in it than a colander! This also meant that most of my gear got a

Shaky Del, top man!

good soaking. Still, a touch of hardship is what I had been used to all my life, so this would be absolute luxury, all things considered. With little idea what I was doing, I decided that I would have to move around a lot and generally get used to the lay of the land. There was also the task of getting to know the other anglers on the lake and over the next couple of weeks I bumped into the likes of Tench Bloke, Rory, Plumb Bloke, Action Jackson and Shaky Del. The latter two I was destined to spend far too much time drinking with, but what a great laugh. After a while I started to feel more at home with the place, and knowing that Keith had got himself a ticket meant that every journey to the lake was like a boys own adventure. It was on my third trip that things started to come together. Keith had yet to make a visit, and was away on holiday at the time, so with the May weather becoming increasingly hot, I had it in my mind to spend the session on the North Lake. Obviously, I would move to the South if I needed to, but it was one area that I had yet to discover and having an off-license just a stones throw from the lake may also have had something to do with my decision, but we won't dwell too much on that. I launched the boat, and once fully loaded and with the holes letting in enough water, I set off. Eventually, I arrived at a swim called the Bus Stop in Sunnymeads corner, it was Friday afternoon and to be honest, just a pleasure being there. I soaked up the atmosphere for a while before deciding to actually do some fishing. If the carp could move unmolested into the bay, then I was sure they would venture into the margin, so this is where I set some traps. Not being able to get into the corner of the bay, I walked down and sprinkled some pellets in the area, at least that would give me some indication fish had been in there, even if they didn't roar off with one of my hookbaits. Nothing happened during the night and, as soon as I was a couple of brews to the good, I decided to head off for a little look around. As I walked into the corner of Sunnymeads, I could just make out a couple of vortexes - were they tail patterns? I really couldn't be sure, so I shimmied up the nearest tree, then I nearly fell straight back out again when, at my feet, was Mary, the largest carp in the land. I stayed and watched her for ages as she slowly made her way toward the pellets I had left the evening before but, as she approached them, it was obvious from her body language that she was not at all happy. Fins up and bristling, she turned and hid herself in a bush a little further up the road bank margins, and there she stayed, with just the tip of her nose breaking the surface. Having read just about everything there was to read about this place, I recalled that she had at least eaten someone's mixers at some point so I raced back to my gear and quickly assembled my floater rod, and with a net and some mixers I eagerly set off. Walking a little way past her I drifted maybe ten biscuits into the area. For a moment I thought she may be interested, but no sooner had they gone over her head, than she started to swim slowly up the margin. I moved as fast as I could into the next available gap and pulted out a few more mixers. This time, and to the accompaniment of my jaw hitting the deck, she rose gracefully and ate the lot - well knock me down with a controller float. I rushed as quietly as possible into the next available gap and once again sent a small pouch of mixers ten yards

There was Mary, the largest carp in the land

out into the lake. This time, though, my float had been cast a few yards beyond them, if she came up again I would twitch it back into position and then, as if on cue, she did just that and I twitched (probably a lot!) the float into her path. She ate the lot again, and rather charmingly ignored my hookbait, before continuing her journey. Two minutes later I had set a trap once again on her intended path, but refrained from casting. What I did was put more free offerings a little further out and hoped she would gain confidence. She nailed the first lot and as she moved on I lost sight of her, so, convinced she was going for the second batch, I launched the controller beyond that and it landed smack on her head! With an almighty swirl she was gone, and I watched as she sent up a bow wave across the lake. Bollocks!! I was a quivering, sweaty, mosquito ravaged mess so I decided to climb a tree and sulk. This was just about the best move I could have made, because whilst sitting in the tree deciding which branch I should throw the noose around, I spotted some carp. Right in front of me, at about 110 yards, was the dot island, and swimming around it must have been most of the Wraysbury carp. For a couple of hours I plotted their route, basically they were doing a figure of eight around that feature and the larger cigar island further to my left, but on each of their circuits I noticed that they disappeared from view in one particular spot. That was all I needed to know, and as I made my way round to the gear I decided that I was going to let them have some bait. Keith and I had decided to carry on as we had at Horton, particles and boillies and lots of 'em so, to that end, the first thing that I loaded into the boat was three rather large buckets of the mix and then a rod. Life jacket on and away I went. It was about 150 yards from the Bus Stop to the spot, and I spent a few minutes looking at the lakebed through my diving mask. To be honest, there was nothing remarkable about it, but if that is where they wanted to be, then that is where I would angle for them. The weed was fairly thick, although not that high off the bottom yet, and so I gently lowered my double pop-up hookbait, directly off the lead, onto the spot. I took a second or two to admire how perfect it looked and then promptly emptied the contents of the three buckets over the area. There was probably about 25k of bait out there now, and I couldn't help thinking that it was probably a bit too much so, just to ease my furrowed brow, I decided to put another rod out there, and with that done I could relax for the first time that day. It was, by now, about three in the afternoon and I was thirsty and then, right on cue, Mr. Thompson appeared round the corner armed to the teeth with cold lager. I greeted him rather like a child would Father Christmas, and so we sat and chatted and drank lots of cold beer. I told him about my day and, as is Phil's way, he managed to stop me fretting about things. If it's going to happen, according to Phil, then it will happen regardless of what we do. That said, it was time to get more beer, and with that he sauntered off to the off-licence, top man! Eventually, he set up in the channel behind the Cigar Island and with nothing better to do we finished off the beer. It was a really pleasant evening, and he was great company, but eventually I had to get some sleep and was soon in the land of nod. The problem was that it had started to rain, and my bloody Delkims were letting in more water than they were keeping out so I covered them up with the polythene bags that my army rations came in, but one of them just wouldn't stop squawking. On the verge of chucking it in the lake, I decided to strip it down as best I could, and try to dry it out. An hour later I must have got it right, because it was once again on the bank stick, albeit with a poly bag to wear, and I was once again in my own bag. At three in the morning I was up, taking an urgent leak, when all of a sudden there was an almighty crash out in the darkness. As soon as I was able I rushed to the rods, and could just make out the activity was in the area of my hookbaits, the game was definitely afoot! Two more fish boshed out as I climbed back into the bag, and it was with some

difficulty that I eventually drifted back to sleep. Around half six, the friggin alarm started squealing like a pig again. I turned over, just about to holler some abuse at it, when I noticed the spool was spinning at a rate of knots. Bloody hell, it was a bite! From the get go, I was convinced it was a good 'un, and nothing the fish did made me feel any different. I was as scared as I was ever likely to be, but the battle raged on. I was wishing Phil would walk into my swim and issue some words of encouragement, but in the end I was glad it was just me and the fish. Getting it near the margins did nothing to dampen its efforts to escape, and for a while it just plodded around, so there was nothing I could do but hope it stayed on, and then the carp hit the surface, and my legs almost gave way - it was Mallin's, I was sure.

With the dog removed, we settled on 38.08

Two pin falls and a submission later he lay in the bottom of my net. The temptation was to rush and get Phil, but I just needed to gather my thoughts and pinch myself, of all the fish to land, it was him. I unhooked him and placed him in the net, in the margins, and once fully secured, I then bolted to get Phil. I don't know what he made of the idiot that gibbered in front of him, but he was soon by my side. We then got hold of Phil Jackson, who was with us in about half an hour. Sometimes captures can be made even more complete when the right people are there, and two finer guys I could not have hoped for. Even Shaky Del arrived to lend a hand. I really hadn't thought about the weighing, but it was suggested that we ought to find out and, with Coral the carp dog trying to get in the sling, it looked as if we had a fifty pounder on our hands, but when Phil got her out of the way we decided that 38.08 was a bit more realistic. In a daze I held him up for the cameras and eventually slipped him back home. Light My Fire!!

It was Sunday morning and soon time to head for home so, with the Titanic loaded up, I headed across the bay, stopping for a while over the area I had hooked the fish. To my utter amazement there wasn't a single grain of hemp or anything left on the spot, it was a poignant reminder of just how much carp can eat. There was also one other job, and that was the ceremonial burial at sea for the buzzers. I had had enough of them, but seeing as we had caught some good fish together I guessed it

Mallin's in all his glory

was the best way to be rid of them. For all I know, they still reside in the middle of the North Lake, and I suspect Mallin's gives them a good kick every time he is in the area for their part in his downfall. What it did leave me with was thoughts of the other two fish in my all time favourite carp list, but for now, they would have to wait. Wraysbury had me firmly in her grip, and I can't tell you how happy I was about that.

I can't tell you how happy I was

A big Wraysbury sky

137

The Banned

Chapter 9

The Banned

Keith had been on holiday in France when Mallin's was in my net, so it wasn't until a few days later that I could fill him in on the details, and what details they were. By the time I had recounted the story for the hundredth time, we were both in danger of spontaneously combusting. The problem we had was that I was having to juggle my meagre time, and he would only be there at the weekends. There was some celebrating to do, and he was the most important guy to do that with, but that would have to wait until his return from France. The weekend following the capture, I was once again Wraysbury bound but the problem here was that everyone else wanted to drink a toast to my success. Although I had got my gear over to Springates Point, and there was evidence of carp in the area, the lure of the pub from hell, The Perseverance, was too great to resist. A few of us rolled out of there around eleven that evening, and an hour later I was standing somewhat unsteadily in my swim. The rods were still in the holdall, and I didn't have the get up and go to unsheathe them, so I simply fell into bed and didn't open my eyes until nine in the morning. Tench Bloke was on his travels and had left a mountain of lager under my bedchair, but I couldn't even look at the stuff. Then Del arrived with a similar amount of the same. As far as I could see, it would have been rude not to share a tin with him, so we did. By midday there was no way I was going to be doing any fishing, but we did get a bit excited when we got a call that Bill Dawson - or Bake Bean Head, as he had become known (sorry Bill) - had landed Mary from No Carp Bay. This I simply had to see so, before I was completely trollied, Del and I got in my boat, then we lugged as much beer and wine round to where the victorious captor was fishing, arriving in the swim just as he was returning the great beast. Hand shakes all round and we popped a cork or two, and there we stayed for quite some time, in actual fact it was dark by the time Del and I decided to head back to our swims. What followed was just about the stupidest thing I could ever have done, but I did it, so here goes. Back at the boat, that was nestling in the margins of the gap that separates the North and South Lakes, Del was just about to save my life. My intention was to simply row the few short yards to the opposite bank and walk to where my gear was, at which point Del insisted that I put my life jacket on, which evidently I resisted for some reason. Eventually, he had me dressed, and much against his better judgment I set off. It was probably around eleven in the evening by now, but it was some three hours later that I eventually had some idea of where I was! I vaguely remember people cheering as I passed them for the umpteenth time, and the fact that I had a couple of cans to keep me company along the way. I arrived, by some miracle, in the margins just to the left of the Rocky Barge, and once I had come to rest I tried to step onto the bank. The next thing I remember was standing on the bottom of the lake in 18ft of water as my boat came to rest right by my side. The life jacket I had on was actually not inflated, because it was a device we used for parachuting called a Personal Life Preserver. It needed a handle pulling and I was having some difficulty finding it, but once I did I was lifted from the bottom and surfaced like a Polaris missile! My overriding feeling was how cold I was, and then some one grabbed me, and pulled me up onto the bank. The next thing I remember was waking butt naked, on my bedchair, with a pile of wet clothes all around me and it appeared that I must have navigated my way back to my plot through every thorny bush on the way, I was covered in so many stings and scratches. I was still trying to make some sense of it all, when my second saviour arrived to see how I was, not well, was all I could mumble, but I nearly shook his hand off when he told me what had happened. To say I was one very lucky man would be a terrible understatement and, to this day, I have never ventured out in a boat again whilst under the influence. A very close shave. The guy turned out to be from up north and I am so sorry, but I cannot recall his name. That said, he did get my carp radar up and running when he told me that he and his brother had seen some carp in the Finger Bays. Really? I pressed him for more details as I stuffed things into the relevant bags. Yep, Mary had been there, as had a few more of the big girls. I was almost salivating at the mouth the more he told me. Eventually, I asked when all this had happened. 'Ooh...I don't rightly know...twer probably about three year ago now'. I slumped back on my bed chair, but couldn't help chuckling at how excited I was for a few minutes. With that, I decided that I had had enough, and ran for home.

As much as I wanted to be there all the time, it just wasn't possible. I did get to have my first session with Keith, however, and with the boat well and truly unavailable, we raised a glass or two to the capture of Mallin's. With that out of the way, more normal service was resumed. I had managed to get a couple of days free in early

June, and fully intended to fish into the weekend, but once again the army buggered that up. We had got hold of some very high-powered walkie-talkies, one of which burst into life whilst Jenkins was still fifteen miles away demanding information! I informed him I was on Bryant's Point, having chased some carp around for a few hours, and he said he would join me shortly but, as is the way at Wraysbury, shortly is a relative word. It was about an hour and a half before he came huffing and puffing into my swim. The world was soon put to rights, as we talked away a very pleasant evening, however, by morning nothing had occurred and nothing had been seen. Keith was keen to move, and as I had to pack up and go to work I decided I would follow him on his travels. Eventually, we ended up in the Drive In Dredger swim, which he really fancied, so I gave him a hand to sort things out. He then jumped into the boat, armed with a couple of buckets of our bait mix and, once above the area, which was about 90 yards from the bank, started spreading some of it over the top. I told him to keep pouring whenever he looked like stopping, after all, he didn't need too much ballast on board for the return journey. I must admit, the area looked bang on, and I wished him luck as I drove away. That night, being the Guard Commander, I had the most boring and insufferable chores to do, and all the time I was expecting a call from Jenks, but my mind was taken off the fishing when, in the dead of the night, I heard a couple of shots ring out. The rear gate to the camp was guarded at all times by two soldiers, and with the heightened security status, every one was as sharp as a razor. What happened was that two joy riders had approached the gate at speed, followed closely by the local constabulary. Now, we had all had the briefing about how a car could be driven to the target and then abandoned, indeed I had experienced it myself previously. Remotely, it could be detonated and it was good night Vienna for anyone in the

Keith ended up in the Dredger Bay

immediate vicinity, so fearing the worst, the young soldier released two rounds into the air, by way of warning shots. It had the desired affect and two very frightened teenagers tumbled onto the pavement. When I arrived on the scene, both the soldiers were giggling, and I couldn't help smiling myself because the car thieves had, quite literally, shit themselves! Even the local Bobbies were finding it hard to be serious. You can only hope that the kids had learnt a very valuable, if not rather smelly, lesson! Once normal, boring service had been resumed, the call I was expecting arrived, just a little later than I thought at seven in the morning. I had to hold the phone away from my ear for fear of some damage being done until, after some time, I heard the words Cluster, and rightfully thought he may have bagged the beast. He had! Early that morning a tench-like take had him on the rods, so he lifted into it, then all he did was reel it into the margins, a quick flip and flop, and she was in the net. At 43lb, Cluster was his sixth forty-pound carp in less than twelve months. It really couldn't have happened to a nicer guy and I was chuffed to bits for him. What that did mean, however, is that I wouldn't be buying the beer at our next meeting! But the capture was just about to be dulled by the biggest of hammer blows. He went for a visit to Horton that Sunday to let a few of the lads know of his good fortune, only to learn that the carp were dying. Eventually, CP's,

Cluster at 43lb

Jack, the Koi and many others were to be found washed up in the margins. As much as it was, at the time, my favourite lake, I had not had the association with it that Keith and the others had had. I listened, and saw grown men cry at that time, and I really could understand their dismay, an emotion that soon turned to anger, and that I could understand even more. Right. I know Keith has had his say, but I would just like to give my ten pennies worth as well. Hindsight is a wonderful thing, and much has been said about the carp that were or were not responsible for those deaths. Putting a load of manky little commons in a net anchored to the pontoon was irresponsible and stupidity of the highest order. Nets simply don't keep viruses at bay. This seems to be the centre of everyone's attention, but not mine. Having spent a fair bit of time there the summer before, I saw things, but unfortunately was not in a position to say anything, and even if I had, the belligerent and autocratic leadership would have simply ignored or banned me. Some carp were stocked from the big lake at Thorpe Lea over the years, and it was obvious that they were compatible with the resident carp so why they couldn't just use fish from there I will never know, but I saw two fish stocked that were not even in a lake when they were chosen. (One was taken from a container lorry in the car park of the Five Bells, and run across the field to be placed in the Church Lake). It was more likely that one of these ill advised and stupid stockings is what brought the deadly virus into Horton. I, for one, don't think the two people responsible were ever punished enough for what they did, and when cross examined by a mob of angry carp anglers, they came out with a load of bullshit, anyway. The irony of this story is that the very carp that I saw come across the field is now one of the biggest and best looking carp in the lake, and if I sound angry then that's because I am, but I feel a whole lot better for getting it out of my system.

We did indeed celebrate the capture of Cluster, and in very fine fashion too, the trouble was, the lake seemed to have gone into a period of inactivity. Try as I may, I could not find a single thing to fish for, other than the always visible stockies, of which a couple of small commons had kindly found their way into my landing net. The fish looked quite superb, but I could never understand why they were in there in the first place, it was perfect the way it was. More fish equals more tickets sold, I suppose, which is a pretty piss poor way of dealing with the home of the biggest fish in the land. Anyway, July turned into August and with it a nice surprise. Keith had won the Carp Angler of the Year and received £2,000 for his troubles and it was whilst we were sharing a stubby on Bryant's Point that we started organizing a party to celebrate. As we spoke, a somewhat errant boat began to appear from our right, launched from the Mad Dog swim. The person involved seemed hell bent on dropping his rigs in my swim, having passed over two of my lines (that were being fished 120 yards out) at about sixty yards. I shouted, which he ignored, and then I shouted some more, obviously he still wasn't listening. The only thing for it was to launch a marker float to get his attention. It sailed out and landed some 15 yards from him, which elicited a shaking of the fist, but still the rig was dropped. Now, I don't go fishing to argue with people, and as the Norfolk Cow Pat made his way back to his swim, Keith and I opened another beer. Ce la vie...or so we thought. Ten minutes later, however, said Cow Pat was puffing and panting at the back of my swim and we were subjected to a torrent of abuse. At first I could handle his inane and completely drunken tirade, but then it got a little personal and I launched myself over my brolly, but he was too far away and ran for all he was worth, as is his way. With Jenks laughing his socks off, I once again picked up my beer, and then he came back. He really wasn't worth bothering with, so we decided just to listen. He started from a little further back this time (yawn, yawn!) and then he pulled a can of nuclear strength cider from his pocket and opened it. The next thing he did had Keith and I in tears. He poured the lot on the floor and told us that that was what he thought of us! How very odd, maybe it was some kind of Norfolk tribal ritual, who knows? I could only think that it was an awful waste of ale but, not content with this, he stumbled back to his plot and when someone entered the swim, he told them that he had sorted both Keith and I right out, then opened another can and poured that one on the floor too. "That's what I thought of them," he said. We could only hope he would get better soon.

He was gone the following day, and so, unfortunately, was Keith. Every cloud has a silver lining, however, and no sooner had I been left alone, than Reg rolled up.

Keith received £2,000 for his troubles

He set up to my right, and once settled and fishing we got down to socializing, laughing and giggling well into the night, and it was no surprise to wake up actionless in the morning. We were wondering where the hell the carp had got to, and were gazing out into a big bay to our left, when one of my rods ripped off, and I mean ripped! It was as much as I could do to lift the rod up, so fast was it going. Playing the fish in from that distance was a fraught business, and it didn't help having razor tongued Reg gobbing off in my ear. Still, I managed to get it into range and eventually Reg lifted the net around my prize. I thought I knew most of the carp that swam in the lake, but this one neither of us had seen before. She weighed 22.10 and was really a stunning fish, and as Phil Lynnot's voice rang out across the swim, I named her Rosie. I was absolutely buzzing, not knowing the fish just made it all the better and it wasn't until the following week that I was to get some idea as to her identity.

Some felt that she was probably one of the fungus mirrors that had, for some bizarre reason, been stocked into the lake a year or so earlier, but I wasn't so sure. The following Friday I set up in the Lawn on the North Lake and, with the rods in situ, I was just making a brew when I got a visitor. I didn't recognise the fellow, who was probably in his fifties, but he seemed friendly enough and asked if I fished the lake much. I then asked him if he did any fishing at all and he told me that he was on his way to a club meeting to sort out a ticket for his barbel fishing later that year. As we talked I felt as if I should know him...then the penny dropped, bloody hell, it was Kenny Hodder! All of a sudden he had to have a seat, and would he like some tea? I really wanted him to stay forever and talk to me about the times that he

I was absolutely buzzing

and Sir Pete had fished the place. Eventually, I remembered that I had a picture of the fish from the week before, so he studied it for a while and was convinced that it was a fish he had caught some fifteen years before. If that is the case, then I can safely say that that is the most special carp I have ever landed. She has been caught two or three times since I left Wraysbury and has become one of the most sought after fish in there, and rightfully so.

Two things happened around this time; boats were banned and all of a sudden carp started falling off. For some unknown reason, the management decided that we were no longer allowed to go afloat. The reasons weren't clear, but over the course of time I believe the blame may lay at my door to some extent as I think word had got back to the office about my near death experience in the North Lake. We had never understood everyone's reliance on them, anyway, although we used them ourselves a lot of the time but, to a man, the rule was ignored, and the only thing that changed was the times at which one was used, but the Third Reich soon got wind of that! Whatever the case, we had a party to go to and I was looking forward to it. I had arrived at the lake on the Tuesday and was hell bent on finding some carp to fish for. I was now on summer leave, so there was plenty of time, the weather was warm, and I did indeed find plenty of fish. The problem was, they were in the dense snags in the Dredger Bay, and no sane man would dangle for them there. To that end, I moved around the area and tried to fish from as many different swims as possible in the hope that they would eventually come out, which they didn't, but I didn't stop trying either! On the Thursday I found a group of commons in a little swim to the right of the Drive In Dredger, I think it was called the White Fence, which acted as the left boundary of the South Lake sailing club. Two of the carp I recognised; Jacko's common, and the floppy tail common, but although the others were of comparable size, I hadn't a clue who they were.

Eventually, they moved off and headed in front of the sailing club, backs out of the water and not a care in the world. I raced around to the Oak Tree swim in No Carp Bay, and fifteen minutes later they cruised around a metal post and behind a large bar some fifteen yards out from the swim, and the more I looked, the more I saw. They had joined Mary and Mallin's in a snag just behind the bar. Game on!

I found a group of commons in the White Fence

With so many fish in attendance, the last thing I wanted to do was use a boat, so I simply positioned a couple of rigs with small PVA bags and light leads, on the back of the bar. I quickly got up in the branches of the big oak tree, and could see I had not disturbed the fish. By first light the next morning I had already been in the tree for half an hour, but it was a while before I could see the bar. The small red splodges that the bags had left around my hookbaits were no longer visible, had I been done? I now had the hump and decided that I would lay a feast out for them once I knew their backs were turned, and by midday the trap was set. Rightly or wrongly, my two hookbaits were nestling in amongst about ten kilos of our little mix and it looked the nuts, so I was ready to make a big impact on Keith's two grand winnings. He duly arrived on the Friday evening and quickly got his rods out. Some early morning boating was going to be necessary but in the mean time, we contented ourselves with a take-away and a chilled out evening. Tomorrow would be a different story, however; we even discussed the possibility of catching a carp while the party raged, and just as quickly dismissed the idea as pure fantasy. Phil, Jacko and Del joined us for the evening, which was nice.

Bright and early, Jenks was off in the boat to do some exploring, whilst I was on look out duties. It took him a while, but once the job was done we could concentrate on getting the furniture set up for the party. My small area of the lake was now full of carp, and some proper chunks too, therefore I was loathe to move too far from my rods. By mid afternoon a dozen or so people were there and the beer had began to

Furniture out, and the party began

flow, then just as I was asking Keith what I could help him spend the rest of his money on, one of his rods decided that it wanted to party. It howled for a few seconds but by the time he had picked up the offending item, all was solid. There was only one thing for it, so Laney paddled whilst Jenks took up the slack. At first it was all very exciting, but a few minutes later we could see his shoulders slump forward as a large lump of weed was swung to hand. Oh crap! Keith simply got on with the party, and with the wine and food quickly consumed, all thoughts of carp were soon forgotten. That was until one of my rods decided to come to the party as well. I lead the pack as I raced to the rod, a few yards away, and battle was joined. The crowd oohed and aahed at all the right times, and Keith made ready with the net, then all of a sudden, a bloody great big mirror rolled a few yards out...and the hook fell out. I stared at the spot for only a few seconds, but when I turned around there was no one in sight, they all knew the feeling, and you don't want people around when you are reaching for the noose. I was sure the fish was Mallin's, and having caught him a couple of months ago, you would have thought it wouldn't be that much of a big deal but it was, and after all that effort the bastard had fallen off. I don't think I have ever been so upset about the loss of a fish but, as Keith so rightly said, there was only one thing to do, have a drink - so I did. The beer flowed, and we all ran around sticks in some crazy, Rob Tough party game. What a great party, and with some of the best people, it really was a great day, but oh, what might have been? As harrowing as those losses were, unbelievably there was worse to come. On the Sunday we all packed away, and with our tails firmly between our legs, drifted off home and although Wraysbury is not far, I still had time to think on the journey. It's probably the time I do most of my thinking actually, because once at home the last thing I want is anything to do with carp fishing! By the time I pulled up outside the house, I had decided to get my arse back there on the Tuesday morning, and so, with much more of a skip in my step, I set off early that morning. The first thing I did was to drive to the swim Keith had occupied at the weekend,

Laney paddled, while Keith took up the slack

In the end it was a great day

and within fifteen minutes I had seen two fish show at distance so, with no further need for investigation, I got my gear sorted. With the boat ban now firmly in place I would have to make the trip as quickly and stealthily as possible and even though my little inflatable was about as much use as tits on a fish I still managed to get two 14mm bottom baits in position on a raised gravel hump, along with a scattering of boillies and particles, before the thing deflated completely. I then smugly rolled the boat up and stowed it in the car just behind me. The weather was fine and sunny and, with the wind trickling into No Carp Bay, I sat back totally confident of some action. By mid afternoon, with no bivvy up, the old tan was getting a good top up when at three o'clock, the middle rod bounced in the rests and the spool went into melt down. The fish kited to the right a little, before everything went solid, so I went through all the normal procedures; slack line, tight line, pulling from different angles, but all to no avail. I even gave Keith a ring hoping he would come up with some kind of answer, the bottom line, was that I, inevitably, was going to have to go after it, but I feared that my little inflatable was certainly not man enough for the job. I rang Tetley and Jacko who, although both working locally, had no boats to offer. So, with no obvious alternative I huffed and puffed for a few minutes until the boat was blown up, stuffed a fag in my mouth just to get the old lungs started again and, with rod in hand and the net onboard, I set off in pursuit of the fish. Unsure if it was still on, I made my way to the area, at which point the carp decided that another weed bed was a better refuge, so at least it was still on. I was over the fish in no time and, just as I got it moving again, water started to trickle over the side of the boat - she was going down...fast! All I could do was loosen off the clutch and head for the sailing club point about 40 yards away. The problem was, every time I did this, once back over the fish and with it moving, I had to go to the point again to blow the damn thing back up. This was getting stupid and just as I was getting a bit despondent, Jacko had arrived in my swim, and began shouting encouragement from the bank. With one final effort I decided that I would just heave the fish to the surface and, come what may, get it in the net. The plan then was to inflate my life jacket and swim to shore, then I would sort everything else out when I had landed the thing. The plan initially seemed to be working as I, once again, got the fish on the move, when, all of a sudden, a large ball of weed came into view. The fish was still on, so I reached down and grabbed the top of my lead core, at which point the tail of the fish was exposed, and I recognised the slightly distorted bottom lobe immediately. Five feet below me was the largest carp in the land, Mary!! The boat, by now, was almost useless but I turned and got the net down in the water; just a little more and I could bundle the lot into the net but then, as I raised her and the weed a tad higher, there was an almost imperceptible knock on the line and, to my utter dismay, she appeared from the weed and swam slowly into the depths. I have no words to describe how I felt at that time, it really was the most horrible experience. I slowly made my way to the point, once again, and just as slowly re-inflated the lifeless piece of plastic, just enough to get me back to my swim. Jacko stayed for a while and we shared a beer but I felt sorry for him, too, because there was nothing he could say to ease my furrowed and incredibly depressed brow. Eventually he had to go, and I managed to get two hookbaits back in position, but, as you would imagine, I wasn't happy. I didn't sleep a wink that night, but just sat on my bed chair more determined than ever to wreak my vengeance upon these Wraysbury carp. There was little point in re-doing the baits, I couldn't have positioned them better and I really didn't want to be out in the boat too much, so there they stayed until, at three o'clock, the same time as the day before, the middle rod did its best to give me a heart attack. This time I was taking no prisoners and even climbed on my bed chair for more elevation. Wrapped in weed, the carp couldn't make any head way, so I kept it moving as best I could but inevitably, some 70 yards out, everything came to a halt again. I was soon afloat in my porous little craft, and quickly over the fish, once again we visited a couple of weed beds but, with no leverage, I simply hung on. Then some of the weed dropped off the line and the flank of an extremely long and scaly carp was exposed - it was Mary's Mate. Then the hooklink snapped.

The depths of despair had never been so thoroughly visited as at that moment. I really needed to speak to someone who would understand, and Jenks got the full brunt of my agony and, as we were expected at a kids fish-in at Horseshoe lake the following day, he suggested I get over to his house for the night. No sooner said than done. He arrived home from work to find me well into his beer supplies and, like the good mate he is, cracked a bottle for himself. We did that until we could drink no more and then, in the morning, we headed off for Lechlade and, to be honest, the weekend was just what the doctor ordered. The kids loved it, and they caught an unbelievable amount of fish, and after that I felt refreshed and ready to get back to the battle, but neither Keith, nor I, could have imagined that there was still a whole world of pain left for us to endure.

The following week my summer leave was over, and the army was demanding a lot more of my time - they never did quite grasp the concept of carp fishing, bless 'em! With Reg and Keith resuming the hunt that weekend, all I could hope for was good news and it came, but in the most bizarre of circumstances. On the Sunday morning, Phil Thompson was in their swim explaining that he had just landed

Mary, so off they went to do the pictures and I will never forget Keith's reaction to the event. He was, for the first time ever, speechless.

Then Princess Diana died, which sent the world into meltdown.

I was still determined to get back to the lake, so the following morning I moved into the Turfs in the North Lake, and the fact that that was where Phil had landed Mary from was completely immaterial... honest! I spent the day spodding out a few kilos of boillies and particles to a small strip of clear silt at about 45 yards range, then shortly after the task was complete, Jenks arrived on the scene. He set up in the Style on the other side of the sailing club and positioned his hookbaits at a similar distance to me, spreading a fair bit of bait over them. Tomorrow was Diana's funeral and we spent the evening discussing how the world had reacted to the news. Maybe

Phil had landed Mary

We were about to get punished... badly!

the big man upstairs decided that we should have been at home grieving with the rest of the planet, because the next day we were about to be punished...badly!

I made a couple of early morning brews and was just carrying them into his swim, when I noticed a very excited Keith, with a very bent rod in his hands. I nearly dropped the lot, but after doing a little shuffle, I made my way to the front of the swim to man the net. He told me he didn't know if the fish was still on, because of the amount of weed involved, then thirty yards out the weed pinged off the line, and a carp made off at speed. He reckoned it wasn't a big one, but I reminded him that it was a Wraysbury carp, and he should be concentrating. He did just that, but only for a few seconds more because the hooklink parted! There was nothing I could say, so, before he had even turned, I legged it back to my swim. All the commotion had got the old bowel very much awake, so picking up my small entrenching tool and bog roll, I made my way through the brambles to take care of business. I was just doing the paper work, when one of the rods let out a one toner and, hoisting up my trousers, I legged it through the under growth back to the swim. It only took a few seconds, but by the time I got there the action had stopped. All was solid and I called out to Jenks that we were going to need a boat, which thankfully he had and although it took some time to blow it up, at least it looked as if it may just stay that way, so off we went. Graciously, the management had relented a little where boating was concerned and we could now use them for just this sort of emergency. With me taking up the slack, and Keith removing weed bed after weed bed from the line, we moved out into the lake but all I could think of was that I was about to lose yet another fish, and probably moaned more than I should have. Jenks just kept on removing weed and, after fifteen minutes, he said that he could feel the fish so I prepared to take up the fight as the last bit of weed was free. He said it felt like a good 'un and, as he released the line, the rod tip pulled steadily round and I saw the flank of a huge grey mirror roll in the deep, clear water.

And then it fell off!

I looked at the tip of the horribly straight rod and let out a huge scream of frustration. What the hell had we done to deserve this? In silence, we paddled the short distance to the bank where I trudged back to my plot, a beaten man, barely noticing Keith creep past my brolly as he made his way back to his plot. Gutted!! As always, we decided that a big and totally unhealthy breakfast may just lift the mood, so we set up on the sailing club lawn and began to tuck in, then, as I was just loading up another mouthful of cholesterol, a buzzer howled in Keith's swim. The third carp of the day had made a mistake and as soon as he had the rod in his hand he said it was a good 'un, and from the way it took off, I wouldn't have argued. The carp sped off to the right, stopping only briefly as it charged through weed bed after weed bed then, just as it seemed he was getting the upper hand, the hooklink parted once again. This really was the worst kind of carp fishing nightmare I had ever witnessed. So they buried Diana, and although we were completely shattered by our experiences, we both felt for the Royal family. A sad day all round really.

As October loomed we had done nothing to redress the balance, but later that month we decided that the four musketeers should gather at Wraysbury. We never really needed an excuse for a party but, as it was Reg's birthday, it seemed the ideal time, and so we arranged to meet at Wraysbury to celebrate. Dave would be there on the Friday and Reg would get there early on the Saturday, but Keith and I got the march on both of them and arrived at the lake very early on the Thursday morning. I was happy setting up in the Rocky Barge, whilst Jenks headed further to my left towards the Rocket, and being a tad lazy that day, instead of embarking on the half mile trek to the swims, we went for the easy option of boating it over the short 30 yard gap that separated the two lakes. Fine angling, even if I say so myself! The risk of expulsion was far outweighed by the ease of the journey and we also carried on the skullduggery by putting our baits out with the boat in the early morning mist. With the job done we could sit back and relax. I mean, who would be watching at that hour? Dave arrived earlier than anticipated, and once we had ferried him across the gap, he set up in Springates to my right; we were all ready for an evening in my swim. Now, early is a very relative term for Reg, and none of us expected him to appear until mid morning on Saturday, however, he woke Keith at seven in the morning, declining the offer of a lift, although he was quite willing for Keith to ferry his gear across the gap. When he was happy, we all took the opportunity to reposition the baits, and then the wheels came off completely.

Unbeknownst to us, our boating antics had been reported to the office by some kindly soul and so Ian Welch, who had been sniffing around the green gates opposite us, had witnessed the whole thing; then the management moved in for the kill.

When Ian arrived in Reg, Keith and Dave's swim, off to my left, all merry hell broke loose and, unsure what to do, I reeled my rods in. Just as I was doing so, a young lad, maybe 11 or 12, stood at the top of the bank above my swim and told me his dad had sent him to get my ticket. Whilst I could see no point in arguing - I had been caught fair and square - I told him to tell his cowardly father to come and get it for himself. All the time I could hear the guys arguing further up the bank and when eventually dad arrived, he stood behind the boy and asked for my ticket. Being a cantankerous sod I told him to come down and get it which, eventually, he did. I have no idea what he thought I might do, but I could see how surprised he was when, without argument, I simply handed it over, then with that done, I decided to go and lend my support to the lads. Things had settled down a bit on my arrival, and just then Mr. Welch disappeared. We didn't know what he was doing, but it turned out he had gone to check Dave's swim and although he had no baited hooks in the water, that was the story that was eventually given and it was clear that Ian really wanted shot of Dave, and this was his opportunity. We were banned on the spot and had to leave, the trouble was, we now had to walk everything back to the cars, which was about a mile away. It was like the retreat from Moscow, and took us an hour or so to complete the task, then as we were loading up, Mr. Welch arrived on the scene, snorting in disgust as he and Dave continued their heated discussion. Dave was blaming him for the Horton deaths, and as he was fishing for the Black Mirror at the time, Mr. Welch told him he would get hold of that fish and Dave would never catch it! I really thought it was going to come to blows, yet somehow we managed to settle things down, but what the bloody hell were we going to do now? I made a couple of calls, and all of a sudden we were on our way to Aldershot. It was the best we could come up with at short notice, and soon enough

Would we ever fish Wraysbury again?

we were set up and angling at Chalk Farm. We caught some fish too, including one of the biggest in the lake at the time, but it was all overshadowed by the fact that we may never fish Wraysbury again. Dave and Keith were eventually banned for life, I got a month's ban, whilst Reg, not seen in a boat, got away with it all - it doesn't take the brains of a rocket scientist to work out who wasn't flavour of the month, does it? So ended the strangest few months I could remember, and although I did venture back once my ban was over, my heart just wasn't in it. So, with the winter fast approaching, I decided to head for pastures new. As I closed the green gates for the last time that year, I promised to return because there really was some unfinished business to attend to. In our four months of fishing at Wraysbury, Keith and I had hooked ten carp, losing seven of them – in Dave and Phil's first year they hooked and landed ten. Sometimes, and there is bugger all you can do about it, you are shit out of luck! It was a funny old year!

It had been a funny old year

We headed off into the Oxfordshire countryside

Chapter 10

The Lord of the Manor . . .

Without Wraysbury to occupy my mind, I must admit to being a little lost, I really didn't know what the hell to do. There was Manor in Oxfordshire and of course Chalk Farm to fall back on, the trouble with the last option was that not all of us had a ticket and, as we were fast approaching November, we hadn't really got stuck into anywhere. I like my winter campaigns to start well before the onset of the cold weather, it's just that our plans had been knocked into a cocked hat by events in the Colne Valley. That said, we all decided we would head off into the Oxfordshire countryside, and see what unfolded, and to that end we did have two aces up our collective sleeves in the form of Mick Dickens and Graham Jarman.

Both of these lads had been involved with Linear Fisheries for a while, and Keith had spent some time with both of these guys, Mick at Zyg Gregorek's place in Devon, and Graham on a couple of French holidays. Indeed, I had met them briefly the year before when we had made our first trip to Manor where they had both been a good source of information, and were as keen as you like. Plans were made, and off we went, and bearing in mind the fish that the lake contained at the time, I was pleasantly surprised to find no one fishing it on my arrival. I had managed to get away a day early from my army duties, and rather sneakily arrived a day before the other chaps were due, which I was getting rather good at. My only problem was that on subsequent trips I would always end up only fishing one rod effectively. Let me explain. I was starting to utilise my time a lot better as far as my army commitments were concerned and being my own boss meant that, once I had completed my task for the week, I could knock off and go fishing. A couple of late nights on Monday and Tuesday, and my desk was cleared, but to be honest, I was never designed to drive a desk and shine my arse, but needs must and all that! To that end I always arrived before anyone else. Which meant I would, more often than not, be on the fish when one of the other 'Banned' members arrived.

Trouble was, none of us were taking the fishing that seriously, and by Friday I would have a neighbour either side of me. I lost count of the amount of times I had either my left or right hand rods reeled in, as Keith or Dave attempted to get as close to the action as possible. That left my middle rod as the only one fishing effectively, thankfully, that was the one that nearly always produced the bites and I could concentrate on taking the piss out of the rest of them for blanking. At the time none of us could have envisaged how much of a struggle Manor would be for Keith and Dave, but for now we were content just to be doing some social winter carping. It wasn't until the second trip that things started to come together.

Once again I had arrived on a Thursday, and after a good walk round and eventually getting sorted, I could sit back and listen to the torrent of abuse from my friends - how did we ever survive before mobile phones? Rather smugly I sat down to wait, and come the Friday, I was still sure I was in the right area of the lake as I had seen a couple of fish show over the bait, and that would do for me. Manor was a different proposition to the lake that is there today, it didn't have half the amount of fish, but what was there were highly sought after. I remember thinking that if I could only bag a couple of them this winter then I would be a happy man, as much as I was able to fish a lot more than I had been for the past twenty years, things were also changing for my friends. Keith, as always, had his full time job and family to take care of. Reg was getting used to the idea of marriage the following year, and his normal full time job. The biggest shock to the system, though, was for Dave. He had recently become a father, and I have yet to meet another man who could have been more proud, but that didn't stop us ribbing him about his lack of fishing time.

By Friday I always had a neighbour either side of me

Parenthood had obviously had an affect on the old boy!

It must be a terrible shock to the system, going from a total free bird to the constraints of fatherhood. Plus, there was also the not insignificant fact that he was putting his first book together. All in all, I was quite enjoying sticking it up 'em on a weekly basis! Just as I was getting used to being on my own, Graham arrived, having blagged a day off, and so the fun began. Calls from Laney and Keith ensured I spent the rest of the day making sure I had enough aspirin for Saturday morning, when Reg was due to arrive, and with all four of us on the bank it was going to get a little rowdy! They would be there on Friday evening, and while Graham and I waited, we saw the odd fish boom out at the distance we were fishing, things were looking good. They got a whole lot better at around four in the afternoon when one of my rods was nearly torn from the rest. Fishing, as I had been, in a silty channel between two long rows of the famous Oxfordshire onion weed, I had been receiving numerous liners as the day went on so I shouldn't have been surprised, but I nearly swallowed my tonsils at the severity of the take. The fish stayed deep at long range

for some time, and it was only with a large slice of patience that I actually got it moving toward me. I remember remarking to Graham that I thought it was a good one, at which point he got the message and picked up my landing net. On and on the battle raged until, eventually, I had a rather good fish rolling some ten yards out and with the net now in the water, I carefully steered my prize towards it. Slowly she slipped over the net cord, and I could let out the usual bellows of delight, after which Graham and I got on with the weighing. He recognised the carp as the Peanut fish, but I really didn't care, and at 33lb I was over the moon, which was a nice way to start the winter off. Keith was only a couple of miles away by now, so I secured the carp in the landing net, as I was sure he would want to have a look. He did, and made all the right noises as I held the fish up for the camera. Let the fun begin!

Graham manned the net

Let the fun begin!

By early evening the party was in full swing, well, we had a carp to celebrate and it was during the frivolities that a certain water in Kent came up in conversation. It was Conningbrook of course, in which lived a carp named Two Tone. Dave had his heart set on going there, but I was a little bit reluctant, because, as much as I wanted to go, I was worried about being so far from home. As it was in Oxfordshire, I was stretching things a little too far because if anything went wrong with Lynn it would take me an age to get there, something I am conscious of all the time. But the thought of one of the largest carp in Britain was too much to resist, and so, from that point on, plans were made for the spring. Until then, though, we still had some fishing to do, and I for one was looking forward to spending a few months with my mates. Talking of which, by Saturday morning we were all wondering where Reg was. Needing supplies for the following night, Dave decided it was time to call him and I could tell from the conversation that Reg was at work, and it was probably the last thing he wanted to do, but Laney insisted and read out the shopping list. Unbeknown to us, the wheel of fortune was now turning rapidly in Reg's favour, and here he is to tell the tale.

For over five years, Horton had dominated my angling life like no other lake before or since. Not only because of the carp that lived within its crystal clear waters but also due to the friends that I had made there, some of whom are still close mates, many years on. During that time, I spent virtually every weekend and all of my holiday entitlement, camped on its banks - "camped" being an appropriate description, most of the time. The Church Lake was not what you would call "easy", but that was exactly what made it such an addictive challenge and each capture so special plus, back then, Horton boasted an unrivalled stock of big carp. Not surprisingly, that meant it was generally busy, particularly at weekends, which happened to be the only time I could fish, other than my holidays. Fishing weekends only was just getting so frustrating. Keith would ring me when he arrived on a Friday afternoon, to let me know who was on and what was happening but, as the afternoon progressed, more and more people would turn up and Keith would text to let me know that yet another swim had gone. By the time I arrived, around seven in the evening, the lake would often be packed. Now, I know this is a problem for any weekender, but at Horton it was often a case of knowing where I wanted to fish, but never actually being able to turn up early enough to get anywhere near it. This was nothing new, of course, but after a while it really started to do my head in and I began to fish other venues, from time to time.

I began to fish other venues

One Sunday afternoon, after leaving Horton following yet another blank, I paid a visit to a lake near Ascot racecourse, which was actually where I had caught my first ever carp, some twelve years before. The carp in question was one of a group of four that I had got feeding on crust in the middle of a huge weed bed and, at seventeen and a half pounds, was the largest fish I had seen on the bank, but also the smallest of the group of four. That seventeen pounder looked so huge and I remember shaking with excitement as to what the others might weigh. This lake is very private and, as a young lad, I had been given permission to fish after getting a summer job on the farm. The owner did not allow anyone to fish the lake, so being able to have a go was always a bit special. Returning all these years later, I was amazed to find the owner remembered me, and even more amazed when he again granted me permission to fish. When I walked down to the lake and found the carp, it was obvious they had grown a fair bit as well, but not only were they bigger now, there were far more of them than I had remembered. A plan was soon hatched, and I baited the area where I had seen them with about a kilo of boillies which I had left over from the Horton session, and planned to return next weekend. The following Saturday lunchtime I returned with Keith, who was well up for a night on an un-fished lake in the middle of nowhere, and so I set up in the baited area whilst Keith settled on the far side, opposite me. What a night it turned out to be. We had four takes between us but unfortunately only landed two, both falling to my rods. They were cracking looking chunky mirrors and, at 35.08 and 21.12, we were over the moon. We had our own little piece of paradise, with big uncaught carp waiting to be bagged and no other anglers to worry about, it really was too good to be true. Oh, what a difference a few days can make. The farm owner rang me the following Monday to see how I had got on and, when I told him what I had caught, he seemed pleased but made it very clear that I was to tell nobody, as he didn't want other carp anglers knowing about his fish and potentially poaching the lake.

"Can I bring a friend with me?', I asked, a little late, but better late than never.

His answer was short and very clear, "No, and don't tell anyone what you've caught".

A chunky looking mirror of 35.08

Oh shit, now I had a problem. I rang Keith immediately to tell him the bad news and, as you can imagine, he was totally gutted. I felt so bad, but Keith understood the situation, bless him, and told me I'd be crazy not to go back and have another go.

So, the following weekend I returned alone, setting up in the swim where I had caught the brace from the week before, and by the time the rods were out, it was virtually dark. Up went the brolly and then it was time to eat, before settling down for the night. Some time in the early hours I was woken by a one toner and, after a prolonged scrap through some very dense weed, I landed my second thirty in as many nights fishing. It weighed 33 exactly but was much longer than the 35, lighter in colour and, like the other two, totally perfect and uncaught. The following morning I went down to see the farmer to get him to take some photos for me. "You were here early this morning" he remarked as we walked back to the lake to do the photos, "I don't want you here at night, you know. What time did you get here?" Um! I told him what he wanted to hear but he knew the score of course and, as I held the fish for the camera, my head was spinning. Here I was, with access to some fantastic, totally exclusive fishing, but with a huge problem. Every take had come during the wee small hours, between two and five in the morning, and now I was being told that I wasn't allowed on the property at night. What was I saying about too good to be true?

For the next couple of trips I decided to stick to the "rules" and pack up at dusk, only to return at dawn the next day, as I was pretty sure the farmer knew I had been fishing at night, so was likely to check up. Fishing daylight only turned out to be a total waste of time as I had expected, so the following Saturday evening I made a point of waving goodnight to the farmer and his wife as I drove past their cottage, only to drive half a mile up the road, hide the van away and walk back over the fields in darkness. I'd left the rods and a few essentials stashed on the lake and, within five minutes of returning, was soon angling again. Then, just before dawn, I walked back over the fields, and drove the van back through the gate as if I had just arrived.

This routine continued for the next few weeks and, each night, I would catch at least one fish, but never any during daylight hours. The carp would just mill about, or sit in the thickest of the weed beds, hardly

I got to know the inhabitants of the lake well

moving for hours on end. This did, however, give me a chance to watch the fish a great deal and, in time, I got to know the inhabitants of the lake very well. In total, there were thirteen mirrors ranging from low twenties up to upper thirties, two small commons, both around mid doubles, one tench and a few perch.

By the end of September I'd caught twelve of the mirrors, ranging from 21.12 to 35.08 (the one I'd caught on the first session with Keith). Unbelievably, I never hooked either of the commons, which was weird, but, not surprisingly I also started to double up on quite a few, including the 35, which I ended up catching three times. Now I'm not trying to give it the big un about what I caught, it was just that the one remaining uncaught mirror I had spotted, had to be close to forty pounds. I regularly saw it with the 35 and it always looked the bigger fish but, for some reason, I never did catch it, although I lost one on my last trip, so who knows?

That summer was one of the best of my angling life

By now, the farmer had sussed my night time antics and had a little word in my ear, so to speak - it was time to move on. I could have continued to fish just the days, but there seemed little point given the fact I was still only catching at night, and besides, I had no intention of catching the same few fish time and time again, which was now happening with every visit. So, what to do?

I still had my Horton ticket so decided to fish just one more winter until the end of the season, and although it was terribly hard, as always, it was also great fun. The social scene down there became the stuff of legends, and many nights were enjoyed in the company of the other worthy nutters who were prepared to endure the winter on its banks. One of my mates from Swindon thought I was mad to give up my ticket, given what still remained on my "wanted list", but I had already managed to catch a few, including my p.b. common and mirror, so I was more than happy. Besides, another challenge was now occupying my thoughts - Wraysbury.

I'd been over to Wraysbury regularly over the last couple of years to visit my old mates, Phil Thompson and Laney. Of course, I'd heard about the great lake but it wasn't until I began visiting Dave and Phil that the thought of actually angling there came to mind, and when I started walking around this incredible lake, getting to know the place a bit, it seemed the obvious next step in my angling. The fact that it contained the largest carp in the land at the time was just the cherry on the cake. Never in my wildest dreams did I expect to catch her, but she was a fish that did like her bait, and she got caught regularly, so there was always a chance. But what really prompted me to get a ticket, was the fact that so few people fished there. I knew it would be hard, harder even than Horton, but that didn't bother me. At least I would be fishing there on my terms, without having to worry about getting a swim on a Friday evening.

I know Chilly has gone into detail elsewhere in this book as to what happened over at Wraysbury, so I won't go over the same ground but, as a result of our ban, I found myself without a target water for my carp angling obsession. Dave and Keith headed over to Kent to fish for a new pretender to the record, Chilly was back on Wraysbury, but with limited time at my disposal I thought it was about time I looked at some of the waters closer to home. I live in a part of the world blessed with many lakes, but very few of them had any history of producing really big carp. That said, the potential was there and with very few anglers and lots of water, it had to be worth a closer look. That summer turned into one of the best in my angling life, although I didn't catch any monsters, the fact that I could fish without any other anglers around made it so enjoyable. For the first time since the Ascot lake, I was able to pre-bait swims knowing that I would get to fish them, without the interference of other anglers. It was heaven. Then, one evening in November, Keith rang to tell me that he and Chilly would be fishing a lake closer to my home that coming weekend, and wanted to see if we could get together for a bit of a social. Unfortunately, I had other commitments so would be unable to fish, but said I would try to come down at some stage to see them. I arrived shortly after dark the following Friday evening, to find two very excited carp anglers set up at the far end of the lake, half way along the south bank. I hadn't seen either of them for weeks and my arrival heralded much banter and general mickey taking, as always. Over the next couple of hours the lads enlightened me, as much as they could, about Manor Farm Lake, and were obviously very excited about the prospect of doing a bit of time there in the near future. From what they had been told, the lake held quite a large stock of carp, the majority being twenties but with some real stunners in amongst them. There were also a growing number of fish over thirty pounds, the biggest fish out so far, being caught at just under forty pounds. Both Keith and Chilly bagged carp that first weekend to around mid twenties, as I recall, so that was even better. It all sounded great but, for some reason, I just didn't share their enthusiasm for the place from that very first visit. Manor still had a gravel workings on the eastern bank, back then, and it seemed that whichever swim you fished, you always ended up facing the workings. The lake itself wasn't overly busy with anglers, and there really were some lovely fish to be caught but, after a few social sessions leading up to Christmas, it became clear that Manor was just like any other water at this time of year. Once the really cold weather arrived, the lake shut up shop, the

Chilly had the bragging rights... and all the beer!

captures becoming very few and far between. I fished it on a number of occasions over the following year, generally in the colder months with Keith and Chilly, and by now Laney was getting up there as well. It was a great place for a bit of a social, and gave us a chance of some better fish rather than sitting on a water freezing our knackers off, angling for doubles all winter. But as time went on, and I got to know the lake better, I was enjoying the fishing more and more on there. Okay, so it wasn't the best looking fishery in the world, but there were some awesome carp in the water and, pretty soon, we all started to really get in to it. Chilly did the most, and caught a proper one in April, bagging Popeye at 39.08. A great result for the big guy, and well deserved, but it did, of course, give him bragging rights over the rest of us which was going to mean he would be unbearable for a while - or until one of us bagged an even bigger beast.

By May the weather had improved, and that meant more anglers venturing onto the banks. At times, through the winter, we could have the place virtually to ourselves, along with Mick and Graham, two mates of Keith's from way back, but as soon as the sun made an appearance so did all those other anglers. We all had plans for the summer anyway. Dave and Keith headed over to Kent in pursuit of the big two tone mirror that would one day hold the British record, Chilly went back over to Wraysbury, while I went to explore the Cotswold Water Park near my home. I had a wonderful summers fishing and while my three best mates angled for two of the biggest and best know carp in the country, I decided to go in search of the unknown and, although I didn't catch any real whackers, I did have some of the most enjoyable fishing I've ever experienced.

That summer seemed to fly past in next to no time and, with work being so busy, I had taken very little time off, so by September I really needed a holiday. The weather was still unseasonably warm and I managed to convince my wife, Kate, into coming fishing with me for a few days. It would be the first time all year that I would fish midweek and so, on the off chance, I gave Linear head bailiff Roy Parsons a ring, to see what had been happening over at Manor. To my surprise he informed

I decided to go in search of the unknown

me that the place was very quiet and, although there had been a few on over the weekend, the place was now deserted. That would do for me. We arrived about lunchtime and went for a look around to see if we could find some fish before setting up. The lake was like a millpond, not a breath of wind, hot, bright and sunny so Kate was well pleased as she was right up for a few days of sunbathing, but the conditions were hardly conducive for angling. Still, never mind, as long as she was happy then that was cool with me. We eventually found what we were looking for, over the far side, and spent the next three days chilling out and relaxing as the fishing was slow, to say the least. It was warm and muggy, with hardly any wind and the only carp I saw were just slowly cruising around out in the middle. I tried chucking zig rigs at them and getting them going off the top, all to no avail. Then, on the fourth day things began to change with a nice breeze picking up from the north west and, although still hot, I started to see a few signs of the fish becoming more active. I wandered over to the workings bank and soon saw a few moving along the margins only a couple of yards out, heading for the back bay, so for the rest of the day I tried in vain to tempt one out of there but, by evening, they slowly began to drift away. My chance had gone. I returned to the swim for some much needed food and Kate and I enjoyed a fantastic meal, washed down with a few glasses of wine. I repositioned the rods just off the workings bank, where I'd seen fish coming into the bay earlier in the day, but this time I baited quite heavily with the remaining bait. In all, I guess I put in about three kilos of Activ-8 boillies and

What a state... but what a fish!

half a bucket of hemp. I'd tried the softly, softly approach; tomorrow I'd stop them in their tracks. We didn't stay up late that night, a combination of a long day in the sun and too much red wine soon took its toll and, all too soon, we were both tucked up. I awoke early the following morning, my head pounding and feeling pretty dehydrated, so despite still being dark, I put the kettle on for the first much needed brew of the day. Sitting at the doorway of the bivvy, cup of tea in hand, I thought I could hear the odd fish crashing out but, in the early morning gloom, couldn't make out where they were. I stayed awake as long as I could but must have dozed off because the next thing I knew, one of the rods melted off. Still half asleep and bare footed, I flew out of the bivvy onto the damp grass like a baby giraffe on roller skates and by the time I reached the rods I was airborne! Half a back somersault later, I landed, the back of my head hitting the ground first. God, I felt like I'd been run over by a lorry, but all the time the buzzer was screaming for attention. Somehow I got up, grabbed the rod and struck. Nothing. Buzzer still screaming. Oh shit, better try this one. The noise stopped, fish on. I remember little of the fight, I couldn't focus, could hardly stand, and all the time Kate was pissing herself laughing.

After who knows how long, I managed to somehow get the carp in the net and it was only then that Kate stopped laughing and realised I was really hurt. My head and neck were killing me, I was soaked to the skin and covered in mud all down my back, just like a giant skid mark, what a state! It wasn't until Roy arrived a little while later, that I was able to sort myself out - well, Roy sorted myself out, actually. He weighed the fish, a stunning mirror just short of thirty pounds, and then took some photos for me, bless him.

The following week I met up with the boys over at Taplow for a charity match. We hadn't fished together since the spring and along with Dave, Keith, and Chilly, a few other friends who I hadn't seen in a while also turned up; it was like being back at Horton. During the weekend we managed to bag a couple between us, Chilly a 23lb and me a 27lb, and we also got talking about the forthcoming winter. The four of us all fancied

We all fancied another go at Manor

another go on Manor, but this time a plan had begun to take shape. We would fish right through the winter and keep the bait going in, in the hope of keeping the fish feeding and hopefully bagging a few as a result. It wasn't until November that we actually all managed to get on the lake at the same time. The normal games ensued during the week leading up to the

I collected Molly the carp dog on the way

session, with us all bluffing and double bluffing as to when we would each arrive. Chilly, true to form, got there two days earlier than he said he would, but I also had a plan which involved booking the Friday off work and turning up on Thursday night – well, that was my plan. Normally, I'd work every other Saturday but due to a mix up at work, the rota got changed which meant I'd have to work that weekend. I was gutted. Keith rang me at work on the Saturday to rub it in,

"Where are you?". "You know where I am you bastard, what do you want?" He then started reading out a shopping list. "Are you mad, if you think I'm going shopping...". Keith then interrupted, "We've run out of beer.". Bastards! I shot home after work, picked up the carp dog, then belted down to Tesco's. It was packed. I charged around as fast as I could but it was murder in there and, by the time I got out, I was in a right foul mood. I'd just finished loading the car when this large

That night was a bit of a social

four by four came screeching backwards through the car park at an incredible rate of knots, directly towards my car. I could see what was going to happen and started screaming at the top of my voice, the yuppie wagon skidding to a halt a hooks gape from my bumper. By now I was out of the car and giving the bloke both barrels. Then the driver got out, almost in slow motion, and the sun disappeared. Moments later, this monster starts bounding towards me. I swear he must have been 7ft tall, 30 stone and God was he ugly. One huge eyebrow went from one side of his, well, face I'd guess you'd call it, to the other. A cross between giant haystacks and Peter Beardsley, and shit was he angry. For the next few minutes he tried chasing me round Tesco's car park but, due to his size and the amount of adrenaline pumping though my body (run or fight, run or fight...RUN!), he never stood a chance. As luck would have it, the owner of the car blocking me in turned up soon after, and I dived into the motor and got the hell out of Dodge.

So, now I'm speeding down the road, constantly looking in the rear view mirror in case the swamp donkey was still chasing me, and trying to remember where all the speed cameras were down the A420, when the phone rang. It was Keith. Chilly had bagged a 33lb mirror - hoorah! My mood changed in an instant, at last something good had happened today. I arrived some time later to be greeted by Dave and one very smiley Chilly who had, very thoughtfully, walked down to the car park to help me with my gear. Strangely, the first thing out of the motor was the beer, but I made sure they were both well loaded before ushering them to the lake, while I trotted along carrying a huge bag of crisps, just in case we got the munchies. Between them, the lads pretty much had the road bank stitched up, but another mate, Greg Richardson, was in the first swim and packing up, so I stopped for a chat. Greg said he would be leaving just before dark, he'd caught a 30lb common the night before and had seen a few during the day - pukka! I dropped my gear with him there and then - sorted - no need for walking around, climbing trees today. I then wandered next door to Keith's for a while to grab a beer and toast Chilly's earlier success. Greg left about half an hour before dark, giving me plenty of time to get the rods out while I could still see what I was doing, cheers mate. I'd fished the swim a number of times so knew the area well, and pretty soon two rods were cast to a harder, slightly shallower area about 70 yards out, while the other was dropped short, down to the left, where a pipe fed water from the workings. The pipe wasn't running but it was a good area nevertheless, if not a bit obvious, and even as I swung the bait out I couldn't help but think that a fair percentage of anglers would have a rod on that spot when fishing this swim. I fished that rod as a single but scattered about a hundred baits over the other two, not wanting to over do it, as I was only fishing for one night, plus I had no idea what Greg had put in.

That night we had a bit of a social. Well, quite a lot of a social as it happens, and Sunday dawned far too early for my liking. Looking at some of the others it was obvious that I wasn't the only one suffering but, after a huge fry up and copious amounts of tea, we all began to brighten up a bit. The southerly which had been blowing for the last few days had now begun to swing round to more of a south westerly and, considering the force of the wind, it was incredibly mild for the time of year. With the wind now pushing straight towards my swim it really looked the one, and in conditions like this the carp just had to be feeding. We all sat around in Keith's plot for most of the morning, from where we could see the majority of the lake, but hadn't spotted any fish at all, nevertheless, you couldn't help but to feel confident in these conditions. Laney and I had decided that there was only one way to get a take, so, having discussed the fact that Cut Tail was the biggest in the lake, I bellowed across the water, "Big fat mirror!", a call that had been heard on Horton a few times in the past. Amazingly, a few minutes later, an alarm burst into

Cut Tail and the Lord of the Manor

life. We all froze for a second, then the penny dropped - it was mine. I ran the few yards to the rods with cheers and shouts of encouragement from the others, getting to them just as the indicator on the middle rod began to drop back to the ground. I raised the rod and frantically wound the reel handle as the line continued to slacken (the fish was swimming towards me at an incredible rate of knots) before eventually tightening, as I struck into solid resistance.

The spot I had hooked the fish from was beyond a fairly substantial weed bed, and the fish was obviously only too aware of that. With the carp locked up solid behind the weed bed I applied steady pressure, but it moved not an inch and, by now, I was surrounded by a load of experts all offering their pearls of wisdom and conflicting advice on what to do next. "For God's sake Reg, pull it in, I'm getting bored!" were Laney's helpful words. The carp must have felt the same as, soon after, the rod tip banged down hard, the line pinged free and I was in proper contact with the fish for the first time, even though it had been on for a few minutes. Once free of the weed, the fish came in without any other dramas, other than making a few short but powerful runs close in, so Keith grabbed the landing net while Chilly stood at the waters edge, trying to catch the first glimpse of my prize. Now, Chilly's a big old boy

and would make a far better door than he would a window, and, combined with Jenks with all that hair, I couldn't see a bloody thing. I was calm, no worries, that was until Chilly saw the fish, "'Oh my God! Oh my God! Oh my God!" he kept screaming. Keith gave Dave one of those looks, thinking I hadn't seen him, and all of a sudden it went very quiet, very serious. Then, moments later, she was in the net, it was Cut Tail, at which point total mayhem ensued! Dave took charge of the weighing, asking, "What's your P.B. Reg?" "Forty pounds, eight", I replied. "Not anymore boy, forty two ten". The bragging rights were now mine, and the following weekend I had an even bigger hangover!

"Big fat mirror!"

Chapter 11

Three Wheels on My Wagon

With Christmas over and done with, I could once again turn my attention back to fishing, and so when Lynn was well enough, I often travelled up to Manor, or when I needed to be near to home, I went back to Chalk Farm. The year had kicked off in Oxford in fine style when our mate, Mick Dickens, landed a truly awesome brace from Manor in the shape of Popeye at 38lb and Cut Tail at 42lb and I was gagging to get back there. Unfortunately, Lynn had many hospital visits in the January and February, and it was whilst dealing with this that Keith and I were asked to do our first slide show. For me this was the

first foray into the world of stardom (cough, cough!) and to say we were nervous would not adequately sum up the sheer dread that we both felt. We would be on stage at the Carp Society conference at Dunstable, which meant that we would have to address at least a couple of hundred carp anglers. Gulp! I am sure that I was included just so that Jenkins had a hand to hold, because I am convinced all they wanted to hear about was Keith's remarkable six forties in a twelve month period. Be that as it may, I was going to be on stage, and the most immediate need was not to make a fool of myself - easier said than done. We arrived at the show fairly early on the Sunday armed with my fishing tackle, although I had no idea where

Mick Dickens and his awesome brace

I was going to be fishing, but it acted just like a comfy rag to know that I was going. We had set the slides up the evening before at Keith's house, and of course we had included some music - Thin Lizzy's 'The Boys Are Back in Town' to be precise. I couldn't help thinking it was all a bit dramatic, but Jenks liked it so who was I to argue? Now, I was used to talking to rooms full of men because of my army career, but nothing can prepare you for the nightmare of addressing a room full of carp anglers, many of whom I held in very high esteem and had infinitely more experience than myself. Still, as Phil Lynott boomed out across the auditorium we went and did our bit and, remarkably, it all went without too much trouble and it was nice to get Dave and Reg up on stage to share the moment. When it was over, all I wanted to do was get the hell out of there; that, as far as I was concerned, was my fifteen minutes of fame and I wanted nothing more to do with it. Strange that, because in the not too distant future, I would once again be thrust back where I really didn't want to go.

By now, Dave and I had tickets for the Brook and I was really in a quandary about what to do. Oxford or Kent? Kent or Oxford? Keith made the decision for me by reminding me of the big fat mirror I would be dangling for down in Kent, and so it was that I made my way to Conningbrook for the first time. As is my wont, I eventually arrived after a few wrong turns, and pulled up outside of Joe's house, but I have to admit that I was terribly disappointed when I stood on the banks. It looked so barren and uninteresting, and did nothing for me at all, there weren't even any trees to climb, and I wondered how the hell I was going to entertain myself. But, I was here and I would do some dangling. There were a few anglers on, none of whom I knew, so I spent my time walking around and the first thing that struck me was how many fish were showing. I could have been forgiven for thinking there were hundreds of carp in there, so often did they crash out and I really didn't know what to do. Eventually, I sat down in the area known as The Island (there are no islands at the Brook; it's just what the area is called) and it seemed to me that they were just moving up and down the lake leaping all the time. Knowing there were a handful of carp in the place left me shaking my head so there was only one thing for it, and that was to set up in a swim that offered me a shot at the middle of the lake. At least if they kept doing what they were doing now, they would be over my baits about a dozen times a day. To that end I loaded up and set off for the far bank and set my stall out in a swim know as Ghosties. The lake was a lot deeper than I thought it would be, but if that was how it was then I would have to deal with it and, after some marker float madness, I had three traps out in the lake. I wasn't at all confident, but reasoned that I did have the rest of the year to get to grips with the place so, with a cold lager in hand, I settled down to wait. For the first time in a long while I had changed my rigs, and was using the Stiff Link Pop up's. I even got Andy Kidd, a mate of Terry's, to give them the once over and he thought they looked okay, so out they went. I 'sticked' out a few 18mm Active 8 boillies, which the gulls gleefully consumed, so single hookbaits it would be then! The wind was coming over my right shoulder, which meant that I only had the faint whiff of the perfume factory over the road and for now I could put up with the smell, but come the morning...well!

Just after dark I had the twitchiest of bites and was soon reeling in a small pike. I repositioned the hookbait and reasoned that this sort of thing happened on most lakes from time to time, but by about mid-night I was releasing my ninth one, and was a little bit pissed off to tell the truth. It was late, I was tired, and to my eternal chagrin I didn't check the hooklink. Around half two, one of the rods ripped off in a rather different manner to the other pike bites I had received and there was little doubt that a carp was responsible when the rod was nearly ripped from

my hand. I played the fish carefully and after a while had it heading my way...and then the line fell slack. Oh Bollocks!!! On closer inspection, I think the pike had damaged the hooklink, and I had paid the ultimate price - Conningbrook one, Chilly nil, a situation that would remain for the next eight years.

When Laney arrived in the morning the wind had changed and all we could smell was the stench of perfume from over the road, mingled with Oxtail soup from the factory next door. It was so bad that it was giving me a headache, and I could see that Dave wasn't too happy about it either. Rightly or wrongly, I decided there and then that I didn't like the place and wanted to go back to Oxford, so I bade Laney farewell and wished him luck, not that he needed any of course!

Single hookbaits it would be then

The following week we decided that we would head off to Oxford, and the clan would gather to celebrate Mick's brace from Manor, now that sounded like fun! As per normal, I worked my butt off and finished my work on the Tuesday evening, so by the following morning I was racing up the M4 toward Oxford. When I arrived, there was just one other angler on Manor, and with a strong southwesterly blowing into the Conveyor Bank, there was only one place I wanted to be. With the other angler, remarkably, on the back of the wind, I set up in the third swim along the road bank, an area I was fairly familiar with, and in short order I had three hookbaits at about eighty yards in one of the silty gullies. A couple of kilos of Active 8 followed them into the pond and the traps were set. For the next 36 hours the fish showed constantly in and around the baited area, but I was left scratching my head. Why no action? On the Friday morning I had just about had enough so I reeled in and went to visit the shops. Once I had accumulated enough supplies I got back to the lake and, in that short time, the wind had veered round to a horrible northerly, and my heart sank. If I couldn't catch one when it looked so good, then how was I going to catch one now? The fish, however, must still have been in the mood because, as I stood and cursed the wind, a good fish showed a little way behind the bait, and so, with all thoughts of a move forgotten, I dispatched a couple of hookbaits back onto the spots. Happy with everything, I got the kettle

We gathered to celebrate Mick's brace

going and waited for my friends to arrive. For once Reg was first, followed later by Graham, and we sat and discussed tactics for a while, until as usual they decided to set up either side of me. Now there's a surprise. I must admit that my confidence was slowly ebbing away as the pair of them went at it with their marker floats, not what I needed, so I was completely shocked when one of the rods let out a couple of bleeps, followed by a full blooded one toner. Well that was one way of stopping them whipping the water to a foam! As soon as I had the rod in my hand I knew it was a good fish, and as the battle went on it did nothing to change my mind. The usual mickey taking soon died down as the fish neared the bank, and as it broke the surface for the first time, Reg immediately went for the net. It then became a little serious as up and down the margins it plodded, with me hanging on for grim death, however, the pressure eventually took its toll and it rolled into the outstretched net, at which point I sent my tonsils into orbit...as you do! We had no idea which fish it was until we rather gingerly looked into the net, and there lay the reason I had come to this lake in the first place. Popeye!! With great care, we got her onto the mat and recorded a weight of 39.08. It seemed amazing that we were here to celebrate Mick's brace, and that Popeye was the smaller of the two. Oh, I could definitely feel a hangover coming on. I quickly rang Roy Parsons to see if it would be okay to sack her, as Keith was inbound and I was sure he would want to have a look. With that done, we got ourselves a celebratory brew, and by the time we had finished it, Jenks was on hand with his camera. They all clicked away for a while

until it was time to slip her back to her home, and with a mighty flick of her tail she was gone. When Mick arrived there was infinitely more alcohol in my swim than fishing tackle, this was going to be a night to remember, and I'm told it was, but I really can't recall too much about it. Just the way it should be!

After that session, I wanted to stay at Manor. I couldn't think of going anywhere else. There were still a couple of carp I really wanted to catch; The Random Linear and Cut Tail topping that

It was obviously a good fish

list, but strangely, the more I fished there, the more unlikely I felt I was going to catch them. Maybe I simply talked myself out of getting them in the bottom of my net, who knows? I sat and watched the Random get caught so many times, I was getting a bit fed up with being on the other side of the camera. An old mate of mine, Greg Ritchardson, caught it one day, and as he returned him I said that I would be having it soon, to which he turned round and said that you have to be good to catch this one. I trudged back to my plot thinking that I was never going to be any good, but then again, maybe he was just a lucky bastard? There is one other story surrounding me and this fish, and I must admit that I brought it all on myself.

Shortly after my success with Popeye, I was at the lake for a couple of nights and, come the second evening, I was all alone on the pond and rather enjoying it when I got a couple of visitors. It was two lads from down Aldershot way, one I got on with very well, the other I could not stand the sight of. They asked me about the place, and did I have any bait I could spare them? I was just about to tell them to piss off, when I realised I may be able to get them out of my hair, so yes, I had some bait, and I thought it would be best if they fished over the other side, as I was thinking of moving there myself in the morning. So, armed with a kilo or two of bait and what they thought was good information, they set off. Whilst, all alone on the road bank, I giggled myself to sleep. A low twenty common in the night made me smile even more, that was until one of my visitors made his way into my swim to inform me that his mate had landed the Random earlier in the morning at 33lb. That will teach me for being such an unsociable git!! And so, winter eventually let go of her grip on the countryside, and spring came along and kicked nature up the backside. It was now that I was to have two very interesting meetings on the banks of Manor. Meetings that would change my life in more ways than

Popeye, 39.08!

Just the way it should be!

"You have to be good to catch this one"

I ever could have imagined. I had pulled up in the car park and was just wheeling my gear onto the lake, but my heart sank when I saw how many anglers were there. I don't actually recall how we got chatting, but soon enough I was sharing a brew with a guy by the name of Adam Penning. To be honest I wasn't at all interested in the fact that he was working with Drennan at the time and was largely responsible for the release of the ESP range; I just needed to know if he knew where the carp were. That was all superseded by the fact that he was a great guy to talk to. We laughed and joked about this and that until, eventually, we talked about anything but carp fishing, which I found very refreshing. It also transpired that he was going to be doing a magazine feature over the next day or so, so I decided I would keep as far out of his way as possible. To that end, after yet another cup of tea, I headed off to the other side of the lake and, as I set up, I couldn't help thinking about the gear he had shown me, best of all though, he didn't have to pay for any of it...bastard! The lake was fishing very poorly, and eventually I ended up back round with Adam, who, by now, had been joined by the editor of the magazine he was writing for, Catchmore Carp. As with Adam, I hit it off with Jim Foster right from the start, so much so, in fact, that by midnight we were one bottle of Jack Daniels and a couple of bottles of wine to the good. This article work looked like bloody good fun to me! Come the morning we were all a little subdued, but I was there to fish, and eventually, after thirty hours on the water, I decided that it may be time to get the rods out, at which point I was joined

We laughed and joked about this and that

by Jim. We talked some crap for a while until eventually he asked if I would write him an article about fishing in weed. Well, knock me down with a tub of pop-ups! I had no idea what to say, why in hells name would he want me to do that? Although he has never admitted it, I am sure that Penning had something to do with it but what ever the case, I agreed, and spent the next twenty four hours worrying about it. Somehow, over the next week, I managed to pen the required 2,500 words and we met back at Manor the following weekend for the pictures, and so it was that I started to write, and, with Adam throwing me the odd bit of tackle to write about, all was well with the world. One of the beauties of life is that we never know what is around the corner, and Jim and I could never have imagined how much fun we were both just about to have.

With all these distractions I must have simply forgot to catch myself a carp or two, and decided it was about

It was always fun to be in the company of Jim Foster

time I did. My next visit coincided with one of Terry Hearn's first trips of the year and we chatted for a while until the carp, as they do, decided to let him know where they were. He was off to the area like shit off a shovel, and very soon, Terry helped himself to a couple, including the Peanut mirror that I had landed in November, at 34lb. I, on the other hand, had to be content with losing what felt like a good fish. Poor old Terry had to listen to me for the rest of the evening - when I have a moan it's best to steer clear until I have cheered up a bit.

It was a few days before I could return, and as I skidded to a halt in the car park, I was determined to set the world to rights. I remember, although it wasn't forecast, that a strong and not very warm wind had sprung up and whilst I wasn't too sure that the carp would follow it, there were two things that made me change my mind. For a while Smith's, the gravel company that owned Manor, had been re-sculpting the out of bounds gravel bank, and during their labours had pushed a lot of gravel into the lake, which in effect, had created a gravel bar and I was sure, knowing how nosey carp can be, that they would have to investigate. The other, and more obvious reason for going to that end of the lake, was that several carp had boomed out in the choppy water, so as fast as my legs would carry me, I was up there with my kit.

With fish in residence, it was a simple case of whacking out two single pop-ups to fish for themselves for a while and one of them didn't stay too long. I was sorting out the accommodation for the night when the bobbin on one of the rods fell to the floor and I wound and wound until, eventually, I had caught up with the culprit. That was the easy part because, once battle was joined, the carp was hell bent on getting to the far side of the lake, a trick it performed on several occasions. It was a while before it rolled in front of me, exposing the most perfect set of linear scales and, a short time later, he was in the net. It was a fish known as the Zip, for obvious reasons, and weighed a pleasing 27lb – there could be no better way to start a session. The fish stopped showing after that, and with no more action, first light found me up the willow tree that marked the entrance to the top bay, and there at my feet were several of Manor's finest. After a while I came up with a plan and set about putting it into action, then with everything in place, the kettle was on and I was happy. I happened to glance down to the road bank a little later and was convinced that Laney was going to join me, however, it wasn't him but Terry, and he decided to angle in the bay up to my right, bagging himself a lovely 29lb mirror a little later, which was a good sign as it meant the fish were still about. We bumped into each other throughout the rest of the day, in the branches of the

It was a fish known as the Zip

willow, and although fish were still very evident, nothing had happened as the evening drew in, that was until a double figure common tripped one of my traps. A good start. In the early hours I was once again called into action, and was soon very awake as my arms were nearly pulled from their sockets. After much tooing and frowing, a rather long and scaley mirror lay in the folds of my net but, at 30.10, he was not a fish I was familiar with, and the capture was made even sweeter when I spoke to Roy Parsons because he had never seen it either - another one of Manor's little mysteries. With the weather warming up nicely and summer on its way, I was hoping for some more action over the coming weeks, however, my itchy feet were once again about to drag me off to pastures new. Unbelievably, I was bored with Oxford and needed to be somewhere else, and as crazy as it seems, that would be the last time I would ever fish there, but it truly is a special place. The problem was now, I wasn't quite sure where I should go.

Terry bagged himself a lovely 29lb mirror

One of Manor's mysteries

By now, Keith had bagged himself a ticket for the Brook and, with Dave now in full swing, I decided that I would go there for a while, but yet again, my vision of carp fishing was just about to upset the apple cart - I really didn't like the place at all. Added to that was the fact that Lynn was getting increasingly ill, so I wasn't too comfortable with being so far from home. As always, she insisted that I just get on with it, and everything would be okay, the problem is, I can't fish effectively if I have something far more important on my mind. The one good thing about the Brook was the anglers that fished there, the social life was absolutely bonkers, so much so that it invariably got in the way of the fishing. A meeting with Paul Forward or Martin Locke, and of course Laney, was usually followed by a mad dash to Tesco's for some cold lager. I remember on one visit, Joe was having a party in his house, and everyone on the lake was invited, and what an incredible night that was. There were whole pigs to cook, salmon, and massive legs of pork and, unsurprisingly, we kicked the arse right out of it, but a good time was had by all. Come the morning, though, and with a rather bad headache, I had to make a decision. My time was precious, and I could not condone that time away from Lynn by simply travelling to Kent and getting pissed at every opportunity. Something had to give, and it did. Wraysbury seemed to be the answer, and soon enough I was making plans to return.

I must admit that it all seemed a little strange that Keith would not be there, but then he was Dave Lane's mate, and would have to stay banned. The first thing that struck me was how busy the place was, more and more people were fishing it. Now, Wraysbury is over one hundred acres in size and you would not have thought that would be too much of a problem, but it was. With so few fish to go at, and considering the quality of the anglers there, it wasn't surprising that we all wanted to be in the same place. I was back to weekend fishing, because that was the only time that Lynn's friends had to be with her, but arriving on a Friday to find all the best places occupied did little to instill any confidence in me. To start with, I spent far too much time in the Perseverance pub and, on the odd occasion, I didn't fish at all. I had neither rhyme nor reason to my fishing, and could not get into it.

We had some laughs though

Worries about losing Lynn, and the fact that in a short while I would be leaving the army, left me in a bit of pickle but, forcing these things to the back of my mind, I ploughed on. At no point during the coming months did I ever feel as if I was going to catch a carp and as much as I hate to admit it, I had stumbled completely off the rails. A trip to Wraysbury was just an excuse to get drunk. I had plenty of things I didn't want to think about, and the bottom of a bottle seemed the best place to be and I have to say that, looking back, I am ashamed of myself, but bloody hell we had some laughs!

By the end of July, I was carting more cans of lager around the pond than I was fishing tackle, and finding it increasingly difficult to get a handle on reality. I arrived on Friday 31st July to find Jacko still set up in the Turfs. In fact, he had been there for about three weeks, having come up with a plan, and was determined to stick to it. His intention was to stay in the swim until he caught one, the problem was that his swim had taken over from the Perseverance Pub, and everyone would turn up with copious amounts of beer; all in all, the ideal place for me to spend my time. I don't want you to get the impression that Jacko was one of those 'I'm on the dole to support my fishing' types because he wasn't. He was running his own business; it's just that he needed to get it out of his system, but the trouble was the plan had not worked as yet. To try and cheer the old boy up, I added my pile of cold lager to his already impressive collection but to be honest we were all a bit worried about him at the time, he was in a bit of a mess, but hey, there was beer to drink...so we did! Phil Thompson arrived, as did Del, and the party went into full swing. The object of our mickey taking for the evening was Jacko's boat. He had got hold of an old sailing dingy with which to do his baiting up, but instead of using buckets to carry the hemp to its desired spot, he had simply cooked it and poured it into the bottom of the boat, and then once over the area he would ladle it out around the marker. He was happy, so he took it all in his rather wobbly stride. By the time it was dark, there was no way I was going fishing, so set up my bed chair some twenty yards behind him, then the next thing I knew, Jacko was running around telling those who would listen that he had just landed the Pug. In truth, he had no idea which fish it was, but soon enough we were on hand to give assistance. It was Mallin's at 42lb and, even before the pictures were done, I could feel another mammoth session on the booze was imminent, and with the fish safely back in his home that is precisely what we did.

The day became a blur, and once again we were all in his swim generally taking the piss out of everything then, suddenly, there was the most horrible noise coming from somewhere towards Horton. It was a rave of some kind, and went on right through until morning. God I hate that music! With all that madness going on, the last thing we thought of was Jacko getting a bite, but that is exactly what happened. As he lifted the rod I grabbed the net, and within a couple of minutes a rather large carp was waiting for me to lift the net around it. He had no idea what he had landed, but I could see quite clearly, so I told him.

"Well done Action, you've got Mary's Mate!!" Which left him speechless, and rightfully so.

With the pictures done and a weight of 41lb recorded, he felt that it only right that we celebrate, I couldn't help thinking that we had done enough of that already, but he was adamant. Who was I to argue? Especially as he said we would go to the Five Bells, and the beers were on him. How we never got thrown out is a mystery, it really was a crazy afternoon, eventually, though, we had to get back to the lake, and I'm not sure how, but we ended up sitting in Jacko's clapped out old van just inside the green gates. I was knackered from the long walk back from the pub, but he was full of it, so much so, that he decided that we should go rally driving around the peninsula, and so, in a cloud of dust and leaves, we sped around skidding everywhere. Whether we were breaking any laws I have no idea, but as we were on private ground we figured it was okay, and how we didn't die I will never know either - complete and utter madness! We eventually got back to his swim, at which point he was keen to show me how good his rods were.

"Look Chilly, I have had these for fifteen years, and they have never let me down". I nodded sagely and agreed that they were, indeed, fine rods, what else could I say? Then he wanted me to see how good they were by grabbing the tip.

"Go on son, grab it and see what they are like". So I did, and he heaved into the rod, which promptly broke into a thousand pieces. He stood and stared at the small piece of butt section left in his hand whilst I, on the other hand, had trouble stopping every rib in my body from breaking, and the more upset he got, the more I laughed. There was only one thing for it, and simultaneously we reached for a beer. I raised my can and said "Well done fella".

It was Mallin's at 42lb

"But Chilly, I broke me fuckin' rod!" Which just sent me into raptures once again...priceless!

Lurching from one drinking session to the next, I was getting more and more depressed about my fishing, and felt so helpless about Lynn. Don't get me wrong, I was having fun, but I couldn't help thinking how much I was wasting my time and, by mid-September, I was simply going through the motions. I had taken to fishing in and around the Bryant's Point area in the South Lake - in the main, I think, because of the entertainment found there. On Sundays the local football team would have a game in the morning, and it was my greatest joy to watch it; Sunday league football is so much more fun than the stuff you see on the telly. I would walk around to the bar, get a couple of pints and sit and watch a load of overweight and hungover blokes kick the crap out of each other, but as nice as that was, it still wasn't getting me any nearer to catching a carp. I thought that was about to change when, on my arrival one day, I spied several fish showing at fairly short range from

You've got Mary's mate fella

56.06 and a new British record

Bryant's Point. In no time at all I had some traps set and sat and hoped that I had done enough, then some time later Kevin Cummings (Plumb Bloke) set up in the Mad Dog swim on the other side of the bay and, as I watched him get things sorted, I felt sure that somebody was in for a bite. The night passed, then I was woken in the early hours by someone telling me that Plumb Bloke had landed Mary so, quickly reeling the rods in, I ran around to see what all the fuss was about. We got the monster out of the water and once on the mat no one could say a word, she looked magnificent, and the scales read out their message - 56.06, a new British record. He had caught the fish before but, to a man, we could not have been happier for him but, after first shaking his hand, I sat back with some incredulity and watched as deals were struck on who would get the exclusivity on the story. Mary,

Chris Ball arrived to witness the occasion

bless her, lay in a sack whilst ridiculous amounts of money were discussed, which made me feel a little sad - is that why we catch these fish, just for the highest bidder? I know more about the game now, but at the time I was gobsmacked. The Angling Times won the day, but that didn't stop Chris Ball turning up to witness the occasion and to be honest I felt sorry for him, he wasn't allowed to do anything. But when he reached over and stroked her flank you could see that Mary was all that mattered to him, and just being there. I had the utmost respect for him that day, and still have. The pictures were done, and the story was told, and then someone mentioned beer...and that was the end of that!!

The annual Wraysbury Christmas party

Shortly after that my fishing time came to a grinding halt when Lynn was rushed into hospital, and all thoughts of Wraysbury were cast from my mind. Max, the Mad Marauder, was going to have to put up with sharing his house with his Dad, and I was going to have to do my best to get Lynn back on the road to recovery. Now, I am not the best at being kept in the dark about things, and this is only compounded by the fact that doctors simply don't have the time to bother about the people at home, and how they are going to cope with the situation. No one wanted to tell me anything, and I wanted to find out what the score was. It all started on the ward, but eventually the argument ended in one of the surgeon's offices, and as the argument raged on a couple of security guys turned up, which probably had something to do with the hole I had just punched in the wall! Thankfully, I knew one of them and the heat was taken out of the situation. Yes, I know they have far more important things to attend to, and did not deserve my short tempered tirade, but it is hard to help to put someone's life back together when you don't know what's happening. I was more reassured after a while, and we all got along fine, but I wasn't exactly flavour of the month. Anyway, from that point on I was kept firmly in the loop, which saved a lot of time, and helped Lynn no end. It wasn't until after Christmas, in early 1999, that I was able to get the rods out properly once again. The annual Wraysbury Christmas party had got me back in the mood, and of course the Perseverance had to put up with us all for one last time. Lynn's recuperation was taking a long time, and to that end I once again turned my attention to the army lake, Chalk Farm.

I turned my attention back to Chalk Farm

The business end of a Wraysbury carp

Chapter 12

Lifes Lessons

The year of reckoning had arrived. For all of my adult years I had led the military life, I really knew nothing else, but there was now eighteen months to my retirement. It seems such a long time when you write it, but in reality it was over in the blink of an eye, and, if I was honest I was scared. I had had a good insight into the civilian world through Keith, Dave and Reg, but I knew that it was going to be a shock...and then some, and I had no doubt that a lot of my time would be spent sorting things out for the future. There is a popular misconception about the army in that we don't pay our way in the world, and are generally mollycoddled. Wrong! We pay tax just like everyone else has to; food has to be paid for, and in fact all of life's little burdens have to be dealt with just the same as everyone else. Couple that with putting your neck on the line from time to time, and it all adds up to a pretty tough life, especially for the families of the soldiers. I often have a laugh at some of the comments I get now-a-days, things like "you need to get a real life", which normally come from some jealous little prick, of course. For most of my army career I had a life that was just about as real as it gets. Lynn and I had been discussing it, with a degree of trepidation, but as always she insisted that I do some angling, which was all well and good, but I couldn't think for the life of me what I was going to do when I got out. I had been writing for a while, which was really just a nice way of supplementing my income and I got some free tackle too, by way of ESP. Adam had been involving me in product development, and I was tasked to test some of the gear, and it was nice to be involved that way. On the bait front, Kev Knight at Mainline was sorting me out, so there was much I didn't have to worry about with regards to my fishing. But, for the life of me, I could see no way that anyone could actually make a living from fishing. No, I would have to rely on my military contacts and get a job looking after some Arab prince or doing one of the security jobs in the Middle-East. It was all I could think of for the time being. Of course, Lynn was suffering now, not only from the breast cancer, but bowel cancer and other related problems and as much as I didn't want to admit it, things were starting to get worse. There was a need for me to stay in the Aldershot area because that is where her consultants were and changing them could have had a dramatic affect on her treatment, which I wasn't about to put at risk.

My life had been as real as it gets

Remarkably ostrich like, I simply buried my head in the sand and one cold and frosty morning, packed my rods into the car, then made the short journey to Chalk Farm. At the very least, I could leave the 'real' world behind for a while. Being so familiar with the lake helped a lot, and the action picked up as if I had never been away, I even got Keith over every now and again, and we caught some carp too. We had managed to get together over the Christmas period for the usual Banned social session, all meeting up at Averley Lakes in Essex, and as usual kicked the arse out of everything. As much as these trips are very light hearted affairs, there is always that element of competition when mates are together and, to that end, everyone fished everyone else's swim and did as much poaching as possible. All culminating in Laney once again rubbing our noses in it with a 28lb mirror. These trips, however, have a different slant to them other than catching carp because friends, genuine ones at any rate, are hard to come by, and living so far apart I treasured those moments.

With Lynn recovering 'as well as could be expected' and the carp playing ball, all was well in Chilly world, that was until late February. It was a cold evening and as I settled down to watch a bit of telly I started to feel decidedly unwell, so unwell, in fact, that I retired early to my bed. Now, I don't do 'being sick' at all. I have never made a doctors appointment, and have only ever been to the medical centre when carried in on a stretcher. What it did do was for Lynn to start clucking around me trying to make sure I was okay...which, I assured her, I was not. I dozed fitfully throughout the night until the pain started to kick in. It felt as if someone was trying to drive a red hot poker through my lower stomach and the light was just spreading across the sky when I gave in, asking Lynn to phone the camp. The army has never really been known for its compassion in situations like this and in time honoured tradition it was decided that an ambulance would take too long, so one of the duty personnel was dispatched to my house in a rather old and battered Landrover. He arrived at our quarters whilst Lynn was trying to dress me, no easy task when you have a twelve stone Great Dane thinking it was all a great laugh. Max was jumping all over me, bless him, but he was a bark and half away from getting a kick in the bollocks!! It was comical; the young private had to

Leaving the 'real' world behind

As usual, we kicked the arse out of everything

wrestle the dog, while my unwell wife had to wrestle me into some clothes, and then I looked at the Landrover. I could feel the pain even before I got in the damn thing. Needs must and all that, and I eventually heaved myself into the front seat, whilst Lynn climbed in the back, and we were off. I nearly battered the driver several times as he gleefully roared over the bumps in the road and by the time we reached Frimley Park Hospital I thought I was close to death. I was immediately rushed into A&E, and left there to writhe around in agony until some Captain had had his Tea and Tiffin, and decided that I was worthy of attention.

I treasured those moments

By now I had the hump, and even Lynn knew what was coming. There wouldn't be any officers in my kind of army, and this fellow left me feeling no different, so as he sauntered in I launched into him with my full repertoire of expletives, and said officer backed off. It was obvious he had called up the heavy mob when a full Colonel swept back the curtain and demanded that he examine me. Fair enough, so he probed about and um'ed and ah'ed for a while and, as much as I told him hundreds of times that my appendix was just about to fall out of my arse, he eventually righted himself and announced that I may have appendicitis...well, no shit Sherlock!! At which point he said he was going to have to do some kind of examination. Lynn gripped my hand a little tighter, not for any comfort that may have afforded, but to stop me hitting the bloke, and then she explained what that examination entailed. I was horrified!

"What, in the name of all things holy, would sticking a digit up my backside tell him that I could not. I am in friggin agony and you are going to do something about it...right now!!"

Remarkably, he turned and left in a hurry, at which point he briefed his Captain that he would have to do the inspection of my arse, because he felt I was going to hit him if he did. It was probably the craziest order anyone had ever been given. I tried to swear Lynn to secrecy, because I knew that Jenks and Co would be merciless if they found out, but the mischievous grin on her face told me that I was in trouble, and there was me thinking I had married a nice girl!

Anyway, they eventually filled me up with Morphine and I drifted in and out of oblivion for a while. The next thing I knew was waking up feeling like shit and dying for a fag. Lynn was at my bedside and pushed me out to a smoking area, where I lit one up and promptly spewed all over the place. I needed to lay down, which is what I did for the next few days, and by the time I got home I was feeling a lot better, and all I could think about was going fishing. Lynn wasn't so sure, so I left it a few more days until boredom got the better of me and she gave in. I groaned and sweated as I loaded up my gear into the car, but once that was done, Lynn reminded me that I had an appointment to get the stitches out. The last thing I needed was to be waiting around in a hospital for some snotty little intern to remove them, so decided that I would have to do it myself. I visited Yateley Angling Centre, where I bumped into Mick Barnes, who, like me, was in the army at the time, and volunteered his services. I declined because I just wanted to get to the lake, I hadn't been for a while and felt that would be the best way to make a full recovery. That's probably why I am not a doctor, because it didn't exactly turn out like that.

Yet again, my friend who lived in one of the married quarters on the side of Chalk Farm, allowed me to park in his drive and I really needed that favour more than ever this time. It was only a short walk to the nearest, and probably most productive swim on the lake, the Little Beech, even so, it took me about forty minutes to get the stuff in there, and by the time I did, I was a sweaty mess, and in a lot of pain. The wind was pushing in there very nicely, and for a moment I was happy, that was until I saw several fish show right on the back of the wind at the far end of the lake. Oh shit! What ever the circumstances, I simply can't fish when I know they are all over the other side so there was nothing for it, I had to move. So, the painful process began all over again. In all, it took me a little over an hour to get everything round there, all the while checking to see if I hadn't left any of my entrails dragging in the mud behind me. Once I had finished, I was actually sick a couple of times, but there were still stitches to remove, and some fishing to be done. First things first and it was out with the scalpel blade. Thankfully, it was just one big stitch running the length of the wound as I snipped off one end and dragged the whole lot out, which was slightly painful, but not too bad. As much as I wanted to fish a rather productive spot at about 60 yards, I knew I would probably do some permanent damage if I tried to chuck a lead that far so, in the end, I settled on a couple of PVA bags at

Now that's what I call a result!

about 15 yards in some holes in the weed. I was shattered and far from well, so literally curled up on my bed and wondered what heaven looked like as I didn't think it would be long before I found out.

I drifted in and out of a fitful sleep until, eventually, one of the rods sprang into life. Getting to the rods was easier said than done, but soon I was holding a very bent piece of carbon. Keeping the butt away from the danger zone, I gingerly played the fish all the way into the net. It was a small mirror of around 16lb, and as I lifted him onto the mat I remember thanking him for not being any bigger because I was sure I would never have been able to get it on the bank. After slipping him back it took me fully ten minutes to regain my composure, but just as I was sorting the rod out, a big fish boomed out in the darkness. I craned my neck around the edge of my brolly and sure enough, the rings were emanating from the very spot I really wanted to fish. This was obviously going to hurt, and I couldn't help wondering if the hospital had enough of my blood to rectify the damage a cast to that spot would undoubtedly do. With a slightly larger lead attached and the bag impaled on the hook, I took up my position. The insanity of what I was about to do did cross my mind for a nano-second, then I launched it. No sooner had the line left my finger than a searing spasm ripped across my stomach. Had someone just shot me? With the line still peeling rapidly off the spool, I fell to my knees. I had no idea if the lead had landed as intended, and to be honest I really didn't care. For all I knew, I was about to spin off my mortal coil, but as I was still breathing, maybe not just yet and it must have been at least ten minutes before I could even tighten up the line and put it on the rests. At which point, nearly in tears, I fell unceremoniously back onto my bed. I was really feeling sorry for Laney at this point, because he was the one that would find me early in the morning, and have to inform my wife of my demise. It's not often that I look at the rods and hope they don't go off, but that is exactly what I did as I tried desperately to get some sleep. My prayers seemed to have been answered, but at five thirty I let out a groan as the long range rod chirped into life. Once again, I was careful where the butt of the rod was, and concentrated on landing what was obviously a bigger fish. Strangely, I had no thoughts of 'I hope this doesn't fall off', just the fact that once in the net I would have to lift it onto the mat. I pulled, and it pulled back for a while, until it rolled into the outstretched net. It looked very big, and felt a whole lot bigger when I lifted it out of the water, especially when it appeared that someone had been clog dancing on my torso all night. At 32lb it was the biggest common in the lake, and it must have been the thought of that which helped me to sack the fish carefully in the margins. I allowed myself a bit of a chuckle...now that's what I call a result!

I curled up once again on my bed, and just as I was drifting off, Laney arrived. Thankfully, I wasn't dead and with some difficulty we managed to get the pictures done. As Jenks would be arriving later on that day, we thought it best if I moved around in front of the houses, as it would make for a better social; the three of us hadn't been together for some time, and I didn't want to waste the opportunity to catch up so, with a very deep breath, I moved around to the swim I had arrived in the day before. Rather pleasingly, Keith had got off work very early, and by one in the afternoon we were all angling. Now, we all know how merciless our mates can be if they can detect the slightest chink in your armour and this situation was no different, so being well aware of my rather homophobic nature, I was subjected to intense bouts of marigold gloves and KY jelly jokes. It is quite amazing how much mileage they got out of the fact that someone had stuck a digit up my backside. Having landed a personal best common, I was somewhat impervious to their gibes and simply concentrated on the angling, plus the beer and food the antagonists had brought with them. Over the next couple of days Dave and I helped ourselves to four more fish each, but Jenks just couldn't get one, even his legendary poaching techniques could not get him a bite. The last couple of fish were the best though, with Laney bagging himself a stunning 26lb Linear, whilst I launched a last gasp single hookbait at a showing fish which resulted in a cracking 29lb mirror. Understandably, the after effects of my operation were soon forgotten and a good time was had by all, well, for a week or so at any rate.

Dave and I helped ourselves to four more fish each

Dave had taken the pictures of my common on his camera, and Kev Green at the Angling Times asked me to send a picture off to him. I spoke to Laney, who agreed to send them off and the following week there was my picture; unfortunately, Dave had sent off a picture of his linear as well, and this had been inset on the picture of the common. All I could hope for was that no one would notice because, you see, Laney did not have a ticket, but once we had been sussed I was contacted by the chairman of the club. I gave him the normal set of bollocks you give when a ban is obviously looming, and then waited for the verdict. I was to be banned for three months for taking a 'guest' but as this period would include the two months closed season, I think I got away quite lightly. There is an interesting story behind all of that, and it has a lot to do with the silly grape vine that surrounds carp fishing at times. If you believed the local folk lore around here, you would be forgiven for thinking that I had been banned from this club loads of times but this was, in fact, the one and only ban I ever received, which should put to rest the jealous prattling of a rather bitter and sad northern exile that has moved into our area. But, isn't there always one of those? However, I do have one small admission to make. At the time I didn't even have a ticket myself. I had become so much a part of the furniture at this lake, that for several years I had not bothered to renew my membership. I know I shouldn't, but it still makes me chuckle!

Apart from doing the odd article now and again, I spent the next couple of months trying to make sense of leaving the army but I really didn't know where to start. Most important of all was my resettlement training to sort out, something that events conspired to prevent me from ever doing. I could never have imagined how unprepared I would be when the day finally came to walk out of the gates for the last time. All that thinking was far too much for my little brain to take in, so eventually there could only be one outcome...I needed to go fishing! As I had no idea what the future held, I decided that I would stick with Wraysbury for the foreseeable, but I did make a couple of decisions, though. My fishing would change once the army was out of the way. I no longer wanted to fish the waters that had been so good to me in the past, to that end, whatever I was doing this season would be for the last time. The challenges of civvy street would be compounded by the challenges of new waters, and so, come the beginning of June, it was time to load up the boat and tackle, then head off in search of a monster or two.

Once again, the lake seemed so busy, but that fact was cushioned by knowing that Keith had once again got a ticket. That said, we hardly fished together because as my army commitments dwindled, I was able to fish more in the middle of the week. I hoped that would help with the fishing, but most of the time my mind was concentrating on

I would stick with Wraysbury for now

other things. There was also the not insignificant fact that anglers on the water were coming in for far more attention from some of the low life's that surrounded it. The only time that it really bothered me was when I became a target for several air rifles whilst set up on Bryant's Point. For two days I had pellets winging around my head, and try as I may I could never get near the culprits but, eventually, as they always do when they get no reaction, they got bored and moved on. There were a couple of frightening incidents though. A mate of mine, Rory, was set up in the Root Nightmare and was taking a bit of an afternoon nap, when he became very much awake. A kid of maybe twelve or thirteen was looming over him holding a large carving knife and, rather nervously, he inquired what the hell was going on. The kid simply replied that Rory's kit was so crap that he wasn't going to kill him to steal it. Charming! We suffered for a while, until they picked on the wrong man. Jacko was set up in the Mad Dog and I was in the Root and we were having a chat in my swim, then when Jacko went back to his, some gear was missing. He had his suspicions, and went to inform the bloke that lived opposite him in Douglas Lane (the road that leads to the South Lake carp park). Sure enough, it was his kids that were responsible and, for the next hour, all we could hear was the kids getting a good beating. Oddly enough, we didn't see them again.

With the season a few weeks old, I arrived to find that most of the guys were set up in the South Lake. All of the prime spots were taken, but with the wind trickling into Bryant's Bay I was surprised that no one had set up in there so I quickly got a bucket from the car and went for a look around. One of the residents of Douglas Lane, whose house backed onto the lake, had undertaken a mission to defoliate that part of the bank, and I must admit it looked horrible as I made my way toward it. That impression quickly changed as I crept up to a stump, there to discover several of the small stockies that now inhabited the lake and I could just make out a couple of bigger shapes a little further out, but my view was obscured by the ripple on the water. I travelled right down to the bottom of the bay and decided that I would set up there and wait for them to get to me so, as cool as I could (I didn't want to alert anyone as to my good fortune), I went and got my gear from the car. Thirty minutes later and I was good to go. Thankfully, I had no need for a boat here; it was just a case of finding a nice spot in the margins for a couple of rods. (I was armed with the new Assassinate boillies and was keen to see if this would break my Wraysbury drought) and had soon positioned two stiff link pop-ups in the ten foot deep margins, one behind a set of pads and the other in front of some reeds. A pound of 14mm boillies would keep the hookbaits company, and the scene was set. I had a few visitors during the day and into the evening then, according to my plan, I refrained from any of the proffered cold lagers. As nice as they would have been, I was now more determined than ever to catch a carp. The odd fish cruised by as the light faded, and I drifted off to sleep, then, up at first light, I started the day by informing the carp what a bunch of bastards they were, and made myself a brew. That was followed by a few more, and I must admit, I thought my chance for the day had gone. The houses were only a few yards behind me, and several of the occupants were out in the gardens doing some chores and as they toiled away I happened to glance up to the entrance of the bay, and was sure I could see someone playing a carp. I walked down to my left for a better look and, sure enough, there was some rod bending action going on. I trudged back to my plot and was just about to sit down for a good old sulk when the rod behind the pads heaved round, the line pinged from the clip and the buzzer howled. I suppose it must have been a very rare occurrence at Wraysbury, that two anglers were playing a fish at the same time, and although my battle was over a lot quicker than the other guy, it was just as tense. I had a few problems with the lilies, but soon had a nice mirror rolling a couple of rod lengths out and, as it neared the net, I could see which fish it was. Measles was making his last bid for freedom, but all I could think about was that he was the first fish I had ever seen a picture of from Wraysbury. Held by Richard Skidmore, that image had been in my mind ever since I started fishing here and, with that, he was in the net and I could exercise my tonsils with a deafening,

"Light my fire!" At which point I turned round to see all the 'gardeners' staring somewhat strangely at me. I tried to explain that I had just landed a Wraysbury carp and how special that was, but with the odd shake of the head, they returned to their houses. How rude, I thought they could have at least offered me a lager! Once I had sorted the fish out and secured him in the landing net, I set off to find myself a photographer. The obvious place was where the other action had taken place, which had ended with the guy landing Mallin's, and once those pictures were done I dragged everyone down to the end of the bay. At 28.12 he was not the

The bottom end of Bryant's Bay

biggest of the Wraysbury fish, but that is not the point. Probably one of the oldest fish in the pond was now being held up, by me, for the gathered camera men and I was the happiest man alive. Keen to tell Lynn of my good fortune, I quickly gave her a ring whilst she was queuing up in the post office with a friend. I screamed down the phone that I had got Measles and she could not have realised what affect her congratulations were having on the other customers as she replied.

"Oh you've caught Measles, oh well done, what a clever boy you are". The place fell silent and everyone turned to look at her, she thought about explaining for a moment, and then decided that they would never really understand. Bless her. Then someone mentioned beer, and as much as I didn't want to be supping ale, it just seemed the right thing to do.

"Oh you've caught Measles, well done!"

A couple of weeks later, I found myself setting up in the Root Nightmare for a few nights. The conversations that I had during the first day revolved around the recent closure of many waters around the Colne Valley, where fish had been dying in many lakes, and as a precaution, and quite rightly so, the controlling bodies decided that to prevent further contamination they should shut their doors for a while. We could only guess what RMC's reaction would be but, as hard as all this devastating news was to take, I wanted to concentrate on my fishing. For the first time that season I was definitely on the fish, I had seen quite a few by the time I had all three rods fishing, and was simply hoping that I would once again hold a big fat mirror. Early the next morning I was out and about looking to see if they were still in the area, when a whole gaggle of 'fun police' turned up through the gates, which did not look good. Being the first in line, I was soon informed that the lake was closed with immediate effect and you simply could not argue with the logic of the decision, so, as the bailiff posse made their way around the lake, I quickly packed my gear away. Far from being annoyed, I could understand the move completely, and now I just had to get on with sorting out becoming Mr. Chillcott. So that is what I tried to do.

The closure didn't last too long and within a couple of weeks I was once again screaming up the M3 with my hair on fire. Now that I was concentrating on my fishing, rather than feeling sorry for myself, I felt right on top of the game. The fishing, however, slowed dramatically (not that it was ever that hectic), and we all settled in for the long haul and, although I had yet to catch another carp, I was extremely happy with my efforts, at least I was now putting the effort in. Lynn had been quite well, and I had all but forgotten about leaving the army, but isn't it always the way, just when you think you have got things cracked, life comes along and gives you a good old kick in the knackers?

I had been at Wraysbury for the August bank holiday weekend, getting home early on the Monday morning, and with everything sorted I settled down for an evening in front of the telly. Lynn and I are 'Trekies' and were both looking forward to the relatively new Voyager series, but as Captain Janeway was just doing battle with some alien, Lynn said that she really didn't feel too well. She tried to shrug it off, and said she would be okay then, just at that moment, she simply collapsed out of her chair and crashed to the floor. I am normally quite unflappable in these situations but this was serious. At first I tried to talk to her, but got no response, Max even tried to rouse his mum, but both our attempts failed. I placed her in the recovery position and checked for a pulse, at least she was breathing and her heart, although weak, was working. The ambulance arrived in very short order and, once

I had briefed the para-medics, they got on with their job and, soon enough, she was off to the hospital in a blaze of blue lights. I tend to get in the way of things when she first arrives at the A&E, so I made sure I got all the bits and pieces that she would need for a normal hospital stay, and then an hour later, I was at her bed side after having been briefed by the doctors. It appeared that she had had a stroke and was completely paralysed and unable to speak, so all I could do was wait and hope, and believe me I did a great deal of that over the coming weeks. It was several days before there was any improvement; the right side of her body being the first to respond, as well as her voice, although the latter was horribly slurred and hard to comprehend. I was assured, though, that things were improving; I would just have to take their word for that, because as far as I could see things were not good at all! So, for a couple of weeks I fed Max my food, disposed of his rather large turds, and worried myself to death. Gradually things got better, but it was very obvious that her left, and most dominant side, was going to be the most affected. Then as the end of September loomed, I was told I could collect her from the hospital and as nice as that was, we both knew that this was only the beginning of her recovery.

The next month or so was taken up with physiotherapy and plenty of doctors appointments and, before I forget, having heard a few horror stories about the Social Services, I will never have a bad word said about them again. They offered support above and beyond the call of duty, a gesture Lynn and I will be eternally

I spent some time walking around Chalk Farm

grateful for, and without that help I have no idea how I would have coped. Around the middle of October, Lynn's voice was all but back to normal, and most of the movement and strength had returned to her right side. The left side was a different matter though, and as much as she tried, it just would not get better. After several meetings, we were told that this was probably going to be how it would stay, which, for someone as active as Lynn has always been, this was a hammer blow. But, and you have probably guessed already, on the journey home she asked when I wanted to go fishing. Remarkable!

I had all but forgotten about that side of things, it just wasn't important any more.

Trouble was, as my wife was fully aware, I was never designed to live in a house and to be honest, I think she was rather looking forward to me getting out of the way. Everything was in a bit of a pickle, and between her and her friends they would try and put right all the mess Max and myself had made of things. Again, the last thing I wanted to do was listen to a load of Lynn's mates moaning about me, so Max and I started to spend a little time walking around Chalk Farm. If I was going to do some dangling then I needed to be as near to home as possible, so to that end, within a few days I was taking a bucket of Response Pellets with me on every trip with Max. During the week there was never anyone fishing, and I started to bait a couple of spots and because they were little fished, it wasn't long before I could see that the carp had been taking full advantage of the free meals. One area in particular, just to the right of a swim called the Dip, had fish in or around it on every trip. Max and I rushed through the door with a little more gusto one day, and Lynn responded with a "when are you going then?" It was Friday and I planned to go on the Monday, which left me the weekend to sort out some cover for Lynn, which was never too hard to find - I had volunteers coming out of my ear holes - and so I formed a plan. I would fish from midday until late afternoon, as often as I could and, as always, Chalky had a few nice surprises in store.

Mirrors of 21lb and 24lb restored my sanity

By the time I had arrived at the lake and in the swim, the spot had received about 30 kilos of pellets and as much as I was there for only a few hours, I was determined to keep piling it in, so within minutes, I had two hookbaits on either side of the area, and followed that with a pound or two of boillies and pellet. I couldn't help ringing home a few hundred times, and in the end I think everyone there got fed up with my calls. So I settled down to wait...and it didn't take too long. Mirrors of 21lb and 24lb restored my sanity, and with a huge grin on my face I packed away and headed home - God, I love carp fishing! I know Lynn was happy that I had now got something else to occupy my mind, (although her friends never quite saw it that way), and so, every other day, I would find myself in the little corner swim. The action got better and better, but some anglers were starting to take more notice of what I was doing, so much so, in fact, that I had to take drastic action. I could no longer fish with my buzzers on, for fear of alerting them to my successes, and I also had to do some strange casting. Sixty or seventy yards out in front of the swim is a Plateau that surrounds an island, and it is where this drops away into the lake that the majority of anglers like to fish. Not a bad thing, because it can be very productive, so in an effort to disguise the fact that I was fishing the margins, on my

Chalky had a few nice surprises in store

arrival I would launch a hookbait out to the drop off and slowly reel it back in. I was hidden by dense reeds, so they could not see me swing the lead to hand and reposition it in the margins, and it worked a treat. I had also taken to baiting up the spot at night, when, unfortunately, there were nearly always a couple of anglers on the lake, who were getting far too nosey, so in an effort to throw them off the scent I would arrive with one bucket of hemp and another that I would fill with gravel from the carp park. I would bait several spots with the gravel, and then do the real baiting up. It was a joy to see one or two anglers had moved onto my pre-baited gravel areas the next day. It may seem a little nasty to do such a thing, but I hate lazy anglers, and have infinitely more respect for someone who is willing and able to do his own hard work. Anyway, I never told them, so they were none the wiser!

With everything going so well on the fishing front, I was obviously keen to keep things going, Lynn was even asking when I was going to do the night. I had no idea, but I must admit that one spot had caught my eye because, around five in the evening, an area of deep water was always being disturbed by leaping carp. On the last couple of short visits I had taken my spod rod with me and let them have a fair amount of bait and this was the spot, if everything was okay at home, that I would do my first night. The next trip down, armed with my spod rod, I set up as normal and within twenty minutes I was holding a double figure mirror, a nice start. An hour later and the same rod was in melt down on the rests and as a much better fish made his bid for freedom, I held on for grim death. It got in every weed bed and all the marginal reeds before I was able to lift the net around what was obviously a good fish for this lake, and at 32.08 it was a new lake record. How cool is that!? I secured the fish in the landing net and tried to decide who should come and do the pictures. Thankfully, Chris Ball had got a ticket for the lake and as he only lived just up the road I gave him a call, and he said he would be there in fifteen minutes. Top man! Everything was back in position by the time he arrived, so we quickly got on with the pictures. It really is great having him around, because I don't know any one else who gets so excited, except for me. You will remember that I was able to park in a friend's house when I was at the lake; well it was his wife that was just about to send Chris into even more raptures. Wendy rang and asked if I wanted a cup of tea, to which I asked if she could bring two and as we were only 40 yards from

her back garden, a few minutes later Chris's jaw hit the floor as a rather tall, very long legged blonde in a mini skirt arrived with a tray of tea and biscuits. She entertained him with her broad scouse humour for ten minutes, before returning to her house, but it took a while for Chris to wipe the dribble from his chin! Then, just as he had done so, the other rod decided to come to the party and it was some time before I was able to scoop up an incredibly long and scaley mirror, and Chris was off again. At 29.02 we were both suitably blown away, then I baited

A lake record . . . How cool was that?

At 29.02 we were both suitably blown away

the spots once more and headed for home but all I could think about was that I would have to do a night soon. That was going to be difficult, however, as Lynn could not dress or bathe without my help, and I just didn't think I could leave her that long. I still had the next day to do, but we both agreed that the following week I should try and do an overnighter. I arrived a little later than I would have liked the following day, but need not have worried because, no sooner had I cast out, than I was attached to yet another angry carp. This time it was a common, and with the help of a passer by, I recorded a weight of 32.08. Bloody hell, on consecutive days I had landed two lake records and I was fast becoming of the opinion that it is far better to be lucky than good - something I still feel to this day. I soon packed away, trying to get my head around doing a night the following week. During the ensuing days I baited the open water spot, and on every visit I saw evidence of fish in the area and I knew, if I played this right, then I may get even luckier!

A couple of days before I set off I had been to the lake and had the rods already in the clips. The spod rod had been in the clip for a couple of weeks by now, so hopefully on my arrival I could get everything in position with the minimum of fuss. I had been baiting with copious amounts of Parti Blend, Response Pellets and 14mm Assassin-8 boillies, and as far as I could tell the time was right. I fiffed and faffed around Lynn so much that I think she was pleased when I eventually left the house, and so, with Sarah, our next door neighbour, wife and doggy sitting, I set off for the lake. Within minutes I was unloading the car, and was pleased to see no one else around. I had only baited the area that morning, so in an effort to keep disturbance to a minimum, I cast the two pop-up hookbaits onto the spots, then house up and kettle on. Worried about Lynn, I must have rung home on a dozen occasions by seven in the evening until, eventually, I was told to just enjoy myself. Not having done a night for some time, I was determined not to miss any of it by going to sleep which was a good job really, as I wasn't about to get any.

The action began around nine in the evening, landing four bream in quick succession, then shortly after they got fed up, the tench moved in, which was definitely not in the script. I was starting to think that there may not be a lot of bait left out there for the carp, but I need not have worried, as shortly after midnight I was connected to my first carp of the night, a double figure common. A couple of hours later I had added two more doubles and things were coming together nicely. They started to get a little bigger at four o'clock when I landed a lovely 24lb

I recorded a weight of 32.08

Big Joe, and didn't she look fantastic

mirror, and judging by the amount of bait it left on the unhooking mat, there was still plenty out there. I sat and smiled to myself and fired up the kettle for the hundredth time that night then, just as the first glimmer of light started to spread on the far horizon, one of the bobbins lifted a fraction. I had just placed my cup down when the line was out of the clip and the buzzer screamed. The demented animal that I was connected to ran me ragged all over the lake and it was some time before I had it heading my way. The problem, now, was getting it over the marginal shelf; it simply refused to come into the shallower water. I just kept the pressure on and let that tire the beast out, which eventually it did. I then heaved it into the outstretched net, leaving it safely in the bottom of the net while I got my head torch. It was a big fish, that much I could tell, but in the light I could see which one it was - Big Joe, and didn't she look fantastic! This is one of the best looking carp I have ever had the pleasure to catch, and although I had landed her before, it took nothing away from the moment. I must admit that I had a rather large lump in my throat as I gazed at my prize; even after all the pain and suffering that Lynn had endured, it was still possible for me to catch such a magnificent beast. At 33lb, I knew a man who would love to see this fish, and within the hour Chris Ball was once again by my side. As expected, he was truly amazed as I lifted her from the water onto the mat, and got some great pictures, before I let her swim off strongly into her home. The chips had been well and truly down, but with some effort I had landed an incredible carp, in incredible circumstances. I was away soon after that, and Lynn was overjoyed. Our outlook on things became brighter for a while, but we could not have foreseen what was just around the corner.

An incredible fish, in incredible circumstances

Chapter 13

One Final Hoorah!

Ever since Lynn's stroke I had been thinking long and hard about my fishing. To stop all together would have broken her heart because all she ever wanted me to do was carry on as normally as possible, so staying as near to home was the best solution I could come up with. This meant that if I wanted to be fishing for big carp, then I was limited for choice. I had already decided that this would be my last season on Chalk Farm (I could no longer live with catching the same fish over and over again), however this only limited my choices still further, but eventually I came up with a plan. The Car Park Lake had been on my mind for a while and I think, subconsciously, that I had already made up my mind to fish it once my army career was over. That meant I would be fishing there come the start of the season in 2000. To that end, I decided to get myself a winter ticket and, as the old army saying goes, time spent in reconnaissance is seldom wasted. I knew the Car Park was hard enough at the best of times, so I could only assume that it would

be nigh on impossible once the cold weather had settled in. Undaunted, I intended to spend as much time there as I could, this would hopefully give me some valuable information about the lake itself especially as, with no weed to contend with, finding features would be far easier. As it turned out, any successes I had there had absolutely bugger all to do with anything I found out at the time. Still, at least I thought I was trying hard! The rest of the fishing time I would do at Chalk Farm, for one final hoorah, and then the wheels came off once again.

It was to be my last season on Chalky

One final hoorah!

It was the 16th November, my brothers birthday as it happens, but that is not the reason I remember it so vividly. Once again, Lynn and I had settled down in front of the telly for the night but a short while later she said that she felt a little strange. I looked at her and immediately the alarm bells began to ring, so I was on the phone straight away, and the ambulance was soon inbound. Evidently, Lynn is flagged, so when her name is typed into the computer the operator is required to dispatch assistance without further questioning but, in the time it took to get there, she had already collapsed. Placing her in the recovery position and desperately trying to keep Max from rendering assistance, I waited and, soon enough, she was in the ambulance and on her way. I suppose there is a degree of becoming sanitised to all this hospital stuff, but I can assure you I have never felt anything but panic in these situations. I sat for some time with my head in my hands and wondered just how much more of this she could take before, eventually, I ended up at the hospital. Things weren't as bad as they could have been, and it was decided that she had had some kind of aftershock from the first stroke. I vowed there and then that I would not be going fishing, even for short sessions, until after Christmas, that way she would get my full attention, and her recovery would not be hindered in any way. It is very difficult to impart just how stressful these times can be for the carer. I know it's a lot harder for those that are suffering, but it was taking its toll on me, for sure. We spent Christmas and saw in the new Millennium at home and in between times I was able to get away for a couple of days to join in the 'Banned Christmas Social' at Averley Lakes Sometimes, it is not about the carp but your mates, and I spent some much needed quality time with them. We drank far too

Sometimes it's not about carp, but your mates

much of course, but on the drive home I felt more positive about the future than I had for a long time. There was one other rather major thing that was occupying my mind, and that was that in less than six months I would be officially leaving the army. I still had no idea what the hell I would be doing, certainly not making a living from carp fishing, of that I was sure! Because of the writing I had been doing

I was getting some assistance from ESP and Korda, in the shape of some free gear, which was nice, but that was hardly going to sustain us in the coming years. Mainline was still providing me with bait, so at least I wasn't going to have to dig too deep into my pockets, so in typical Chillcott style, I simply buried my head in the sand and tried to carry on as normal. Easier said than done.

I did my first trip to the Car Park Lake, and although it was shrouded

I tried to carry on as normal

in winter gloom, I got the feeling that I was going to enjoy myself here. With only the odd angler on the water, I spent some time finding out all about the lake, and the old marker rod got a bit of a beating. Realistically, if I wanted to catch a carp then I would have to do so at the army lake which, in between caring for Lynn and having to do all the house related things, I had been visiting as often as possible. The odd night was all I could manage but I did get a fair bit of action until, towards the end of February, I made the difficult decision to sever my contact with the lake completely. It's just that I wanted one final session that would leave me on a high. I could not fish twenty four hours a day, so the plan was to fish from early evening until the following morning and in that way I could take care of business at home,

and not be worrying all the time. I had just taken receipt of a prototype bait from Mainline that ended up being called NRG so, in an effort to really put it through its paces, I decided that I would use as much as I could carry and see what happened. So, five nights and I would never angle there again and with no one really fishing the place I could settle on one spot to introduce the bait, which just happened to be the swim that I had my horrible appendix session in, a couple of years before. As always, the lake was incredibly kind to me, and over five

As always the lake was incredibly kind to me

nights I caught thirty three fish, but the lake saved the best until last. Now, we have all heard the stories of uncaught monsters, or the mythical common, well Chalky had one of its own. Over the years I had spent a fair amount of time at this lake; I had fed its inhabitants in the margins, and had become very familiar with all of the carp. Coupled with the fact that I had seen just about everyone's pictures of the fish, I think it fair to say that I had a rather unique view of what was in there, however, for all those years, I had seen on many occasions a carp that was somewhat different to the rest. He was rather scaleless, a lot deeper in the body, and had absolutely no intention of ever eating anyone's bait! I can recall so many times when I had fish feeding in the edge, he would turn up, take one look at his greedy brethren, and bugger off. As far as I knew, he had never been landed.

I realised, as I pushed my bank sticks in on the Friday night, that this would be the last time. It was a sad moment, and once the hookbaits and bait had been positioned, I sat back to reflect. The lake had been so good to me; it had carried me through some dark and depressing times and I felt as if we had grown up together, and it was so strange to think I would never fish here again. In a somewhat sombre mood I settled down for the night, which was a lot quieter than the other four, that said, I was returning my third fish around four in the morning. I couldn't get back to sleep, so contented myself with several cups of tea. There was an eerie silence as the light sliced its way over the horizon, and just as I was thinking it was all over, one of the rods simply ripped. In fact it was going so fast that the alarm couldn't keep up with it. Lifting into the fish made no difference at all, and it

Sadly, I would never fish here again

carried on its journey to the island. Having to get there over the plateau meant that it sent up a huge bow wave in the shallow water, which was all very spectacular. Then, just as I thought it would make the snaggy island margin, it changed direction and went for the deeper water. There, a more normal, although rather manic, fight ensued and it felt an absolute age before I had it anywhere near the net and, mercifully, once there, I soon scooped it up. As I peered into the net, the fish rolled onto its side, and there lay the carp that I had seen so many times, and that no one had ever caught - this remarkable little lake had saved the very best till last. It was an emotional moment, and I took a minute or two to suppress the lump in my throat before quickly reeling in the other rod. That was it, it was over, and I could think of no better way to end it all. At 29lb, he was not the biggest fish in the lake, but to me, the most special. A friend and I quietly did the pictures before he headed off to work, and then I was alone. The gear was soon in the car, and I turned for one last look. Thank you Chalk Farm, I shall miss you.

I am not the type of guy that can dwell too long, and my maudlin mood was soon lifted by a call from Lewis Read. I had known Lewis for a while, but it wasn't until I had been to the Car Park Lake that I got to know him well. Around the time that I had been landing my final army lake fish, he had landed the first fish of the year from the Car Park - The Dustbin at 38lb - and he will never really know how much that one capture fueled my fires. I fished on there until the end of the season, but nothing else was caught. That said, the lakes grip on me had started to tighten. I would be back in June...and I just couldn't wait!

Not the biggest in the lake but the most special

Section 3

Like a Bat Out of Hell . . .

Hawley Lake, was on the Garrison ticket

Chapter 14

Single Minded

I t was now March of 2000, and apart from the Car Park to look forward to, I had no idea what to do for the spring. By now I was on, what is affectionately known in the army, as gardening leave. I had done no resettlement training, and the Brigade was far too busy to be worrying about little old me. It was sad to think that my rather frantic military career was going to simply fade into history but, not one for too much fuss, I wasn't that bothered. The thing that did concern me was how I was going to keep Lynn and myself. We had no savings, although I would be receiving a rather generous army pension and, if you coupled that with the large payout I would receive, it appeared that things weren't too bad. But that lot was not going to see me through the rest of my life, not comfortably anyway. I needed to sort out some work, but the problem as I saw it was looking after Lynn, and the fact that it would be hard for me to hold down a normal job. Not that I wanted one of those either, if I wanted employment then it was going to have to be something that got the old adrenalin pumping. I had already been approached about work in the body guard industry, and had plenty of contacts to keep me interested. As much as that would have been interesting, I would have to work to a very stringent time table, and I wasn't sure my life could cope with that. Lynn and I discussed all this at great length until, of course, I got bored and wanted to go fishing. So, once again I buried my head in the sand, and thought about where I should go.

My magazine writing was, by now, in full swing and as always I was on the look out for somewhere different to do the articles. One lake sprang to mind and that was Hawley, on the Garrison ticket, situated just outside of Yateley, on army land, at Gibraltar Barracks. I had fished there for a while many moons ago, and had some success with a few of the Leney strain carp that lived there. The biggest of these, a wonderful linear (that I never caught) had disappeared a long time before, and as far as I could see there was only one of the originals I had yet to catch, a fish called Crinkle Tail. The water had, over the years, also received numerous illegal stockings from various places in the area, a situation that has, thankfully, been halted. There had also been a large introduction of fish from a finger lake (legally) that was separated from the main lake by an old Bailey bridge. All in all, it seemed like a good place to spend the spring, and while away the days before the hunt for Heather began. My time was still very limited, but I set myself two goals - one was to catch Crinkle, and the other, to land sixty fish in ten nights. Why I came up with that number I will never know, it just sounded good I suppose. So with that in mind I went off for a recce. The lake itself is probably about sixty acres and was, unbelievably, dug by hand during the war, by German prisoners, for whatever reason I have no idea, but they created a marvellous environment to train soldiers. The Royal Engineers have been there ever since and, of course, this provided one of the hazards when fishing there. A sailing club and a water ski school proved to be much more of a pain, however. With the average depth being no more than five feet, the sandy lake was always very murky. That said, on my first visit I spotted a load of fish all over the place, the spots of most activity being in the areas where the army and the ski boats were at there most active, so that is where I started my little campaign.

I had taken to baiting up either end of the ski run, where the boats turned, and also

March on the Car Park lake

in front of the area that the army used to launch their craft. It was quite remarkable to watch the water everytime the areas were disturbed by a propeller, the carp leaping until the boat came back. It didn't take the brains of a rocket scientist to realise that they were taking advantage of the disturbed lake bed, however, for the foreseeable future, there would be a load of my bait available along with the natural food that had been dug up. After a few days of this, I just couldn't wait any longer to get my rods out. I had been introducing the bait via the spod, and with everything in the clip it was a simple case of baiting up and positioning a couple of hookbaits, and it didn't take too long to get some action. The plan wasn't to fish ten days straight, but rather one or two nights a week, and things started off very well. After only a short time I was twenty fish to the good, with most of them being between 15lb and 20lb, although there was the odd bigger one, topped by a 24lb common. I was having fun, and with Yateley firmly in my mind, that was all I wanted for now. It was then that I gave Jim Foster a call from Catchmore Carp,

There was the odd bigger fish like this 24lb common

(that title had changed to Total Carp by now), and suggested we do a feature at the lake. He was always such good fun to be on the bank with, and I was looking forward to the latest instalment in his crazy love life. If you ever meet Jim, don't forget to ask him about the fore skin splitting incident, it will have you in tears in more ways than one, believe you me!! I had been having some success fishing underneath the Rhododendron bushes, and to that end we were going to do an article about that. The spot I had selected was not a swim, but a small gap in the bushes, hidden by a big oak tree. We had a very small area, the size of an unhooking mat to work in, so Jim had to do all the pictures whilst in the water in his boxer shorts. I was in much the same predicament, should I be lucky enough to hook one so, I waded out in my boxers to position the rods. With the rods set up out in the lake, we sat down to wait and it didn't take too long. We both jumped out of our skins when one of the rods tore off, and out into the lake we went. Once I had the carp away from danger, Jim waded even further out to get some shots before I maneuvered the fish into the net and secured it quickly with the bank sticks. We were covered in silt and soaking wet, and I remember giggling that we must have looked a strange sight. It was a bit cramped to do the pictures where we were, so decided to go and have a look for a better place - and then we got arrested! As we both burst out of the bushes, I looked along the length of the tarmac track

I waded out in my boxers to position the rods

that ran behind us and my chin dropped. There, to the left of us, was a ten man army patrol, and to the right was an MOD police van with four of them in it. Oh Lordy, this didn't look good. Two grown men soaking wet, appearing from the undergrowth in their underpants, immediately had their attention. The army patrol just stood and sniggered, whilst the MOD plods quickly had us surrounded.

"What have we got here then gentlemen?" but, before I could reply, we were spread-eagled against the side of the van.

"Been having a little fun, have we?" I tried desperately to explain, and if they would let me, I would go and get my ID card. But they weren't having any of that, oh no! We spent the next ten minutes being grilled. Did we know it was an offence to practice lewd acts in a public place? This was all getting very embarrassing, and only brought to a close when I was allowed to show my army credentials, and explain what had happened. The story, of course, filtered back to my barracks, and for a while Jim and I were referred to as The Fish Shop Boys! We did get the shots of the fish in the end, but it was very amusing to do so under the close scrutiny of the MOD coppers.

A gay old carp!

I eventually got over the embarrassment of it all, and continued with my fishing, which all went rather well. But, when I had reached 58 fish, I was starting to wonder if I was going to see one of the few originals left in the lake, and more precisely, Crinkle Tail. I turned up for my final session, heading once more for one of the baited areas, and very quickly got a couple of rods in position, but I couldn't help noticing that the area I was casting to had been laid out for some kind of military action. In fact, it was a practice day for some soldiers who would be passing out very soon, rehearsing for the day they would show their mums and dads all they had learnt in training. By ten in the morning I was getting a little worried, as eight assault craft were circling in front of me, fully laden with recruits, who were just about to assault the very beach, a rod length in front of where my hookbaits had come to rest, and as the boats stormed the beach no more than four feet over my area, I slumped into my chair. These crazy bastards were just about to ruin my chances, remember this was the last night of the ten I had allocated here. With weapons on fully automatic and battle simulation explosions going off all over the place, you would be forgiven for thinking there wouldn't be a self respecting carp within a mile of here...but then, what the hell do we know? As the last of the men leaped onto the sand, one of my indicators let out a short series of bleeps and, convinced I was about to land a personal best soldier, I stood by the rod. Everyone was now out and fighting the imaginary enemy, which was strange. It got even stranger when that rod ripped off and I was connected to an angry carp. As the war raged on, I was concentrating on my own battle with an island to the left causing a few problems, but I soon managed to get the fish within netting range. I was sure I caught sight of a strange tail at that point, and once it was in the net I could see that I had, indeed, caught my target fish - Crinkle was mine. At 29.10 I was over the moon, but as much as I really wanted that fish, I think I will always remember her because of the insane circumstances in which she was caught. How Bizarre! Oh, and I did get my sixtieth fish, when I landed a lovely fully scaled a little later. Then it was home for tea and biscuits!

All that was now occupying my mind was the Car Park Lake. I wanted no distractions, but as always, life was about to give me some things to think about. I had been into the barracks and done the final paper work, and apart from handing in my ID card, there was nothing left to do. I eventually did that at the end of May, two days before the season started at Yateley. Twenty two years of my life had gone in the blink of an eye but, as sad as I was about it all, I had no time to dwell on it. Lynn and I needed somewhere to live, but we would be allowed to stay in the married quarters until I found accommodation for us. As far as I was concerned,

At 29.10, I was over the moon

Number sixty

that would have to wait for a while, because I was just about to set out on the hunt for Heather. The inactivity that Lynn's two strokes had caused had also led to complications. She was now in desperate need of an operation, but that would have to wait until numerous tests had been done, and she gained a bit more strength. And then of course there was Max. With his mum now confined to a wheel chair, there was no way she could take him for a walk and, as much as the lazy git would have slept on his sofa all day long, he needed exercise. Yateley being so close to home, it wasn't too much of a problem, but I would have to be away for more than the allotted ninety minutes. Then RMC and, to a great extent, the rest of the syndicate, came to our rescue. I would be allowed to be away for as long as necessary, and no one had an issue with that, a gesture for which I will be eternally grateful. There was one other rather pressing need, and that was to get rid of my reliance on alcohol. Although I don't think that I have ever been an alcoholic, I must have been getting damn near to one. I had never reached for a drink during the day (unless there was a carp to celebrate!), but once the sun was over the yard arm, it was game on, the bottom of a bottle being the best place for me to hide and forget all the things that were going on in my life. There were two problems with that - if Lynn got ill there was no way I could drive back from wherever I was and, of course, my own health. As fit as I was, it would eventually take its toll, and I just couldn't allow that to happen. I had bought myself a bottle of Jack Daniels with which to celebrate my new found freedom, and that very bottle is still sitting in my kitchen, un-opened. I wanted to take on this new challenge with a clear head, and so I kissed goodbye to those crazy drink fueled days...well almost. You see, I do like a drink, and at times I can still kick the arse right out of it, but I don't like being that way anymore. It was hard, but I had a mission, and I couldn't do it if I was pissed!

And so the season began. With no restrictions on time, the lake was constantly packed out and, very often, it was just a case of turning up and occupying any swim that was free. As much as that can be a horrible waste of time, I needed to be there to stay in touch with what was going on. It was easy to keep

up with what the anglers were doing, and in the crystal clear and weedy water, it was easy to see what the fish were up to. The hard bit was getting a swim so that you could actually fish for them. One of the pleasures of fishing the lake at that time was that most of the members simply left someone to get on with it if

It was always easy to find the fish on the Car Park

Little John and Arfur, he had them jumping through fiery hoops

they were having a bit of a result and, straight from the off, one man was head and shoulders above the rest. To put it simply, he had the lakes residents jumping through fiery hoops! We all stood back and watched as 'Little' John Coxhead racked up an impressive tally, all of which was going on in the Back Bay. I remember well, the day he caught Arfur, we all stood around without saying a word, so spell binding were his results. It was that day that I made a decision, I had been fishing some of the more popular swims, but that really revolved around hookbaits in areas that every one else was fishing, and I was becoming increasingly bored with this style of angling. I wandered back to my swim, Dessies, and sat and thought for a while. The season was two weeks old, and John had caught most of the fish already, what I needed was to find some opportunities for myself, and fish to my own strengths. John had now finished in the Back Bay, and this was the area I started to take more interest in. Now, although the lake had been getting quieter and quieter, I still needed to be a little careful about giving the game away.

The more static approach didn't seem to be working

The Back Bay had lost much of its fascination with everyone, in the main because of John's results. I don't think anyone thought the fish would get back in there, and neither did I, to be honest, but one day I was in a tree overlooking the area, when Heather strolled into the bay. She, and one other fish that I could not really see that well, visited two spots on the Works bank. That, as they say, would do for me. At the time, I had been using a lot of caster and as much as I was being plagued with tench and bream, I felt that a margin spot may respond better to their use. To that end, I baited both areas with a handful of casters, a handful of Response Pellets and a few crushed and whole 14mm Assassinate boillies. I had a short section of pole with a cup on the end to do this, and both spots were marked with a nick on a tree and a scratch on the pole. It was just a simple case of loading the cup and threading it through the trees. Job done. This operation was carried out under the cover of darkness for the next few days and, sitting and watching for a while after each introduction, I was amazed how quickly the fish responded. The last time I did it was on a Saturday night, and the plan was to return on the Sunday afternoon to actually fish the spots.

As I pulled up into the car park, it was obvious that the lake had fewer anglers on and, as handy as that was, I still needed to be a touch nonchalant about what I was up to. Quietly, I got my gear round to the works bank, and placed it behind the

As you can see, it wasn't easy to get to my rods

small gap in the undergrowth that I would fish my rods in. I then made my way around the lake and caught up on the weekend's activities, of which there was very little so, arriving back at the bay, I quickly got myself up a tree to see what I could see. There was one fish that was just cruising around, but when he returned to the large weedbed in the centre of the bay, I spotted a couple more fish. Game on!

The spot to the left was a gravel slope, which I would fish at the bottom of, in about five feet of water, and the other was a small hole in the weed about two and half feet deep. Sorting the left one first I attached a

14mm bottom bait to the rig and waded carefully along the margin. Very conveniently there was a small twig at the top of the gravel and I put the line around that, which allowed the five foot lead core leader to run unobtrusively down the slope. A handful of the bait concoction, and I made my way the ten yards back to my swim, all the way hiding the mainline under the lilies and weed. I did exactly the same with the right hand rod, the only difference was that my 4oz running lead was balanced on the edge of the drop off. If a fish picked up the bait then the lead would run down the lead core, a situation I hoped they had not

I hid my mainline under the lilies and weed

encountered before. There was little need for bobbins, and with the line slackened off completely, I sat back and waited for events to unfold.

Being such a sociable lake, I spent much of my time trying to ensure any visitors kept a low profile. My last guest of the evening was Lewis Read and he was congratulating me on my fine angling, but that had nothing to do with the traps I had set. A few days before I had made him a brew, to which I added a couple of sweeteners, and he was disgusted. How the hell did I think I was going to catch a Car Park fish if I didn't have real sugar in my swim? Well this time I had rectified the problem and had added some sugar to his brew.

"Now you will catch one" he said, as he finished his drink and departed. Oh I do hope so!

As night began to close in on the lake, I spotted the odd fish drifting into the bay and, as you may expect, confidence was high, which meant it took an age to get to sleep, but eventually I was knocking out the Z's. The next thing I remember was tumbling down the overgrown slope trying desperately to get to the howling buzzer. I picked up the rod and marched straight into the lake, and so the battle began, and what a battle it was! The fish had almost made it to the mini back bay by the time I had gained any kind of control, I simply couldn't let it get in there, and held on. For a second or two the rod kept on arching over, and then the fish rolled. I had stopped it, but then it ran to the right, coming to a halt in the very weed bed that the carp had been using as a daytime shelter, and with a little bit of effort I managed to get it moving once again. The fight was played out within the confines of the bay, until eventually I was able to lift the net around a large amount of weed and lilies, plus a bloody great big carp. In the gloomy morning light I had no idea which fish it was, and it wasn't until I had carried the fish up the slope and on to the mat, that the leathery flanks of the Dustbin were revealed. Si Gibblin was on hand to help with the weighing, and we settled on 40.04, oh deep, deep joy!! My first fish from the lake. It is so hard to explain how marvellous that feeling was. I had read so much about the place, and you never really think you will ever get to catch one, but I had, and boy was I happy. I secured him in the net in front of the steps

The Dustbin at 40.04. Oh deep, deep joy!

swim next door, then the photographers arrived and I held up a large slice of carp fishing history and my, didn't he look fine. Having finally become Mr. Chillcott on 6th June, this was the first carp I had landed as a civilian. Once back in his home it was time for me to do the same, so I baited the spots and

With the Dustbin returned, it was time for tea

with a huge smile on my face, drove out of the gate.

I was actually on borrowed time now. Lynn's operation was imminent, and we got more of an idea what was involved at the doctors the next morning. There was little I could do for now, so, at Lynn's insistence I went back to the lake. Remarkably, the area was free, in fact there was no one anywhere near it, I could only hope the Dustbin hadn't told his mates about me. With my gear back in position I went to the back of the bay and climbed a tree, and there in the same weedbed were several large carp. I stayed there for a couple of hours and it soon became obvious that they were still visiting the same baited spots then, once they returned to the weedbed I got the rods ready to go. Same as before, I placed the baits and remembered

Same as before I placed the baits

thinking how much bigger the right hand area was from the last time I had looked at it. It also struck me how exciting it would be to see a fish get hooked in such shallow water, and so, with the traps set, I made myself comfortable. Young Dave Ball was down to my right in the Dug Out, so I had a little company for the evening, which I really needed because I was so excited. I don't think anyone that has ever fished there could honestly say that they were positive of a bite, but at that moment I was quite convinced one of the traps would be sprung by morning. Again, sleep was hard to come by, but I must have drifted off at some stage and the run, when it came, was an absolute one toner. The bramble bushes made my journey to the rods a rather painful one, especially as I did most of it on my backside, then, as I picked up the rod, I noticed the huge bow wave going out across the lake. On and on the fish charged, visiting just about every weedbed along the way and it was an awful long time before I felt I had any control whatsoever, but eventually it was heading my way. I had never had a carp fight so hard, it was ridiculous. By now I was up to my waist in the lilies and slowly sinking into the silt, and still the damn thing would not give up. Then the flank of a monster broke the surface and, as quickly as I could, I got the net under it and heaved for all I was worth.

Light My Fire!!

I heard Dave at the top of the slope and he enquired as to which carp it was. I had no idea, so I simply bit through the line and rolled the fish up in the net. It was big, that much I did know, and I handed the bundle to Dave who took it to the unhooking mat. As I stumbled out of the bushes he uttered one of those immortal lines, lines that are designed to make all rational thought impossible.

Every one came round to help

"It's Single Scale".

When I landed Mallin's from Wraysbury, I mentioned that he was the first of a great trio of carp that I desperately wanted to catch, well here was one of the others. Oh Chillcott, you lucky bastard!! Both Dave and I were a bit on the shaky side when we hoisted him up on the scales. He reckoned he was 44lb, but

Single Scale all 43.12 of him

with a wobbly needle I settled for the lowest point, which made it 43.12. Good enough for any man. Once again, I secured him in the Steps swim and reached for my phone, I simply had to let Lynn know what had happened. It was 0500 and I made her cry. Again, amid the heartache, there was something very special to celebrate, and as I was to constantly remind her over the coming six months, I would always have those Single Scale moments to bring a smile to my face!

I will always have those Single Scale moments

Sonning Eye

Chapter 15

In the Blink of an Eye

For the next month or so, I drifted around the Car Park trying desperately to find another opportunity. There was little trouble finding the fish, but invariably they would once again be in front of Little John as he continued his rampage across the lake. There were several times I could have moved in on his hard work, but it just didn't seem right. If I wanted to catch another one then it would have to be on my terms. There was also one other very distracting occurrence that happened around that time, and that was the capture of an unknown (well, it was initially) 52lb mirror.

Andy Dodd had landed the huge beast from a massive lake on the Oxfordshire/Berkshire border, Sonning Eye. In a bizarre twist of fate, the carp had a much enlarged right eye (possibly blind), and from that day forth he became known as the Eye. Very little was known about the place, but it wasn't long before Laney and Keith had come up with a plan to fish there, it was all very exciting stuff, and the

phone lines between Crawley and Aldershot went into melt down for a while. I desperately wanted to go up there then, but with Heather on my mind, I couldn't think about that just yet, instead I listened as the pair of them told me all about it. Chrissie Pearson was also keen to get in on the action and, all in all, it sounded like some kind of boys own adventure! I did drag myself away from Yateley one weekend to have a dangle with Jenks, for no other reason than I really had been missing his company, and what a strange session that turned out to be.

The boys had been having some success at the far end of the lake, on a rather straight, but incredibly long, bit of bank. The swims there had been labelled the Two

Sunset over the Two Buoy swim

Buoy, Three Buoy and Four Buoy, and was where most of the bars, that ran the length of the lake, ended up. All in all, an ideal place to catch carp. On our way around to that bank, however, we spotted a lot of fish in a small bay; I say 'a lot of fish', but that is a relative term for Sonning, because as far as we knew there were only between eighty and a hundred carp in 350 acres! But, if that is where they wanted to be, then that is where we would fish for them. We watched for an age as they paraded up and down the margin, but eventually kicked ourselves into gear and set some traps, at which point, one of the Reading and District bailiffs turned up. We sat and looked on in amazement as he simply walked into a swim to our right, and then took more than three hours to set up his base camp. There was a television to sort out, aerial and all, then a big tripod was erected, and the scales fitted whilst, all the time there were carp sunning themselves under his feet. I cannot think for one minute that he had seen them, because the next and last thing he did was to put the rods out. After all the effort of getting the housing situation right, we thought we would at least be in for some fine angling, but no. Three single hookbaits were launched out as far as he was able, an operation that took all of three minutes, and put him about 90 yards from the nearest carp! Once that was done, he retired to his bivvy for the next twenty-four hours. I did have a chance meeting with him a while later, and all he did was moan about the fact that he

Keith rounded off the session nicely

couldn't catch a carp from the place. I nodded as sagely as I could whilst he recounted his tides of woe, and returned to my plot shaking my head. Bless him. Keith rounded off the session nicely with a 17lb common, to which our odd neighbour responded by saying that it was only a small one. I was just about to tell him that carp fishing such places had little to do with the size of the fish, and more about the achievement of catching one, but I didn't get the chance because he was off back to his marquee... Eastenders was due to start.

A few days later all thoughts of carp fishing were cast from my mind. I had been at home for a couple of days, and it was obvious Lynn wasn't well, and when she eventually collapsed, I was once again at her bedside for many days. Eventually, they were in control of her condition, and the consultant decided that he would have to operate. This was the big one and really did sound horrific, so I took a few months off to sort things out, and make sure that her recovery was complete before setting off in search of a monster or two. As always, she was putting me first and insisted I go, but I just couldn't. What did cheer me up though, were all the stories filtering back from Sonning. Keith had landed the most stunning Linear of 33lb - it was great to get one of those early morning manic calls from him - and Laney was, well, just being Laney really, and catching on every single trip. Top of the pile though, was Chrissie because he had landed the Sonning Forty at a little over that mark. Things, as they say, were shaping up nicely. As good as that all sounds, the guys were subject to the local green eyed monsters from time to time and things got so bad in the end that Chrissie, in his own inimitable way, sorted it all out. Rather pleasingly, things settled down after that!

It wasn't until the beginning of November that I could once again dust off the rods, and go fishing. It was all a bit too late for Sonning, that place was going to be hard enough in the warmer weather, but having a Reading and District ticket gave us access to several other waters, and one went by the name of Pingewood. A couple of local lads had alerted us to its potential, and like you would, we were keen to investigate, so Laney and I made our first foray on a cold winters morning. The lake itself is used by a water sports centre which, thankfully, had shut up shop for the colder months, and what this meant was that we could fish an area that had been out of bounds during the summer. Having beaten Dave to the lake, I was all

Keith and his Linear at 33lb

set up and angling in between two jetties on his arrival, with fish having been very evident there all the time I'd been setting up. He set up some way off to my left, and we settled down to wait. The night was interrupted by a couple of small commons for both of us, and just on first light we were sharing a brew. This was the first time I had ever used a remote sounder box with my alarms, and what happened next was a bit of a joke. My third rod, the one positioned near the jetties, was just behind my bivvy, then, all of a sudden, a piercing scream emanated from somewhere. We both looked at each other and for a few seconds had no idea what was going on. The penny eventually dropped when Dave headed off at full steam toward my rod, at which point I nearly knocked him into the lake as he held me back.

"Look at that", he said, "how fast is that spool spinning?"

For the life of me, I don't know why I didn't just pick up the rod, but we both stared in amazement. It was only a moment or two, but I thought it maybe time to lift into the fish and let battle commence, and what a great battle it was, although all the way through, Laney wouldn't shut up about how fast the spool was whizzing round! As he manned the net, I manoeuvred the fish toward him and in went a stunning linear of 27lb; we decided then and there that we liked it here.

The following week, Laney bagged himself a wonderful, prehistoric looking twenty-nine pound mirror, and although I struggled for a while, things turned for the

Top of the pile was Chrissie with the Sonning forty

The spool was a blur

better as Christmas approached. Unlike today, the bank that runs along the motorway was out of bounds (it has subsequently been back filled, the lake made smaller, and every area easily accessible). What I wanted to do was to fish as far out

as possible, and with as much bait as my body would allow me to put out. In the centre of the lake was a large orange buoy, and some fifteen yards to the left of this is where I concentrated my efforts. At 130 yards it was no easy task, but it didn't half keep me warm. The first attempt was a bit of a disaster with bream, bream and more bloody bream. I had included a fair amount of Response Pellets in my spod mix and they loved 'em, but the problem I had was that every time I introduced the mix, you could hear carp booming out over it all night long. The first session I did, I believe I had in excess of fifty bream over the two night stay but,

I concentrated my efforts in the Yellow Buoy swim

despite that, when I returned a couple of days later I decided that I would stick to the same plan. By one o'clock the following morning the will to live had almost deserted me - thirty four bream had made my life hell and I was just about to leave the rigs in the butt ring when I heard the first carp of the night crash out. It was cold and the air pressure extremely high. That, along with the motorway lights illuminating the rings the carp left, had me quickly repositioning my rods and an hour later I hadn't had a single bleep, at least the bream had taken the rest of the night off!

I was supping another cup of tea, and watching a heavy mist settle over the water, when one of the rods ripped into life and as I leant into the fish it made little difference, it just carried on going. I was just thinking that it was probably going to end up on the M4, when everything came to a grinding halt. Try as I may, I couldn't get the fish moving, and the stalemate lasted an age but, determined that the weed would not lose me this fish, I came up with a rather drastic plan. The adventure people had sunk their fibre glass boats in the margins to keep them out of sight during the winter, and it was one of these that was going to save the day. So, with some effort, and a good half an hour later, I had managed to drag one onto the bank. I was one big sweaty mess and took a moment to get my breath back, then trotted to the car and grabbed my life jacket, and got ready to go after the fish. I must admit, it was bloody freezing and I was beginning to doubt the wisdom of what I was about to do, that said, if I had pulled for a break I would have been heartbroken if I had woken in the morning to see the buoy bobbing around with a tethered carp on it. No, I was doing the right thing, and without further ado, put the landing net in the boat and started to reel my way out to the fish. I needn't have worried about the buoy, because I didn't get over the fish until I was some twenty-five yards beyond that and, as is the way in this kind of situation, the pressure from above soon had the fish on the move. It towed me around for a while until I was only twenty yards from the centre of the out of bound bank when, all of a sudden it hit the surface and sent up a massive sheet of spray as it turned and dived. "Blimey that looks like a damn fine fish" I heard someone say. It made me jump and I cautiously looked around. It was three o'clock in the morning and there was no one else on the lake, so I concentrated on the fish, surely I was hearing things? Eventually, it rose to the surface and then simply slipped it into the net.

"Oh very well done old fellow" said the extremely posh voice once again. For the second time I nearly jumped out of my skin.

"Who the bloody hell is that?" I shouted.

"Watched the whole thing, damned exciting". It was surreal, here I was with a good carp in my net, having a full blown conversation with someone I couldn't see anywhere on the bank. Apparently he had broken down on the motorway, and had wandered a few short yards to the lake whilst he waited for recovery.

It was then I discovered I had another problem, no oar, and I was starting to drift out into the lake, and at this rate I would have been there for a week before I got back to my plot. I sat down to work out what to do next and as I did, the wooden seat cracked and I fell into the bottom of the boat. Now that was handy, one of the sections of the broken seat looked remarkably like a cricket bat, an ideal paddle for my return journey! It was still attached to one side of the boat, so I stood astride it and tried to lever the piece off, getting a bit heavy handed, but eventually it came free. The problem now was that my efforts had caused the boat to split from just under the rowlock all the way down to the keel. The water didn't appear to be coming in that fast, so with a thirty pound parachute hanging out the back I started to make the return journey across the lake and was half way there when I began to realise that something may be a little wrong. The water, by now, had just about covered my nether regions and that, along with the cold and all my hard work, was starting to take its toll. As fit as I was, I couldn't help wondering that I may just die and I did, fleetingly, think about releasing the fish, but hell, I caught it and I wanted a picture! Another half an hour went by, and with the water now up to my chest I was within spitting distance of the bank, so near that I decided, in my infinite wisdom, that I could wade back.

I jumped over board and simply disappeared from view. It was so cold I thought I had mumps as my knackers had relocated themselves in my throat, then, coughing and spluttering, I managed to heave myself onto the bank. I was freezing, but attended to the carp first, and at 30.04, all the effort was well worth it. I popped her into a sack and then sorted myself out, which took most of the next two hours, but at least I was dry and relatively warm. I hadn't replaced that rod, and as the light was filling the sky I supped a brew, looking at the remaining one on the rest. I was just

All the effort was well worth it

about to ring a mate to come down to do some pictures, when the rod bounced, and line peeled from the spool. The fight was as dour as the other was exciting, and in no time at all I found myself looking down on another good mirror, and at 33lb that is exactly what he was. I placed him in another sack and he came to rest a few yards away from his mate. The only thing left to do was to re-sink the boat and no one would be any the wiser and so, with that out of the way, I managed to make the call and an hour later the fish had been photographed and were back in their home. Why I am so bonkers, I have little idea, but it ain't half fun at times!

With Christmas fast approaching I sat down to think about what I wanted to do with my fishing. The Car Park Lake was still high on my priority list, but Sonning was calling too, and the fun my friends were having there was making me a little jealous. I was desperate to join them, but having to stay local I decided that I would venture over to Yateley in the New Year and see what was what.

RMC had, for some time, been revamping the Pads Lake; fish had been stocked, and the water quality greatly improved and I had, in fact, done the odd article on there the previous year. In early January I bumped into Ray Varndel, the head bailiff and all round Yateley leg-end, and he suggested that I give it a go and see what the winter potential might be. Not one to be looking a gift horse in the mouth I readily agreed, and I could keep my eye on the Car Park next door whilst having some fun along the way. Being relatively shallow and with an amazing one hundred carp in

It ain't half fun at times!

The revamped Pads Lake

its two and a half acres, I suspected that this might all be a bit of a hoot...and it was! These sort of situations are ideal for testing out new things, so I intended to do just that, and it was all rather encouraging when, on my first visit, Ray landed a 32lb mirror, although he really didn't do much after that. This was handy, because it meant that I would pretty much have the lake to myself for a while. It was obvious that carp would be caught, they had received very little angling pressure, and with most of the carp being of the Fishers Pond strain, a liberal helping of pellets would ensure that my rollers were rattled on more than a few occasions. That said, there were a few carp in there that really did hold my attention. They had been introduced from a RMC lake in the area, and were much older fish with a lot more character,

Ray had landed a 32lb mirror

so the plan was to catch a couple of those. I had been messing around with casters for a couple of winters, and those, along with some 10mm boillies and Response Pellets, would form the basis of the baiting. This worked very well, and after a short while I had caught loads of them up to about 27lb. Fishing into areas that the pads thrive is a blinding way of being on the fish in the colder months, they just like being there and it was whilst I was fishing the In-between Pads swim that I was to find out one more useful bit of information. Simon Scott and Ben Gratwick had been working over on the Match Lake with the Sparsholt students and, one lunchtime, they came over for a visit. Both of them still had their dry suits on and I invited them to go out and have a look. You would think the last thing you need in your swim is a couple of blokes bobbing about, but when Ben disappeared from view I knew they had discovered what I was looking for. In a lake that is about four feet deep on average, it was nice to know that there was a deep hole of six foot, and from there on in I concentrated there.

The following week I had been reading an article by Bob Nudd (clever blokes these match guys) and he had been telling me about introducing maybe ten casters every minute or so to bring the carp up in the water. As much as I wasn't going to be fishing up in the water column, I thought it may give me an indication if the fish were there or not, so, with two hookbaits in the hole, I sat and fired out ten casters and ten pellets every five minutes. I was just getting to the point of writing Bob a shitty letter when I noticed a subtle sub-surface disturbance. After another five minutes I had seen several more. They were definitely there, and when I stopped putting them out I surmised that they would have to drop to the lake bed if they wanted more food. Fifteen minutes later and I was playing the most angry fish and I am truly glad someone was there to witness it, because the speed and ferocity of the fight was breath taking. Eventually, I somewhat unceremoniously bundled a

I caught loads of them

lovely common into the net, its tail was ridiculously big and it was identified as one of the fish I wanted to catch from here. It had never been hooked before, and the pictures were a bit of a worry because it was so tensed up. At 24lb I was chuffed to bits and quickly got it back in the pond, then started to do my trick with the caster once again. An hour later, this had drawn the carp up to the surface again, and again I stopped putting out the free offerings. Sure enough, within fifteen minutes I was bent into another fish, a dogged fight ensued until I got it into the net, and in the bottom was the biggest fish in the lake. It was one of the fish from up the road, and at 34.06 my fires were well and truly lit! Unfortunately, the poor animal has to run around these days with the name Chilly's Fish, for which I can only apologise. Anyway, it was a nice way to end my little dabble there, but for now though, I had bigger fish to fry (or so I hoped)!

Whilst waiting for the Car Park season to begin on the first of June, I was hell bent on spending some time at Sonning. The trouble was the weather, it caused so much havoc for a couple of weeks, and I wondered if I would even have a lake to fish. Talk about April showers, it didn't stop raining for ages. I tried hard to get there as often as possible, but every time I did, I was met with a wall of water, and it was very difficult to see where the River Thames started and the lake began. Several times I had to return home praying for the rain to stop. It did so eventually, and slowly the water level dropped...then it froze! What a frustrating time that was. All in all, it was several weeks before I could set up and do some angling.

It's tail was ridiculously big

It's now called Chilly's Fish, poor animal

The first time I ever set eyes on the place was the year before, and while on my way to a 'fish with the stars' (cough, cough!) event at Horseshoe Lake, I had stopped off for a look. I didn't see a soul whilst I was there, and simply sat at the end of a strong south westerly wind on a spit of land that became known as Punishers Point. It was sunny, and I sat and watched as carp after carp showed, with the waves crashing over their heads. It was a remarkable day and I promised myself, should the chance arise, that I would fish there come the first big south westerly wind of the following spring.

Well here I was, ready to go, and after first negotiating my way around the mad dog from the houses that backed onto this area of the lake, I surveyed the situation. There is a small lagoon behind the point, and after the dog had settled down I made my way quietly towards it. To my absolute amazement I spotted a carp, and not just any carp - it was the Eye herself, and she was sitting no more than a yard out just beyond some reeds. With her were two other fish, a common of about 20lb and a mirror of similar size. I stood and watched them for a while until the big 'un turned and made her way out of the narrow gap at the entrance to the lagoon, her two buddies following in an orderly line, and I lost sight of them as they made their way into the main lake. White horses were racing through the 20 acre bay, generated, of course, by a lovely south westerly. The dark, forbidding clouds rolled over head, shedding a little rain from time to time, but the carp were there, and showed me how good they were at leaping out of the water. Once again, the game was afoot!

Not having fished this bay, or indeed, the lake before, I was keen to do a little investigating with the marker rod. I eventually found a small plateau at 50 yards just round to my left, and this was where I invested about 10k of 18mm boillies and three hookbaits. With the house up and the kettle boiling, all was well with the world, then, sometime later that day, a mate of mine, Dessie, turned up and I could tell by his face that he wanted to be where I was. It really did look that good. Eventually he set up on the other side of the lagoon, but he was someway from being near

All tucked away in Punishers Point

the action. The night was quiet and I woke feeling a little disappointed; surely I should have got a bite? Supping probably my third brew of the day, I noticed one of the lines pick up slightly in the water, and I was left in little doubt that a carp was on when the bobbin smacked into the rod, and the reel became a blur. I hadn't noticed them before, but someone had put some bamboo canes on the high points of a couple of bars, and these were just about to cause me no end of problems.

My first Sonning carp. Wow!!

Once the fish had reached the first one, he simply ran around it a few times until everything was locked up solid. Thankfully, Laney had arrived a little earlier and it was whilst I was going over to Dessie for some help that I bumped into him. There was a small boat stashed some way down to my right, and soon I was afloat and after the carp. Although the water was terribly choppy, I was able to simply pull the cane out of the water and untangle the line, and not long after that a vaguely familiar common lay in the bottom of the net. I struggled back to shore and, with Laney's help, we weighed the 20.12 fish and he had his picture taken.

My first Sonning carp. Wow!!

I mentioned to Dave that I was convinced it was the common I had seen with the Eye the day before. How near I had been to the big 'un with my first bite, I wasn't sure, but a little while later I was sure I was very close indeed.

I had repositioned all the hookbaits, and a couple of hours later I was still sat staring

I smiled broadly for the camera

at the rods. The bite, when it came, was a very bream like affair, but the battle was not, and unbelievably, I was connected to my second Sonning carp! The wind had really got up by now, bringing a lot of the floating weed with it but, as much as it hindered proceedings, I eventually scooped up the carp, plus a fair amount of weed. On the mat I cleared everything out of the way, only to be confronted with the mirror that had also been with the Eye; again the fish weighed just over 20lb, and again I smiled broadly for the camera.

For once I kept Laney busy with the camera

It doesn't get any better than that!

With three nights left of my allotted time, I really couldn't have been happier, and although it wasn't said, Dave and I could sense that the big girl was out there somewhere. To be honest, I was just happy to be getting bites, so once again the traps were set, but it wasn't until the following morning that one of them was sprung. From the off this felt like a different prospect, and the long searing runs were challenging the old sphincter muscles to the limit, then it started to kite rapidly to the left, and as much as I tried I couldn't stop it making the sunken branches of a nearby island. Once again Dave was there to lend assistance and, as I stood with the rod in my hand, he made his way out in the boat. With some difficulty he managed to release the fish and soon after that I had it in the net.

I think it fair to say that we all want to catch a big carp, but every now and then something ends up in your net that takes your breath away for other reasons. There, before us, lay the most stunning fish I have ever had the pleasure to land. I am still not sure how to describe it; 'triple row fully scaled heavily scaled plated thing' is

What a trip it was

The wind had taken the carp to the far end of the lake

what I came up with in the end. It really was shocking and at 27lb we posed in the drizzly weather - it doesn't get any better than that.

With fish showing regularly over the baited area, I was sure of more action, and I got it. The next bite produced what was to be my biggest Sonning carp, although probably not the best looker, a 32lb common that was reeled unceremoniously into my net, and was one that Dave had had the year before, at a few ounces lighter. That was followed up a couple of hours later by a brilliantly coloured scaley 22lb mirror, and I sat for a while dumfounded at the amount of fish I was catching, it just wasn't meant to be this way. The action then slowed and it wasn't until the following afternoon that I got another bite. I was on the phone to Paul Forward at the time, and he was dispatched into the bushes when one of the rods chirped into life but, unfortunately, the fish came adrift just shy of the net. It wasn't big but I would still have liked to have seen it on my mat. Oh well, you can't win them all. I got even, an hour later, when the last of the fish for this session made a mistake, the scale perfect 26lb common making a perfect end to the trip, and what a trip it was. The drive home from any session had never been so sweet.

The following week, Dave and I were once again on the prowl. He was set up in a swim called the Secret, whilst I contented myself with being in the Mattress, both looking a good bet as the westerly wind piled into that area. The following morning, however, the wind had changed and the northerly air flow, I was sure, had taken the carp the mile to the far end of the lake. At half four in the morning, I was

If they weren't here then they didn't live in the lake anymore

loading up the car and making my way round to the bank onto which the wind was blowing. Laney was only just behind me, and the first thing we spotted was carp, as the powerful waves broke onto the bank, exposing their backs. We angled there for the night, but nothing happened, and by the next morning we were on our way out of the gates. I had no idea at the time, but my next trip would be my last ever, apart from one social session with Jenks towards the end of that year.

Lynn had once again fallen very ill, but the trouble was that the procedure to sort

My first visitor, 21lb common

things out was going to take a massive effort by her consultancy team. As always, though, until she had the date for the operation, she insisted that I go fishing. I really wasn't sure if I should go, but again we were playing that delicate juggling act. I arrived at Sonning to find a nice westerly blowing and decided to set up in the Secret that Laney had been occupying the week before. There is a small inflow stream there that was absolutely gushing water into the main lake, and I surmised that if the carp weren't there they really couldn't be living in the lake any more. With as much confidence as it is possible to have, I set up a couple of rods and dispatched them to the area where the turbulent water started to settle down a bit.

Liberally baited, I sat down to wait for Laney to arrive and, after giving me several minutes of abuse, he decided to fish a little further down to my left just by the ski club. The whole of our margins were covered in what I call carp anglers ice cream, you know, the white frothy stuff that is driven in on high winds and, as sure as we could be of action, we were soon set up and angling. Dave quickly had a small, fully scaled mirror in the net, courtesy of a fine bit of angling, but I had to wait a while longer. Late in the night I got my first visitor in the shape of a 21lb common and, for the only time, I was a little miffed at the size because, for ages, there had been several very big carp showing over the spot, still thems the breaks, eh? Dave waded in with a couple more, and we eventually settled down for the night. Again, I was woken in the early hours by a 21lb mirror, and two hours later I was roaring out of the gates at a hundred miles an hour.

The pain had eventually taken its toll, and Lynn had had to ring for an ambulance, and so that was to be the last fish I ever caught from the place, but what a couple of weeks it had been. Not in my wildest dreams!

For the foreseeable future I would be looking after my wife, and there was nothing more important than that.

Not in my wildest dreams!

Chapter 16

Jam Side Down

Remarkably, Lynn's recovery took a lot less time than we had thought. Not only had the operation sorted out a whole host of problems, it had also given her some quality of life that she had not been able to enjoy for several years. She had also had to put up with me messing everything up in the house and breaking things, so I don't think a fishing trip for me could have come any sooner, and to be honest, I think Max was also a bit fed up with me taking up all his space. Now, if the family wanted me out of the way, then fair enough. The season started on the Car Park, and for a couple of weeks I was content to be getting a feel for the old girl once again, but just as I was getting into my stride, we had to move house. I couldn't have expected Lynn to do anything - she didn't have the strength - so the whole sorry task looked like it would have to be done by me. As I have said, I am really not designed for this sort of thing, and I could see a huge disaster looming on the horizon.

Enter one Mick 'Barney' Barnes (now CEMEX Anglings General Manager), who really was a knight in shining armour. Living only two doors away from us in quarters, he offered his services, for which he will never really know how grateful Lynn and I were, and within thirteen days we were all set up in the new accommodation. Thankfully, Mick volunteered to put up all the fittings as well, because if I had done it I have little doubt that they would have fallen to bits many moons ago. All of his handy work is still functional in our bungalow, so cheers Mick! There were, however, a million and one things to do, so I fitted my fishing in and around my housey chores, but only owning one screw driver, a hammer and a roll of masking tape also limited my effectiveness. Things haven't changed to this day to be honest! With all this going on it was hard to concentrate on my fishing, but there is one thing that pleases me almost as much as me catching a carp, and that is my friends successes.

Whilst in the turmoil of moving I was delighted to hear that brother Chrissie had

Chrissie and the Eye at 57.08

landed the Eye, at an all time high of 57.08. Everyone was delighted for him, all the amazing hard work he had put in having paid off. There were successes close to home too. My mate Craig Dunn, who, along with his Bristol buddy, Bill Fowler, would travel up every weekend to fish at Yateley, had his efforts rewarded with the capture of Chunky from the Car Park - again, everyone was just happy for the guy. Then, at long last, I managed to see the legendary Basil in the flesh. The previous year I had got to know Simon Croft, as he would often stop in for a chat on his way up to the North Lake. I remember well the day he came into my swim on the Car Park having just lost the mighty fish close to the net. There was little I could say to cheer him up, but when he left my swim he seemed more determined than ever. A year later, and I was running as fast as I could up to him to help out with the pictures. I have always gazed in awe at this carp, and I must tell you she looked a million times better in the flesh. I think Simon was off to University shortly after that, and I bet he spent much of his time there with a silly grin on his face. Top man!

Chunky and Craig Dunn at the Car Park lake

My one and only meeting with the legendary Bazil

All of this was getting me no nearer to catching a carp for myself, however. With Little John now on the North Lake, his place had been taken by his good mate Steve Pagulatos. It always seemed that every year one person would get the lion's share of the action on the Car Park, and Steve had simply taken over where John had left off. Now, he had caught Heather a couple of times, and you would be very surprised at the lengths he went to, not to catch her again. I was set up in the End Works swim one warm and sunny day, with just about every carp in the lake feeding on my spots, spending all of my time hanging out of the tree waiting for the bite that would surely come. On the second day I was pulling out what remained of my hair, when I got a call from Steve. He had what he thought was the Dustbin taking Mixers at the other end of the lake. Worried that he may have mistaken it for Heather, he wanted to know if she was still pigging out on my bait. Oh yes, I assured him, but he still came round to see for himself, then, fifteen minutes later, he was back in his swim, launching his controller to the Dustbin.

And then he got a bite. In the horrendous weed he was quickly in need of the boat and, once over the fish, it was a relatively simple case of getting it into the net. Unbelievably, it was Heather; she really did fancy that boy, so had simply followed him back up the lake and the first thing the Leather clad bitch did when she got there was take his hookbait.

God, I hate women at times!

It took me a while, but eventually I got into some rhythm, and one area was really taking my fancy - Dessies. It gives great access to a very pronounced bar in the centre of the lake, and I spent as much time in there as I could. Just to the left of the bar was a spot that interested me, and after a few days work I eventually had fish visiting it, things were looking increasingly good. This situation went on for a couple of weeks until, eventually, I decided that I would put a hookbait there. It may seem strange that I didn't do it before, but I just felt that it would be better to let them keep on feeding there without any lines to hinder them.

I was visited early one Friday morning by Fat Al, and I asked if he would like to move in for the weekend, to which he readily agreed. My hope was that I would be able to move back in on the Sunday, but I stared at my phone the whole time I was away, scared to death that he would have caught one from there. Fortunately it didn't go off, so eventually I packed the motor and made my way to the lake. It was one of those journeys without a single hick-up, you know the sort of thing, no red lights and not much traffic so, by the time I had my gear on the barrow, I was convinced I was having one. Al was all but packed up as I arrived, and by about two in the afternoon I was on my own and setting the traps. The two hookbaits went in without a hitch, the lines were slackened off, and there were fish ghosting in and around the bait. This was it!

At half past four my phone chirped into life, and as I answered it I could tell that there was something seriously wrong. Lynn could hardly speak so I told her to stay exactly where she was, and rang the ambulance. I would get to Frimley Park Hospital as fast as I could, but I needed to leave my gear in situ. Spike, the head bailiff, said there would be no problem with that, and that they would all make sure it was safe. With my hair on fire, I beat the ambulance by a couple of minutes but wasn't allowed near her at first because things had really taken a turn for the worse. I just can't explain how harrowing that was, for all we knew Lynn was about to die. The doctors and nurses were doing all they could, but all I could do was sit and wait.

I stayed at the hospital that night, and rang Spike early the next day, asking if it would be okay to pick my gear up around midday, because I had to go home and get a little sleep. Nothing had improved with Lynn, and I was just getting in the way so, once I had freshened up a bit, I made my way to Yateley, and as I rounded the corner to the swim I could see someone waiting. No names, no pack drill here, but the young lad didn't even ask how my wife was, he was just so intent on getting in the swim. I cleared everything out and he moved in, and to my eternal shame, all I could think of was that he was going to have one. I dumped my stuff at home, and after a quick wrestle with Max, I was back at the hospital. Things had still not improved, and nobody looked at all happy, so I decided to stay the night once again.

I had left my phone in the car, and early the next morning I went to see if I had had any calls. There was a message, and it said that the guy that had moved in had had Heather at over 48lb.

I was crest fallen.

I was still unable to speak to Lynn, which was probably fortunate, because exactly the same thing happened the next morning, this time he had landed the Dustbin. Ugloe at 33lb and a 28lb common completed his haul for the week in that swim. With a wife that, for all I knew, was dying, all I could think of was wallowing in my own self pity. How very, very sad. Lynn was conscious a couple of days later, and I found it hard not to let my bitter disappointment show through.

It was at that moment that I made a decision; my obsession was taking over my life, and I was somehow losing the reason we all go fishing in the first place. It is supposed to be fun, and for a short while I had let the capture of Heather and a few other fish almost ruin everything that Lynn and I had worked for. It was then that I decided never to let it take over my life, ever again. In fact, I told her that I really didn't want to go carp fishing at all, and I was hanging up my rods for good. It just didn't seem important any more, and with no distractions I could concentrate on her recovery.

For a couple months I never even thought about fishing, I wasn't bothered if I never went again. I had to meet up with Viv Shears, the then RMC fisheries manager one day, and whilst we chatted he told me all about Sandhurst Lake at Yateley. They had been stocking the place and generally sorting it out, with a view to opening it the following winter, and did I fancy giving it a go? For a kick

Viv told me all about Sandhurst Lake at Yateley

A lake full of fish that had never been fished for!

off it would give RMC an idea about the fish there, and we could big it up a little. There was no pressure and it actually sounded quite good fun, so with that thought in mind I started to get things ready. I had no idea at the time, but my fires were just about to be re-ignited.

It was around then that I got the call all of us had been waiting for, Laney had landed the Eye at 55lb. Which, understandably, helped to fan my flames some more, so a few days later I was making my way to Sandhurst.

It was a little bit silly, but damn good fun!

Now, it's not very often that you are confronted with a fifteen acre lake absolutely stuffed full of carp which have never really been fished for, is it? To that end, I had filled every available bit of space in the car with bait, I was going to find a spot in the middle of the lake and let 'em have it! Knowing nothing about the pond, I set out on a voyage of discovery with my marker float and the first thing that struck me was how shallow it was, but there were plenty of features. Eventually, I selected a swim that offered very good coverage in the centre of the lake (I believe it is now called the Palace) and, with three rods in position, I scattered 10k of boillies in the area. I would like to have sat down and relaxed, but that wasn't going to be possible for the next two days because, basically, I caught one, on average, every hour or so. It really was a little silly, but bloody hell it was damn good fun! I suppose the biggest I caught was about 18lb, but the size of the carp really didn't bother me. I did exactly the same thing the following week, and it was at that point I discovered exactly why I love carp fishing so much. Barney joined me one day as he was walking his dog, and in the couple of hours he was there, I landed eight carp. We stood and laughed

the whole time, it was madness, and very often all three rods were going off at once. I started to fish other swims, with similar results, but I was starting to wonder where some of the bigger fish were. I think I had landed a couple of twenty pounders by now, but had heard stories of a couple of original carp, one being a thirty pound common, and the other a lovely mid-twenty linear. Those then became my targets, but try as I may I could not catch them, and then Barney arrived to fish. Unsure where to go, I suggested he try down the other end because a few fish had been showing down there, and off he went. The next thing I heard of him is that he had landed the linear, followed shortly after by the big common at 32lb!

Barney and the Big Common

Why I hadn't moved round to where he was, I have no idea. You live and learn eh? I did manage to get amongst some of the larger fish eventually, the biggest of which was a fish that became known as Cracker at 28lb, and one fish that has had to spend the rest of its life being called Chilly's Fish (poor thing) at 27.10, but I was still after one of those originals. Then I learnt that RMC had decided to open up a couple of swims on the island, and once the work was completed, Viv asked if I would like to join him for the first session on there. Well, I wasn't about to say no, was I? Early the next morning I played and landed what was for me the best looking fish in the lake, The Drop Scale Linear at a little over 28lb. It was that one capture that made me start to look at my carp fishing a little more seriously, and once again I started to think about what I wanted to do.

I really wanted to go back onto the Car Park, but was unsure whether I could trust myself. I couldn't handle getting that obsessive once again, its just that I really needed one last go, and there were a couple of other things on my mind too. My mate Colin Davidson had appeared on the front cover of the Anglers Mail the previous year, with a stunning 35.10 common from Frimley. He is the first to admit that he knew nothing of the water, and on only his third trip had landed the biggest one in the lake. Be that as it may, that fish took my breath away, and I had promised myself that as soon as I could, I would go after it. Frimley is only a few minutes from my doorstep, and the more I thought about it, the more I liked the idea. Remember, Walkers big common had been the main driving force behind my carp fishing, and having one that big, so close to home, was going to be too hard to resist.

The best looking carp in the lake

Horton was another place I began to think about, or more precisely, Shoulders. The lake was making a remarkable recovery from the fish deaths a few years before, and whilst it will never be the same lake again, some of the originals remained. With spring fast approaching in 2002, I had a game plan for the future. For now though, I just wanted to keep on enjoying myself, and fish a few different places.

The Sandhurst thing soon fizzled out, and I spent a little time back on the Pads Lake. RMC were really working hard to prepare for the opening in a few months time, but even the nettings and swim construction didn't put the fish off. It really was enjoyable. I even went down to Ringwood for a couple of trips, why I don't know, but I caught a few fish there too, the biggest being a 27.10

A stunning Ringwood mirror

mirror. There were also a couple of recce trips over to Frimley Pit 3, although I didn't want to fish it until the winter, I just wanted a look and to see how the land lay over there. It was very productive too, and I caught a load of carp.

All in all, from the depths of despair, I had reinvented myself with a fantastic voyage of re-discovery. I proved to myself that the carp don't necessarily have to be that big in order for me to have fun, and more importantly, I could contain my obsessive side, and simply go angling for me. I fully expected it to get a little serious from time to time, because with two targets in mind it would have to. It's just that I enjoy all other aspects of life, and I never want carp fishing to get in the way of that!

Result of a recce to Pit 3

Static at Yateley, i'ts not something that I enjoy

Chapter 17

Stiffen up the Sinews, Summon up the Blood

With the sad news that Basil had passed away the year before, it was obvious that the Car Park Lake was going to be busier than ever. I wasn't even sure I wanted to be fishing there really, especially as I was trying to stop myself getting too wrapped up in my fishing again. It's a bit like parachuting really, if someone dies or is badly injured then the best way to overcome any of your anxiety is to simply go up and do it again, before you even have a chance to think about it. In a crazy sort of way, fishing back at Yateley was all part of my therapy...or so I thought. Surely nothing would be stupid enough to get caught with so much pressure on the water? As it happens, I was the one that ended up with egg on my face, as four of the fish graced the banks before I had even cast a rod in there. From the kick off then, I was one step off the pace and things simply stayed that way until I made a decision.

With so many anglers on the lake it was impossible to find any opportunities in the edge, which meant that I was going to have to fish in a very static way. It is not something that I enjoy that much, although I could think of no other way of doing it. I began to use a lot of bait, and over the next few weeks I really started to fill the place in, boillies, pellets and particles all figured in my plan - invite everything to the party and see what happened. Tench and bream that's what, I didn't think that there were so many in the lake, it was all rather frustrating. On many occasions I could see the odd carp visiting the areas, but just as I thought they may settle, a little red eyed monster would upset them by taking off with my hookbait. I persevered for about six weeks, but once again I was starting to lose the will to live. Waking up and staring at the same trees every morning was driving me mad, I was looking for an excuse to leave and I found it toward the end of July. The fish started to spawn, and as I always do, I reeled my rods in. I have never understood why anglers continue to fish when the carp are doing this, the risk of damaging them when they are at their most vulnerable is great, and I believe it best to leave them alone to get on with it. A few years before, I had witnessed the most horrific thing when a very large carp was foul hooked in the belly whilst spawning, and that resulted directly in her death. I didn't know it at the time, but my Yateley fires were barely a flicker by now. I would fish it again a few times, but never with as much enthusiasm, as I was just about to take my first tentative steps in the hunt for Charlie's Mate, the big Frimley common. My intention had been to fish Frimley during the winter, but whilst the fish at Yateley had their annual sexual rampage, I thought it would be a good idea to get some more information about the lake, but I could never have imagined just how much this mission would take over my life for the next few years.

I stopped off at home to pick up some bait supplies, and take Max for his morning walk. I was still having to perform this duty every day, with Lynn now being totally reliant on a wheel chair, a situation that would not change. Knowing the Frimley fish had spawned the week before, I reasoned that they may just be up for a good post coital nosh up so, with that in mind, my poor car groaned as I headed off.

The view from the Double Boards

Having had a brief look at the lake in the spring, when the trees were still bereft of leaves, I was shocked at how striking the place looked in its full summer glory. Mind you, it was stinking hot, and by the time I had humped the bait and tackle to the area that interested me, I was in a bit of a state, so sat in the shade and tried to recover, whilst watching the water. As far as I could tell, just about every carp in the lake were sunning themselves around an exposed bar, and I didn't know it at the time, but the swim into which I was about to move my gear was to play a large part in the dramas that were about to unfold. The Double Boards commands the most water of any of the swims on Pit 3, and with a whole host of features to go at, it was a magnet for both carp and carp angler alike.

Once I had my breath back I sorted myself out, and as with any new water, the marker float went into action. With so many carp in the area I was a bit wary of going mad, but I needed to know what was out there. At the bottom of the exposed bar the gravel turned into silt, and this is where I positioned three hookbaits and about 25 kilos of my bait. I had no idea what was going to happen next, and this for me is one of the greatest things about carp fishing, the unknown. How boring would it be to simply turn up and catch carp all the time? So, with my first brew in my hand, I worried about the amount of bait I had put in, but I really shouldn't have.

As expected, the fish showed no sign of feeding whilst the sun was on the water, but once it had set someone must have rung the dinner bell. At 1030 that evening I was playing my first carp, and for three nights the action was almost non-stop. I had seven carp everytime darkness set in, but I was wondering why there were no bites in the day. I awoke on the second morning, after an hours kip, to see several fish head and shouldering in the open water, and sat and watched for a while as a couple of fresh pop-ups nestled in amongst them, but no bites were forthcoming. I searched in my bag for a small washing tablet bag that was hidden there, and after filling it with thirty boillies, I pegged it in the margins to soak until the following morning. Another frantic night was followed, once again, with carp leaping in the open water so, as quick as I could, I baited two rods with the washed out baits, and launched them into the area. These were followed by half a dozen free offerings, and before I could switch the buzzer on, the first rod was away. A lovely 25lb common eventually slipped into the net. Now, I am a firm believer that one carp is lucky, but two is skill, so to that end I quickly repositioned the rod. Again I didn't have long to wait, and was soon slipping a nice double figure mirror back

The action was non stop

to his home. It seemed as if I had come across a tactic that would work nicely when the action was slow, and so, thoroughly wrecked, I packed away and headed for home. I was going to like it at Frimley, and the hunt for that big common had started off in fine style.

I returned to the Car Park the following week, but my mind was elsewhere. I had received a call from my good friend, Tim Paisley, and during that conversation he had asked if I would like to represent my country at the World Cup being held on Lake Raduta, Romania. I thought about it for a nano second before biting his hand off at the shoulder. Would I ever!! He also asked who I would like to share this momentous occasion with. Again, that took a fraction of a second, and as soon as I had ended the call from Tim, I quickly gave Jenkins a ring. I really thought that if I looked out of my window in the direction of Crawley, I would be able to see a small thermo-nuclear explosion. Man, was he excited!

Now, I know that we weren't selected by some process of elimination, and hadn't exactly earned the right to go, but representing our country is something that Keith and I would have killed for. Preparations for that were going to take over my life for a while, and the phone lines between us went into melt down. That said, I tried desperately to concentrate on my fishing, but it just wasn't happening. I drove away from Yateley wondering if I would go back, Lynn had two massive operations coming up, the first of which would be shortly after my return from Romania. It

The hunt for the Big Common had started in fine style

Viv and I had a few up to low twenties

was then that I decided to solely concentrate on Pit 3 at Frimley as, being only a stones throw from my house, I could get home quickly if needed. The stakes were not quite as high there, but you would have to be a sad man if the thought of several upper 30 commons didn't make you just a little moist.

I had arranged to do a night with Viv Shears so we could catch up on things, and have a bit of a social, and by the time he had left we had landed a few fish each to low 20's. As soon as I was alone I moved up into the first swim on the lake, that covers some lovely pads, and quickly landed a couple of nice fish, both a little over twenty pounds. I had been looking down the centre of the lake, and had seen several much larger fish boom out in that area, so I packed my gear away and went to investigate. Because I was unsure exactly where they had

Dear old Daisy at 29.06

shown, I was guessing to begin with, but I did find a very interesting feature. It was almost like a wall right in the middle of the lake and ran for more than ten yards. With the marker positioned in the middle of it, I trotted back up to where I had come from, and joy of joys, the little red flight was bang on the spot. With a skip in my step I was back round there in a flash and started to introduce some bait, well lots of bait actually. 15k of NRG boillies and about 5k of Response pellets eventually found its way to the spot. Now if that didn't get at least a couple of the big girls excited, then I would eat my spod rod!

All night long the liners kept me awake, but I did manage to fall asleep eventually, then one of the rods did rip off in the early hours, but my buffoonery meant that it fell off almost immediately. I had been in such a deep sleep, that I tipped my bed chair up and got tangled in the sleeping bag, so it was no surprise that I was soon reeling in an empty hook. I gave the nights activities a bit of thought, maybe they were simply getting away with it so, like you do, I shortened the hooklinks and attached some far heavier leads. That seemed to do the trick as a 16lb common, followed by one of the most wanted mirror carp in Frimley, rolled into my net. The mirror was a fish called Daisy, one of Donald Leney's finest, and weighed a rather pleasing 29.06. The poor old girl had a somewhat interesting history, having lived in a number of lakes before finally settling in at Frimley. I gazed at her in awe, a proper slice of history for sure.

Along with my dog walking, I had some business to take care of the next day, so it was mid-afternoon before I could get the rods in the water once again. With a little more bait on the spots, I was sure of some more action but I wasn't quite ready for what happened next. Between 1130 and 0430 in the morning I had twelve takes.

At 29.12 I could hardly be disappointed

At one point I had commons of 21lb and 24lb in the net at the same time. A 16lb'er followed shortly afterwards, then a few minutes later I again had commons of 24lb and 26.08 nestling in my net. The night was becoming a blur as several more mid-twenty commons hit the spreader block, and just as I thought it could get no better I had a titanic struggle with what I was convinced was my first 30lb carp from the lake. Totally empty from their spawning activity, she didn't quite make it, but at 29.12 I could hardly be disappointed, she really was a cracking looking fish. Shattered, but entirely happy, I packed up the following morning, if this was anything to go by, then the winter was going to be very interesting indeed!

For now though, all I could think of was the World Cup and stopping Jenkins from spontaneously combusting through the excitement of it all. This was going to be fun! And I can think of no one better than Jenks to tell the story.

We were, at last, bound for Romania

'Let's Rock!'

The plane accelerated away along the runway and, as the huge jets lifted the wheels from the tarmac, my clock clicked to 1.00 p.m. - Friday 13th at 13.00 hours and my erstwhile companion, seasoned in 22 years of jumping out of aircraft, swore profusely and declared to anyone who would listen that we were all going to die! We were, at last, bound for Romania – Lake Raduta to be precise - to contest the Carp World Cup, and I had to smile at the irony of our take off time. For the past month, Chilly had kept me appraised of every single near air collision, and when he heard that our departure date had been brought forward by 24 hours to the aforementioned date I thought I would probably have to sedate him with an elephant dart to get him on the plane – much like B. A. Barracus in the A-Team. It had been a couple of months previously that Chilly had called me at work, not an uncommon occurrence, and casually mentioned a call he'd had from Tim Paisley. This, also, was not an uncommon occurrence so I was not really prepared for what came next.

"He's putting a six man team together for the World Cup in Romania and he asked if I knew anyone who'd like to represent their country!"

The next few seconds stretched to the far horizon before he continued,

"Then he asked me if I thought you would fancy it."

The stream of words that issued forth from me were mainly unintelligible but the gist was 'What? Yes! F&&%% hell Yes! YESSSS!'

After I'd told everybody a dozen times over the next few hours, I calmed down enough to ask if I could actually have the time off work 'cos I actually had no holiday left. My boss, Nic (bless him), said there was no way he would stop me, and he'd even pay me for the week as well – top man.

Somehow, over the next couple of weeks, it was decided that I would design the badge to go on the team shirts and fleeces and I came up with the '3 carp' design, instead of the 3 lions. It went down well and we looked the dogs danglies when we had the team photo's taken (in fact, I've still got the polo shirts to this day, and my daughter, Christine, has the England fleece).

Obviously, over the next month or so, the phone lines were red hot between Crawley and Aldershot as we went through every possible scenario. We discussed different baiting strategies, different rigs, what clothes to take, how we would transport all the gear, and who would do the cooking. A lot of these questions were answered by Tim, who did a sterling job of organising bait and tackle, so all we had to think about was end tackle and music. There was no way we were going to spend five days on the bank without a bit of music to lighten the mood, so I rattled through my CD collection and took enough to last us a month! Along with this I took some small, portable speakers and CD player so everything was set.

The next thing on the agenda was to find out as much as we could about the huge Lake Raduta, so Carpworld's were scanned for any articles to pore over, and diverse anglers were contacted for any information that may be of help. The main theme that was coming through was that you would definitely lose fish, no matter what strength of line you used, as some of the snags were in fact sunken forests and villages! We soaked it all up and thought it would come in handy but, in hindsight, it mattered very little as we knew most of it already, but it helped to pass the time for the few weeks before the off.

For some bizarre reason, Laney had 'volunteered' to drop me and Chilly off at Heathrow so all we had to do was be ready. Oh, we were ready alright, probably both of us by about four in the morning with our flight not due to take off until midday – just like little boys on Christmas Eve.

When we arrived at the Terminal, most of the guys were already there, about thirty or so of 'em, and all looking suitably excited. We shook a few hands then took over a part of the departure lounge with all of our rod holdalls. The mayhem was short lived and pretty soon we were being called to board the plane, at which point the Para got really twitchy. We'd been warned that there was a bit of a delay and he commenced telling anyone that listened that we would take off at bloody 1300 hours – how right he was.

Three hours later, however, we were checked into our hotel and all memory of our flight of doom was washed away with the first ice cold beer of the evening. We met quite a few of the other competitors, including some wonderful South Africans and a dodgy pseudo Afrikaan from Leicester! The night was full of humour, bon homie and copious amounts of liquor and it was at a very wobbly 4.00 the following afternoon that Chilly and I emerged from our room. Everybody was congregating in the lobby of the hotel, or more precisely at the bar, in preparation for the draw at 6.30, and soon the 200 or so protagonists were ushered into the room where the draw was to be made. After much preamble the first name was drawn from the hat and it was none other than the dodgy pseudo Afrikaan – Davo. All the Brits gave him a raucous welcome and then we were into it. Many names seemed to be drawn before any of the Brits were, and it was noticeable how conservatively all the other teams were taking the whole affair. Not so us boys, though, and when the first of our lads was drawn from the hat all the other teams were left in little doubt that we were present!

Then – "Chillcott and Jenkins". We roared even louder as the big man rose and turned to the gathered throng, beckoning for more noise. He got it in bucket loads, then strode to the basket full of swim numbers. He tore open the envelope, looked at me with a smile, then announced to the expectant throng at the top of his voice, "That's a Mercedes!!"

Oh, how we whooped and hollered, and I had to smile at our swim number. 85, my house number.

After the gamesmanship, we had a good look at where we were situated. It was at the bottom of one of many large bays, the Church Bay I believe, and not many people fancied our chances in there. Oh well, we were here now and there was no way we were going down without a fight, so let's get on with it!

The evening took a more sedate route than the previous nights and we were in our room by eleven, asleep by midnight and up at 6.30. The next few hours were spent chatting, a bit of breakfast, cup of tea. A very welcome bottle of Coke had been left unattended for just a little too long and the opportunity was not to be sniffed at, then, eventually, we were on the coach and away. We all just wanted to get on and do some fishing now, sod all the other palaver.

An hour or so later and we were bumping down the track to the lake, stopping at a not inconsiderable Hotel Raduta. Still, we had not really seen the lake and now it was time to get sweaty and distribute the bait and tackle that Mainline and Fox had despatched a few weeks earlier. I must say well done to Kev Knight because, within an hour, all six of us in the Carpworld/Mainline/Fox team had all of our bait, food, bivvies, bedchairs and assorted items of end tackle and spods, plus enough pop-ups to re-float the Romanian economy! Once all of our gear was allocated, we all waited around for the small fleet of dodgy jeeps to come and collect and deposit us at our swims .Then it was our turn, into the jeep and off on a four mile magic carpet ride to our swim. Once all the gear was unloaded and the transport lost in a cloud of dust, we looked at each other, smiled and warmly shook each other's hand.

"Let's rock," I said.

"Let's!" replied Chilly.

We surveyed the water in front of us, which looked huge; probably half a mile to the far bank. If a big wind sprung up and blew our way we'd probably end up in

Fox and Mainline had sent enough gear to re-float the Romanian economy

Chilly strode forth into the lake

Bucharest long before the others! The surrounding terrain was, to say the least, open, and from the hill behind us we could quite easily see the far horizon, which we thought might have been Poland! Our only neighbours in the bay were a few hundred yards either side of us, so we were sure to be unmolested – maybe.

It was midday and the match started in two hours, so it was out with the plumbing float to see what wonders lay before us. As Chilly strode forth into the lake to unleash his first cast, a carp left the water two hundred yards out and we hoorahed. Half an hour later we barely mentioned the tenth similar occurrence. At one point a grass carp had swum behind Chilly, and I thought briefly of netting it (it was probably a mid-20 and looked very poorly) but that wasn't Cricket so on with the real game. We had been advised to look for between 8' – 14' but that would have been a luxury and after an hour of casting, Chilly's marker float was rising no more than four feet at 160 yards! His third cast had left a marker float attached to a particularly nasty snag 140 yards out, which proved to be most fortuitous as it marked that spot all week. The wind was coming from the south and was pushing straight at us from left to right and causing the line to bow horrendously. This caused me to misread my first few casts with the marker and I thought that I had found seven or eight feet at about 100 yards, but after some very careful plumbing (pulling the float down to the lead rather than letting it up) I was still happy to find an area a little over five feet in depth and this would be where I would concentrate my initial baiting. My tackle consisted of 12'6" 3.25lb TC rods with the Long Cast Baitrunners (an absolute must for this sort of fishing), these I'd loaded up with 12lb mainline and finished off with 45lb Quicksilver leaders and a yard of 45lb lead core. 3.5 and 4 ounce leads on safety clips got me to where I wanted to go and the E S P Big T size 5's and 7's all stayed well buried. I was going to vary my rigs and ended up using two different ones - one was a combi-link with 3 -4" of 25lb Mask to a small flexi-swivel, then 2" of Quicksilver to the hook. The other was 6" of Kryston 15lb Snakebite with an inch stripped back below the hook. All were fished as pop ups with the two most successful being N R G and Pineapple and usually very well dipped. All I had to do was get them into the lake.

Then it was 2 o'clock.

Let the games commence.

"Don't get too despondent if you don't catch for a while. They will come to you if you keep putting the bait in."

This was the advice that Tim had given us earlier in the day. I stood in the water, ten minutes after we had cast out, and proceeded to launch boillies from the throwing stick.

'Bleep'!!

I turned around to look at Chilly, who in turn was looking at me. Between us were his rods, fished beach caster style with tips high in the air. Only, one of the tips was getting lower by the second and, before the alarm could sound once more, Chilly had thrust the rod into the air and I watched it hoop over. I just laughed out loud and thrashed the water with the throwing stick in sheer delight. Unfortunately, just as I got onto dry land to get the net I heard him swear as the first of many carp that week found the safety of the snag, the rod pinging back as the line cut. We looked at each other, despondent for a moment, then simply howled with laughter. We were going to catch carp!

In retrospect, we missed an opportunity then, because, instead of continuing with single hookbaits for the next couple of hours we carried on with our game plan and proceeded to bait the granny out of the swim for a couple of hours. Consequently we had no further action until just on darkness (7.30) when, as a Polish or Romanian magazine team came in to do a bit of filming, Chilly had another single bleep. Once again the snag was victorious and we started to doubt our chances. Those doubts were banished an hour later when he bullied the next fish from the snag and into my waiting net and, although only a mid – 20, its capture was greeted like that of a record breaker. We were off the mark and, a few hours later, another slightly smaller fish joined it on the sacking pole. Just before dawn it was my turn, but the carp was barely bigger than the lead and added nothing to our total! The night had been chilly, tiring but successful, however, as I sat there with the first cup of tea of the day I wondered how I was going to survive if this was how it was going to be. I was knackered! I had a headache, I'd caught no carp to talk of and we hadn't even been going 24 hours. Whilst all this was going on, my son Vincent was a couple of days into what was to be an amazing session. Fishing a large southern pit for the second season, he had been baiting heavily since the beginning of the season and had caught a few carp to 38lb (a p.b.) but this week was to surpass all that had gone before. As we drove to Heathrow I had sent a text to him to say we were on our way, and he replied that he had just caught a 24lb Common. This was followed by a 29lb Mirror and today I had learnt from Laney that Vince had caught a 38.10 Mirror, another p.b. This was turning into a good week and brought a surge of energy to my groaning muscles.

"Come on, boy, let's get some bait in the water," commanded the Sarn't Major, so up I got and trudged slowly into the cold water to start the day with a good

Another pb for Vince at 38.10

And then there was Chilly

spodding! An hour or so later I was into a bit of a rhythm and was happy with the spread of bait. We were using Grange and N.R.G. boillies, both 18mm, but once air dried they were down to almost 16mm, which caused a problem getting real accuracy. It was still quite windy and I knew that it was pointless trying to put all the bait at extreme range because if the wind really picked up I would be unable to reach it, so 80 -100 yards from where I was spodding (20 yards out in the lake) was good enough for me.

Then there was Chilly!

And people say that Frank Warwick can cast! I'm sure he can, but I'd like to see him cast a spod in excess of 150 yards, consistently, for two or three hours at a time, twice a day for five days! There is extreme casting, then there is what Chilly was doing, which is obscene casting. When he was at Orchid earlier in the year he had cast a plumbing float a huge distance and, on seeing it, proclaimed big caster Marsh Pratley, had told Chilly to clip it up and had then paced out the distance, stopping at 167 paces! Now, in most people's strides that is going to be about 160 yards, and Chilly, having left the line in the clip since that session, had hit the clip fairly early on in his plumbing of the Raduta swim, and it was just short of there that he found the snag that he was fishing to the left of. Whatever, I watched him for five days, and have no doubt that very few other teams would have caught what we did from that swim because nobody could have fished the way Chilly did.

Right, that's enough of your ego massage, mate, what about me? Well, at last I had a take in the early afternoon and into the net went a twenty pound common to the same sort of vocal commotion as Chilly's first fish, and within a couple of hours it was joined by two more and we were really rocking. Chilly was beginning to see the problem with fishing near to the snag by now, having hooked three more fish but landing only one. The snag obviously held some sort of attraction for the carp and the closer that he cast to it, the more action Chilly received, but the more likely he was to lose the fish. This was getting frustrating and also a little worrying because of the amount of tackle we were leaving in the carp, so he began to put his hookbaits and spods further to the left, in a bid to entice the carp away from the snag.

The marshals came round twice a day to weigh any fish, and also with an update of the match positions and, on Monday evening, we were top of the world!

First! Me and Chillcott!!

Oh, what a day that was, however brief, probably only a matter of hours, but what a feeling. We just kept looking at each other and laughing, one or the other of us swearing quietly or saying, "Now, you're not getting too despondent are you!?"

Vince had landed a 35.06 white linear

That night was the only one that we failed to catch anything, the take to my rod producing my only lost fish of the week when the hook pulled almost immediately and, by morning, we knew that our fifteen minutes were up!

But we just soldiered on. We came up with an idea to get the boillies further and it was all down to Shaun Harrison. I had read an article he did recently about re-hydrating baits and, although this was for a different purpose, I felt that we could re-soak the boillies and get them back up to 18mm. So,10 kilos of mixed baits into a bucket, filled with fresh water, two 500ml bottles of Hempseed Oil and a couple of drops of Pineapple Flavouring. Leave for twenty hours, then chuck 'em as far as you can. And it worked a treat, cheers Shaun! And more news from home spurred us on with a text from Dave saying that Vince had landed a 35.06 white linear, a fish he had seen on numerous occasions, oh boy, was he going to be pleased!

So, more throwing stick, more spods and, later that day, more hollering. We'd had a few visitors over the first couple of days, mainly foreign journalists, and that afternoon Phillippe Lagarbe from Media Carpe came around with the weighing crew. I'd taken a portable C.D. player and some small speakers with me for a bit of light entertainment, and Santana was drifting out of the bivvy when Phillipe arrived. We chatted about all things rock, and then drifted back into the carp side of things, and he had a few interesting things to say before leaving and wishing us well. He probably hadn't been gone a few minutes when one of Chilly's Gladiators nodded and he whacked into it and made his way backwards as best he could. This was the furthest left of the three rods and gave him the best chance of guiding it away from the snag, but I still stood behind him quietly murmuring "Come on. Come on." over and over again, before bending to get the net when I saw him

advance purposefully forward and, with a terse "Come on, Jenks" I was summoned to arms.

This appeared to me to be a better fish, the rod tip being pulled down forcefully on numerous occasions, but soon I could see swirls ten yards away as the fish made its final surges for freedom. I don't know what it's like with you guys, but with us there is constant banter as

We whooped and hollered!

the fish is being played. Even if it is just the 'It's okay' mantra, there is always something. So it was here, until I saw the fish's mouth and my own mouth went dry! I could have put my fist in that mouth and I had to net this fish. NOW! It rolled a couple more times and not a word was said between us. Then it was in the net and an unintelligible string of nonsense came screaming, roaring, gushing forth! It was no monster, that we knew, but it was by far the biggest we had landed and, boy, were we pleased. We thought it was probably a mid-30 so phoned the marshal's to come and weigh it. When they arrived, an hour or so later, I told them that I thought it was probably 16 or 17 kilo's, so one of the guys said that they would weigh it in the

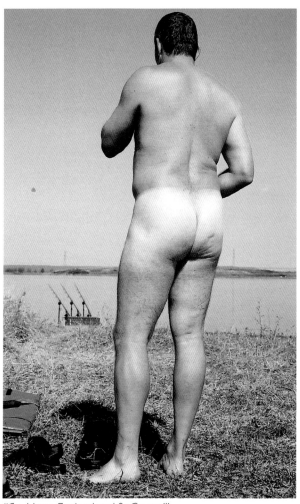

"Cry Harry, England and St George!"

morning! Chilly was in the lake baiting up again, but suddenly he was striding through the waves like Neptune and, before he reached the shore, matey had phoned for help, saying that we had landed a 20 kilo fish – actions speak louder than words! The team arrived with Phillippe in tow and despite the fish weighing just over 33lb, we still whooped and hollered, especially as I had caught another one pound carp to compliment it!

We seemed to be getting into a bit of a rhythm now. Bed when we were tired, eight or nine in the evening. Then snoring shifts, me for the first couple of hours whilst Chilly lay there devising interesting ways of making me stop, then the roles reversed for the next couple of hours! Sometime in the early hours I would get one or two takes, then we'd wake at about 7.30. Cup of tea, fag for Chilly, genital husbandry for me then, with a purposeful "Stiffen the sinews,

Summon up the blood" from me, Chilly would rise and, completing the sentence with "Cry Harry, England and St. George!" we were once more into the breach! (And don't think I'm kidding, I am deadly serious).

An hour or so spodding or sticking would be interrupted by our first food delivery of the day, normally some very welcome chicken salad sandwiches. These were washed down with a cup of tea before we were back into the lake for another hour or so. We finished at 11.30 in the morning because Chilly's first

Goran the goat herder

action of the day came soon after midday, and would normally be followed by two or three more chances. MacDonald's would arrive at about two in the afternoon, just as we were getting peckish (MacDonald's were one of the sponsors for the event, if you hadn't guessed) then it was back into the lake at about six for a further hour of baiting, coming out just as another MacDonald's arrived! We didn't eat all of them, honest! Mary Paisley had put together a very comprehensive food parcel for all of us and we ate really well despite the Mac's!

So that was the routine, but it wasn't just the Big Mac man and the carp weighing squad who kept us entertained. The track behind us was the Romanian equivalent of the M25, and there was a steady procession of livestock and their owners passing by all day long. Goran the Goat-botherer and Sherban the Sheep-worrier were regular commuters twice a day, harrying there respective herds with sticks and kicks, but then there was the amazing Cow Shouter coming past at least four times a day. He would harangue and bellow at his totally oblivious charges, smiling all the while as he did so. We got to talk to him on a couple of occasions, although 'talk' is probably a bit of an exaggeration. Mainly, our discourse consisted of me and Chill shouting and pointing, and the cow-shouter smiling inanely and letting out the odd barked command to his herd of smelly ungulates. After that, each time he passed us he would bellow something unintelligible and we would smile affably whilst calling him something very Anglo-Saxon – ah, peace and goodwill to all men. On the flip side of that coin was the team of Eastern Europeans fishing a couple of hundred yards to our right. They were a couple of youngish lads but their team mascot was something else. She was a stunning looking lady with legs up to her armpits and everything else that should go with that package! We'd admired her from afar, but on one occasion one of the guys came along to us with her in tow as translator. Man, they could have asked for anything they'd wanted, what with her being dressed in some very short shorts and a rather fetching top. All they wanted, however, was a bit of advice and some bait, which we gave them in bundles! As she wiggled back to her swim we pondered a few ways that might suffice as payment for our services – I mean, how could she have failed to fall for the prospect of a night under the stars with a couple of smelly, English fishermen. Surely, it's what her dreams were constantly filled with? But, strangely, she never returned and we could only surmise that her henchman had forbade her the life of luxury she had always dreamed of. That could be the only possible answer.

Doing an interview for a Yugoslavian author

One afternoon, this lovely Yugoslavian guy came up with a Dictaphone and asked if he could ask a few questions, which he'd already done with a few of the other English guys. We were in the middle of answering these questions (which he was hoping to write a book from) and had just told us that we were World Carp Leg Ends, when I had a screamer to one of the rods. He then proceeded to take photos of everything, including a close up of the fish's mouth before Chilly had netted it! Close, very close but it did prove that we were, indeed, Leg Ends! But it was our leg ends that were beginning to suffer.

We had both brought sandals to wear into the lake, but when a buzzer screams at night you just run straight into the water without thought of footwear. The problem was that the lakebed was littered with all manner of foot slicing objects, from rocks and shells to broken bottles and splintered leg bones! It was one of these objects that caused us to move with less haste when, after a mid-afternoon dash, Chilly emerged with a gaping wound to the sole of his foot. I suggested sewing it up with a length of Quicksilver, but that idea seemed a bit radical so we opted for a wash in clean, hot water and a couple of plasters. He's a big boy, he'll be alright! After that we left our sandals next to our rods at all times and when one of us got a run, the other one would put the rod holders sandals on, before putting on his own sandals and following with the net (from further down the bank I would think that the Eastern beauty was confirming her fears about the feelthy English, what with one or other of our heads at waist height at different times of day and night!). Very up close and personal, but a lot healthier. The other problem came from pulling our sandals from the cloying silt every time we went out to spod or stick, and eventually we had to wear socks before putting on the sandals –all we needed now was a knotted handkerchief and a deck chair and we would be the ultimate Brits abroad. But, by Friday morning, we could hardly walk properly and my feet still bled for a few days after returning home, every time I got out of bed. Oh well, it's only carp fishing.

This was turning out to be a great week to be a Jenkins

By Wednesday we were settled into fourth place, and Vince had caught another 35lb scaly linear, having lost a 30lb Common at the net a few hours after catching the white linear. This was turning in to a great week to be a Jenkins, and providing that we could keep catching three or four fish a day over the last couple of days we thought that we had a good chance of retaining fourth position. We were 50 or so kilos behind third place and the same in front of fifth which equated to about 6 or 7 fish (unless a couple of whackers came along) so we had to try to ensure that we kept landing the fish. The problem was that Chilly was losing as many as he was landing and we couldn't afford for that balance to go the wrong way so we had to think up a change of tactics. Chilly, therefore, decided to plumb about five yards short of the snag marker in a bid to give himself a bit of an edge and consequently found a nice hard area in about four and a half feet of water. In this situation braid would have provided a massive edge, but it was banned as a mainline, only being allowed as a leader, so it was time to get brutal. Hit and run!

The idea was that, as soon as he got the merest nod on the rod tip, Chilly would strike and run backwards as far as possible, which was about 30 yards. The

I yelled at him to keep running

baitrunner was off and clutch wound up tight and, after almost four hours of non-stop baiting (with a much appreciated Jimi Hendrix accompaniment drifting from our bivvy out across the lake), he sat down at midday and stared intently at the rods. The kettle had barely boiled for the first cup of the afternoon when he was up and off! He struck the rod and ran back, but slowed a little too early and the fish just made the snag. Bugger! When he repeated the process half an hour later I yelled at him to keep running and he nearly disappeared over a nearby goat herder! But the ploy worked, as it did three more times in the next few hours (unfortunately the last one came off through our own fault, which we won't dwell on) and when the marshals arrived we had 23 kilos to weigh in. The latest list showed us in a ciabatta sandwich, 34 kilos behind the Italians in third and about the same amount ahead of the Italians in fifth. The 23 kilos could have moved us within 11 kilos of third but we didn't know what they had caught during the afternoon so just tried to concentrate on retaining fourth place. What was also encouraging was the fight for the team title because we could see that Frank and Bob were twelfth and Tim and Steve were seventeenth, however both teams only needed to catch one more fish than those immediately in front of them and they could both jump three or four places. As much as our thoughts were on our own position we hoped that both the other pairs would enjoy some significant action during the night.

The last baiting of the week

As the evening wore on it was soon to be my turn, so I took to the water with the throwing stick to commence the last of the baiting for the week. I'd only been out there for ten minutes when it was nearly all over.

Let me explain.

We were at the bottom of the bay and about 350 yards to our left were a Romanian team. They were about 100 yards up the left hand bank and obviously had some very shallow water in front of them because they were wading a very long way before casting. This had posed us no problem until that last afternoon when, unable to watch Chilly hook another carp, the guy waded out a good 150 yards before trying to launch his hookbait into the area that Chilly had been fishing all week. He fell woefully short but his intention was all too clear and Chillcott was not happy!

" OII!! You poaching @**$@! £%%^%^@ *^&**%!!!" He strode out of the lake in just his shorts, thighs like tug boats pumping away and chest so far out you could have balanced a beer keg on it!

"I'll be back in a minute, Jenks" he barked, and I suddenly had a vision of me and Chilly in a vat of pig swill!

Nostrils flaring like a charging bull and a snipers glint in the eye he strode menacingly along the bank to discuss the border dispute with the now land-bound angler. I could hear every word, and all of them were spat out like six-inch nails from a nail gun! They didn't need to speak English to understand exactly what the big man was saying, and when the other three guys in the swim all stood up it was indeed a red rag to a raging bull!

"COME ON THEN!!" he roared as he stepped towards them, "All four of you! NOW!!"

Suddenly, three of them sat down and the fourth picked up his rod and rapidly wound in his rig. How very diplomatic!

Chilly strode back round to our swim with a huge grin on his face and, rubbing his hands together, declared,

"Ah, that's better boy. Now, let's do some carp angling!"

I just shook my head, smiling, and wielded the throwing stick once more.

Due to the inaccuracy of a throwing stick at that distance and in the cross winds which we were sometimes experiencing, I had been happy to spread all three rods across a thirty or forty yard area, but tonight was the last night and I felt that I needed to ensure at least one more carp, so I had to concentrate the bait more, and the only way I was happy doing that was with a catapult. But not from over 80 yards. I had to get nearer, so I did. Borrowing Chilly's idea, and his hooded top, I put it on back to front and filled the hood beneath my chin with three or four hundred boillies. Then picking up the Fox Boillie pult I waded out forty or so yards until I was just at knee depth (my knees happen to start at my nipples!) and proceeded to fire three or four boillies at a time out to the required area. Half an hour later, and with my arms hanging out of their sockets, I waded ashore much happier with my baited area and began preparing our last meal of the week.

We were tired, expectant, happy, worried and every other emotion you could possibly imagine and, by nine o'clock, ready for bed. Chilly retired first and I sat looking out towards the far bank, where the second and third place guys were situated. A shooting star fizzed across the sky, like many before it that week, and I requested just one more carp. PLEASE!

Then I joined Chilly in the bivvy and tried to will myself to sleep but it was impossible. My mind was like a mixing deck, with a thousand thoughts all vying for first place to be heard. The lack of snoring from across the way led me to believe that Chilly's mind was in a similar turmoil, but neither of us said a word. For what seemed like a thousand hours we built up a palpable energy, a cloying tension that you could almost taste and underlying it all was the knowledge, the absolute certain necessity, that we needed one more carp – and it was down to me to catch it. I must have dozed off because I awoke to the sight of Chilly walking back into the bivvy after his usual midnight pee. Unaware that I was awake he muttered, "We ain't gonna bloody catch one!"

My thoughts entirely, and my stomach tightened at that fact.

A second is a very strange thing, it can last for just a second or almost an eternity. BLEEP!

Within a second I had covered the fifteen yards to the rods and my hand hovered over the left-hand rod. An eternity later I saw the indicator lift a fraction and heaved the Ethos into the air, feeling the carp on the other end thump its head in annoyance. Chilly was by my side and, after hearing my grunted confirmation that I was "in", he put on my sandals for me and soon followed me into the lake. As with the 33, very little was being said, we just wanted to see the net full of carp, whatever the size. I don't know how long it took, only a few minutes, but long enough, then the cloying envelope of tension was burst like a mere soap bubble as Chilly screamed his joy. In the net! We'd done it and our emotions burst forth like a sundered dam.

We couldn't stop talking, the kettle went on and we talked some more and drank in great draughts of relief. It was three in the morning and we were wide awake and laughing heartily.

Home for the week, and the scene of the final night tension

An hour later we attempted some more sleep and I was awoken just before Dawnski by a screamer to the right hand rod and soon landed another 21 pounder for a fine brace. We had two more hours left and I willed just one more, but my shooting star had kept its side of the bargain and there was no more. Half an hour before the end, our marshals came round to shake our hands and tell us that we were definitely fourth, we hadn't needed the night time carp after all, but what the hell, it was a night we will never forget.

The week took its toll on everything... it was hard!

We had used 40 kilos of boillies, 40 kilos of Response pellets and hemp pellets, muscles we didn't know we had, blood, sweat and tears. We had come into it wondering whose throat would be the first to be ripped out as nerves stretched and fatigue took its toll, and we had emerged, after one of the most memorable weeks of our carp fishing lives, closer friends than either of us could ever have thought possible.

The Camaradarie was fantastic

And we had come fourth in the world. A position I could only have dreamt about, if I was honest. I'd thought that if we could have finished in the top thirty we would have done very well, Chilly had higher aspirations, but not by much. The final table showed us just 16 kilos behind the third placed Italians, but they had lost as many, if not more, fish as us so it was a fair result for all concerned. Unfortunately, our other two teams couldn't catch the required carp in the last night and we ended up third in the team event, but still not to be

The breathtaking Presidential Palace

sneezed at and by far the best of the British teams. But there was still more to come. We returned to Raduta's hotel for a couple of hours and the camaraderie was fantastic, especially when everyone stood to applaud the victorious Austrians. Then it was back to Bucharest, but the trip back was a little fraught because, no matter where you are in the world, Friday afternoon traffic is always a real bitch. This didn't help a few of the lads, whose bladders were a might smaller than their drinking capacity, and after one unscheduled toilet stop, there was to be no more until we had navigated the traffic-strewn city streets and reached our hotel. This state of affairs brought ever-increasing looks of anguish and pain on a couple of well known faces until all that was left for them to do was the classic 'pee in a bottle'! The relief was obvious, although the disposal of said bottle less than subtle – let your imagination fill in the gaps.

After a very welcome shower, it was back into the coach for another twenty minutes, weaving through more Friday evening traffic (with much emptier bladders) to take us to the presentation, but were we in for a shock when we got there.

It was held in the Presidential Palace, which is the second largest building in the world behind the Pentagon! If the event was held in England, the equivalent venue would be Buckingham Palace, believe me! And there were me and Chilly in our Union Jack shorts – love it!

It was wall to wall, floor to ceiling marble and crystal chandeliers. All the walls were adorned with huge oil paintings which were, doubtless, worth a small fortune.

The sin of it was that, on our journeys to and from the lake, we travelled on rutted, dusty tracks, past ramshackle huts and villages where the measure of a mans wealth was by the number of teeth in his head, and whether he owned a goat! This whole building was like a diamond encrusted lifeboat in a sea of poverty and squalor.

That said, we weren't there to judge the previous regime, and would surely not have even been in the country if it had still been in power.

The next couple of hours was surreal, especially when we were called up to get our prizes, with the British boys bringing the house down for us; cheers lads.

Now, just a small whinge, and one which Tim Paisley alluded to at the time, and that was the prizes. We didn't go out there for prizes, we just wanted to do as well as we could, but for some of the guys there, the last thing they needed was rods and reels. The American team had had to pay £1200 excess baggage to get to Romania, and their brilliant fifth place was going to cost them a further £200 - £300 to get the gear back. Much easier to take back 8000 euros, which they should have won up until two weeks before the competition, at which point Mr. Raduta decided that he wasn't going to give cash prizes, but he'd left it just late enough for anyone to make the decision to pull out. Chilly and I should have won 10000 euros, instead we won six rods and six reels, some dodgy alarms and a strange watch. For an hour or so we were, for the first time that week, a bit pissed off, then I turned into Delski Trotter and set up my own little market stall in a small corner of all that opulence, and pretty soon we were Romanian millionaires. We even managed to get rid of the dodgy alarms to some Macedonian guy back at the hotel. I nearly ripped his arm off when he offered me £100 for the two sets of four, but he was no mug because an hour later he came up with two pieces of paper and asked Chilly and I to put our signatures next to that of Tim Paisley and Steve Briggs. He then put one of each signed sheet into each box. Not such a plonker, Rodski!

The final evening in the hotel bar was just great. All those people from so many different countries all speaking a common language. The guy who had been Rodney to my Del boy was a Polish guy called Przemek Sydor, and he was well chuffed with his result. He had been fishing next to Chris Woodrow and Rene Hawkins who had given him a few boillies to try out. He'd put one out, fired out a few round it and a little later had bagged one of only two mirrors caught in the match, at 35lb he was over the moon and will love the Essex boys forever! I swapped my England shirt with a Croatian and also had to negotiate a suitable swap with a Romanian for my Union Jack shorts. At one point it seemed that I would get the very tight trousers off of his lovely wife but, in the end, all I got was a kiss on the cheek from her and he got my shorts, but it was fun trying!

And so to bed, at three in the morning, phoning Laney just in case he had forgotten that we had come fourth in the world! We were remarkably okay a few hours later and by midday were shaking Laney's hand at Heathrow airport and on our way home, tired but very happy.

And so it ended, but the effect on both of us had been more than we could ever have imagined, not least in the knowledge that we were "@&*(@** global!" as Chilly declared to me after being accosted by an American who actually knew his name (and mine)!

All of the people we met were so friendly, but then when you share a common interest, or obsession, it is so much easier to get on, no matter what language you speak. The fact that so many of them knew most of the English boys was a bit of a buzz, and also that they all had such great respect for English carp anglers. We met loads of people who we should have stayed in contact with but, as usual, we failed to keep that part of the bargain. I'd just like to say it was great to meet you all and I look forward to the next time more than I thought I would. There are, also, so many people who do so much preparation work for this sort of event, and who rarely get a mention, so a great big thanks to everyone who helped us get out there, enabled us to fish and stay comfortable, and fed and watered us whilst we sat out there enjoying ourselves; it was all hugely appreciated.

And finally – we went forth and came fourth, and that, as my great Para mate would say, is huge!

We collected our prize and the boys brought the house down

The peace and tranquility of Frimley

Chapter 18

Lights, Camera, Action

The Raduta trip took so much out of me that it was hard to actually get going again. Although my Mum had travelled up from Plymouth to stay with Lynn whilst I was away, I really needed to spend some quality time with her so, for a few days, I simply unwound and chilled out, but when Lynn's hospital visit was delayed, I started thinking about doing a bit of angling. Whilst I had been away, the Car Park had been fishing fairly well, producing three fish and, as much as I wanted to go to Frimley, I just couldn't help heading off to Yateley. I spent a few frustrating days chasing Arfur around in front of Trumptens and The Beech swim, but again my heart wasn't in it. Eventually, I packed my gear away and opened the gate, not knowing that this would be the last time I would do so with the Car Park Lake in mind. When I left the army I thought I would be able to give it the time it deserved, but life, as it normally does, had conspired to make that time limited. I had caught two of its magnificent residents, and although Heather will always remain my ultimate enigma, it still holds a special place in my heart.

The only other option was to go back to the peace and tranquillity of Frimley. Lynn's hospital appointment would come through soon enough, and I needed some time to sort my head out. There was also the fact that I would be fishing for a few big fat commons...all in all, just what the doctor ordered.

I don't think the fish here had ever seen the amount of bait that I was applying, and to that end, it had taken them by surprise. How long that situation would remain was unknown, but whilst it was working they were going to get it! Of course, much depends on putting it in the right area in the first place, so, with Heather firmly pushed to the back of my mind, I decided that it was Frimley or bust.

I arrived at Pit 3 and, unusually, I only spotted one fish, and with just that to go on I set up in a swim which covered that area. I then lay a veritable banquet before them, but for two nights the fish refused to be tempted, apart from several large bream. After returning my fourth slimy little devil at around one in the morning,

I set up in a swim that covered the area

I decided that enough was enough so I reeled in the rods. If they wouldn't tell me where to fish during the day then in all probability they would give their location away at night so I prowled around the lake for about four hours until, eventually, a fish crashed in the inky blackness. I was over the other side at the time, and as I hastily made my way back to my gear, I heard several more in the same area. It was now five o'clock, and there was no time like the present, so I moved my stuff the short distance down the lake.

The fish continued to show, and as they were so obviously in residence and also appeared to be feeding, there was little need to frighten them off by introducing a load of bait; I simply launched a couple of stiff link NRG pop-ups at the next two fish to show, and sat back with a brew. As the first light of day made its way wearily across the sky, the activity stopped as abruptly as it had begun. I left the rods for a while longer just in case the carp moved back into the area, but an hour later I was convinced the chance had gone. Keeping the disturbance to a minimum, I soon discovered a couple of likely looking spots and, two hours later, I was happy that they had been baited exactly how I wanted them. With the lines marked and in the clips, I paid a quick visit to the shops for some fresh supplies and, on my return, I was rather surprised to see what looked like a group of divers on the opposite bank. The mystery was solved when one of the RMC employees paid me a visit. He explained that the lake was supposed to be shut down for the day; someone had obviously removed the signs at the entrance.

I couldn't think for the life of me who could have done such a silly thing, and told him so, as convincingly as I possibly could!

Satisfied that I wasn't the perpetrator of the crime, he allowed me to keep on fishing, and wandered off. I was a bit worried about sticking a hook in one of them, so I decided to have a wonder round and see what was going on. I was tempted to take some bait round and ask them to scatter it over my spots, but as I was fishing when the lake was supposed to be shut, I didn't want to push it too far!

They were actually looking for a weapon that the army had lost, and their information indicated that it may be in one of the Frimley pits. I had a little giggle to myself at that; someone in the mob was in deep shit, that was for sure. As it happened, I knew a couple of the lads and wondered if they would do me a favour. They were working an area that I had never seen anyone fish, due to the fact that it has incredibly deep and particularly stinky silt, so I asked one of them to have a look at the silt and see if there were any harder areas. He came to the surface two or three times with a few handfuls, some of it thick and bursting with life; the area was marked down for further attention. Back in my swim, I positioned the hookbaits and waited for events to unfold. The night was fairly eventful with

There was a group of army divers on the far bank

commons of 21lb and 26lb, and the most glorious 25lb fully scaled. Business at home kept me from the lake for a couple of hours in the morning, and whilst I was away I couldn't help thinking about the size of the carp I was catching. Don't get me wrong here, I would have been a very sad man if I wasn't happy with the fish that I had already caught, it's just that I didn't seem to be getting amongst the larger carp, although I had seen them regularly in and around my baited areas. Back at the lake I decided to put both the hookbaits a few yards either side of the bait, not directly on it.

Then something strange happened. The left hand spot was very tight, so in an effort to ensure the rig landed exactly where I wanted it, I used the marker rod. With that in position, I lay my rod on the reeds, and as I turned, I caught a glimpse of two blokes in a swim on the other side of a bay, 50 yards to my right. One of them looked as if he was being attacked by a swarm of wasps, there was so much arm waving going on. Poor man! A couple of minutes later, the other guy, one of the bailiffs, appeared in my swim. We exchanged pleasantries and he informed me that I might get a bit of bother from matey next door because, apparently, he wanted to fish the area I was in. The bailiff had explained that the water was already being fished, but he wasn't sure if he had been understood. Anyway, as I wasn't doing anything wrong, I continued with my plan, then, a few minutes later, the fellow stormed into my swim.

One of Frimley's fully scaled stunners

"I want a word with you", he said, somewhat aggressively.

"Really? Not if you speak to me like that", I said.

"I have a bait right out there where you are casting your marker" he whined.

His inability to cast a very long way meant that he had towed his hookbaits out, via a remote controlled boat, to an area he could never have fished conventionally. I explained that the swim I was in covered that water. Now, as plain as that description of the situation may have been for a normal person, it was not good enough for him.

"You are scaring all the fish with your marker", he said.

I replied, "No I am not. If I am scaring fish then I am only doing so in 'my water'. OKAY?" At which point, things took a turn for the worse.

"It's not your water, it belongs to RMC".

This was starting to get a bit silly, I explained as best I could what the expression 'my water' meant, but matey boy was having none of it.

"What's your name", he demanded.

"What the hell has that got to do with anything?", I replied.

"I want to know your name". Desperate to get rid of the idiot, I told him.

"Ian Chillcott".

"Ah, that explains everything".

"Tell me", I said, "exactly what does that explain?"

I could hear his solitary brain cell working overtime on that one, but it failed to respond and he changed tack.

"You should have come round to me and asked where I was fishing".

"No", I said, "You should have come round and asked me where I was casting, since it is so obvious that this swim covers those spots".

"For that I apologise", he said.

"Great, now we seem to be getting somewhere, fella". I had spoken too soon.

"But my hookbait is out there and you are scaring all..."

"FRIGGIN HELL, SHUT UP YOU IDIOT" I growled.

Good heavens, give me strength. With the biggest scowl I could muster, I ordered him back to his swim to reel in the offending rod. I now had the right hump and, turning back to my rods, I refused to speak further. Any more of this and drastic action would be needed. I haven't seen him since, and hope I never do. Strange man!

Whilst I am on the subject of strange people, there was one other occurrence that worried me...well for a second or two anyway. A few days before this session, I had to go to Horton for a meeting with Viv Shears, and when I arrived he was in an animated conversation with one of the Kingsmead bailiffs. Someone had been out of order and it looked like they would have to remove him from the venue.

"Maybe I will have to ban him" he said, and turned to me.

"Talking of bans, it looks as if we will have to ban you as well, Chillcott".

Bloody hell, what had I done now? Unable to keep a straight face, he burst into fits of laughter. I keep lots of different baits in my car, in case I go somewhere else and need something a little different, and in amongst that bait were a couple of tins of tiger nuts. Some sad, sorry and spineless little maggot had taken photos of the back of my car and sent the pictures to Ian Welch at the RMC head office in an effort, I presume, to get me banned. Tigers are banned on Frimley, and that is precisely why they were in the car. Anyway, whoever the pitiful little git is, you gave everyone a good laugh, so please don't think you wasted your time completely! This, unfortunately, wasn't the last of this type of incident either, but it confirmed that I was getting things very right on Pit 3. I could only hope that Charlie's Mate agreed. As soon as the idiot had left me alone, I got a couple of hookbaits onto the spots, and put the kettle on. I also noticed that said idiot had packed up and gone home, I really hope it wasn't something I said! A short while later, I was staring longingly at my rods when one of them let out a single bleep, the bobbin moving almost imperceptibly toward the rod. I stood and made my way forward, glancing automatically toward the area of the hookbait when, halfway there, an absolute monster of a common leapt clear of the water, the line cracked out of the clip and the buzzer howled. Normally I am not too bad in these situations, but knowing exactly what was on the end had my knees knocking from the start. I have no idea how long I played that fish, but the battle raged on and on. Up and down the margins it chugged, but eventually the pressure took its toll and, at the first time of asking, it rolled into the net. I took a moment to compose myself, but soon got the fish on the mat, it was enormous and also the most perfect common I had ever seen. At 35lb I raised my head to the clouds and thanked who ever was listening up there for their help. A little while later I was holding up a stunning personal best common for the cameras. Now I was starting to get somewhere.

When everyone had departed, I realised I hadn't recast the rod, and with that done I was once again back in the ball game. Someone had very kindly left me a bottle of red wine, and as the evening closed in I raised a glass to big English commons, wherever they may be. In fact, I think I did that several times, as you do!

At first light I swang my legs off the bedchair to fire up the kettle, and whilst I waited for it to boil, the same rod tore into life. For some time I was just watching the spool empty of line, I couldn't do a thing with it. Again the fight was protracted, but time and pressure saved the day, and a large common ended up in the bottom of the net! This fish was a completely different shape to the other and with shaking hands I weighed her. At 32.02 I smiled for the camera and packed away.

Christmas was fast approaching and the action carried on as before and, although I didn't get any more of the really big fish that year, I was having so much fun that I didn't care. Just the way it should be. With the New Year kicking into gear I was obviously keen to reacquaint myself with the Frimley fish, but life was just about to engineer another small change in direction.

My first trip was going very well, with me managing to bag several fish up to 29lb, and as I was settling down for the second night, my phone chirped into life. I speak to Chris Ball a fair bit, so I wasn't surprised to see his name on the screen. We talked of many things, until he came to the point. Carp Fishing News and Angling Publications were putting together the first ten part TV series dedicated to carp fishing, and they wanted me to be part of the set up. Wow, little old me was going to be on the telly! I was chuffed to bits, but couldn't help thinking that they could have chosen a better time of year to do it. I literally had to drop every thing I was doing, and concentrate on this; if we were going to make this work then we

The most perfect common I had ever seen

With shaking hands I weighed her at 32.02

were going to have to catch some carp. Easier said than done. I also had the added distraction of Charlie's Mate, which had just been landed at a little over forty pounds for the first time. My whole carp fishing existence had revolved around a common of this size and now I was having to turn my attention elsewhere. Oh bugger!

And so it began.

"A winter carp for the cameras from a water you have never fished before", were my instructions. "Not too much to ask is it?"

Well yes actually, but there is nothing I like better than a challenge, and so we decided to head off to Linear Fisheries Oxlease Lake, on a nod and a wink from Roy Parsons. It had been doing the odd fish of late, so in for a penny and all that, I set off for Oxford wondering what the hell I had let myself in for. When I got there I picked Roy's brain some more, and after a good look around, set up in a plot that gave me a good amount of water to work in. I positioned everything with just one bite in mind, and by early evening I was feeling a little more confident as a few fish had showed in my part of the lake. Tim Paisley was down for the night, although not fishing, so it was good to listen to his plans for the filming. As we turned in, I said one final prayer to the carp gods and was soon in the land of Nod.

Three bleeps at 5.45 a.m. had me out of the bag and on the rod in seconds and before the line had even been taken from the clip I had the rod in hand and was playing the first carp of the series. Playing any carp is a bit nerve racking, but this was the first time I had ever done so with a TV series in mind. Soon enough, though, I had him in the net and it didn't look a bad one either. At 22.12 he was, at that moment, the best carp I had ever caught! With the rest of the day going off without a hitch, Tim asked me if I could do something the following week with my old mucker Adam Penning.

So it was that I found myself heading off into deepest, darkest Oxfordshire a few days later. With both of us now working for Drennan, we had access to a very private estate lake, and this is where we decided to do the next instalment of what had become known as 'Mission Impossible'.

Several fish up to 29lb

The water is set in an old Capability Brown estate, and a more beautiful place to spend some time fishing would be hard to imagine. Knowing the lake a lot better than me, I listened intently to Adam's advice, and so we set up in an area that he felt gave us the best chance - with no fish sightings it was all we could do. The weather was horrible; high pressure, cold, and most of the time it was hard to see the rod tips, so bad was the fog. We couldn't have the camera crew there at night, mainly because of the conditions, so if we were lucky enough to bag one then it would have to go into a sack until morning. During the evening we talked about the history of the fish in the lake, and I remarked that I would love to catch a carp I had seen him holding in an article. The fish was called Number One, because in the stocking records there is a small black and white picture of it with the number 1 written alongside. The conversation always got back to that fish, and I really couldn't get it off my mind.

At that moment in time, the best carp I had ever caught

The conditions could not have been worse

Now, I am not sure if Penning is frightened of the dark or not, but he had recently been to see a movie that had scared the life out of him. Every movement in the woods behind us was greeted with him saying, "What was that? What was that?" A little while later something landed with a bang on top of my bivvy and he nearly had heart failure. As I went to look, he even told me to be careful! It was the wing of a pigeon, and this almost caused him to have a fit.

Laugh, I nearly swallowed my tongue!

He had also been asking if I thought any of the trees would fall down in the night, which reminded me of a story that might either placate him or just tip him over the edge.

Many moons ago I had been part of a four-man patrol in the jungles of Brunei, and dead falls are an occupational hazard there. It wasn't surprising to see several hundred tons of Teak falling through the under growth. We had, as operational necessity dictated, put our hammocks up an hour after last light, and in the morning we would be packed away an hour before first light, and ready to move. The officer we had with us, well, we'll call him Captain Black, was prone to a bit of a lay-in and the three of us were almost ready to depart, when he eventually responded to our pleas to get up. We had moved away a little and were waiting for him in a small riverbed, and as he walked away from his hammock, scratching his nuts and yawning, an almighty 'Crack' had us looking his way. A few seconds later a massive tree smashed straight through the hammock he had been asleep in only seconds before. As calm as you like, he scratched his nose and turned.

"I say Gentlemen, shouldn't somebody have shouted 'TIMBER!'"

I really thought he was the coolest bloke I had ever met, but Adam looked as if he was going to be sick as he panned around him at the forbidding Giant Redwoods behind us. I was just about to relive another story when he suggested he tell me more about Number One. There is nothing better to shut me up than a story of a carp I want to catch, and over another bottle of wine I had just about convinced myself I was having it. So, with Numero Uno on my mind, I drifted off to sleep.

At around five in the morning I got a very slow drop back, and quickly lifted into the fish. I wasn't too sure at first because it felt for all the world like a tench but it soon woke up after that, and I was left in no doubt that a carp was on the end, Adam trotted up to lend a hand, and I needed it. There are no swims on the lake, and I was fishing my rods through some reeds but, not wanting to drag the fish through that lot, I waded out in my underpants until I was in open water. Adam launched the net out to me, and I prepared to scoop up the fish, the only trouble was, I was sinking rapidly into the silt, and if I wanted to land the damn thing then I would have to do it quickly. Rather unceremoniously, I reeled down hard and simply heaved it, amid a load of spray, into the net. The night was so dark, there was no way I could see what I had landed, so I collapsed the net and handed it all over to Adam. With the fish safe, I could concentrate on getting out myself, at which point I saw his head torch on, and a huge range of expletives rang out around the lake.

"You ain't going to believe this boy, but its Number One".

I truly believe to this day, that I willed that fish onto my hook, it was amazing. Quickly, we weighed him and sacked him up ready for the cameras arrival.

Time for tea, and lots of it! When I did retrieve my prize from the margin and opened the sack, my jaw nearly shattered into a million pieces as it hit the deck. He was stunning - one of the best looking carp I have ever had the pleasure to catch. The 'mission impossible' couldn't have gone any better, and I was looking forward to receiving my next set of orders, which would obviously self destruct in five seconds.

Thankfully, I was able to go back to Frimley and do a spot of fishing for myself over the next week or so. Evidently, there had been very little out since my last visit, so I hadn't missed much and I was looking forward to having an early morning chat with Charlie's Mate, but really I just wanted to catch something. I was daydreaming of big commons as I made my way to the lake, when the bloody car broke down. I should have sorted it out there and then, but as normal carp anglers do, I simply left it were it was, transferred my gear into a mates car then carried on to the lake.

"You ain't going to believe this boy, its Number One!"

Good angling! All I wanted to do was chill out, but I can never seem to do that until the rods are fishing as best as I can get them. Thankfully, two fish showed in the very swim that I had deposited my gear, so I didn't have to think too hard about location and, an hour later, I was happy.

Now, all that rushing around had got my system into overdrive and I was in desperate need of a 'shovel patrol'. The swim that I was in was ideally suited to this

Len got it all on film

task because just at the back of it is a small stream. It was a simple case of picking up my little entrenching tool, some paper, and leaping over onto the soft ground beyond. What followed was just about the most embarrassing thing that I have ever endured. I bet you guessed there would be a shit related story didn't you?

Anyway, off I went and, although I knew there would be no one around, I had a quick look just to make sure. After digging a hole, it was time to get on with the job in hand and, with the unload complete, including the paper work, I stood up and noticed three people standing staring at me, about 20 yards away. Armed with clipboards and rucksacks, I had no idea what they were there for, but I was wishing the ground would open up and swallow me. How embarrassing was that? All I could do was pull up my trousers, fill in my hole, then picking up my shovel, I raised a hand and shouted as loud as I could.

"Good morning!"

Once under cover I ran as fast as my somewhat embarrassed legs could carry me. What a shocker! I did my business under the cover of darkness from there on.

The session was a good indicator that I could still fish how I wanted to, and the bait was piled in. A double, a 26lb common and a very chunky fish of 30.02 made things complete and as soon as I could, I headed for home.

The very next day, Lynn got a call from the hospital; a bed was available and they would be operating straight away. Someone had unwittingly told her that I was due to do the final part of my 'mission impossible' thing the following week, and once again she was upset that I may not be able to do it. However, she has a very clever technique for such occasions and much of that is to do with her powers of recovery. The operation wasn't a big one, as far as she was concerned, but it did have far reaching ramifications. Everything went well and, after she had fluttered her baby blues at the consultants, I was asked to pick her up after only five days. Remarkable! She was already making a miraculous recovery; I could only hope that would continue. The trouble was, I wasn't about to be a part of that, because as we drove home she asked when I was heading off to Frimley to do the filming. At the time I wasn't sure, but two days later I found myself lugging my gear around Pit 3 on the look out for a carp or two. I could find no sign of the fish, so selected the swim that had produced the most carp of late, The Double Boards. Not the best location you will ever hear about, but I was happy. As per usual, all three rods were fished at the base of the exposed bar at about 80 yards, and a liberal scattering of bait was spread over all three. Time to put the house up, kettle on, and sit back and hope.

At the start of any session you are hoping for some action, praying that a big fish will come along, but with cameras inbound my hoping and praying became more intense. Around midnight I started to get the odd liner, some of them quite savage, and also hearing the odd fish crash out in the baited area meant confidence was high. It got a whole lot higher a while later when I landed the first fish of the night, a 16lb common. Four more fish followed that one, the biggest being 22lb, but unfortunately I was informed the camera crew could not get to me.

Great, all that effort and none of it was going to get on film. They did ring to say that they could be down first thing the following morning and that I should retain anything else I caught. The day was quiet and, after repositioning the hookbaits just before dark, I once again settled down to wait, but it wasn't until six in the morning that I was called into action. I quickly unhooked the 19lb common and got the rod back in position, and half an hour later I hooked what I hoped was a fish for the cameras. We battled away for a while before I scooped up a nice common of 25.02; now this one was going to get on the telly, so I secured him in a sack and waited for the crew to arrive. Sometime later we filmed the segment and the job, as they say, was a good 'un. I was tempted to go home, but with the lure of a winter thirty for the cameras, I stayed exactly where I was. Little did I know what was in store.

This chunky 30.02 common made things complete

Some time in the early hours I landed a 16lb common, and once returned to his home, I climbed back into my bed. A severe frost had developed and I was absolutely freezing. I could only have just dozed off, when a blinding take had me very much awake. The fish felt big and heavy, and it was some time before I could get it anywhere near the net. I had a sneaky suspicion, as it made its first roll, what it was but I dared not think about that and, after five more minutes charging up and down the margins, I managed to steer it into the net. I had no doubt that I had achieved the target and a 30lb common lay in the folds of my net. Scraping the thick ice off the unhooking mat I laid the beast on it, and she span the scales round to a healthy 32.04.

Light My Fire!

Once I secured her in the margins I climbed straight back into the bag and was back out of it within seconds, then, for the second time that morning, my arms were nearly pulled from their sockets. As with the previous fish, this one took an absolute age to bring to the net. Even in the darkness I could see it was big, but it wasn't until I grabbed my head torch that I could see exactly what I had landed - it was one of the few fully scaled fish that live in the lake. Shaking like a leaf, I managed to unhook her and prepare the scales and the more I looked at her the

Chris went into raptures, as I knew he would

more beautiful she became; weight was immaterial really. I settled on 30.02 and she came to rest in a sack alongside her mate. It was an hour later that I eventually got hold of Chris Ball and Len Gurd; they would be with me shortly.

I really couldn't believe what had just happened, and sat drinking tea watching the light fill the sky, whilst the icy cold of the night gave way to a warm and gloriously sunny day. I don't know about it shining on the righteous, but it was certainly beaming down on one very lucky carp angler. Just to put the icing on the cake, I landed a 24lb common a short while later, and my friends, Rick and Odd from Yateley, were on hand to lend some assistance. Both of the fish looked truly stunning in the winter sunshine, and Chris Ball went into raptures, as I knew he would. Eventually, I was left on my own and, after slowly packing up, I headed for the gate.

With all that out of the way, I could now concentrate on my own fishing, and a date with a rather large common.

The fish looked stunning in the winter sunshine

All was well at Frimley

Chapter 19

Goodbye Old Friend

With everything going so well at Frimley, I could see little point in changing anything. My only problem was that I felt no nearer to catching the big girl than I did when I started. Let's be honest here, there are so many carp in Pit 3 that it is rather hard to simply select the one I wanted to catch, and once the bait has been cast, it is something of a lottery as to which one picks it up. All the fishing here has to be done from recognised swims, so there was no chance of stalking, although some of the 'out of bounds' areas were a little bit of a grey area. That said, and much to everyone's annoyance who accused me of it, I never once fished or caught a carp from a restricted area. I hoped March 2003 would herald the start of the spring and the weather would improve, but if anything it got colder and many times I thought of reeling in as the cat ice formed in the margins. The chance of being cut off, and leaving the fish trailing tackle sickened me, but they wanted to eat whatever the weather, and who was I to disappoint them?

The situation with Lynn was not getting any better, we knew that she would soon be back in the operating theatre, and now Max was not well either. Once again, I felt like a juggler with all four balls in the air at one time. It was difficult to know what I should do for the best, so as ostrich like as ever, I tried to carry on as per normal. Whilst not nearly as important as the first two problems, I also had to contend with the dreaded tuffties. Word spreads around the tufted duck community as quickly as news on the carp fishing grapevine, and their numbers were increasing on a daily basis with the promise of free food. I had, by now, taken to doing all my baiting up after dark to ensure that the carp were getting as much of the bait as possible, I had also taken to placing my hookbaits some distance from the main baited areas. This tactic seemed to give them a little more longevity, it was also a tactic that was producing some of the bigger fish, so I wasn't too bothered about having to do it, and that is how I had set up on this occasion. I was concerned about the ice forming in the margins, maybe I should call it quits, and just as I contemplated reeling in, I received a very slow take. I let the fish roar around in the centre of the lake for as long as I could, because of the ice, but it soon became obvious that I would have to be a tad more inventive if I wanted to get it in the net. So off came the tracksuit bottoms and socks, and in I went. JEEZ, it was bloody freezing, but I strode out regardless, clearing the ice as I went. It wasn't long before I had cleared a path, and clambered back onto dry land. I couldn't feel my legs,

The Frimley carp fed whatever the conditions

and had to keep checking to see if they were still there! Rather more quickly than I would have liked, I bullied the common into the net, and thankfully the head bailiff wandered into my swim as I was trying to get my circulation going again. He took charge of things, and we eventually weighed and photographed the 28lb common. Once it was chugging off back into the lake, we sat down for tea...and lots of it! As we chatted, we couldn't help noticing how much the air temperature was warming up, maybe it wouldn't freeze after all? I went to sleep confident of more action and hopefully, not having to take another dip, that was until six in the morning, when once again I was in danger of getting frost bite. By the time I had sorted out the mid-twenty common, I finally convinced myself to go home, this was getting a bit ridiculous. Then the unthinkable happened.

I had been at home for a couple of days, and had just returned from taking Max for his walk. For some time, he had been having trouble with his breathing, and now it had finally taken its toll. He collapsed in the front garden, and it was sometime before I could get him in the house and onto his sofa. Now, I am sure that for some of you, a dog is just a dog, but Lynn and I have no children, and he had become such a massive part of our lives, much like a son. You may, therefore, understand our heartache a little better when I tell you he was my best friend, and had kept

I was once again in danger of getting frost bite!

Lynn company through all her illness related inactivity. He helped her around the house and into the garden, by always being at her side and, for Lynn, with a husband that was away so much, he was always the shoulder on which she could hold onto for support. There was also the not insignificant fact that I used to share with him all of my carp fishing secrets, and I am sure he was totally bored with me telling them to him. I had lost count of the times I discussed my thoughts on rigs and bait with him, when all he wanted to know was when he was getting his food, but it helped me to talk to him about it.

We had always said that we would not keep him alive just to satisfy our own selfish needs, and to that end, I talked at great length to the vets. He was so popular there that one of them just couldn't bring herself to come and do what needed to be done, but eventually, Max closed those big old eyes for the last time, in his own home.

Lynn and I have never suffered so much, and he has left a massive hole in our lives, one that will never be filled again. I was totally blown away by how so many people in the army and carp angling communities showed their sympathy and, for weeks after, we had every space in the living room taken up with sympathy cards. He had touched more than just Lynn and I with his passing.

For the fun, joy and wonderful memories he has left us with, I thank him. Gone, but not forgotten, old friend.

Adjusting to life without Max was going to be hard, but I just had to get on with it, not that I felt like doing that for a while. Lynn was determined that I should get out fishing, and back into some sort of rhythm, and although I went to the lake a couple of times, I couldn't get my head into gear. It was freezing up during the night and

staying that way through the days, and I didn't fancy fishing anyway. A week or so later, the weatherman promised that the forecast was set to change, with some serious stuff coming in from the Atlantic, big south westerlies and rain. Now if that didn't get me out, nothing would! That said, as I left the house the following morning, I did so with a heavy heart, this was going to be hard.

Gone but not forgotten old friend

As soon as I was able, I was once again set up in the Double Boards, with the predictable spread of bait at the base of the exposed bar. The wind picked up, the rain came and, for the first time in a long while, I was bursting with excitement and I wasn't about to be disappointed. Surprisingly, the first bite came at six the next morning, I say surprisingly, because the fish had been booming out over the bait all night. What did shock me was that it was an 18lb common, but this seemed to be the way every session kicked off. No sooner had I returned him, than one of the other rods screamed for my attention, but the damn thing fell off shortly after battle was joined. I took a few minutes to reposition all three rods, and was just putting the kettle on when I was called to arms once again. This fish fought more like a tuna than a carp, and it was an age before I could guide him into the net. On closer inspection, I wasn't surprised to see a rather large carp, and a mirror to boot! I weighed him at 29.14, and secured him in the net, as I had a mate coming down within the hour, and I really wanted a picture. Luckily, a bailiff came along a little later so he did the honours, the carp being identified as Spike, a rarely caught fish that hadn't been out for over two years. Frimley mirrors are highly sought after, and this was one of the finest.

The tufties appeared to be leaving me alone for now, so the following night I didn't put any more bait out, and hoped that the situation would remain the same. That said, I did have another one of natures most annoying creatures to contend with; a young swan had taken up residence on the lake, and was just about to cause me no end of problems. One thing that always amazes me about these birds is that they have actually survived the evolutionary process. Most animals get by because they have a brain, and are camouflaged to some extent, so can someone tell me why something that is white, and stupid in the extreme, has survived for so long? Anyway, this bloody thing took my lines out on three separate occasions, and each time I simply put the line in the

Spike, one of the rarely caught mirrors

Probably the most stupid animal on the planet!!

clips, then launched them back to the spots. The third time however, once the line was clipped up, I left them there and visited the off-licence. A bottle of their finest red was just the pick me up I needed, so with the rods back out, the white mutant got bored and took up residence on the far bank.

I awoke at first light, and the first order of business was to blame the swan for my fishless night, but I had only been awake for about an hour when one of the rods decided to put me out of my misery. An obviously large fish ploughed its way up the lake with me hanging on for grim death, and it was sometime before I had it heading in my direction. Steadily, I kept it moving, then carefully steered it into the net. Once weighed, at 33.12, I gave Nigel Sharp a ring, as he was working just up the road and we got some shots done. Interestingly, he said it was a fish he had never seen before, and he knows a thing or two about the place, which made the capture even more pleasing. All I could think about on the way home was Charlie's Mate, surely he would be mine soon? Mmmm...a common to equal Walkers fish, that is all I ever wanted.

While I was away from the lake, Nigel slipped into a swim across the pond from the one I was concentrating on, and landed himself that very carp! He had been after it for some time, and I was truly chuffed to bits for him. At 41.06, Charlie's Mate had obviously been making the most of the bait I had been chucking in, but when would my turn come? I really didn't want to stop putting the bait in, as it was obviously working so well, and not being able to do any stalking meant that I couldn't dictate proceedings at

I gave Nigel Sharpe a ring

all. So, I was just going to carry on going, same as before. In fact, in an effort to keep the fish feeding, I had taken to baiting up during the evenings that I wasn't fishing. There was little doubt that I would be helping others to catch, but they were so on the bait, and I wanted to keep it that way. Trouble was, on the very next trip, I saw and heard nothing for a couple of days and this worried me a little so, eventually, I drove over to Gold Valley Lakes and got

When would my time come?

myself a few pints of maggots; maybe they would get the carp in the feeding mood. Back at the lake, I Sticky Magged them into small balls, and fired them out onto the spots, then, with the rods back in position, I took a look in the small bay to my right. With the sun shining brightly, I thought that the fish might be taking advantage of it, and sure enough, as I peered through the reeds I spotted a carp; it was Charlie's Mate, and she looked huge. A while later, probably sixty of her friends had joined her at the tanning salon and I watched them for hours, until the heat of the day started to die off. It was then that they began to move out and, most pleasing of all, they were headed straight towards my baited area. The night was very quiet and still, which only accentuated the sound of a large fish crashing over my baits at one in the morning. Swinging my legs out of bed, I sat and watched as five more fish boomed out, and it wasn't long before the bites began. Five fish by first light had made my decision with the maggots a good one.

I mooched around for the day, but once again I could find nothing to fish for, although many of the carp had turned up in the bay. The traps were set, only this time I dispensed with the maggots because, as much as they had re-invigorated the area, I have always thought that their continued use tends to make the fishing more difficult; I wanted them eating boillies. I needn't have worried because the action kicked of as before, and several commons up to 26.12 made for another hectic night, but it was the last two fish that really make Frimley what it is.

Just before dawn, I stood and marvelled at the speed with which my spool was spinning, on and on the carp battled, and the harder I pulled, the more it pulled back. My arms ached for what seemed an eternity, but with some degree of difficulty, I managed to bundle it into the net. I laughed when I saw the size of his tail, little wonder the 29.02 common had fought so hard! A few minutes later I was doing exactly the same thing, but although the fight didn't last as long, the ferocity of its runs left me breathless. It was one of Frimley's rather unique mirrors and, at 27lb, he was definitely a bit of an animal.

You could be forgiven for thinking that all I had to do at Pit 3 was to cast a bait out and I would reel in a carp. Sometimes, it seemed that way to me, but what a series of captures fails to convey is the amount of hard work involved. For many years I fished with my friends, and baiting up and pooling information was something we all revelled in, the captures my friends made being greeted as if I had caught them myself, it was a tremendous time. Working closely with other soldiers had taught me that trust and camaraderie are vitally important aspects of success. Of course, that revolved around keeping people alive, but I was starting to miss fishing with my mates. Since leaving the army, our circumstances have changed

Another hectic night

and, having more time for fishing means that I can fish during the week, a time when Keith would inevitably be driving a desk at work. Reg had his young family to look after, and was starting out on an adventure that would keep him out of the country for long periods. Dave went after the carp he longed for, although his young family, and a change in his work situation, would soon knock that into a cocked hat, which all meant I was now fishing on my own. It's not that I am some kind of unsociable git, far from it, it is just the way things have turned out. There were a couple of good points that came from my solitary existence, and one of those was that I had no one to blame for any failures, but myself. Most importantly though, I could orchestrate things to the way I wanted them. Trouble was, the work load increased ten fold.

During my time in the army, I had achieved all I ever wanted to, and that was about as hard, physically and mentally, as it is possible to get. Now all I needed was to somehow transfer that will power to my fishing. It has meant that I have, on numerous occasions, pushed the boat out too far, at times when I should have been taking things a little easier, but I really can't help myself and if I am going to do something, then it has to be done to the best of my ability, or it just ain't getting

It was one of Frimley's rather unique mirrors

done. It is very much like every other aspect of life, generally, the more you put in the more you get out of it, and having thrown myself at every single one of life's opportunities, I was a dab hand at adapting my enthusiasm to anything I wished. That's why I know it is so important not to think that carp fishing is the sole reason for my existence. I have a life, and I want to live it. In saying that, when I am fishing, I want to get into it as much as I possibly can. I often hear some comments about the way I am on the bank, and much of that has to do with my military background. Having spent my life jumping out of aeroplanes, I had to have the ability to survive on the minimum of equipment, it stands to reason, therefore, that I can live on the bank without all the trappings of a camping holiday. I take as little as possible, because I believe lots of gear will hinder my ability to move, and be proactive. I also don't give much thought to hygiene either, after all, we are not on some kind of fashion parade, so what does it matter what I look like? I have, over the years, been several months without a proper wash, my only concession being cleaning my teeth with salt when ever possible, a military necessity. I am fully aware that carp fishing means a lot of different things to different people, but there is little good moaning if you don't put the effort in, in the first place, and having everything but the kitchen sink in your swim is a sure fire way of hindering you achieving your goals. And let's be honest here, some anglers that cart all the latest gear around are doing so because they think it makes them look good, but there is no doubt whatsoever, that the thing that makes you look good, is holding a big fat carp up for the cameras. Concentrating on the last few feet of your terminal tackle and where you put it, is the key to getting it right. Hard work is the only way to make a success of this game. Whether or not I am the hardest working is very debatable, but I believe I do enough to be able to look myself in the eye when I am shaving in the morning, although not when I am fishing, of course! There is a down side to being the kind of person I am, and that is boredom. Not with the fishing itself - I can sit

I had to have the ability to survive on the minimum of equipment

there for as long as it takes - but with the venues. I have never stayed long in any one place, preferring to keep moving around, because looking at the same old trees for years at a time would send me round the twist. That is why I change the places I am fishing so often, I may not have caught the fish I was after, but as long as I have had some success then I feel I have nothing to prove.

Which, in a round about way, brings me back to Frimley. I was starting to get bored, and although seriously looking for somewhere to be for the summer, I was totally under the spell of Charlie's Mate, so I knew that I would be back. It was nearly time to move on, though with the fishing going so well I was content to

Hard work is the only way to be successful

stay a while longer. In any case, I had enough distractions in my life to keep my mind occupied, it would be Frimley until the end of May, but where the hell was I going to go next?

With that thought swimming around in my brain, I continued to enjoy myself, although it has to be said, the fishing started to slow up for a while. The area that I had been concentrating on was coming under increasing pressure as the spring ticket holders arrived. I really can't blame them for wanting to be in the Double Boards, it had been producing the goods for me, but by then, I think it had gone

beyond its best. As the carp had moved on, I set out to find them, and even though the fishing wasn't that good through the early part of the spring, it was fun because of the proactive nature of moving around.

Due, I think, to our success at the Romanian World Cup, Keith and I had been invited to the World Carp Classic at Armance. Once again, we would be part of the Angling Publications team, supported most magnificently by Fox and Mainline.

I continued to enjoy myself

Rather pleasingly, the team was bolstered by Laney and Keith's son, Vince, so if the fishing was pants, we were at least guaranteed to have a great social. As it turned out, the former was the case. I have little time for match fishing for carp, I much prefer the 'me versus the carp' way, that said, these big world events are such a good laugh, and the pre-match drinking is legendary, what with all the different nationalities there. Anyway, late in April the four of us set out for France. Remarkably, the journey went without a hitch, apart from Dave getting the nozzle of the petrol pump stuck in Keith's car. Despite the laboured efforts of four grown men, we could not get it out and, in the end, the garage owner, a very frail lady, sorted it out in seconds, much to our embarrassment. An hour later we were settling down to a giant carp party, which made the draw the following morning a very subdued affair. Keith and I eventually drew a swim, which both of us knew was a

no hoper. That didn't stop us trying, but we could tell it wasn't to be, and neither was it for the vast majority of the field. So few carp were caught that I really couldn't see the point of the whole thing, mind you, the organiser made a fortune, and at the end of the day, I think that is all that mattered to him. I had one other worry, and that was whilst I was away, Lynn had been taken into hospital, so all I wanted to do was get home. Thankfully, the day arrived and as soon as we were able, we sped out of the gates and headed for good old Blighty. I won't be doing another one of those in a hurry, that's for sure!

Back at Frimley, I reckoned I had only a couple more sessions left in me before

The draw at Armance, but I won't be doing that again in a hurry

Avez vous un brain cell?

I would turn my back on the lake for a while. I spent a few hours just having a stroll around, and reflecting on what had gone on over the past few months. Life without Max was a depressing place to be, and as hard as I tried not to think about it, even going home, which I normally relish, was tainted by not being knocked down by an eleven and a half stone Great Dane as I came through the door. More than ever, I tried to keep Lynn busy when I wasn't fishing, there can be little doubt that the loss of her soul mate had affected her in a different way than it had me. One thing that did bring a smile to my face was that, in the depths of winter, I had Frimley almost completely to myself during the week and I began to relish those long periods when I might not see anyone for a day or two. The fishing, although beyond my wildest dreams, was secondary to the fact that I had a tranquil pit, full of the most stunning carp I have ever had the pleasure of catching, all to myself. The warmer weather was drawing a lot more anglers out of their winter hibernation, and for the past few weeks I was never really on my own. Oh, for some frost and cat ice once again! Still, ever was it thus, and I was a bit surprised not to have caught one of the three big commons in the pit but, unfortunately, that is just the way it goes sometimes. The statistics of my time there made for some pretty impressive reading, but that is a personal thing, and I won't bore you with them here, and so, with the reminiscing over, I decided it was time to catch a carp. Unfortunately, the fish refused to give the game away and I had to make my best guess, and any swim is as good as the next when you are doing that so, with three rods out doing the business, I tried to settle down. That was never really going to happen, because until I am completely happy, I find it impossible to rest. To that end, I stayed up all night waiting for the carp to tell me if I should move or not and it wasn't until 0230 that I heard a fish crash out so, grabbing my cigarettes and a bucket, I legged it down to the next swim. I sat there for a good thirty minutes and was just about to go back to my plot, when another showed. And then another and another and, for a while, there seemed to be one in the air every minute or so. With nothing in front of my rods, I quickly reeled in and moved the short distance, and with the fish so obviously in residence, I cast three hookbaits to the areas of most activity.

Completely knackered, I collapsed onto my bedchair and crashed out but I had been asleep for the grand total of fifteen minutes, when a small common had me scrambling around in a bit of a panic. I slipped the little rascal back and climbed into bed once again, not opening my eyes until a couple of hours after first light. With nothing moving, I made a quick trip to the shops and returned to lay a feast before the carp and with that little chore out of the way, I sat back with a brew and waited. It wasn't until the early hours that I was awoken by a take and, in short order, I landed three commons, the biggest of which was 23lb. I retained that fish in the net for a couple of self take pics and was just sorting the rod out, when one of the others blistered off. Although not spectacular, the fight was dogged, and for some time we did battle but, having only one net with me, I had to try and get the 23 out of the net, which I eventually did with some difficulty. With the net now being far easier to manoeuvre, I quickly scooped up my prize. Thankfully one of the

I was happy with that!

bailiffs, Gary, arrived and we recorded a weight of 34.02. He actually wanted me to weigh it again because the fish looked so much bigger, but I really wasn't that bothered. At the time, this was probably the fifth biggest fish in the lake, and I was happy with that.

I did have one more session on Pit 3, landing a couple more of her stunning fish, but for now, I knew my time was done for a while. Along with the restrictions life had put on me, I really could not have been happier. There was one last thing to do before I made a decision about the future, and that was a junior event organised by RMC at the Blue Pool near Reading. I really do enjoy these sort of things, and at the very least I am able to put something back into the sport that I love so much. I shared this event with a young lad who went by the name of Kyle Spires, and we had the most marvellous time catching plenty of carp. Something else it gave me the chance to do was to have a good chat with my friend, Viv Shears, and whilst we chatted, he brought me up to speed with things at Horton. Not having taken much interest in the place for some time, I was very interested to hear how the stockies had thrived in the lake. Of course, we talked about the originals, and Shoulders was discussed at great length. It had been six years since I had cast a line there, maybe now was the time to start my ultimate quest for the mighty beast. I spent the rest of the month thinking about him, and by June 1st, I was sure I had found a home for the summer.

Come on Shoulders, light my fire. I needed something because, of late, the flames had been somewhat subdued by the loss of my greatest friend, Max.

We had the most marvellous time

I had been thinking long and hard about Horton

Chapter 20

Back to the Future

Along with Horton, I had been thinking long and hard about the Car Park Lake. Although I hadn't done as much time there as I would have liked, I really couldn't see me fishing there again. It truly is a special place, and to everyone I fished there with, thanks for the memories.

For me, though, life is far too short to be sitting on the same lakes year after year, and having had the massive restrictions that army life has on an angler, I wanted to fish as many waters as I could, given that I now had infinitely more time at my disposal. It wasn't until the night before the off that I eventually made up my mind to go to Horton. I had not fished there since the 1996/1997 season, and many people were quite surprised that I had decided to fish there once again, some even believing that I had caught all the big ones before (I wish!). It really is a different place now, some of the great history fish still swim in its waters, and the recent introductions were piling on the weight. The old juices were starting to flow, and I hastily threw some gear together for the start, the next day. Horton and the quest for Shoulders it would be then!

Of course, it just wasn't about him either, there were many other fish that I would desperately love to catch. The Parrot, the Thorpe Park common, Tetley's common, the Wood Carving and the Dumpy Mirror were just some of the originals that still carry the flag for their sadly-missed brothers and sisters. There were also the Fishers Pond fish that have thrived in the wonderfully rich environment that Horton offers, and with many of those now fast approaching mid-thirties, they could hardly be classed as stockies any more. So we drew for swims, both Viv and I came out late, and we settled on two of the more unpopular swims. As we set off with our gear I noticed that

Welcome back!

the Weedy Bay was empty and, being one of my favourite areas a few years back, I couldn't help wondering if I should be moving in there. I pushed the thought to the back of my mind, I was here for a bit of a social with my friend, sadly something we do too little of. The lake itself had matured a hell of a lot since I last fished there, and looked absolutely wonderful in its fine summer livery, however, it was what was below the surface that was just about to shock me. When I had last cast a marker float out here, it was very often the case that you never got it back; the weed back then was incredibly dense all over the lake.

I made my first cast, a long one, because there was no one fishing opposite, and slowly reeled it in. It did not pick up a single strand of weed, and the subsequent twelve casts were met with the same result, which I found odd. Weed is not everyone's cup of tea, but I absolutely love the stuff; the more the merrier! I felt a little confused, I had geared myself up to be fishing in the holes in the weed and setting subtle little traps. Without weed, the fishing can become so 'spotty' at times, and it takes a while to find the areas that the fish are willing to feed on. There was nothing I could do but adjust to the conditions, for now though, I was just content to have the rods out and soak up the atmosphere.

The night was uneventful, and I was up and about early, looking for signs of carp, and I didn't have to look too far because many of the fish were bang in front of me!

Trouble was, they were on the surface about 16ft above my hookbaits. While I was searching the bivvy for my mixers, Julie, Viv's girlfriend was making her way up to us with an offer of some breakfast and, en route, she had been waylaid by a very agitated Derek Rance. For those of you that don't know, Derek is deaf and dumb, but this has never hindered him when it comes to catching carp. He had indicated to Julie that he had landed a carp, but was unsure which one. I didn't even know he was on the pond, but he had moved into the Weedy Bay late the previous evening, so I trotted down to him and there in the bottom of his net was the Parrot. As you would expect he was chuffed to bits, and I managed, somehow, to sort things out.

She weighed 41.06 and behaved very well for the pictures and, as I made my way back to my swim, I ruefully shook my head, what might have been if I had followed my gut feeling? That's the way it goes sometimes, you just have

What might have been?

to get on with it. My mood was lifted a little by the sight of dozens of carp in my swim, lots of them grass carp, but there were a few mirrors there too and, although Viv and I managed to get the odd one taking mixers, it just wouldn't happen. One thing that may surprise some people was that an hour after her return, the Parrot turned up in front of us, and in her own peculiar way, started to slurp the odd mixer. It is very often the case that, when these big girls want to feed, even a capture won't put them off their stride. Handled with the minimum of fuss, she had not been put off by her brief visit to the bank. Strange, but true.

When the session ended, I was determined to return as soon as I could, and although I hadn't been sure how I would feel about fishing the lake again, I had really enjoyed myself. The next time, though, I vowed to get myself on the score sheet. I had a home for the summer.

After a short sabbatical with my parents in Plymouth, I returned to Horton fully refreshed and ready to do battle. Word on the street was that particles, in all their various forms, had dominated the fishing the year before, and everyone was now piling them in, hoping for a repeat performance. While I would have been a fool not to get on the band wagon, I was determined to include my Active 8 boillies and Response pellets into any mix that I was using. On my arrival, I was a bit disappointed to see the lake was still suffering from the start of season rush, there

really weren't that many options, but I set off for a good look around. It's naughty, I know, but I had soon put a little bit of kit in three swims that took my fancy, and as there was no one else on the move, it didn't seem too bad. After a few minutes deliberation, I had narrowed it down to one but, when I got back to the lodge, my phone rang and I sat on the bench to take the call. That lasted about five seconds, because as I said hello a big fish crashed out in front of the Spindly Tree.

Phone call terminated, kit loaded up and I was round there before you could say 'leaping carp'. The first thing on arrival was to sort a couple of rods out, the two Active 8 pop-ups from last week still seemed to be okay, and just as I finished checking their buoyancy, a carp broke the surface 30 yards out. One of the rods was hastily dispatched into the rings it had left, when, as if by magic, another one showed 20 yards to the right, so, with both rods sorted, I slackened off the line and lay them on the

Line slackened – rods on deck

At 22.08 he made an excellent start to the campaign

deck. A cup of tea was in order, and it was while I was brewing up the second, that I heard a strange sound and, as I span round, I could see one of the spools was a blur. I was on the rod immediately, and for the first time in six years I was connected to a Horton carp. I probably took things far too carefully, because it took an age to get it into the net, but at 22.08 he made an excellent start to my campaign. I repositioned the rods and scattered a dozen boillies in the general area, confidence was high, to say the least, but it wasn't until the following afternoon that I got another chance.

I had a few people in my swim at the time, when I received what looked like a big liner. It did the same thing a few minutes later, only this time the bobbin held up tight to the rod. Whatever it was, was definitely on, and I told the gathered masses that it was probably a bream. I changed my mind quickly when it sped off to my right at high speed.

"Grass carp," I declared. Then, when I felt a little head shaking, I convinced myself it was a tench. Thankfully, it popped up just off the marginal trees and I could see that it was indeed a carp, and a good one at that. With a little more pressure from me, I guided the fish into the net being manned by one of the on lookers. On closer inspection I realised that it was the Dumpy mirror and, at number five on my Horton hit list, I was rather blown away. She span the scales round to 33.06, an all time high, and with a couple of extra cameramen on the case, she was soon back in her home. Now we were cooking!

When I was fishing here before, two fish in a week would have been a right result, but what I didn't comprehend at the time was just how productive Horton could be. Content with what I had caught, I set about fishing a couple of other swims, a bit of homework for the future and, while on my travels, Barry Davis moved into the swim I had vacated and helped himself to five more fish. It was a valuable lesson, and a mistake I would try desperately not to repeat. I didn't catch anything else that session, and by the time I returned there had been a few more fish out, including Shoulders. It was hard for me to get my head around how many fish were being caught, this was taking some getting used to, and I must have done five laps of the lake before I settled in a swim called the Lookout. The occupant was just moving out, he had caught nothing, but as the wind was about to change and come charging up this end of the lake, I hoped the fish would move with it, if they did, then I would be waiting for them. The session turned into a very frustrating time, the wind took a little longer than anticipated, but by day three my longed for easterly arrived, and things started to look a bit better. Early the next morning I was awake and looking, but by eight o'clock I got that horrible feeling that nothing was going to happen, so popped round to the next swim and shared a brew with Paul Maulder. We chatted for a while until I started getting the odd liner, time to get back and hover over my rods. For two hours I watched carp after carp head and shoulder

Number five on my Horton hit list

over the baits, and all the time I was getting these strange lifts on my bobbins. I couldn't understand why I hadn't got a bite, then all became clear later, once the activity stopped, and I swung the first rig to hand. My heart sank, I had heard of it happening to others, but never to me. There, neatly embedded in my lead core, was my little size 10 hook. Oh shit, bollocks and bugger!! I trudged down to the lodge for some supplies, which gave me the chance to get my head together. By the time I had returned to the swim and topped the spots up, I was more determined than ever, I just hoped I wouldn't have to wait until the following morning to get my revenge.

With everything sorted I once again shared a brew with Paul, and although the poor lad had to listen to my tides of woe, it really is only another carp angler that can understand these things. Anyway, he made all the right noises, and I felt a little better as I went back to my plot. I hadn't been there a minute before the bobbin lifted a fraction, and did the same thing a few seconds later, surely I couldn't be that unlucky again? Eventually it lifted and held up, that would do for me and, as I raised the rod, the satisfying thump of a carp was transmitted down the line. Although not a spectacular fight, I had to keep the fish at range. I wanted it to be too tired to take advantage of the stringy, grass like weed that was flourishing in the margins. All went to plan and with Paul manning the net, I guided the fish in. It was a common, and a good 'un to boot, so I bit through the line and prepared the mat, sling, scales and of course, the camera. A stunning common called Pimple was held up for the snappers, and one very happy carp angler smiled over the top of her chestnut shoulders. She is one of Horton's old guard, and nearly as old as me, and although I would never suggest that carp fishing owes me anything, I felt that I truly

I felt I truly deserved this fish, Pimple 32.08

deserved that fish. I packed up the following morning, desperately thinking how I could get back in double quick time.

Two days later found me prowling the banks, but I didn't have to go too far, as a couple of fish showed in front of One Up, so, securing the swim with my bucket, I now had one hour for a leisurely stroll around the lake. Nothing else took my fancy, so I quickly got my gear from the car and, as I was not exactly familiar with this swim, I spent a fair amount of time mapping things out with the marker. One spot was horribly obvious, the sort of area I try to avoid normally, however, of late it had been producing fish; I would have been foolish not to have a bait there, but I was looking for something a little more subtle for the other rod. Much of the lakebed was covered in a very dark, almost black silkweed, and although it looked uninviting, it did hold a lot of natural food, but, after a while, I found

It took me six hours to empty the buckets

a small strip of silt that was slightly less 'choddy' than the surrounding area - just what I was looking for. The usual particle and boillie mix was spodded out, all 25kg of it, and it took me six hours to empty the buckets! I was absolutely knackered, and whilst I would have loved to sit back and will Shoulders onto my hook, I couldn't. I have to wonder, sometimes, why some people go fishing at all; their actions defy belief at times. I couldn't believe it when the bloke opposite stood at the front of his swim and launched a marker three times at my spots, then every hour or so he would stand up and attempt to do the same thing again. It was only because I was standing by my rods that he didn't. Once he had spotted me, though, he threw his rod down, and amidst much ape like arm waving, retired to his bivvy. This went on for thirty six hours and culminated in him rising at 0805 and, with fish showing over my areas, he would then cast his marker three more times. With the manoeuvre complete, he simply leant the marker up against a tree and retired back to his bed. Charming!! Now I don't go fishing for a punch-up, I go because I love it, and I didn't want to march around there and front him up because I knew what would happen. There was also little point in shouting because he would not have been able to hear me, so I waited for a bailiff to go round and tell him what the score was. I had no further bother, but I now know why this fellow gets in such a mess wherever he angles!

With the swim now devoid of any activity at all, I topped up the spots with a little more bait, but couldn't help thinking that any chance I had may have been ruined. Come the evening I was wondering if it wouldn't be a good idea to move, the lake wasn't that busy, and with a few hours of light left I had plenty of time. Then, as I was actually making my way to the rods to reel them in, I got a rather twitchy bream-like bite. Not wanting to take any chances I lifted into what ever it was and, at first, all I could feel was a very heavy weight - there was no sign of life, so I just kept on pumping it all towards me. I was sure that at any moment a bream, covered in a ton of silkweed, would pop to the surface. You will understand, therefore, my surprise at seeing a very long scaley flank break the surface. Oh Lordy! I remember Keith saying, when I told him I was making a return to Horton, that I would be doing a bit of chub fishing. I had assured him, if I wanted to do that I would head off down the river, from which you may have guessed that a grass carp was not high on my agenda of fish to catch. Be that as it may, I was now attached to one that was at least four feet long. It was just a case of guiding it into the net, at which point I expected it to go mad, but even the mesh on its flanks didn't seem to register with this one. Which was a good job really, because I have no idea how I would have handled this long, fully scaled snake if it had. At 38lb it was, at the time, the third biggest one ever caught, and I must admit to being very impressed with the way it looked. Thankfully, it swam off strongly as I returned it so, all in all, a rather unique experience, and then, of course, I smiled and waved across the lake to my would-be antagonist, and put some more bait out before settling down for the night.

Waking at four in the morning, I felt totally refreshed; there was the odd bit of activity in the area, which steadily increased as time went by so I was a little surprised that I'd had no action by eight o'clock, but I need not have worried as, soon after

A fully scaled snake of 38lb

that, the rod on the subtle spot burst into life. A lively battle ensued until I scooped up one of the Fishers Pond fish; at 26lb he made a nice start to the day, and I couldn't resist another little wave and a smile at matey boy across the pond.

From his gibbon like reaction, I don't think he was that impressed! With the rod quickly back in the ball game, I didn't get any time to dwell on my success, as the other rod roared off. There was little doubt that this was a better fish, slow and hard it fought all the way into the margins, where the stringy weed caused me a few problems, but after some nifty rod work I had a rather large and dark mirror rolling on the surface, and recognised him straight away; it was another of Horton's historic originals, Black Tail. As much as the stock fish would undoubtedly be the future, it was these fish that I was here to catch.

I was so excited I nearly spontaneously combusted on the spot! She looked truly magnificent, all 32.08 of her, as I held her up for the attendant cameras. A very special fish and a very special moment. Try as I may, I didn't get any more action, and the following morning I happily packed everything away, not forgetting to give matey boy one last wave of course!

With things going so incredibly well, the last thing I wanted was more distractions, but I had promised to do another junior fish-in at the Blue Pool for RMC, and that is where I was heading, though once the event was over, I would be straight back to Horton. I spent two fantastic days in the company of young Jake Galbraith, and we caught a cart load of fish on zigs. A top weekend, but as soon as it was done,

She looked truly magnificent

A top weekend

I was racing up the M4 dreaming of Shoulders and all his mates. It was one of those journeys that always bolsters my confidence. No traffic jams, no red lights and most remarkable for me, no getting lost! All in all, a very good start to the session, and with a spring in my step I set out for a lap of the lake, bucket in hand. The lodge end was packed out, with all that pressure it was the last place I wanted to be. As I arrived at the far end, towards the Dog Bay, I spotted one other angler, which was more like it, and I settled on the Shoulders swim, probably my favourite on the lake. Knowing that the horrible black weed was home to any amount of natural food, I was looking for areas that it was thickest, and once found, I set out a feast fit for a forty pounder. A mixture of particles with crushed and whole boillies were delivered with the spod, and three hours later I was happy. I got even happier half an hour later when the wind decided to change, I now had a lovely easterly pumping into my area. All that was needed now was a big fat mirror to complete the picture.

I was angling well, everything felt right, kettle on...come on Shoulders!

An uneventful night was followed by an equally uneventful morning, that was until one of the rods ripped off out of the blue. All was going well, but once again the stringy marginal weed was going to be a problem. Thankfully, Colin, who was fishing in the Lookout swim to my right, came to my rescue. We both had to strip off and go after the fish, which he somehow managed to bundle into the net. Top man! I always get a bit twitchy when I think a fish weighs 30lb exactly, so I made the call of 29.15, but Del had arrived and wanted an accurate weight and he was adamant that it was 30lb on the nose. Oh well, if he was happy then so was I, and with that, the Little Peach and I posed in the morning

I set out a feast fit for a forty pounder

The Little Peach at 30lb exactly

sunshine; what a good start to the proceedings! The day was turning out to be very hot indeed, and after topping up the spots I sat in the shade to cool off. It wasn't until the following morning that I was once again called into action but, this time, however, the marginal weed claimed its first casualty. The line had become encrusted with the black horrible stuff, and I was unable to apply enough pressure to get it to the net. Swearing and cursing, I repositioned the rods and waited.

I was just making myself a brew when a friend of mine, Odd, arrived from Yateley, and then the heavens opened. As we cowered in my bivvy supping a cup of tea, one of the bobbins pulled up tight then, in the blink of an eye, the line cracked from the clip and the buzzer howled. I slipped my way to the rods and, somewhat unsteadily, battle was joined. I had convinced myself that it was a small fish towing lots of weed around, until the leadcore cleared the water at about 20 yards to reveal that there was no weed - this was a bit of a lump.

Things got increasingly frantic from then on, as I coaxed the fish toward the problematic ribbon weed, at which point I jumped into the water to get a better angle, and the fish surfaced. It was then that I knew which fish I was connected to. Odd was just about to join me with the net, but there was no time for that.

"Throw me the friggin net, throw it", was all I could shout, which Odd duly did.

I was at full stretch and, inch by inch, I drew the Parrot toward the spreader block until, after what seemed an eternity, she was in and I peered down on the most fantastically ugly carp in the world! Being one of the most recognisable carp on the planet, she formed a huge part of our angling history, I just couldn't believe I had actually caught her.

LIGHT MY FIRE!!

Light My Fire!

I spent the next few minutes running around like a headless chicken, until I calmed down enough to sort things out. I could have quite happily had our picture taken and released her back to her home, but someone suggested we had better find out what she weighed, and so it was, that 41lb of pure ugliness and a not dissimilar angler posed for the battery of photographers. She didn't make things easy for me on the mat, but with enough pictures to sink a battle ship, I slipped her back in the pond.

The most fantastically ugly carp in the world

The World needed to know, so I set about my mobile phone with a vengeance!

I spent the night in a complete daze, I tried to sleep but it was impossible, and found myself walking up and down the banks muttering that I had caught the Parrot, and I never thought I would be able to say that! By morning it looked as if the fish had disappeared, so if they weren't in front of me, then I would have to go and find them. I arrived, after some time, in the RIP corner and there at my feet were about 25 carp, 30 minutes later and my gear was there too. I spent a while watching the carp mooching in and around the reeds, before setting a couple of little traps, but by three in the morning I was convinced they were no longer there. Grabbing my marker float I set off, stopping in the odd swim to do a little homework, but by the time I arrived in the Dog Bay I had seen nothing, so sat myself down and had a smoke.

Just as I was getting up, a movement caught my eye in front of the Gate swim, directly opposite, then a minute or so later I spotted the head of a carp quietly break the surface close in. That, as they say, would do for me, and although the area was fairly busy, that swim was free so I belted round there with my gear.

I found them in the R.I.P. corner

The Shoulders swim, as you would imagine, had been quickly occupied as soon as I left it, but as yet the guy had had nothing. I sat quietly and surveyed the area in which I had seen the fish, two more showing by way of confirmation, and soon enough I was looking for a couple of spots for a hookbait. Both rods were fished no more than two yards from the bank, and both were baited with about ten grains of hemp, and a couple of crushed boillies. They were obviously here and feeding, so there was little need to go mad.

I set up as far back from the water as possible, and settled down to wait then, later that night, I found myself sitting bolt upright on my bedchair and quickly looked at my watch. It was 0350 and I had the most amazing feeling that something quite special was just about to happen, a feeling that was so overpowering I struggled to put the kettle on. The tips of the rods were out of sight, the line was as slack as it was possible to be and with no bobbins on the line, the take, when it came a few minutes later, simply flew from the clip. With great care I battled away with the fish. The runs were savage and long, which meant that it was a while before I had it anywhere near the bank but, due to the marginal weed, the only option was to get in the water again, and soon enough I had drawn the fish into my net. I was a little surprised, on looking in the net in the half-light of dawn, to see what appeared to be a mid-twenty common, but it wasn't until I peeled back a bit more of the mesh that a further 18 inches of rather large common carp came into view.

Bloody hell, Chilly boy, what have you got here?

With the fish resting safely in the bottom of the net, I ran the short distance to wake Ollie, who was fishing on Kingsmead directly behind me. This may seem a little strange, but while I was playing this fish, I had spotted three fish top over the spots in front of the Shoulders swim and, knowing that the guy who was there was leaving that day, I asked Ollie to man the net, then ran up and put my bucket behind his bivvy. The swim was secured for a move later that day. Good angling, or so I hoped. Quickly, we sorted the fish out and unbelievably, another one of my dreams was being held up for the cameras.

I held up another of my dreams for the camera

At 37.12, the Thorpe Park Common is one of the best looking commons in the land and I shook my head in wonderment as I returned her. I never thought I would be able to say I had caught this fish either...but I had!

By mid-afternoon I was all set up where the session had begun, back in the Shoulders swim, and Viv had moved into the swim I had just vacated. I then spent the evening boring him with my stories, but it was just great to share the moment with someone who could really understand what those fish had meant to me. Knowing the spots, I had got everything sorted with the minimum of disturbance. I was hopeful, of course, but I didn't believe it could get any better than that - well, not until 0800 the following morning, that is.

Viv and I were sharing the first brew of the day, and as I was recounting more stories for him, out of the blue one of my rods ripped off. The fight was unspectacular, and soon Viv was holding my prize in the net, but all I could think of was getting a rod back onto the spot, as two carp had showed whilst I was playing the fish. Leaving Viv in charge, I reeled in the other rod and launched it at the spot, landing it exactly where I wanted it to, and I slackened off the line. A short while later I was holding a 26lb mirror up to have his picture taken and had only just returned him, when the re-cast rod was away. This one felt a little better, deep and hard, the carp fought for what seemed like an age, and once again it got caught up in the stringy weed, at which point Viv simply marched out with the net, and scooped everything up. I couldn't quite place him at first, but Viv knew it was the Boxer, another of Horton's stunning jewels. I had caught this fish once before at the end of the

96/97 season, in fact he was the only one of the bigger fish in the lake that I had landed after the fish kill, but I was not in the least disappointed with this recapture, in fact I could not have been happier. The morning sunshine bounced off of his scaly flanks as Viv took the pictures, and at 32.06 he was the most fitting end to one of the most memorable sessions of my life.

A fitting end to a memorable session

Lynn knew exactly what the capture of the Parrot would mean to me, and so, along with a couple of friends, had decked the bungalow out with balloons and congratulation banners. Crazy kid! She could also tell what was on my mind, and without me asking, told me to get back once I had scrubbed up. I would be little good for anything else...I was on fire!

Thirty six hours later I was back at the lake, and as soon as I had skidded to a halt in the carp park, I grabbed a bucket and set off for a tour of the pond. I didn't get very far before I saw a fish show about 60 yards out from a swim called One Up. Not surprisingly, everyone was up the other end, where I had caught the fish the week before, so I was able to move my gear in undetected. The south-westerly wind was increasing in strength and the swim really did look the kiddie and, as nothing more showed, I decided to get to work. I wanted to try one of the more obvious spots, because it had done a couple of fish for me before, however, I needed something a little different for the other rod. A small silty strip at about 60 yards fitted the bill nicely, and then I started with the bait.

Some may think it crazy to go putting 40lb of bait in, but it was a tactic that was working so well. All the fashionable talk was of using little traps and just fishing for a bite, well, fashion has never caught me anything, and I was going to do it my way. Along with a couple of other guys, we had caught the lion's share of the carp this year. A few hours later I was knackered, but happy, and there was no doubt in my mind that one, or both, of the traps would be sprung by morning.

I drifted off to sleep with the patter of rain on my bivvy, and I must have needed that sleep, because I didn't wake until 0700 in the morning, and by nine I was

scratching my head because of the lack of action. Surely the fish would have moved on this wind?

They had, and thirty minutes later I was playing the first fish of the day, which, at 26.06, was just the start I needed. With nothing happening with the rod on the obvious spot, I reeled that in, cast it at the area I had just had the take from and, no sooner had I attached the bobbin, than that rod was away too. This one looked a little bigger than the last and I wasn't surprised to see the needle settle at 30.04. Things were looking good!

Things were looking good

Paul Moulder stripped off and manned the net

I took a couple of minutes to get both rods accurately on the spots and to put out a little more bait but, by now I had a swimful, and they were hell bent on depleting my tea supplies. I wasn't sure if I would be getting any more action, but the crowd hollered their delight when I got another bite. The fight was one of the most vicious affairs I had ever had, and we were all convinced a monster was responsible but, eventually, it kited on a very long line and came to an abrupt halt some twenty yards up to my left. Paul Moulder was manning the net and had already started to strip off, I did the same and the pair of us marched into the water but, with the Horton margins being very deep and very steep, it took us a while to get along side the fish. It was a little hairy, but needs must and all that. The crowd was increasing in numbers by the minute, and they all followed us slowly up the bank and fortunately one guy, a Belgian angler by the name of Nick, had the presence of mind to grab my camera and get it all on film. The boat had been called for from the lodge, but it wasn't needed as thankfully, I got the thing moving, and Paul lifted the net around

I tried my best to take a bow

it. The gathered masses let out a massive cheer, and I tried my best to take a bow. Extracting us from the water had everyone in fits of laughter, but eventually, we sorted things out. You may well be expecting me to tell you that it was a monster, it wasn't, but with so much attitude, I was hardly disappointed with the 25.02 mirror - Sid James and the Carry On crew could not have made a better comedy.

I was expecting a monster

I still had a couple of days left, so I baited heavily again but, by the time I had settled down for the final night of my stay, only a small mirror had taken advantage of the feast. I was used to not getting action until late in the morning, so it is understandable why my early morning brew was sent into orbit as the silty spot produced a bite a little earlier than expected. In the pouring rain I quickly netted a nice mirror and, as fast as I could, weighed him. At 28.08 I wanted a picture, so secured him in the landing net in the hope that the rain would stop, but no sooner had I got the rod back in the ball game, than it was away again. I was in a spot of bother now, because with the net already occupied I would have difficulty netting anything, what with the stringy weed to contend with. Thankfully, the fellow in

31lb, but what a mess!

the swim next door lent me his net, which Barry took hold of and readied. At full stretch, we got the carp over the net and, as he lifted, there was an almighty 'crack!' - the handle had broken and I glanced at the guy it belonged to. Oops!!

With no time to dwell, Barry strode a little further out and finished off the job. It was a good fish, and along with me apologising to the bemused fella next door, we settled on 31lb. What a mess! The fish was placed along side his mate in the margins, and I got the rod back in action. Amid a torrent of abuse, I was soon playing another fish, but this one I recognised immediately, it was the Dumpy Mirror once again, weighing 33lb and, unbelievably, I saw two more fish show over

the spot, and couldn't help thinking that I may get another one. I was sure that I had overcooked the casts, and spent the next few minutes worrying about it. I shouldn't have bothered, because a couple of minutes later I was once again doing battle. Everything went to plan and I was holding my third thirty of the morning at 30.04. This was as crazy as a big bag of crazy things! All I could think about as I closed the creaky old gate, was when would I be opening it again. Surely Shoulders would make a mistake soon?

As crazy as a big bag of crazy things

Events conspired to keep me away from the lake for over a week after that, and when I did return I was greeted with the news that hardly anything had been caught. Indeed, even fish sightings had been very scarce. As usual, once the going got tough, a lot of people had pulled off, only to return when someone started to catch again. It's a strange attitude, because I believe you have to fish through the hard times, and then at least you will be there when it does kick off, not just trying to get in on everyone else's hard work.

With the lake quiet, I set up once again in One Up and, with the guy in the Plateau swim next door leaving the next day, at least I had some options. A very quiet night was followed by an equally quiet day, and despite looking as hard as I could, nothing happened to make me move. I did, however, spot a couple of fish moving over the plateau, and as the swim was empty, I launched a bait out there, followed by a couple of spods of slop. Early the next morning that rod was screaming away in the rest, but as I picked up the rod, it was obvious the fish had found the weed. All was solid for a while and I was just thinking of calling for the boat, when something started to give. The fish, eventually, released itself from its weedy shackles and proceeded to beat me up, and then it hove into view. Now, although I didn't like the fact that the Fishers Pond fish were still being called stockies, the truth about fishing Horton is that, if honest, you really want to catch the old history fish that still swim in her waters. Very high up on my personal list of 'must have' carp was one called Starburst, and although he may not be the biggest in the lake, he sure is one of the most sought after. You will understand, then, why my knees started to knock when I realised what fish I was playing. Oh please don't fall off! Thankfully he didn't, and soon enough I was posing with Starburst, all 29lb of him. Things were definitely slowing down though, and I couldn't help thinking I had probably got the best out of this lake, but I had to keep trying.

You may find this a little hard to believe, but I was starting to get a touch bored with Horton, not the fishing itself, but by being in the same place all the time. I have no idea why I am this way; I just needed something different to do, and while I thought about my little dilemma, I carried on. The most noticeable thing was that the fish were

Posing with Starburst, all 29lb of him

not responding to the big beds of bait, and in an effort to get the bobbins moving again, I travelled light and moved around a fair bit, setting little traps, and hoping, really. My more proactive approach brought rewards when all around were blanking, however, as good as that may have been I could neither find, nor catch, the fish I really wanted. Despite several of the Fishers Pond fish taking pity on me, and a few grass carp, I knew I would have to get away soon, but the decision was made for me a little earlier than expected.

I had been fishing in the Shoulders swim for the night, and had landed a double figure mirror then, as I settled down on the second evening I was joined by, the then, Kingsmead head bailiff. While he was there several good fish boomed out close in behind me on the Mead, and he suggested that I get a bait in there quickly. I was unsure if it was the done thing, but as he was the boss, who was I to argue? With a rod in each lake I drifted off to sleep only to be woken a short time later by the Kingsmead rod. We battled away in the darkness until I got the fish in the net, and it didn't look a bad one either, so I trotted up to the Lookout and asked if the guy could do some pictures, which he kindly did. I have a feeling that, because it was a little over 30lb's, the little green eyed monsters decided to make things difficult for me. The following day, I was subjected to nasty little comments and innuendos, the problem was, none of them would say anything to me, and

I hate that. Even the Kingsmead head bailiff disappeared off the scene, but not before informing everyone that he had not given me permission. I suppose I should have stayed, but I just couldn't be bothered with all the bollocks, and so, with my ultimate target still not finding his way into my net, I packed up and left. It was a while before I would return.

The dilemma now was that I had nowhere to go. I held a season ticket for Dinton Pastures, but that only allowed days and although I went up there a few times with Laney, I really didn't fancy it. Harefield was also paid a visit, but that was never going to happen either. What I really wanted was to be fishing with my mates again, and it just so happens that they had a ticket for somewhere I could go, but them green eyed monsters were out to get us there too.

Days at Dinton, but I just didn't fancy it

I spent some time in the wilderness

Chapter 21

When Obsession Starts to Win

I cannot shy away from the fact that I have a very obsessive nature, and as much as I had enjoyed my time on Horton, I was fully aware that it was starting to rear its ugly head again. If I had let it, the hunt for Shoulders would have taken over my life. It's not that I don't enjoy carp fishing when I am in that mode, but I do have a life, and I am damn well going to live it. Carp fishing is only part of my existence and by letting it take over, I will invariably let other aspects pass on by. At this stage I was now making a living from it all, but determined that it should remain fun, which I am pretty sure is why we all go fishing anyway. So, with winter fast approaching, I decided that I wanted some of that fun.

The ticket that Keith and Dave had was for a forty acre syndicate lake, from where they had been catching loads of carp, and some big ones too, but the problem I had was that the lake was full of predominantly leather(ish) carp. Alarm bells had been ringing in my head when I agreed to go and fish there with them, but I just had to find out a bit more about the carp, and where they came from. It took me some time, but eventually I was introduced to a fellow who used to be a park ranger, and was heavily involved with the lake some thirty years before. As he lived near to the lake, I decided to pay him a visit, which turned out to be a good news/bad news situation. You see, he was in the army during the Second World War, and had fought his way across the desert under Montgomery's command on several occasions and, knowing that I was an ex-serviceman meant, that before I could get to the point, I had to do battle with Rommel for a couple of hours. All interesting stuff which I found fascinating, but I had to sort of force the conversation round to the lake.

Did he know where the carp came from? Yes he did, and he even had the stocking records to back up what he was saying. Rather pleasingly, and at variance with what some people say (probably because they can't get a ticket), all the carp that swim in its water were born in this country, and you cannot ask for more than that. I even managed a visit to the site of their birth, by way of confirmation. They had been stocked some twenty five years previously, in an effort to satisfy an intensive match fishery, but the carp had grown and soon became unmanageable for the light tackle match men, so the carp syndicate was eventually formed, and has stayed that way ever since. One down side of their exposure to size 20 barbless hooks and being packed into keep nets, was that some of them had been left with horrendous damage to their mouths and fins. Thankfully, the syndicate that had been formed stopped this happening, and has left a lake full of hard fighting, and very big, carp. I knew one of the members, who went by the name of Shorty, and it was he who I first went fishing there with. Keith would be arriving later on that day, and I was looking forward to discussing a load of old bollocks with him. The three of us had a great night, and talked of anything but carp. By morning nothing had happened, but I wasn't bothered, as the evening had allowed me to push all thoughts of Shoulders and Charlie's Mate to the back of my mind. Keith had to be away early, and once he was gone, Shorty suggested we go and do a little stalking. Fine by me, so off we went, arriving eventually at the other end of the lake. This water is incredibly deep and I was shocked when my lead landed in about 18 foot of water no more than two rod lengths out, and this was supposedly the shallow end! Undeterred, we both flicked out the one rod that we had brought with us, and scattered a handful of boillies around each.

We were just discussing our ailments, you know the sort of thing, aching knees and backs, when my rod hooped around viciously. Soon enough, a common of maybe 10lb was in the net, and as it was my first fish from the water, I got a couple of shots before he scampered off to his home. Same as before, I set the trap and again we waited, but not for long. My recast rod hooped around for the second time, but this battle was not quite so one sided. The fish stayed deep, and for fully five minutes I could do nothing with it but, because of the depth, it felt like pumping a cod up from the deeps, and it was sometime before I had it near the surface. Bloody hell, it was a cod, a leather cod to be exact, and it looked big. Shorty was on the net and I steadily guided the fish in, but now we were

My first from the water

in a bit of bother. We hadn't brought any scales with us, so Shorty volunteered to go and get his, while I held the fish in the net. He returned not looking too good after his exertions, and we weighed the fish at 34.04. Like two old men we sorted out the pictures, me with my bad back and him with his aching joints, at which point we decided to return, we needed a rest!

A 34.04 leather cod

One thing for sure though, I liked it here...a lot!

Back in our respective plots, we sorted everything out and, by evening, Shorty and I were sharing a fine bottle of red and a Chinese meal. By ten I was laying my weary head on the pillow, smiling inanely at the fact that I had caught a 34 on my first visit. I couldn't have been asleep for long, before I was attending to a very bream-like bite but, not wanting to take any chances I lifted into the fish. Very un-bream like, my arms were nearly torn from their sockets, and battle commenced! Again the fish stayed deep, and it was sometime before I could gingerly lift the mesh around it. It didn't look that big at first, so I left him in the net and sorted out the scales and sling, but then as I lifted him from the water, my aching back indicated that it

may be a little bigger than I thought. It was, and at 37.02 I smiled the smile of a contented man as I held her up for the camera, manned by Shorty. I even managed to catch a few small commons up to 23lb during the rest of the night.

Packing up around nine in the morning, I wasn't sure how often I would be able to fish here due to the fact I would have to be guested, but I really wanted to get back as soon as possible.

The area I had caught the 37 from was near to where Keith and Dave had been steadily applying their bait,

I smiled the smile of a contented man

an area that they were assured no one wanted to, or indeed had, fished during the previous winters. That was until they both started catching carp of course, at which point the knives came out. I had joined Keith for a weekend, one which was wholly unsuccessful for me, but Jenks bagged himself the most glorious mirror of 35.06, and it was while we

The most glorious 35.06 mirror

laughed and giggled about the capture, that he told me about some of the rumours going around the lake. Some members had been complaining about the amount of bait that the boys had been using, and generally accusing them of breaking every rule imaginable. It got so bad that one of them even tipped a load of rubbish in Laney's swim and tried to get him banned. Anybody who knows Dave will know that that is the last thing he would ever do, you would be hard pressed to find his footprints in any swim he had just left, let alone any rubbish, and to top it all, the antagonists were now queuing up to fish the swims they were baiting. Having caught a few carp myself, I was soon being dragged into the sorry affair.

After my ninth night, I was driving home when I got a call from the management. Evidently, I had been accused of breaking just about every rule in the book, and shouldn't I be banned from fishing there? It really was the straw that broke the camels back, I had just about had enough of all this crap, and made the decision not to fish there for a while. It wasn't that the idiots had frightened me off, it was

Sharing some time with a friend

because I didn't want those that were inviting me to the water to be targeted. Everything that is wrong with carp fishing in this day and age, is because of jealousy and I can only think that, because Keith, Dave and I write in the magazines, that the green eyed monster started to foam at the mouth. How terribly sad!

At which point I really had no idea what I wanted to do. The army is a very close knit community, and as much as that can cause some friction at times, there was none of this continual bitchiness that I was constantly coming across in Civvy Street. If I wanted to carry on doing what I was doing, then I was going to have to thicken up my skin a little, but it started, what was for me, a long period in the wilderness. I have never really been able to get my head around how most people want to have a go at whoever is successful in this carp fishing game. Live and let live I say, but very often that statement falls on deaf ears!

To try and cheer myself up, I went up to Oxlease Lake with Adam Penning a couple of weeks later and I can't tell you how much that one session buoyed me up. Adam was doing a feature for Improve Your Coarse Fishing and he wondered if I would like to be involved? It really wasn't anything to do with the feature, it was all about sharing some time with a friend. We caught a cart load of the little fish that Linear had stocked into the lake, and his feature turned out well, but the session was remembered for one very funny reason. Adam was playing his twelfth carp of the day, and just as he got it in the net he asked me to take care of it because he desperately needed to use the toilet. Off he ran the short distance to the port-a-loo, and at that moment my mischievous little brain kicked into gear. I had to make sure that no harm would come to the fish, so employing the two camera men, I wrapped the little mirror in two unhooking mats. We carried it the fifteen yards or so to the loo, and I quickly whipped open the door. Adams face was a picture as I placed the fish at his feet. It was all I could do, through the tears of laughter, to

place the fish in his hands, and we cracked off a couple of shots. Don't worry, the fish was never in any danger, except perhaps from the fumes. God knows what he had eaten the night before, but the smell almost killed us all!!

Refreshed, I had another guest session on the syndicate lake, but the atmosphere was so bad I really couldn't enjoy myself. That said, I did promise myself, once all the silliness had settled down, that I would apply for a winter ticket the following year. It was just that the lake presented me with another interesting aspect of carp fishing, and that was distance. As far

There was no danger, apart from the smell!

as I could see, he who could chuck the farthest, caught the most carp. Although I could chuck a lead a very long way, I wanted to see just how far I could go. That session provided me with a 33lb leather from a cast that was as long as I had ever made, but I knew I could do better. I left it alone after that, but my name had been added to the waiting list.

I'd left it late, but I decided to try and get back into the Frimley thing but, coupled with the fact that my heart wasn't in it, the fishing was very hard. The carp had forgotten about the joys of eating boillies and had responded to the sudden influx of gallons and gallons of maggots. Now, as much as I had used them to revitalise my areas the previous winter, I had never succumbed to using them all the time and, thankfully, I had a mate, Paul Bidmead, who was just as determined as I to keep the boillies going in. We caught the odd fish of course, but the maggot revolution had changed everything. Both of us ploughed on regardless, although I would be kept from the banks for lengthy periods because Lynn was having to have a series of operations. As always, I found it very hard to concentrate on anything else, but in between the hospital visits and at her insistence, I did as much fishing as was

Paul and I kept the boillies going in

I did as much fishing as possible

possible. Which wasn't very much actually. I even started to do a little angling on Frimley's Pit 4, and as much as the carp would play ball, the bird life was almost unbearable. Being a whole lot more weedy than Pit 3 next door, only seemed to focus the flying vermin more on the clear areas I was fishing, and it wasn't long before I had given that up as a bad job.

It is very difficult to put into words how terribly lost I felt at this time. The situation with Lynn was hugely worrying, and coupled with the fact that I had no direction to my fishing, I could not for the life of me find a way out of this situation, but things did start to improve when I went down to Chilham Mill as a guest at the 'Fish with the Chaps' event. As normal, Chris Logsdon and his wife Lynn had made us all feel welcome, and of course, I could spend some time in the company of friends, and what a weekend it was. Far too much red wine, but just the pick me up I needed. There was also the not insignificant fact that I landed a then, lake record.

With Laney running around all over the place, I had been left on my own. Everyone else had followed Dave, because as they said, they wanted to see how the expert did it! As I sat and wondered what it would be like to be an expert, my old mucker Viv Shears came around for a chat.

The scales told a different story, 39.04

We were just putting the world to rights, when there was a hell of a commotion in the reeds 60 yards across the lake from me. This was followed a nano-second later by the shrill call of my alarm. The fish cut a massive swathe of reeds down as it tore off, and I was left hanging on for grim death. The battle was so protracted that both Viv and I thought that maybe I was attached to one of the lakes catfish. That was until a bloody great mirror hit the surface, and we got a bit more serious from that point on, until Viv deftly lifted the net around the fish. Our original estimate was about 35lb, but the scales told a different story, 39.04.

Light My Fire!! I hollered at the top of my voice, like I do. We sacked her in the margins to allow the photographers to get round to me, Chris Logsdon wouldn't believe me at first, but I eventually convinced him to come and have a look. It was absolute madness in my swim after that, at least 30 people had come round and,

eventually, I was in the lake doing some returners...and then I was given an early bath! And of course I had to rub it into Laney; whilst everyone was following the expert, the 'real' expert had gone and caught a lake record. We looked at each other for a second or two, before he hollered "Red wine", and once again that was the end of that. I even bagged a couple more that weekend, so at the very least, it proved I could still catch a carp or two.

By way of celebration, they threw me in

Tucked away on the island

I stayed with the Kent thing for a while, but I wasn't happy, and in an effort to get as far away from the madding crowd as possible, I headed off to Northhampton. My old army buddy Mark Denton lives in the area, and had been, for sometime, waxing lyrical about a couple of lakes up that way. He had lived there all his life so he was very familiar with the places and had been having a dabble on a particular lake of 45 acres, where he and a friend had caught four fish, up to 28lb. As far as we knew they had never been caught before, and that was all I needed to know.

I duly arrived, and as soon as I got there the first problem arose, how the hell was I going to get my gear to the lake, after all, I had a rather large inflatable boat with me. An hour later, having scratched most of my skin off on the brambles, I was ready to set sail. I must have drifted around for hours, because it wasn't until early evening that I spotted a couple of carp, both mirrors. They were grubbing around just in the margins of an island so, as quietly as possible, I pulled the boat out of the water and stood and watched them for a while. It was fascinating, and the hairs on the back of my neck bristled at the thought of catching one of them. A while later they drifted off and I went to investigate, the spot was as clean as a whistle and surrounded by weed, so that was one rod sorted. The other was placed a little way down the margin to my left and I can honestly say that I had not been so excited in a very long time.

It slid over the net cord bristling with indignity

At first light I sat gazing over the lake. 45 acres all to myself, not another angler in sight, and a lake containing carp that I had absolutely no idea about. Just about everything I have ever wanted from my fishing. All I could think of were anglers all over the country fighting for swims, and I giggled to myself - this was heaven. Did it matter that I wasn't fishing for a 50-pounder? Did it hell, I could not have been more contented. As the daydream continued, I nearly swallowed my tongue when the rod fished to the 'spot' absolutely melted off and for a fraction of a second I was unsure what was going on, but I did manage to pick up the rod, and battle commenced. From the head shaking I was sure it wasn't a big fish, but it would not give up until, eventually, the double figure common, if somewhat reluctantly, slid over the net cord bristling with indignity. I have most certainly caught far larger carp than this one, but I cannot think of one that filled me with so much joy and, just as I was packing up, I fought and landed another common of similar size.

The sight that greeted me on my next visit, as I stumbled out of the bushes, took me a little by surprise. 75% of the lakes surface was now covered in weed, and as I boated out to my little island I was singing Guns and Roses' 'Welcome to the Jungle', which seemed to sum up the place nicely. As I rowed around, I spotted several carp sunning themselves, and also a couple of nice areas to put a hookbait, and so, with the spots marked, I set up once again on the island. The wind picked up from the South West and the cloud began to build, all in all it looked incredibly carpy, and all was well with the world. That was until the tench and bream decided to make life difficult. It wasn't until two in the morning that the slimy little gits had had their fill, and I could eventually drift off to sleep.

How long I slept I am not entirely sure, but just before first light I became very much awake as the left hand rod absolutely howled. With one foot in my boat, I tried to gain some control, but more often than not, the carp let me know who was the boss. In the inky blackness we tried to out-manoeuvre each other, and due to the confined nature of the swim, I had to climb into the lake. When the fish surfaced for the first time, I got the landing net in position but, stubbornly, it refused to come to me, so I just kept the pressure on until it could resist no more. Then, carefully, I lifted the mesh around it, resting the fish over the back of the boat, before getting everything ready to receive her. I bit through the line and rolled the net down, not turning the head torch on until she was on the mat and, when I did, I am sure my heart missed a few beats.

Uncaught and unknown

Black and beautiful and never having been landed before, it really was one of those pivotal moments in my life. There was no one there, of course, but even if there had been, I am not sure I would have had anything to say. Carefully, I unhooked the beast and, for the record, she weighed

Unfortunately I have never been back

29.12. It's strange, but as nice as it is to have your mates around you at times like this, it seemed fitting that it was just me and her. I needed a picture of course, and someone kindly came over, forty five minutes later, in the meantime I sacked her in the deep margin and we sat and watched the light chase away the darkness. As crazy as it sounds, I didn't stop talking to her the whole time we waited then, with every care in the world, we got some pictures. It was difficult because of the lack of light on my little island, but even if I didn't get the best shots, I will always have the memories of a very special carp. As with all things, I only got to fish there a couple more times before things started to change. It was never the same again, and, unfortunately I have never been back.

Still unsure of what I wanted to be doing, I decided that a look at Horton might

I carried on as before and even caught a carp

just reinvigorate my carp fishing. I don't want anyone thinking I wasn't enjoying myself because I was, but I could not have realised how much I didn't want to be at Horton. There were a lot of new faces, and the atmosphere had changed completely, however, if I really wanted to catch Shoulders then I would have to fish there. One other thing that changed was how many carp were being caught off the top. Now, I love surface fishing, but I was totally convinced that Shoulders would never be caught that way, and simply ignored it all and carried on fishing the bottom. How wrong could I have been? Having been caught once or twice off the top from his former Longfield home, in the twelve years since he had lived in Horton he had never succumbed. That was until Nigel Sharp put a floater in his path and bagged him. Good angling! It was shortly after this that I arrived at the lake, and during the first few days I saw maybe ten carp fall foul of the old dog biscuit. He wouldn't get caught that way again, surely? Anyway, I carried on as before and even landed myself a carp. I think it's now called the Big Leather, but what ever it was, I was happy. Following it up with Hazel the common the next day, I was sure I had made the right move, and that was confirmed when, on the third day, I landed Starburst once again at 30.06.

With things going so well you would have thought I was happy, but I wasn't. Lynn still had two big operations to endure, and as I was going to France the following week, I needed to spend some time with her to make sure her strength was up. The trip across the channel was one of the first I had done, and as I was going with my friend Tim Paisley, I was looking forward to it. We were going to the Great Lake at Goncourt, a bit of an unknown quantity, but in reality I just wanted to chill out, and that is exactly what I did. I caught a load of carp, and what stunners they were, not what I was expecting from a French lake at all. The lake, at the time, had a real air of mystery about it, and was definitely not a runs water. I had also never fished

with an echo sounder, and spent some time refining my skills. All in all, it was just what the doctor ordered, and I came home fully refreshed. There was now a need to stay local, so I turned my attention back to Frimley, at least then I would be on hand should Lynn need me. So, with Shoulders getting caught a few times from Horton, I set out once again to chase my other obsession, Charlie's Mate. I had been keeping track of things at Pit 3 and one very noticeable fact had come to light. In most cases when she had made a mistake, she would invariably be the only fish caught by that angler in that session so, to that end, I decided to change the way I was using my bait. I didn't want to be baiting up all the time, and I felt that if she was a loner, then I would be better off setting little traps, and by not inviting everything to the party, it may just give her the confidence to feed.

I turned my attention back to Frimley

Commons and mirrors to over thirty pounds

So, with the baiting at a minimum, I set out more in hope than expectation. Unfortunately, depending on which way you look at it, the plan didn't work out too well.

Eleven fish to 31lb over two nights!

Arriving for my first session of the winter, I set up in a swim called the Fallen Tree, knowing that at least it would give me a good view of the lake. Shortly after dark a 19lb common was being returned, which was a nice welcome back. As I was only here for a couple of nights, I thought it may take some time to get back in the swing, but no, the carp kept me busy for the full 48 hours. Commons and mirrors to over 30lb are not to be sniffed at, but I couldn't help thinking that what ever I did at Frimley, the carp were going to like it. Still, mustn't grumble eh?

So convinced was I that the big girl was a loner, I remember turning up early one morning to find loads of fish boshing out at one end of the lake, and sure that she wouldn't be with them, I set up as far away as I could. Unbelievably, the shoal came and found me and I landed eleven fish to 31lb over two nights! The action continued that way for the next few weeks, but I never felt as if I was getting any nearer to my target, however, I did catch a carp that was number two on my list of must haves. It was an hour before first light when I turned up at the lake, so it was sometime before I noticed some signs saying that a boat would be in use during the day. A while later, a couple of the bailiffs were afloat and informed me they were going to retrieve lost

The bailiffs hard at work with the rake

tackle from the marginal trees and the islands. What I liked most was that they had a rake with them, and so asked if they would give my swim a good seeing to. That they did, and when they had gone I positioned three hookbaits and some free offerings right where they had disturbed everything. I was a little surprised to only get one fish in the night, but a huge splash had me swinging my legs out of bed half an hour before first light. I put the kettle on and watched the ripples hit my bank, and whilst I waited for it to boil, three more fish boomed out in the darkness. Surely it was only a matter of time?

The take, when it came, was a rather twitchy affair, and the battle wasn't overly long, but I never once thought it was anything but a big fish. Having to net it in the reeds that surrounded the swim meant that at first I couldn't see what was in the net but, having got the mat ready, I bit through the line, and steered the fish toward me. It was then that I could see the width of its shoulders and, for a moment, I thought it was my obsession, but when I saw a couple of mirror carp scales, I realised it could only be one fish.

Gums had at last fallen foul of my traps and, at 37lb, I was ecstatic. She really is one of the characters of the lake. I believe it was at that very moment when I eventually got my head out of my arse, and decided that I really should be angling for my dreams. I had spent more than a year wandering around in the wilderness, not knowing what to do, or even how to do it. I had been running away from myself, as much as I had been running from the green eyed monsters. I needed to be fishing for myself, and everyone else could go take a running jump!

Gums at 37lb, I was ecstatic

The search for Shoulders it would be then

Chapter 22

Shoulder Arms

Time slipped on by, and as 2004 clicked over to 2005, Chillcott had made a decision. Well almost.

Which fish did I want to catch the most, I thought long and hard, Charlie's Mate or Shoulders? Although the image of Walkers common had been with me since childhood, it was that Shoulders fella that I had probably looked at the hardest, and the longest. We all have different things we want to achieve from our carp fishing, some would probably pick Two Tone, The Burghfield Common and Heather as their top three, whilst others would undoubtedly include the Black Mirror and the Fat Lady. For me though, the list included, as I have said before, Mallin's, Single Scale and last but not least, Shoulders. With the future for Lynn becoming more and more uncertain, I felt that with Frimley being so close to home, I should leave it alone for a while. I could always fish there when there was a need to be nearer home. The search for Shoulders it would be then, and I would resume my quest once the deep waters of Horton looked like producing a bite or two.

That January was one of the warmest on record, but as February arrived, the artic winds began in earnest, and the wild life didn't know what was going on. Through the first couple of weeks of the year I watched grebes going through their mating rituals, but as the easterly winds started, the poor sods didn't know if they were coming or going...literally! So, with only six weeks of the season to go, and regardless of the weather, I began fishing Horton.

It may seem a little pointless when you know you really have no chance of a bite, but I was determined to be there when it kicked off. If I had turned up when they did start having it, I may not have been in a position to take advantage of the situation and, during the second session, I was encouraged to hear that Darrel Peck had landed a 32lb mirror, the first fish out since November. I soldiered on with my eyes glued to the water at all times, very often the signs are so subtle and I didn't want to miss a thing, over the next week or so there were definitely two areas where

I was seeing the most activity. One Up and the Captors swim were where my attention was being drawn, but as I arrived on my next trip, both swims were occupied. I did see a small occurrence in the Lookout, however, and that is where I deposited my gear. This visit coincided with a magazine interview I was doing, and if I was honest, I really didn't want to be doing it. I needed to stay focused, but needs must and all that, so when the guy arrived, just as I was sorting out a couple of rods, I explained that I wanted to get them out first, before we chatted. Once again I was looking for the weediest areas, if weed is the right word, because the bottom was still covered in that horrible black stuff, but the carp seemed to like it, so who was I to complain? With two hookbaits in position, and a couple of spods of 10mm Fusion Boillies and Response Pellets over each, it was time to have a cuppa and a chat.

We hadn't even got half way down the brew, before one of the bobbins pulled up tight and, as I was using back leads, I was unsure if it was a liner at first. I must have looked at the damn thing for ten seconds before the penny eventually dropped and, lifting the rod, I felt the satisfying thump of a carp - now that was handy. For an age, the fish simply chugged around at range, but eventually I made some head way. The Lookout swim is very high above the water, so as the carp made its first visit to the surface, I could clearly see which one I had hooked.

It was the Dumpy Mirror, and she rolled around a little more until I was able to lead her into the outstretched net. Although this was the third time I had caught her, along with being a nice way to illustrate the interview, she also proved that I was getting things right. It really was all the encouragement I needed to keep on going. At 33lb I was well chuffed, but the rest of the session was actionless, although one Fishers Pond fish did get caught from the Church Bay. Things, as they say, were starting to happen, however, the next couple of sessions were dour, very boring and extremely cold.

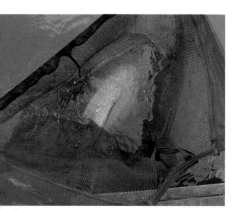

Dumpy in the net

I had been studying the long range forecast at every opportunity and it seemed, at long last, that things were about to change. Warm south westerlies and rain were on their way, and as I suspect every carp angler would, I was wringing my hands with glee. That euphoria, however, was short lived because on the very weekend of its arrival I would be at the Five Lakes Carp Show...Oh bugger!! Normally, I really look forward to this show, but the whole weekend was filled with talk of the weather, everyone felt the same, and I just couldn't wait for it to end. All I could think about was that someone would catch my obsession, and I don't think I have ever looked so long and hard at my mobile, praying for it not to ring. The last thing that I had to do, on the Sunday, was a talk with Lee Jackson and Laney. Being a panel affair it was hosted by Chris Ball, and his final question to us was what were our immediate plans? I smiled inwardly to myself, I was now about to tell the very man who I had first seen holding Shoulders in the Anglers Mail in 1988, and the audience, that I was going to catch it that very week. As soon as I was able, I was out of the door, and with Lynn gripping the dashboard, I raced towards home. Don't ask me why, but I had totally convinced myself that I would achieve my goal that week, and I feverishly packed the gear ready for an early morning start.

I had Mat Woods coming down on the Tuesday, to do some pictures for a Crafty Carper feature. Be that as it may, I was here to catch Shoulders, and he was going to have to fit in around what I was doing, and so, with all thoughts of articles firmly pushed to the back of my mind, I set out on a lap of the lake just as the light was filling the sky, on the Monday morning. Having seen fish in two areas, my plan revolved around one of those spots, but as the lake was quiet, I spent a little time wandering around. Eventually, I came across Beadle, who was set up in Springates point and we shared a brew. Then the first fish showed, followed shortly after by another, so I quickly got hold of Wady, who was in the Lookout, and asked if he would put a bucket in the Captors swim for me, which he duly did. We had no idea at the time, but I was going to have to ask him for an even bigger favour in a couple of days. With the swim secured, I could concentrate on drinking the rest of

A recapture, but I was getting it right

Beadles brew kit, and that done, I set off to get my gear and set up. There was no need to rush so I took my time; I wanted everything as perfect as I could get it. The Captors has a very big gravel feature in front of it at about 60 yards, and while I am sure the carp swam over it frequently, I wasn't convinced that that was the ideal place to fish. Just beyond it, and in slightly deeper water, the silt began, and it was here that I positioned my two hookbaits. Being fifteen yards apart, I then set out a feast good enough for a big old forty pounder, well, at least I was in a positive frame of mind! Although I had spotted the odd fish, nothing happened over the next 24 hours, and it was a welcome distraction when Mat arrived around midday on the Tuesday. He was staying until the following lunch time, and RMC had faxed Angling Publications to say that he could fish that night, something that was to come back and bite us severely on the backside. By early evening I had re-positioned the hookbaits and freshened up the spots, thinking all the while that I could not have done a better job. How the hell could Shoulders resist it? Time would tell.

I should have realised, at this point, that something was amiss, because we got a rather irate call from, the then, fishery manager to tell Mat to reel in and move back from the water. He really wasn't that bothered, complying immediately, and I checked with Mat once again that he had the required permission, which he assured me he had. Why on earth were the management getting so vexed about it all? Very odd.

I was awake early the next morning, and Mat and I sat sharing a brew. I was puzzled that I hadn't received so much as bleep over the past two days, but it was such a nice

That was probably a bite!

morning, we decided to get on with some more pictures. It really can be quite boring doing this sort of thing, and just as the will to live was leaving me, and Mat was photographing the identical rig that lay out in the lake, I got a single bleep. I looked quickly at the rod, but it was a few more seconds before the indicator pulled up to the rod. I was convinced it was a liner, when all of a sudden the line was torn from the clip and the buzzer howled. I reasoned, accurately as it happens, that that was probably a bite!

As soon as I lifted the rod from the rest, I could tell a big fish was responsible, it's plodding and lunging while at range was typical of a larger carp. I was content to just let it do its thing for a while, until it started to kite to the right, and headed for the Weedy Bay. I didn't want it getting in there, and had to apply a little more pressure than I would have liked in order to get it coming my way, then, feeling a bit more in control, I drew the fish along

My heart was in my mouth

the margin, until I felt a rather sickening grating on the line. For a second or two, everything locked up, and with my heart in my mouth I once again pulled a lot harder than I wanted until, all of a sudden, I was back in direct contact and the leadcore cleared the surface. The fish rolled, but I could only see a large creamy belly at this point, and remember mentioning to Wady, who had joined us, that it was one of the bigger Fishers Pond fish...he didn't look so convinced. It was the next time the carp surfaced that all rational thought left me and, as he dived once more for the lake bed, a large crinkly tail was exposed.

It was Shoulders!

Up to that point I had been in control, even getting the net in position, but now I was shaking like a leaf and afraid...very afraid. I rather nervously asked Wady if he wouldn't mind doing the honours with the net, which remarkably he agreed to do. Then, to the accompaniment of my heart

It was Shoulders!

Wady did the honours with the net

pounding wildly, my longed for prize slid straight into the folds of the mesh. There was no need for me to look and confirm what had just happened, because I knew, after all those years the mighty Shoulders was mine!

I cannot ever hope to convey the host of emotions I went through over the next couple of minutes, I really didn't know whether to laugh or cry. Lynn shed a load of excited tears, and I took care of the rest, running around like a demented idiot. Eventually, I calmed down enough to get things sorted out. Most people on the lake came round to congratulate me and lend a hand, for which I shall always be grateful, it really did make the occasion that little more special. I hadn't even thought about the weight of him, it really didn't seem important, but when Jerry Hammond and Barry Davis held the scales up, we all agreed that 42.15 was just about right. In a daze, I held him up for the cameras, and much as I didn't want to, I had to let him slip from my hands and back to his home. With the passing of the Parrot a little while ago, Shoulders is the only one left of the infamous Horton 'A' team. He has survived all that we have thrown at him, truly the King of carp!

And then the management tried their best to ruin things. About 20 minutes after everyone had left the swim, Mat and I were quietly sharing a brew, when the fishery manager walked into the swim. Unaware of what had just transpired, he simply said well done on hearing my news, but something was wrong. We were told to report to the office down by the lodge, and a couple of minutes later we were making our way there like a couple of naughty school kids. I have no idea why we felt that way, because we had done absolutely nothing wrong. With Ian Welch in full head master mode, we were told to come in and sit down. I was treated to a very insincere well done on Shoulders, and then the shouting started, no discussion, no debate, and certainly no room for either of us to say a word. I listened as the tirade

I didn't know whether to laugh or cry

continued, and all I could pick out of the crazed gibbering, was that Mat didn't have permission to be set up on the lake. I could feel the red mist descending over me, and that meant I was very close to punching someone, especially when Ian said I would be losing my ticket! Knowing that any violence on my part would inevitably result in a lengthy, or indeed, total ban, I marched out of the office, but all I could hear was Mat being slated mercilessly. This was ridiculous, I went back in and tried to sort things out. 'Evidently', me losing my ticket was not what was said, but Mat would no longer be welcome on RMC venues. I did ask why they had felt it necessary to congratulate me when they so obviously didn't mean it. I had never been so unfairly treated in my life, and when I checked with Angling Publications, they did have a fax giving Mat permission to be there, and to fish. The fact that it had arrived late was not their fault, and by trying to cover up their own inadequacies by blaming us just showed how far things had got out of hand. Still, I had achieved what I wanted, and I wasn't going to let some misdirected crap spoil my day! The following morning I headed out of the gate, and closed it for the last time. I have no reason to return, because to put myself in front of Shoulders again would only lessen the impact of this capture. It was special, and so is that incredible carp.

Now, when you normally get home, I guess most fellows are confronted with a wife that wants things doing around the house, or the kids need this mending, and the grass needs cutting. Well, as soon as I got back from Horton, Lynn insisted that I get back in the car and go to the Car Park Lake. She believed I was on a roll, and I would be daft not to 'go for it'. I must admit, on the drive home the thought had crossed my mind; there was every chance that Heather could be out before the end of the season. I soon pushed the thought into the dark recesses of my brain, for a kick off I was happy...very happy, and secondly, the person that was encouraging me to go was the woman who had to sacrifice so much, for me to go chasing my dreams. No, she needed a break from it all, and in true Chillcott style, I unleashed the old Harley Davidson.

Truly the King of carp!

You will hear me say, on many occasions, that there is more to life than sitting by the side of a lake, and my bike plays a large part in helping both of us to unwind. I love the idea of going fishing, along with all the excitement of getting to the lake, but I would hate to have to wake up everyday to think that I was just fishing. How immensely boring would that be?

So, for three days Lynn and I got our knees in the breeze, and I contented myself with collecting as many flies and wasps in my teeth as possible. All was well with the world. As much as I would have loved to keep on doing the same, there soon came a time when I wanted to get the rods out once again. I was now in a bit of a dilemma, I didn't want to fish at Frimley through the summer, that was for the winter time, but I did have one area on my mind. Having recently spoken to my old army buddy, Mark Denton, who lives in Northampton, he said he had another lake to have a look at. Evidently, I would be extremely unlucky if I saw another living soul all the time I was there. Now that sounded like fun, and the following week I packed the boat into the car and pointed myself up the M1. Unbelievably, as I was making my very early morning journey, my phone indicated I had a message and it said that Heather had been out; I really must listen to my wife a bit more in future!

Not being that familiar with the area, I wasn't sure what to expect, but I eventually arrived huffing and puffing by the lake. It was beautiful, and as I inflated my boat, a small common cleared the water about 40 yards out. Without a bivvy, or indeed a swim, in sight, I decided that I would give it a go for a while. Unfortunately, as hard as I tried, all I could catch were the commons, in fairness I didn't see anything

Knees in the breeze

bigger, but just as I was thinking it was time to move on, Mark came down for a visit. We talked for a while before he mentioned a very small syndicate that I may be able to fish and I was all ears, but was also thinking that they would not want someone like me on their water. I couldn't have been more wrong, and in only a few days I was the proud owner of a ticket for the Melchborne and District Piscatorial Society. What an absolutely marvellous name for a fishing club! The name itself conjured up pictures of classic estate lakes and creaking cane rods, I just couldn't wait to go and have a look. With only ten anglers allowed to fish the place, no one really had a clue what was in the lake, it was that air of mystery that made it sound so bloody exciting.

My alarm clock had me out of bed at three in the morning and, after hurriedly stuffing the rods into my car, I was soon making my way through the Northamptonshire country side. As the roads narrowed and the houses became more and more spread out, I concentrated on avoiding pheasants and pigeons. When I arrived at the estate, making my way around the sprawling mansion I had my first glimpse of the lake. I was high above it, and for about ten minutes, gazed at the most tranquil and peaceful scene; just maybe I had at last found my little piece of heaven. I snapped out of my daydream, at last, and set out on my first walk around, at which point, you may be wondering what the hell I was doing making a one hundred and twenty mile trip from my house, which is situated in the heart of big carp country? Well, carp fishing is so much more than catching big carp, for me anyway, and yes, I could simply sit on any number of waters near to home, and wait for it to happen, but how terribly boring would that be? I love the unknown, and the excitement that creates is the biggest buzz of all for me. Carp fishing, much like the rest of my life, is about experiencing everything, and this little lake was another high point on the journey. One small problem I had was that I needed to do some pictures for a feature, and to that end, I had got permission for Mat to come down. Under pain of death if he revealed its whereabouts, we had arranged to meet the following day. After a couple of hours I had seen no carpy activity and settled on an area that would give me access to both of the island margins. They were lovely and gravely, but the rest of the lake was covered in deep silt; I would cross that bridge when the need arose, but for now, I was just happy to be fishing and soaking

up the incredibly quiet environment. The evening was filled with the most abundant wild life I had seen in a long time. Owls swooped between the islands, and the sounds of death being issued in the woods, to my right, continued throughout the night. Having no idea what the carps reaction to bait

My little piece of heaven

would be, I thought it best to let them have a fair bit, so 8 kilos of Fusion boillies and Response Pellets had been spread over the three rods and, as darkness descended, the line bites started, and savage ones too. But I had to wait until six in the morning before I got my first bite, and what a bite it was.

So fast was the carp moving that the buzzer had difficulty keeping up with it, and even my intervention made little difference. Piling on the pressure to try and turn it, seemed to make it even madder and I am not sure who was more knackered once he was in the net, but one thing I did know, I was the happier! My smile broadened even more as I lay him gently on the mat, there on his right flank were two large 'C' shaped scales, and to this day he is still known as the Crafty Carper, and knowing that Mat would be there in a while, I slipped him into a sack. At 21.08 I couldn't think of a better way to start my little adventure, and two more double figure mirrors tripped up later that day, before it was time to head for home. All I could think about on the journey was when could I get back? Even if the water held no monsters, it was still a marvellous little bolthole for me to escape the madness that normally surrounds the waters I fish.

Two days later I was back, and walking through the early morning mist on the look out for a carp. I didn't want to get into fishing just one swim, and was determined to find out as much about the place as possible so, this time I fished the other side of the islands, but by morning nothing had happened - time for a little more investigation. I hadn't got 20 yards down to my right before I saw a group of six carp milling around a large weed bed no more than a rod length out. Now, this area of the lake has no natural cover, so I had to crawl up to it on my hands and knees and, for a while, I sat and watched before they gave the game away. There was one spot that they constantly dipped down on, and that was where I would put a bait so,

No better way to start my adventure

carefully retreating to prepare a rod, I attached a small PVA bag and was ready. Back in position, I waited for the carp to reach the other end of the weed before gently lowering the rig down and, with the leadcore nicely concealed at the base of the weed, I slackened off the line and put the rod down. At which point my bloody phone started to ring, I had forgotten it was in my pocket, and quickly answered it as I made my way back from the waters edge. It was Penning, and he was keen to see how I had got on, I think he was as excited as me about this new water! Once out of earshot of the fish we nattered about this and that, until I said that I felt like Walker fishing at Redmire for the first time. We then started talking about the famous fish that had lived at that wonderful little pool, and were just discussing a mid-twenty common called No Pelvic's, when my rod hooped over and the spool began to purr. Adam was

Truly a spooky moment!

unceremoniously dispatched into the long grass, and I engaged in battle. It wasn't the most spectacular fight, and after only a couple of minutes I had a nice looking common in the net. Imagine my surprise, however, as I parted the mesh to see he had no pelvic fins, he also weighed 26.02, about the same weight as his rather famous namesake. Truly a spooky moment!

Mat was once again down for my next, and last, visit for a while and I even got him permission to fish. He has an amazing tactic, it's called 'the bag anywhere trick', and it was this he had employed to catch himself a stunning 25lb common. I landed some smaller fish, but it was this trip that convinced me that there were some bigger fish present. One of them was a stunning mid thirty fully scaled, and I promised myself that I would come back and catch him. Unfortunately, I didn't realise how long that would be, I had some business to take care of, and it would keep me away for two long years.

A bag anywhere and a 25lb common

Sunset on the St Lawrence

Chapter 23

A United State

had arranged, some time before, to have a trip to France, back to Goncourt Great Lake to be exact, with a good friend of mine, Steve March. We would be accompanied by his mates (and now mine) Bilbo, Hattie, Colin, Paul and Sandford but, having been there once before, I was extolling the virtues of its scaley, and not very French looking, carp. At the time, it was still an untapped venue, and by the time we were ready for the off, all of us were gagging to get going. The trip, I hoped, would give me a chance to think about another exciting adventure I had been invited to take part in, and that was the World Carp Cup in America. Tim Paisley was, once again, putting a team together, and had asked if I would like to be part of it. Would I ever, and most pleasing of all I would be partnered by my old

Misty morning at Goncourt

mucker Adam Penning. On hearing the news, Adam was ecstatic about the thought of representing his country, and the phone lines between Essex and Aldershot had been in constant use for some time. It was shaping up to be an incredible trip, and we couldn't wait for it to begin.

Back to the French trip, and things didn't get off to a good start to be honest, because I am okay with a map and a rifle in my hands, but route maps are a different story. It got so bad that, as we slipped over the border into Belgium, I was starting to wonder if we would ever get there! We got separated a while later, and had to hang around for a couple of the guys as they had started to head into Paris, so although it took considerably longer than expected, we eventually arrived at the Goncourt complex. Somewhat wearily, we sorted ourselves out, and with the swims selected, the angling commenced. Having had previous experience, I was keen to look at one particular

Steve March returns the beast

area of the lake, and before I set up I paid it a visit, armed, of course, with a bag of boillies. The intention was to bait up, and then we could all enjoy some stalking. With that done, we set up for the first night, which fortunately was punctuated with the odd fish. Come the morning though, and after shaking off the affects of a little too much red wine, Steve and I headed off to sneak around the baited spots from the night before. It was obvious that there were a stack of fish in residence, but in order not to spook them we took our time. Standing behind a small bush, slightly higher up the bank than Steve, I could tell him when the carp had turned their backs for him to get a rig in position. We really were like a couple of kids at Christmas, it was so exciting, I could see his hand nervously hovering over the rod as I gave a running commentary on the fish's movements and, although I wasn't even angling I was all of a quiver myself. A couple of minutes later, as three very large carp approached the spot, I warned him to be ready, and no sooner had the words left my lips than the water exploded as an angry carp made off. Shaking like a leaf, Steve hung on for grim death, and in the confines of the small bay things were a little fraught for a while, but soon enough he was in control. I could see everything from my vantage point, but deliberately neglected to tell him how big I thought the fish may be. He didn't have any idea as I scooped his prize into the net, but his face was an absolute picture when he realised. His personal best at this point was 32lb and he had just beaten that by a country mile.

The trip was a great success

At 41.04 I thought he was going to swallow his ears as he held it up for the cameras, one of the best moments I have ever witnessed in my carp fishing life! The rest of the trip was a success all round, and we caught a cart load of carp. We had dined and drank royally, and by the time I was back in Blighty I was ready for the American adventure to begin. Those that know me will testify to my hatred of carp matches, they just don't seem to enhance what carp fishing is all about for me. I have always felt that it should be me against the carp, and throwing in an element of competition between anglers ruins the whole thing. That said, there is something about these big international events, and I would go so far as to say that my time spent in Romania with Jenkins, was just about the most enjoyable weeks fishing I had ever had. To that end, although we had some serious intent, Adam and I set out to enjoy ourselves as much as we could.

The St Lawrence specials in action

Before we could even think about the fishing, though, there was so much to sort out. Thankfully, Kev Knight had plenty of dealings with the people that ran organised trips to the States, so that side of things was easily sorted (although I suspect Kev would tell you otherwise!). Fox also made a monumental effort and got everything that Adam and I would need freighted over, we even had a set of rods made up, the St Lawrence Specials, based on the Matrix rods I had been using for some time. It was a nice touch. Tim kept everyone up to speed on a weekly basis and the excitement levels just kept getting higher and higher, but there was one problem for me, however, and it was starting to overshadow all the preparations. It may surprise a lot of you, especially as I have spent most of my life jumping out of planes, that I hate flying but, believe me, I would much prefer to jump out of the damn thing, than land in it!

Then the day of departure arrived, and we all met up at Heathrow, it was the first time that our team had all been together; Tim Paisley, Steve Briggs, John Lilley, Rob Tough, Adam and myself. We were all issued with the team clothing, and lest I ever forget, thank you Tim, God knows what it must have cost to get the squad of six to America and into the competition. Thankfully, the flight was uneventful and we didn't crash, much as I had expected to, and the wheels soon came to a halt on Canadian soil. Once the customs at Ottawa airport had been cleared, we set off to sort out the hire cars - well, I thought they were cars, but when the guy at the desk said that one of the vehicles was a Dodge I immediately bagged it for Adam and me. I thought it would be the best way for us to make our entry into the States, like you do. Knowing that Tim

The team relaxes

has a bit of thing for anything black, I was a little nervous as we were led to our transport. Yep, you guessed it, the Dodge was black. His face was a picture as we loaded up the beast, still the deal had been done, but that didn't stop both of us giggling like a couple of kids as I roared out of the parking lot.

It was my job to guide us into America, which went remarkably well, all things considered, that was until we got to the border crossing, where all the talk between the Brits and the Guards was about creepy crawlies. Jeez, they said, you ain't spendin' time by the river, you'll get eaten alive! Adam was mortified, he really doesn't like insect life, and I chuckled as we drove on. Yet again, I probably didn't help, because all the way to our destination I told him about the things I had come across around the world. It made sense for me to tell him that my body had once been infested with blow worms that took an age to be rid of, and that I had any number of other bugs living in me from time to time. I was just about to tell him the story of a mate of mine who had a leech down his 'japs eye' when I glanced across at him. Even in the glow of the dash board I could see he had gone a strange colour, he really is a magnet for biting things, so I stopped winding him up...for a while anyway!

Sooner than we thought, we arrived at the 8-Ball Hotel in Massena, and after a good night's kip, it was time to get to know the area. The draw was to take place at the Akwesasne Mohawk Casino, and the match HQ was at the Donald Martin Civic Centre Arena in Waddington. Once we were happy with that, it was time to take a look at the river itself. I had heard so many stories about how big it was, but it's not until you stand on its banks and see for yourself just what an imposing sight it is, that you realise.

Bloody hell, it was huge! some two miles wide in places, with massive ocean going tankers chugging up its length, but I tried my best to force the image to the back of my mind. We would have to draw a swim and simply deal with it from there. Adam

Adam surveys the scene

and I got separated from every one else at this stage, can't understand why, and eventually ended up looking at one of the creeks that fed the main river and it was at this point that I started to fear for my life.

We parked the truck and made our way along the bank, spotting, as we went, our first St Lawrence carp, then as we turned a bend we were confronted with a rather large pick-up truck with what looked, for all the world, like the Beverley Hill Billies inside.

They had small spinning rods propped up on sticks and as we neared them, a giant of a man slowly walked toward us. He was wearing dungarees, and sporting the finest ZZ Tops beard I had ever seen. Spitting a rather large lump of tobacco infested gob at our feet, he said.

"I guess you'll be some of those there carp fishermen then".

We nodded, and stared open mouthed as he unsheathed a knife that Crocodile Dundee would have been proud of.

"When I gets one of those pesky carps, I gets my knife and slits him from his ass to his chin and throws him back in the river".

A comment that, I had no doubt, was aimed at shocking us. Unfazed and with a completely straight face, Adam replied.

"Well, when I catch one, I drag it by its tail across the bank, smash it again and again against the nearest tree, kick it around for a while, stamp on its head and then throw it as far as I can into the bushes!"

I was in pain because I was trying, rather forlornly, not to laugh, and the sight of that bleeding great knife in his hand was quite worrying. He was upset that he had been out done on the 'carp killing front', and I glanced toward their truck where a couple more of the 'good old boys' had appeared. With Adam trying to get the next instalment across to the fellow, I hurriedly dragged him away, as I could already hear the theme tune to Deliverance ringing in my ears! When we were out of sight we belted for our Dodge, and in a cloud of blue smoke, made good our escape.

The next day we concentrated on getting all the supplies we would need to sustain us, and highest on Adams list was mosquito repellent. We must have visited every shop for miles, relieving them of all their stock and pretty soon we had an impressive collection. He did have the bag on about one thing, and that was that some of the teams had got hold of a contraption that ran on gas, and was guaranteed to kill every biting critter within a hundred yards. As everyone was admiring their acquisitions in the car park of the hotel, Chris Woodrow produced the mummy and daddy of all devices, but unfortunately for him, when he read the instructions they discovered it had to be run from mains electricity.

We didn't laugh much...honest!

Anyway, with Adam now convinced he could keep the world's mosquito population at bay, he started to relax a little more. We did some more shopping and even escaped from the convoy that

Jingo all the way!

we were continually driving around in. I wanted to know just how much damage I could do to the ozone with the truck, and spent a while watching the petrol gauge move faster than the vehicle!

Then we arrived at a local KFC. The first thing that staggered us was the size of the portions, there was four times the amount of anything I had seen in the UK, and judging by the size of the clientele, I could see that they had been taking full advantage! As I started to tuck into mine, Adam remarked that I looked like Henry V111 eating his food. I remarked that if he didn't shut up, I would do to him what old Henry had done to several of his wives.

"What's that then, you going to do me up the tail pipe son?"

It caught me so unaware, that I was unable to control myself and sent a whole mouthful of KFC flying onto the nearby window. I couldn't stop laughing, and when I noticed the couple behind us starting to giggle, things just got worse. Within a minute, although most of the diners had no idea what was going on, the whole restaurant was in fits of laughter. In the end, I was under the table, completely and utterly out of control; we had to get out of here...quick! As we fell out of the door, two rather nice Harley Davidson's pulled up in the car park and I was just going to have a look, when I noticed the riders were two of the largest and butch women I had ever seen. Adam, now in full flow, called out in his loudest voice.

"Bloody Hell, its dikes on bikes!". I fell to my knees as one of them headed toward him.

"Help me," he said, "I'm going to die here!".

I was of no help whatsoever, because I was in the throws of breaking every rib in my

body, and it was all I could do to bundle him into the black beast, just before man-woman was about to tear him limb from limb. Yet again, I sped away as fast as the truck would take us, but the scene was set. If nothing else, this was going to be fun.

That evening, we unpacked all of our gear and started to prepare our tackle, Fox and Mainline having done us proud. With everything split between the three pairs, we left each other to get ready for action and, by the evening, all that could be done had been done, so it was time to head off for the draw. The Akwesasne Mohawk Casino was

The glitz and glamour of the draw

a most impressive place, with all the glitz and glamour you would imagine of an American gambling joint. Not that that is my kind of thing, so the first port of call was the beer bar and, from then on in, it was all a bit frantic, but the American Carp Society (ACS) had all bases covered. Not that I was aware of it, but evidently the evening went off without a hitch. Adam and I managed to draw swim 101, and spent a lot of our time trying to find out as much about it as we could. It was situated in a town called Ogdensburg, and that was as much as I knew as we returned to our hotel. Little did I know how attached I was going to get to that place, and the people that lived there.

It looked good

Come the morning, there really didn't seem to be that much of a rush. We needed as much rest as we could get but, by eleven, we were in the marina, via a very circuitous route and several stops for a McDonald's, of course. We would be allowed to bait up at one in the afternoon and the match would begin at three so, for a couple of hours we were on our own, but that was all about to change. We were paid a visit shortly before the off, by someone who I will not name, who runs a carp fishing business in the area and I wouldn't want everyone to know he has little idea about the river he guides people on! He came to tell us that we were in the third best swim on the river, and was sure we would do well, by the time he had left, we were convinced that we had a good chance – oh, poor deluded souls!

The first major obstacle to overcome was the flow. It wouldn't allow you to find out what depth we would be fishing in, because the marker would eventually appear 20 yards from the spot it landed, and I had to guess, in the end, that it was about 25 feet.

Then there was the problem of where to introduce the free offerings, because there was no way to gauge where they would come to rest. The best I could come up with was lob 'em out, and chuck a load of bait in, and hope that was enough to stop any passing carp on their way to the river to our left. Well it sounded like a plan to me!

It was now that the people of the area became aware that a new kind of circus had arrived in town and, over the next few hours, it was difficult

There was a new kind of circus in town

to even move around the swim, because so many people had come to see the clowns. We eventually asked the local police if they could put up some tape, but that did little to deter these oh so friendly people. A degree of normality had been restored by evening, and with Adam covered from head to foot in 'mosie' repellent, we tried to settle down. His worst nightmare never appeared the whole time we were there, but we did have one rather innocuous bug to contend with. The Shad fly is only found in two places on earth, one being a place in Egypt and the other being the St Lawrence River and, when they are in full swing, which would have been about a month after our departure, there are billions and billions of them emerging from the river every minute. Evidently, the snow ploughs that are used to keep the roads clear in the long winters, are employed to scrape them off the roads in the summer, so abundant are they. That night, we sat and watched as they crowded around a street lamp, and it was all very spectacular. But what a life they lead, born without a mouth, they emerge from the water in massive swarms, and spend the next twenty four hours trying to find a mate, then die. What we did work out, during one of our more boring moments, was that they spend 90% of their lives trying to get laid. If you can't eat anything, we thought it wasn't too bad a way to spend their time.

Although nothing happened in the night, sleep was hard to come by, we were just too excited I suppose. By 0630, though, the first of our regular visitors arrived, followed closely by the marshals. Nothing had been caught in our section, and as we had somehow lost our radio, we had no other way of finding out.

That is when Lynn, back in the UK, came to our rescue. The ACS had set up a marvellous web site and she could get all the information we needed, and regularly updated us via text. One thing that did become obvious was how ambitious the match had been. Several teams had not even made it to their swims at this point, because they needed ferrying to the islands they would be fishing from. Even then, the water conditions were so severe that it was a complete waste of time. We thanked our lucky stars we were sorted, but then we got a good kick in the nuts. Just to our

left was a small hut, built onto the marina wall, and we watched a guy unlock the door and go in. We ventured over for a chat, evidently it was a station for checking the environment,

"Oh Lordy, what you doing fishin' here, you won't see a carp for another two weeks. Too cold, and the river is runnin' too fast".

Just to make us feel even better, every time someone came to the swim they would say,

Our marshals for the week

We kept the bait going in all the time

"Jeez, you bin here two days and you ain't caught nothin' yet?"

They really knew how to make us feel good!

By Tuesday evening it was obvious we would struggle, but Tim and Steve had drawn a swim near to one of the creeks that the carp were spawning in, and had already amassed an incredible total, 800lb if memory serves me right.

We needed to catch some carp, and we needed a plan. It was an extreme thing to do, but we felt that instead of putting out bait once a day, it may be better if we had bait falling through the water all the time. This would entail staying up for most of the night, but needs must and all that, so that is what we did. Now, for those of you that don't know Adam, he has a slight problem when he can't get much kip, me, well I just get on with it. I have had to live with that for most of my life, but Adam gets sort of touchy when he's not getting his full quota. This was about to cause a few problems, and I don't want anyone to think that I am having a go, because I am not, its just the way it turned out.

That night, we sat on the high marina wall to our left and, via a baiting spoon, we trickled maize into the water. I must admit, by five o'clock I was losing the will to live, and moaning Mini was getting very angry but, although we were starting to get a few liners, there were no bites, and then we simply had to get some sleep. It was light as my head hit the pillow, and as it did, one of my rods ripped off but, unfortunately, after only a few seconds the carp had made it to the jetty to my right, and it was lost.

Oh bollocks!!

No time to dwell, though, because a couple of minutes later the other rod was hollering for my attention and, although this fish weighed a little over 12lb, it proved that we could get something from this swim after all. The first thing to contend with that morning were the marshals and, having metamorphosised into Aaay-dum and Eye-on by now, they arrived calling out these names. We needed the fish weighing, but Adam was

He gets a bit touchy when sleep is in short supply

At least we caught a few

having none of it, he just zipped down his door and refused to come out. Bless him! Once the weighing was out of the way, the wonderful people of Ogdensburg turned up to feed us, which happened every morning, and although I ate just about everything they brought, his Royal Tiredness would have nothing to do with them. I tried to snap him out of it, but the lack of sleep was really getting to him. That didn't stop us from trying, though, and on the Wednesday night we were once again on the marina wall doing our thing. The difference, this time, was that once the liners began, I caught a couple of carp, one of 29.14 and the other 23lb, and although it wasn't a lot when you looked at what Tim and Steve were doing, we were now only a pound away from taking the lead in our section. Although still as cranky as a caged tiger, Penning decided to socialise a little more that day, and it was while we were chatting to a group of guys, he nearly got his head blown off. Let me explain.

One of our regular visitors, who we had christened Fat Larry (all 30 stone of him),

I was determined to catch some more carp

was a weapons instructor, and had various pistols secreted around his rather enormous body. Adam asked if he could see one of them, and Larry unloaded an ornate revolver before handing it over to him, at which point, Adam stood up and shoved the gun at Larry's chest. "Give us all your dollars, fat bloke" he jokingly cried.

Suddenly, moving with as much speed as his bulk would allow, Larry drew another, very much loaded, gun from its holster.

"I am quite within my rights, and accordin' to the constitution of the U-ni-ted States of America, to blow your freekin' head off son, so hand me the weapon, real slow now".

The colour drained from Adams face, and he did as requested. Larry now had a major hump, and Adam ran for the cover of his bivvy - sensible move really.

Sleep is not so important to me, and by now I could tell that if I let things slip, we may possibly end up trying to rip each others throats out. But I was determined to catch some more carp, and much to Adams disgust, we once

Sleeping Beauty stumbled into action

again set up on the wall. As I constantly reminded him, we were English men and made of much sterner stuff than everyone else, although by now I was starting to doubt that myself.

With no action in the daytime, we decided to drive over and see Tim on the Thursday and although it was obvious, by now, that they would win the competition, we thought a visit might just give them a little spur on to continue in the same vein. It certainly gave Adam and me a break from trying to kill each other, and we returned a bit more refreshed. Once back in our swim we sorted out the rods, and whilst doing so, had our first sighting of a carp. It was about ten feet out from our bank, directly under Adams rods, and he soon had a rig and some bait on the spot, although his rods were still facing skywards. He then retired to try and get some sleep, but I just couldn't nod off and lay on my bed looking at his rod tips when, all of a sudden, one of them was nearly touching the water, as a carp sped off with his hookbait. It was the most spectacular run I have ever seen and eventually Sleeping Beauty stumbled into action and landed a double figure

common. For the first time in a while we laughed, but unbelievably, that was the last time he spoke to me until we got back to the hotel in Massena. We were both at the end of our tether, so I just let him get on with it.

And so, the last morning arrived, breakfast had once again been delivered, and I sat chatting to a marvellous Native American lady. She had, unfortunately, lost her son about three months

The final morning and the crowds arrived

I took my time

before, but wanted to tell me all about her culture, and was amazed that we returned all the fish we had caught. She then went on to explain the way in which animals have such a bearing on their lives, it was truly fascinating stuff, and to cap it all she had carved me a carp with 'catch and release' engraved on the side - a remarkable lady, from a rather remarkable community.

I was slowly falling in love with the place, and happy to see so many of the town's people turn out during the final hours of the match. It had been hard, very hard, but we had the section win to look forward to. Surely no one could beat us to that? When the marshals arrived for the last time, however, we were informed that the Hungarians had landed a 'car bootful' of carp in the night. We both felt cheated, and even though it wasn't even a big prize, it was what had sustained us, and helped us to keep it together but then, with minutes of the match remaining, and with probably 50 or 60 people in the

It left us a couple of pounds short

swim, one of my rods screamed into life to the accompaniment of a huge cheer. Having never played a fish in front of so many people, I took my time, but eventually Adam got it in the net, which was met with another enormous roar from the crowd, and we did our best to take a bow. It left us a couple of pounds short of a section win, but the match was over and it was time to return to the hotel.

I would just like to say a big thank you to the people of Ogdensburg, I for one will never forget you all!

Back at the hotel, Adam and I were now speaking, but all we could say was how

Tim gets a well done from Adam

difficult it had been. He really is like a brother to me, and I can forgive him just about anything, so we just needed to get out and blow the top off a few cold ones, then all would be right with the world once again! Then Tim and Steve arrived to a massive ovation, and although Penning was having a wash and brush up at the time, I went and dragged him out too. Once everything was sorted, it was off to the

Casino for the awards ceremony and it really was fantastic to see the boys pick up their hard earned trophy - and I sang my loudest rendition of the National Anthem ever.

What a night, what a week, and as much as Adam and I would have willingly ripped each others throats out at times, I couldn't have shared it with a better bloke. Then I realised I would have to get on an aeroplane once again, to get myself home but, as we cruised along at 39,000 feet, I started thinking about my fishing back home, what the hell was I going to do for the summer? In the end, I reasoned that if I was going to be chasing a monster around, then it might as well be the biggest one out there so, as the wheels touched down, the decision had been made; I was off to Conningbrook to chase Two Tone around for a while.

I was off to Conningbrook

I watched the sun rise on a new adventure

Chapter 24

Ashes to Ashes

It took me a lot longer to get over the America trip than I thought and, of course, there was the gear to sort out. Everything was in such a mess, but within a week I figured I was ready to rock. Information was a little thin on the ground, and with no idea what to expect at the Brook, I decided to just do what I normally do. Boillies and Response Pellets had, for as long as I could remember, caught me fish from every water I had visited and I could see no reason to think that they wouldn't 'do the do' down in Kent. It was also my first outing with the new Illusion flouro mainline, something I was sure would make a huge difference. Lastly, I threw a few tins of sweetcorn into the bait bucket; I was as ready as I would ever be, so set the alarm for three o'clock one warm and muggy evening in June. I am always the same when starting out on a new campaign, which meant that sleep was very hard to come by, but I eventually nodded off. The alarm clock let out its first bleep, but it didn't get a chance to do another one, and launching myself from my bed, I was out of the house within minutes - I was desperate to watch the sun come up on another adventure.

It had been seven years since I last set foot on its banks, and was unusually nervous about seeing the place again. The last time I was there the banks were so open, and I really hadn't liked being there at all. It may well have been because I was still in the army, and the fact that Lynn wasn't at all well, but whatever the reason, I had not given it a good go.

Pulling up in the car park, I grabbed the water bottle, and made my way to the waters edge and the sight that greeted me as the sun poked above the trees was quite incredible. The lake had changed dramatically; all the little spindly trees had grown up and fully matured, so much so that it looked an entirely different lake. I made my way up past the sedges toward Joe's point and beyond, when I came to another interesting feature. For reasons that did not become clear for a while, Brett's (the company that owns the lake) had cut a ten yard wide channel into the lake

The newly cut channel

behind and it was something, I was sure, that would influence the fishing, after all, we were now angling on a 35 acre lake instead of the original 20 acres. As you would expect of a lake that held the British record, on a Sunday morning it was very busy, and I bumped into a few friendly faces. Leroy Swan, Simon Bater and myself shared a brew as the day became warmer and warmer; they even brought me up to speed with what had been happening, but I left them to it after a while, and headed off to the new side where I could only see one person fishing, and that just happened to be Paul Forward. Having known him for years, but not having seen him in ages, it was good to catch up. He also mentioned that he had had several fish in and around his swim the day before but, as nice as that was, I couldn't help thinking how much this side resembled the Conningbrook of old. I wasn't sure I liked it, but when the odd fish started to drift towards him, the whole thing looked a lot more interesting.

By eleven o'clock, and with more and more fish arriving, we were joined by Little John who works with Paul. He had been fishing the Brook for a number of years, and again I tried to get as much information out of him as possible, and one thing that seemed to be very obvious - none of the local guys thought that Two Tone would be caught from the new side any time soon.

By now Paul had sprung into action but, unfortunately, he had to do so with

constant piss-taking from me and Little John. He had some of the fish taking floaters, whilst others were grubbing around in the margins, and of course, they all needed to be angled for, and we sat and chuckled as his antics became more frantic as the day wore on. Now, although we were having a good laugh at his expense, I would have been doing exactly the same thing. It was all very frustrating, then got even more so when a huge boat was launched up toward the channel, and once a large outboard motor was fitted, they started chugging around. Couple that with several swimmers steaming into his swim, and Paul was soon ripping out what little hair he had left. One of the bathers eventually swam between his rods and climbed out onto the bank, and then we found out why the

It was good to catch up

lakes had been joined. There was going to be a triathlon taking place around the area, and Brett's wanted the swimming part of the race to be held on one of their lakes. Conningbrook had lost the toss, and the newly formed channel gave competitors the distance they needed but, as it happens, on the day the whole event was a bit of a shambles. After a couple of hours the water sports activity ended and the lake was once again quiet and then, unbelievably, Paul got a couple of fish taking mixers, and the circus was soon back in full swing. By early evening it was time for him to leave but there was still the odd fish around and it was suggested that I get my arse in the area. I was off like a rocket, and within ten minutes I returned post haste with my barrow, just as Paul reeled his last rod in. We said our goodbyes, and all of a sudden I was on my own.

The swim itself is a point that juts out at the far end of the new side, which means that there is a bay either side of it. I spent some time looking around, eventually deciding to fish a rod in each bay, with one off the end of the point and, with none of the traps more than a couple of yards from the bank, it was a simple case of lobbing out a few broken boillies, a handful of Response Pellets, and a few grains of corn. With all that done, I could sit down and relax. The day had been a real scorcher and tomorrow was shaping up to be even hotter, no need for the brolly, so I set up my bedchair and brew kit, leaving everything else on the barrow. When

Sunset in the point swim

you set out to fish a place like this you know it is going to be hard, but with that comes a tremendous sense of excitement, which is probably why it took so long for me to get some shut eye, then, at some ungodly hour, I was wrenched from my slumber by a screaming buzzer, the one fished into the right hand bay and, somewhat bizarrely, I watched a bow wave travelling in one direction whilst I ran in the other. Once the rod was in my hands, I tried to get some sort of control, which is hugely difficult when you are shaking like a leaf! Soon enough, I had turned the fish and had it heading my way, it hit the surface soon after that, and although I could see it wasn't Two Tone, my knees kept on shaking. After all, this was my first Conningbrook carp! What a moment that was as I got him into the net, there before me lay a very old, but fantastic looking mirror. I cared not what he was called, it was a carp from the Brook, and the first salvos of the campaign had been fired.

Nine hours on the water and I had bagged one!

Still quivering, I weighed the fish at 20.05 and, thankfully, Tom trotted all the way round to do the pictures in the early morning light. Bloody hell, I hadn't been angling for more than nine hours, and I had bagged one already. For the next few hours I crept around hoping that the fish would return to the margin. The wind, although not strong, was coming straight at me and it really did look good for another bite. The first fish of the morning I spied was a 30lb plus common called White Tips, and in double quick time I had got a rod in a position that I thought gave me the best chance of catching him. Not wanting to hover over the rod and risk spooking the fish, I went and sat on my bedchair to drink a celebratory brew but,

One eyed Willy, for obvious reasons

half way down the cup, the rod on 'the spot' flew from the clip and it was one of the most savage takes I have ever seen. I could see it was a common and it fought like there was no tomorrow, but it wasn't the common I was expecting it to be. Still full of fight, I managed to steer it into the net, at which point I had to pinch myself, carp number two from this difficult lake lay in the folds of the mesh. He may not have been the biggest, but One Eyed Willy is certainly one of the characters, and at 20.11, I held him up for the camera, manned by my mate Leroy. I really couldn't have asked for a better start to proceedings, and although the following 24 hours went by with no action, I packed away a happy man. I would be back just as soon as I was able.

The early morning drive the following week passed without a hitch, and I immediately went for a look at the new part of the lake. There were plenty of anglers on the old side, but the new side was angler free. With a mist rising from the water, I crept into a small gap in the shrub lined margin, and no sooner had I got comfortable on my bucket, than a carp rolled a rod length out. It was difficult to see because of the green algae that was forming, but I could tell that there were several other fish present so, happy that they were there and feeding, I crept as quietly as an excited carp angler can, out of the gap, and once away from the lake, ran like a lunatic toward my car. Fifteen minutes later I slumped to the ground, having parked my barrow twenty yards behind the spot. Wheezing and sweating, I tried to quickly set up a rod, which was easier said than done, when I could still see the odd vortex being sent up!

But, after some time, and plenty of cussing, I gently lowered a hookbait into the area, followed as stealthily as I could by a handful of corn and pellets then, with the line as slack as you like, I switched on the buzzer and retreated to my barrow for a brew. I was just thinking about filling the kettle for a second cup of tea, when the single rod went into melt down mode. It was such a surprise that it took me a second or two to respond. All I could think about as the battle raged on was how hot it was, and what was a fish doing feeding in conditions like this? With the weed yet to take hold, I had no problems drawing the carp into the net, at which point, I was treated to a round of applause from the Doctor and Bill Dawson who were fishing just the other side of the channel, Bill calling across that he would come round and do some pictures for me.

The shockingly good looking mirror weighed 21.06, again not one of the monsters, but who the hell cares? I rang Keith, and burbled my story down the phone, he had a ticket too and at some stage we would be angling together. It had been so long since we had been on the same water, and with the success I had been having, I couldn't wait for him to get there. Along with putting the world to rights, as we normally do, there was also a small matter of the cricket.

Not one of the monsters... but who the hell cares?

I began to think more about the old side

The Ashes test series was just about to get under way, and not only are we great cricket fans, there was also the not insignificant matter of sticking it up the Aussies. As hard as tickets were to come by, Keith had got us a couple for one of the days at Lord's, and also the penultimate day of the last test at the Oval, although, later on, and with some considerable wheeling and dealing, he managed to get hold of a pair of tickets for the last day, too. Interestingly, having been speaking to Paul Forward, we learnt that he and his wife Dawn would be there on the last day to, although none of us could ever have imagined the drama that was to unfold around that fateful day.

Now, I would be lying if I didn't say I was there to catch Two Tone, and that is probably why I changed the way that I was fishing. I actually think it was a big mistake, I should have just been happy to be catching, but believing I knew it all (silly boy), I started to set out my stall with him in mind. I began to think more about the old side of the lake, and whilst the weather was hot and not a lot happening, I started to investigate some areas. What I was looking for were clearish spots that I could cast to, should the carp be in any particular area and, in that way, I could keep the disturbance to a minimum should the chance arrive.

For a couple of weeks the lake went into shut down mode, and whilst the sun became merciless in its intensity, we anglers began to come up with more and more inventive ways of keeping our lager cold. It is really handy having a Tesco's super store only half a mile from the lake, and I bought an assortment of cool boxes and tons of ice during that time, which was all pretty handy really, because whoever's swim you arrived in, there was always a cold one on offer. With the lake being so quiet, the trips to Tesco's for breakfast became more frequent, and were also guaranteed to be a laugh when you had Derrick Ritchie for company. Mind you, with that bloody music pumping out of his swim every morning, he wasn't exactly going to enamour himself to everyone, but that's another story! Whilst we were all looking for the next bit of entertainment, the old weekend warrior, Jenkins, helped himself to his first Conningbrook carp.

The weekend warrior helped himself to a carp

While I was away one weekend, he had got bored with sitting around doing nothing so, grabbing a rod, he set off on his travels until, eventually, he found a group of carp and flicked a zig at them. A few minutes later he was holding a 22lb common up for the camera, and I let out my loudest cheer in Aldershot, I really do get so much satisfaction from my friends catching.

We had lost to the damn Aussies!

Toward the end of July, the weatherman said that things were going to improve, south westerly winds and rain were on the way. Halla-bleeding-luya! The news was soured a little, however, by the fact that we had lost the first test at Lord's, those damn Aussies were full of it after that. Having been there to witness it left Keith and I in a pretty sombre mood, but that would soon change. Cricket aside, the weather heralded the start of an action packed few days at the Brook, and not just for myself. Simon Bater had helped himself to five fish over a couple of days from the Island swim, which was just reward for a tremendous amount of effort, and with that news still ringing in my ears, I raced through the early morning drizzle as fast as my old Mondeo would take me. The first thing I needed to do, after first parking my barrow in Joe's Point, was go and congratulate Simon on his remarkable haul. Over a couple of brews, he told me how events had unfolded, and while we talked I saw a fish show out in front of the swim I had secured. Good angling! It was now that I could take advantage of the work I had done a few weeks ago.

Whilst on my travels, I had discovered a lovely area about 50 yards out from the point and slightly to the left so, two casts with a bare lead and with the lines in the clips, I was good to go. Soon enough, two Fusion pop-ups were nestling on the spot and for company I had catapulted out around 2 kilos of 10mm and 14mm boillies. I sat under my Evolution rubbing my hands together as the rain increased, now we were dangling! As the barometric pressure dropped still further, I spotted the odd fish and tried to stay up as long as I could, which, if I was being honest, wasn't that long actually. The next thing I remember was standing in the rain clutching a bent rod, as an unseen carp tried to make good his escape. It eventually found a weedbed, and the laborious task of winching it all back towards me began. Slipping and sliding in the mud, I resembled a one legged man at an arse kicking party as I tried to strip enough weed from the line to allow me to retrieve some more. This process was repeated several times before I could just make out the end of the lead core leader, at which point I guessed the carp must be in the lump of weed just below

Like a one legged man at an arse kicking party!

that. With some difficulty I shuffled the lot into the net, and after a minute of ripping weed out of the way, I discovered I had caught a common carp. Again, he was no monster, but it proved that I was still getting things right.

I was joined that evening by Paul Forward, Pet Food Paul, and Little John, and a mighty fine evening it was too. The weather still looked spot on and it was with some difficulty that I got to sleep, waking at first light and, before I had even got the kettle on, I'd spotted two carp show over the spots. For the next two hours I couldn't drag my eyes away from the area, then, shortly before eight o'clock, I saw the sight I always hoped I would see.

Without a sound, the largest carp in the country rose from the water and slipped silently back down into the depths.

When he did exactly the same thing five minutes later I thought my heart would explode. I was so nervous that I turned and stared at the back of my bivvy, surely this was it? Two minutes later the bobbin cracked into the rod and I was away - now this was bloody frightening! The problematic weed slowed the fish's progress until, eventually, the inevitable happened, and it became stuck fast. Thankfully, I could see Little John's car chugging up the track on the opposite bank, and he soon got the message as I jumped up and down, waving like a lunatic, and he was with me in minutes. I had completely forgotten about Mr F, who was fishing up to my right but, soon enough, in the pouring rain, John and I were off and after the fish. As is the way of these things, once over the top, it was soon free of its weedy shackles, at which point John cleared the line and, after a couple of elegant pirouettes, we managed to guide the carp into the net. We could see that it was a mirror, but his identity was to remain a mystery for a while. Back on the bank, Mr F soon made some sense of the situation, and the Old Lake Fish turned the scales round to 24.12. Eventually, with the pictures done, and after slipping him back to his home, I punched the air once again...I was still getting it right. An extra night didn't persuade the big fella to come back for more, but things were going far better than I could ever have hoped for, as long as I was getting action, the more likely I was to catch him...or so I thought!

Hospital visits for Lynn kept me away from the lake for a fortnight, but by the time I got back I was raring to go. Unfortunately, my next session coincided with the weather being hot, still and quite frankly, boring. Only the odd fish was spotted and they were just lazing in the weed, it looked so uninteresting that I called a halt to proceedings after one night. As much as Lynn had wanted me to go, I now had an excuse to spend a few more days at home and the rest, I hoped, would do her good. The following week I was prowling the banks at some ungodly hour, and although I had seen a small fish on the old side, the wind was pushing through the gap into the new lake, and I wanted to have a really good look around there. I am mighty glad I did, because, as I stood on the high bank behind the Island swim, I saw several fish mooching around close in. They weren't feeding, but swimming aimlessly around, and I sat and watched them for ages. As it got lighter, I could

I punched the air once again

Damper had White Tips directly behind me

start to put names to them:- The Long Common, The Friendly Mirror and White Tips. In fact I saw most of the fish I could name, but no Two Tone. Although there were people around, I was loathe to tell anyone, so as quietly as possible I got my gear round there. Little John was the first to suss me out, and as he crept up behind me, I invited him to have a look. He seemed just as excited as I was, and wishing me luck, he trotted off to ponce a brew somewhere else. For two days I stayed there, and for two days the fish simply refused to feed, but as soon as they moved out of that side of the lake, they must have got the urge for a boillie or two. Damper landed White Tips directly behind me, so I wandered over to see the impressive carp lying on his mat, and after giving it some verbal for not allowing me to catch it, we got on with the pictures. With Jenkins inbound for the weekend, the cricket was really getting in the way of my fishing, for a kick off I didn't want to be far away from my radio, and whenever Keith was out of range of his, it was up to me to keep him

"Bring me my scalpel!"

posted. This day was no different, and by the time he had left work, the Aussies were 160 for 2. I hate texting, but had to tell Jenks that wicket after wicket was falling, in fact, by the time he got to me, the Aussies had lost a further six! It was a fine and social weekend, but the only other excitement was me having to extract a hook from Keith's finger, and of course discussing how we were going to thrash the Antipodeans. Bring me my bow!!

As with most carp anglers, I have to try and balance my time, and I needed to sort out a few things at home. Two weekends from now there was going to be a leaving party for Joe, who was, after many years, moving away. I had a charity event to go to as well, but a call from the hospital was going to change all that, and it looked very much as if I would not be able to attend the penultimate day of the Ashes series either, but Lynn as usual was having none of that! They wanted her to come in and have some tests and, with a big operation looming, things needed to be sorted out. Because we had no idea how long she would be in for, Lynn insisted that I go fishing for a couple of days, and to that end I was practically booted out of the house the following Sunday. Well if I must!

As luck would have it, Keith was still on the pond. He had been fishing the new side almost exclusively on his weekend visits, but although he was seeing plenty of fish, he was yet to get some action from there. I was keen to have a look at the area where I had seen them on my last visit, and sure enough I spotted the odd fish, and as I was sorting out a couple of spots, Keith popped round for a brew before he left. While we chatted we got a call that Topper had landed the Long Common from the Lawn on the old side, so we got round there in double quick time, and helped with the weighing and photos of the great fish. Topper is rarely lost for words, but on that morning he was dumbstruck. Suitably fired up, I bade Keith farewell and returned to my fish spotting, which eventually led me to set a couple of traps close in. By morning, though, that familiar feeling of failure was once again upon me, why the hell couldn't I get a bite? I did spot a couple of fish show much further out in the lake, but I felt I could not angle any better than I was; a mistake really, because I should have investigated that area straight away.

Later on that day, I was having a good walk around the lake and eventually came to the Perfume Bay. As soon as I climbed the tree there, I immediately spotted two commons heading toward the channel, and I nearly fell out of it when I spotted Two Tone right behind them, travelling in the same direction. I trotted round to the gap just in time to see him disappear into the new side. This was the first time that anyone had seen him do such a thing, and I legged it back to my gear as fast as I could. I stayed put for the night, but come morning I was sitting watching fish after fish showing down the other end but by the time I had got my gear round to the point, the activity had stopped, so I set out to investigate. The first cast revealed a silty channel in amongst some savage weed at 70 yards, a further four casts

Topper was speechless, and rightly so

and I was sure I had got the area sussed. All that was left to do was to trot round to the swim I had been in the night before, and check the marker was in the right position. It seemed a little too far to the right for my liking, so I went back and repositioned it, and a quick check revealed it was on the money. With two Pineapple pop-ups nestling in amongst twenty spods worth of small boillies, pellets and corn, I settled down in the very first swim I had fished a couple of months before. With the final Ashes test about to begin, I contented myself by watching the kestrels expertly catching mice in the long grass that surrounded me.

Come morning, I was waiting for the light to fill the sky with my eyes glued to the lake, but by seven o'clock I hadn't seen a thing and was beginning to think that not moving the day before had cost me the chance of a fish. By way of a distraction I spotted Smudge, one of the regulars, making his way towards me with his cup in hand and, over several cups of tea, we sat whilst I recounted my tides of woe. It didn't look remotely like anything was going to happen, but then, just as I was turning the conversation round to cricket, the middle rod flew from the clip and the buzzer screamed. The fish powered off, and there was little I could do to stop it, that was until it hit a large weedbed, where upon everything came to a grinding halt. I tried all the normal tricks, but it soon became obvious that I was in need of a boat. There was one small inflatable in the Island swim and, without prompting, Smudge ran off to get it. Five minutes later he returned huffing and puffing, but as soon as we put the little craft in the water we could see it was never going to be man enough for the job. He immediately volunteered to run all the way round the

Everything was on the money

other side to retrieve the boat that was stored on Joe's Point. It really was an effort above and beyond the call of duty, but it seemed an age before I could see that boat coming through the channel, with Smudge and Derrick Ritchie making full steam towards me. Poor old Smudge looked as if he was going to have a heart attack at any moment, so it was left to Derrick to ferry me out toward the fish, and, all the way out we were ripping weed off the line. Neither of us realised how bad it had become, there was acres of the stuff just below the surface and, once over the fish, I had to apply a bit more pressure than I would have liked but, eventually, it started moving, though the fight was far from over. For some time the common (that much we had been able to see) towed us around in circles, but the pressure eventually took its toll and Derrick scooped my prize into the net. After first taking a moment to catch our breath, and ensuring the carp was okay in the net, we set off for dry land. The small crowd that had gathered let out a round of applause as we arrived on the shore, and Damper Dan held the fish in the water, while the rest of us sorted things out; none of us could have imagined that in only a few days time, Dan would be standing in exactly the same place looking down on a carp considerably larger than mine.

Dan could have had no idea what was about to happen

The scale perfect 28.12 common looked stunning in the early morning sunshine. Smudge deserved a medal that morning, because if it were not for his efforts, I don't believe I would have landed that carp, and to finish off his days work, he cracked off some great shots for me. I think I owe him one, eh? Once the fish was back in the lake, there was just enough time for me to rush home and get Lynn to the hospital for her tests, and by early afternoon she was once again occupying a hospital bed. All she worried about was that I would not be able to go to the charity match, and that I may also miss the last two days of the cricket. Remarkable! By Saturday evening the vampires had taken their quota of Lynn's blood, and although we would worry about the results for a while, she insisted that I get straight on the phone to Jenks and tell him that we were off to the Oval the very next morning.

Bring me my arrows of desire!!

Sunday arrived and we boarded a train bound for the Oval. We had a corporate suite for the day and, amongst trays of champagne and truffles, we nervously waited for the action to start. We needed to dispatch the Australian batting line

Bring me my arrows of desire!!

up, but the cloud was building and we were unsure how much play we would get. We met up with two of Keith's work colleagues, Will and Paul, and while we supped the first cold lager of the day, the gladiators made their way into the arena. When you view cricket on the telly, it is easy to think that the crowd is too

A cold, nerve calming, lager

far away to see much, but from our position, high up in the stand, we could see everything as the English bowling attack set about the Aussies with a passion. Hoggard, Harmison and Flintoff, quite literally battered them into submission, and Keith and I cheered until we were hoarse! England came into bat, remarkably leading by 6 runs, and when bad light brought play to a premature end, we were 34 for 1 wicket. The Ashes series was on a knife edge, all we needed to do was bat through much of the following day, then victory would be ours.

Keith and I, rather unsteadily, and to the words of Jerusalem, made our way back to his place. What an extraordinary day it had been. We raised a few more glasses that night too, and with rather fat heads, rose early next morning to do it all over again. After battering our way through the commuter madness, we were one of the first to arrive at the Oval, and rather nervously, we sat alone in the stand for some time. You may well be wondering what all the fuss is about here, but Jenks and I live and breathe cricket, and this day represented everything. Much like a football supporter watching the England football team play Germany in a World Cup Final, this was our day of reckoning. Whilst the ground was filling, we eventually managed to find Paul Forward and Dawn, then together we shared a nerve wracking day of

We sat alone in the stand

drama. When a couple of wickets fell, Keith and I groaned, then Kevin Peterson strolled to the crease. After a few early scares, he set about the Aussies with gusto, oh how we cheered. I was so nervous after the lunch interval that I sat behind the stand for a while on my own, but the roars of the crowd drew me back. To be truthful, we foolishly thought that the Aussies had no chance, but shortly after tea our hopes were confirmed, and then 22,000 people let rip with the loudest rendition of Jerusalem I have ever

Bring me my chariots of fire!!

heard, and we were still singing hours later. The small Ashes urn was presented and the players did a lap of honour, no one wanting to leave the ground, least of all Keith, Paul, Dawn and myself. But we had done it, the Ashes, after 16 years, were back where they belonged.

Bring me my chariots of fire!!

Later that evening, just as I was pulling up outside my house, my phone chirped. It was a message from Damper Dan, he had landed Two Tone at a record weight of 65.02, and from the new side as well. I really could not have been happier for him; it was a fine bit of angling. Now, bearing in mind that I had gone to Conningbrook to catch that very fish, you may be surprised when I tell you where I would rather have been.

At the Oval, that's where, and I wouldn't have had it any other way!

For some time, I had been preparing for my participation in a match between England and France. The location made the fishing side of things pretty disastrous, but the pomp and circumstance that surrounded the whole event was incredible. I do like to use every opportunity I get to sing the National Anthem, none more so than when we won the match! Sadly, that had very little to do with Adam and I, who were once again partnered for the event. I tried desperately to make him sleep, but to no avail, and by the time the match started, I knew he was once again in cranky mode. We had drawn a swim on the river (there was also a lake), and on arrival in our 'swim' it was obvious we would have to do some heavy work. After several hours of defoliation, we were ready to go, but it didn't start off too well.

We had some heavy work to do

The mood was lightened considerably

Adam was in his 'I need some sleep mode', as he went at it with his marker float, and he was still doing it several hours later. I breathed a sigh of relief when he eventually announced that he had found a place for his fourth rod. He asked me for an 'H' block marker, which I duly handed him, forgetting that it was clipped up at about seven feet, the depth I was fishing the last time I used it. Out he went in the boat, and once over his twenty five foot spot, he threw the marker over the side. It started to unravel, and very quickly hit seven foot, at which point it disappeared from view. The air turned blue as he described how another snag had been added to his swim.

Laugh, I nearly swallowed my tonsils. He stormed back to the bank, positioned a hookbait, and that was the last I saw or heard of him for a few hours. The mood, however, was lightened considerably when that very rod screamed off, at which point he played and landed our only carp of the match. This is precisely why I hate match angling, there was nothing we could do, you can't move, and by the end of it, all we could think about was killing each other once again. There was one moment of typical Penning though.

While we were there, the local anglers had been talking about there being a few Black Bears in the woods which dominated the surrounding area of the river. I had all but forgotten about it, but one day, whilst he was out in the boat redoing his rods, he screamed back at me in the most urgent manner making me jump.

"There's a friggin' great bear behind your bivvy, run...run...run!!" Yeah right, I thought, but his voice became so insistent that I started to take him seriously. I suggested, in a rather nervous appeal, that he should come back and get me.

Tim and Kev proudly collected the trophy

"Move to your right, hurry, hurry..."

So I did, and very quickly too! The sight of me running around flapping like a budgie got too much for him in the end, and he sat in his boat weeping with laughter. I felt such a prat, but Adam had got his revenge for the marker catastrophe. Bless him!! The final night of the trip arrived and, with it, much George Cross waving and National Anthem singing, as Tim Paisley and Kev Knight proudly collected the trophy.

Yet again, another experience was chalked off the list on my carp fishing journey, but on the way home I had to decide where I was going to be angling this winter. I really wanted somewhere I could relax, and as luck would have it, I had received my winter ticket for the lake that I guested on with Keith and Dave the previous winter. Whilst I may well have wanted to do some chilled out fishing, there was one very good reason for wanting to fish this particular lake - distance. On the few visits I had made before, I used nylon as a mainline, but was keen to see if braid would get me those extra yards and, never having used the stuff before, this was a good place to see if I liked it. There was also the problem of not being able to use a leader of any type, so once the rods had been loaded up with some 20lb BS, Submerge Plus, I was ready to rock and roll.

The first session was all about getting used to the braid, but I didn't end up fishing anywhere near the distance I thought I would have to. The rods had only been out for a couple of hours, when I received a savage take, there was no steady pulling over of the tip and a couple of pre-emptive bleeps that are normally associated with nylon, oh no, this was flying! Although the fight was a little scary, I rather enjoyed losing my braid virginity, and the 28lb mirror

I was ready to rock and roll

The 28lb mirror made a good start to proceedings

made a good start to proceedings. I was even happier when a 27lb mirror followed a short time later but, as good as that was, I really wanted to see what distances I could hit with the braid, so on my next outing I chose a swim purely because I would have to fish as far as I could chuck a 4oz lead. There was also the fact that it is the nearest swim to the car, and that I could bait up by hand from the non-fishing bank. All in all, it fitted in nicely with my chilled out fishing. As action was expected mainly through the day light hours, I trotted round to bait up and quickly set up two rods, then all that was left to do was make a couple of mighty, sinew snapping casts and I was in the ball game! The day turned into an absolute blur as I got bite after bite, and one thing for sure, by the end of it, all my fears about braid had been exorcised. I'd had eleven fish up to 34.08, and once in my bed, I slept straight through until eight the next morning, then I had to do it all over

Eleven fish up to 34.08!

again! To be brutally honest, the fishing was not at all difficult, and followed the same pattern all the way up to Christmas, although there was one interesting story that unfolded, and revolved around the biggest fish I caught that winter.

I was set up in a swim that gave me good access to the middle of the lake when I acquired a couple of neighbours up to my right. I watched the nearest one unleash his marker float and get to work, then, not long after, I heard him call his mate and say that he had one on. Having not seen him cast a bait, I wondered what was going on, so wandered up for a look. He explained that when he was happy with his spot, he had put the rod down to sort out the rods when, all of a sudden, he had heard the clutch on his marker rod spinning. To his amazement there seemed to be a carp involved so he carefully played the fish into the bank, and I quickly made my way down to the water with the net. As it hit the surface all became clear, there was a massive ball of braid wrapped up in his marker line, and it was this that had snagged his line. It was a big animal too, but as he had not landed it properly, there was no way he was going to weigh it, but we still had some work to do. Unbelievably, the fish had not been hooked at all, but the braid attached to someones 'crack off' had wound itself around the carp's bottom lip. It all looked a little gruesome to begin with, but as I cut the stuff away, there really didn't seem to have been much damage done, thankfully. I had to squeeze the bottom lip out a little, then we filled it with some medication, and in no time at all she was powering off back into the lake. Job done.

A couple of weeks later I was once again testing every sinew in my body, launching baits to the horizon when, a little later on, I got a bite. This was one very angry fish, and it was some considerable time before I had it anywhere near the net but,

as I drew it over the cord, I knew exactly which fish it was, only this time I could rightfully find out how much she weighed. The bottom lip had healed nicely and at 39lb I smiled, feeling like a modern day Androcles as we had our picture taken; I like to think she paid me a visit by way of a thank you. The lake switched off quite dramatically after the Christmas holidays, but I wasn't about to find out when it would switch back on.

Life was just about to change once again.

I felt like a modern day Androcles

I had some great times on the Copse Lake

Chapter 25

A Line in the Sand

In January 2006, the fishing at the syndicate lake had all but come to a halt. I couldn't help thinking that I should have been at Frimley, after all, the water contained the one fish that I was now so desperate to catch. In the end, however, I believe I made the right choice, because I was just about to get a telephone call that would change the way the rest of the year panned out.

One cold January evening, I found myself speaking to a lawyer who represented a publishing company, and would I consider writing a technical carp fishing book for them? I am, sometimes, very guilty of jumping in with both feet and paying scant regard for any consequences. This time, however, I told the fellow that I would have to give it some thought. For many years I had been writing 'how to' articles, which at times can be remarkably similar to pulling your own teeth out with a set of rusty old pliers. I really wasn't sure I could write a whole book without slitting my wrists! That said, it ain't every day you are asked to do such a thing, and so the decision was made, but I could never have envisaged just how long that process would take. From that moment on, until early November, I worked every single day (all bar a few natural breaks in proceedings) until it was complete. Lynn proofed it all, as I made my eyes bleed at the computer screen until, after a while, I actually started to enjoy it - remarkable! Also, I had to satisfy two magazine articles a month, and I was determined to honour that commitment, but I hate doing anything just for the sake of it, and wanted my writing to be up to date and relevant, which meant that I would have to go fishing.

CEMEX Angling (formerly RMC) had been redeveloping the Copse Lake at Yateley, and in an effort to find out what the fishing was like, I had been given permission to do some angling there. All of it revolved around articles that I needed pictures

I had several trips to Rainbow Lake

for, but I did have some great times over there with my old buddy Mat Woods. The main thing that stopped me going stir crazy was that I had been invited over to Rainbow Lake in France and, during that year, I had four trips booked; two arranged by my mate Barry Cole, and the other two by my good friend Tim Paisley. At this point, I simply must say that foreign fishing does little to get my juices flowing, and whether anyone wants to admit it or not, the chances of catching very big fish are multiplied a thousand times, because there are so many of them out there. In saying that, and due in no small way to the controversy that surrounds the venue, I was keen to have a look and discover what it was all about. I truly enjoyed

I truly enjoyed my time there

my time there, and on all but one occasion, when I really did dance with the devil, all the fish I caught were from open water spots, with little danger of having to go and retrieve every carp I caught from a snag. There are so many fish in there that I found if I baited away from the dangers, they would eventually come and find me. Hell, I even got loads of chances to fish with the free-spool facility on my reels engaged; a full blooded run at Rainbow is a rare thing! I spent a week in January, one in February, and another in April, culminating in a fortnight in June. The latter, in hindsight, was far too long to be leaving Lynn on her own, but that won't happen again. I caught some monsters too (well, to me they were), but the trips were holidays, and I treated them as such.

Tackling Carp was a living, breathing reality

With the last trip out of the way, I knuckled down to finish the book, and by October, Tackling Carp was a living, breathing reality. I couldn't possibly be prouder of the way in which it turned out, but once that was done, all I could think about was doing some fishing for me and I had somewhere in mind that just might allow me to relax, and get back into the swing of things. The few visits I had made to the Copse meant that, at times, I would be fishing very near to the Match Lake. It may surprise some of you that I had only fished there once before, bearing in mind how close it is to my home, and its wonderful history. On many occasions I could hear fish booming out in the night, and even investigated a few spots after finishing an article. Two years previously, the lake and its occupants had suffered greatly, in no small way due the misuse of bait boats; snags and those wretched contraptions should never be allowed to meet! But through a great deal of hard work, none more so than the bailiffs, the lake was once again coming back to life. I didn't want to spend long on there, but I just had to have a go before, once again, turning my attentions to that big old common in Pit 3.

Mat and I had arranged to do one last feature on the Copse and, once it was done, I immediately moved my gear the short distance to the Match Lake. Again, I had heard fish in the night, only this time I had gone over to look at the areas of activity. One swim covered the area, and as soon as I was able, my barrow was parked in the Golf Tees swim. The weed looked horrendous and it was a while before I had found what I was looking for; a large, clear area, surrounded by wall to wall green stuff. Once I had positioned a couple of hookbaits as close to the edges of the clear spot as possible, I went at it with the spod, and a couple of hours later I was supping a brew, content with my efforts. It felt strange not to be thinking of yet another day, tapping away on my keyboard, and I was overjoyed that I didn't have to switch that damn computer on for a while. As darkness fell, and I settled down, the liners started, and continued throughout the night, so I was a little surprised not to get a bite until the early hours. The weed made for a very fraught time, but I eventually managed to lift my net around a nice common and, at 21lb, it was a good start to my period of new found freedom. A couple of hours later, I was out of the gate and away, Lynn was due at the hospital, and on discovering that she may well need another operation, I decided to take my foot off the gas peddle for a while. We had no idea when she would have to go in, but I didn't want to be on a mission when the time came. In the meantime, and at her insistence of course, I got myself back to the Match as soon as I could. I needed to see if I was just being my normal lucky self with that common, or was I getting things right?

I am not a lover of preconceived ideas about what swim I should be fishing until I reach the water, preferring, instead, to have a good look around and let the fish tell me where I should go. I did, first of all, grab the Golf Tees and once I was happy that my gear would remain dry, I set off for a couple of laps of the lake. Nothing was

The weed was horrendous

Scale on the Shoulder at 29.10

seen, so I sorted myself out, and fished exactly the same as I had done the week before. Around mid-night, and amid a load of liners, I got my fist bite, but as I pumped the ball of weed back to me, I was unsure if there was anything on the end. Once I had carted the 30lb of weed to my unhooking mat, I eventually discovered a stunning little Sutton stockie of around ten pounds, small he may have been, but he represented so much more than that, as he was the future of this lake. I spodded out some more bait and settled down once again, but even though the liners were quite frantic at times, it wasn't until half five in the morning that I was doing battle. Thankfully, the lead released almost immediately, which meant the fight was conducted on the surface, and away from the weed. At one point I was sure I had hooked a catfish, so hard did it fight, but eventually, the flank of a good mirror broke the surface and, once in the net, I could see that it was one of the originals. At 29.10, my photographer identified the fish as Scale on the Shoulder, a proper history fish, but things got even better as I sorted myself out for my final night.

It looked bigger and at 31.07 she was!

Exactly the same as before, I had set my traps, but this time I didn't have to wait too long for a bite. The weed played havoc with proceedings, but thankfully, it soon fell off, and a more normal fight ensued. As it came into netting range, I couldn't help thinking that it looked even bigger than the last one, and at 31.07 she was! Steve Fantuzzi came up from Yateley Angling Centre, and identified the carp as the Bum Snag fish. What an awful name for such a marvellous creature, I couldn't help thinking that perhaps that devious fellow, Micky Gray, had had a hand in naming this one! With all thoughts of book writing erased from my mind, plus the capture of two of the lakes most famous carp, I was now ready for the world once again...let the games begin!

Due to my almost compulsive need to move on, I was sure that this would be my last winter in search of Charlie's Mate; I just couldn't envisage myself staying on the same water for any longer. What I did commit myself to was giving it one final bash, a no holds barred attempt. At least if I did fail, I couldn't accuse myself of not giving it my all, but then, just as I made my decision, I got side tracked once again.

Rather stupidly, I went to Sandhurst

Nigel Sharpe had started doing a little time on Sandhurst Lake, just up the road, along with a couple of other guys I knew, and rather stupidly, I decided to have a go on there for a while. I believe it is a testament to the fact that I was thinking about Frimley the whole time I was there, why things went rather badly. It had, according to those in the know, been fishing its head off, but my arrival managed to get every carp in the lake running for cover. For three weeks I smashed my head against a brick wall, but all I caught was bream after bream. It wasn't that anyone else was catching either, because they weren't, and on the second morning of my third session I realised the folly of this decision. I had been watching some bubbles come up over one of my spots for an hour, when a rather large mirror poked its head out, sending up a great swathe of bubbles. Now that was very nice indeed, what wasn't so nice was a large lead landing on the spot a minute or two later, followed shortly after, by another, and as if that wasn't enough, a bait boat came chugging into view, heading directly to the spot. By the time its load was delivered, I was already starting to pack up. Although the two anglers, and I use the description very loosely, obviously lacked a brain cell between them, they ultimately did me a favour because, at that moment, Charlie's Mate became the only carp I thought about for the next three months.

The following week I set out for Frimley, arriving shortly before five in the morning, and after wheeling my barrow

Rods out at Frimley

onto the lake, I set off for a good look around. After a couple of hours I had only seen one fish and, like you would, I set up in a swim to cover that area. The plan was to fish boillies only; the big girl liked them, so that is all she would be getting from me. At the time, Frimley was dominated by the use of bait boats, and so in an effort not to make the baited area look like it had been delivered by one, I spread the bait out as much as I could. The night was incredibly mild, and some time in the wee hours one of the rods ripped into life; I had almost forgotten what a blistering take sounded like, and nearly jumped out of my skin! I had also forgotten how hard Frimley carp fight, so it was some time before I had the fish subdued, and ready for the net. The 19lb common was soon returned to its home, and for the first time, in a very long while, I was completely comfortable with my fishing. It was good to be back! At seven o'clock I was once again marvelling at the way these carp fought, and it was with some relief that I netted another immaculate common of 21lb. A mate was fishing round the corner, so I held the fish in the net, and called him to do some pictures, but within minutes the repositioned rod was away again. Thankfully, I had two nets set up, having learnt some valuable lessons from my previous campaigns and, pretty soon, another common of 22lb was held up for the camera. No more fish were landed that session, but for now I was happy...the thrill of the chase had begun!

Don't ask me why, but I was determined not to be drawn into fishing one swim for the duration of the winter. The Double Boards had always been so good to me, but for some strange reason, I never felt as if I would catch the one fish that I wanted from it. With this in mind, I arrived for my second trip, but no matter where I looked, the Double Boards always appeared to be the best option. Once in the swim, I made the decision not to fish the exposed bar but to concentrate my efforts

The thrill of the chase had begun

at no more than forty yards. For a kick off, it made baiting up so much easier, and history indicated that it was an area of the lake she liked. A couple of small commons suggested that I had found spots which carp were prepared to feed, and I was content with that. I still tried to fish different areas, responding to what the carp were telling me, and on the next visit I was rewarded with a 21lb common, plus one of 31.02. Coming from a swim that I had hardly fished before, I was happy that the bait was working so well. The following week I decided that my days of fishing different areas were over, as I got a first hand glimpse of how focused on the Double Boards the carp actually were. I had taken up residence in a swim called the Fallen Tree, which is twenty yards to the left, and a few hours after my arrival a young lad called Sam turned

I was happy the bait was working so well

up and occupied the ever popular swim to my right. Apart from a couple of bream, the night was uneventful, but at first light I saw three fish show to my left and it looked as if they were moving down the lake toward us. They passed me by completely, of course, settling over Sam's baits, and over the next couple of hours he landed an 18lb common and one of the lakes biggest fish, Shoulders, at 34.14 - a new pb. Not wanting to sit and hope, I moved as fast as I could round to the far side of the bay to Sam's right and soon had some traps set, with a scattering of boillies around each, but the weather had soaked me to the skin. In typical army fashion, all I could do was jump into my sleeping bag, and attempt to dry out. The rain stopped later on, thankfully, and then the bites began. Having landed two 18lb commons and lost one of similar size near to the net, I was just drying things out ready to pack up, when I landed a fish of 21lb. Now, although these weren't big fish, I was hugely encouraged by their capture because it proved that I was reading the water well, and angling efficiently, so I couldn't ask for more than that. With everything packed away, I reached down to unclip the bobbin from the last rod, and as I did so, I couldn't help noticing how tight the line was, the penny finally dropping when the line sped through my fingers. Now that was probably a bite! She tried her best to beat me up for quite a while, but I got the upper hand and slipped her into the net eventually. Steve Mogford, who had been on Frimley for a while, turned up and helped me out with the pictures, but we had no idea, at the time, just how much help he would be for me, a couple of months later. At 33.10,

She was a fish I had never seen before

not only was she the biggest of my campaign so far, she was also a fish that I had never caught before, and that would do for me.

During the Christmas break I was determined to take my foot totally off the pedal and relax, which is exactly what I did. It gave me time to think about what I was doing, and as far as I could tell, all I needed was to 'keep on keeping on'. The one thing that was throwing a bit of a spanner in the works, was that the carp were refusing to show themselves. During the previous two winters I had done, I became convinced that the carp spent more time out of the water than in it! Now, though, I was having to react to the slightest indication, and for as long as I could keep them open, my eyes remained glued to the water. With all that in mind, I started 2007 full of confidence, but that quickly dwindled as the bait boat users began making my life hell. I wonder if the manufacturers of these devices could see their way clear to include a couple of brain cells in the packaging, it would make my life a lot less complicated! That said, I did winkle out a small mirror, so at least I was on the score sheet early in the year.

After all that, I decided to concentrate on the Double Boards, as its layout meant that I wouldn't have to defend it against the Henley Regatta boys. I concentrated my efforts on the short range spots and, once set up, all was well in Chilly world. That was until I got a visitor a while later, who informed me that Charlie's Mate had been caught a couple of weeks before at 43.04. Whilst I was happy for the captor, I found it strange that he did not inform anyone, I have no idea why, but considering there were a few anglers on there to catch that one specific fish, it

I had to just keep on keeping on

seemed a little odd. The other down side to the capture was that she had once again fallen to a bait boat full of maggots. I distinctly remember saying that she loved her boillies...hadn't she read the script? It was at that moment that I decided to up the baiting levels. I would work off my frustrations trying to break as much catapult elastic as possible!

And so, a couple of days later, on one cold Sunday evening, I set about putting my plan into action. There was no one on the pond, so I wouldn't be affecting anyone else's fishing, but just as importantly, no one

I decided to up the baiting levels

could see what I was up to. An hour, and two sets of catapult elastic later, I had delivered six kilos of Pulse boillies to the short range spots from the Double Boards. I did the same thing the following evening, but with half the amount of bait, ready for my arrival in the morning. Once in the swim, two rods were cast to the baited areas, while the other was fished in the margin to my right, and then the wind came. It had been forecast, of course, but I wasn't as prepared as I should have been and much of the night was spent with the bivvy flapping in my face, so I pushed a

few extra pegs in and pulled the bag over my head, hoping for the best. Bloody hell, it looked quite scary! It wasn't until six in the morning that I got my first bite, and I was pleased to see that it was the baited spot that had produced the goods.

Playing a carp is a fraught experience at the best of times, but it takes on a whole different meaning when you have a gale going on around you. As half a tree floated past, and with branches crashing around my head, the battle continued, until I eventually led the fish into the outstretched net. Then, just as I did so, the close in rod called for my attention. I quickly made sure that my first visitor couldn't escape, and picked up the

The first of a stunning brace

Hell, I love carp fishing!

other rod but, this time, I slipped on the boards at the front of the swim and I found myself kneeling in the margins, having taken buffoonery to a whole new level. To my complete surprise, I somehow managed to net the fish without further ado. The whole swim was a scene of complete devastation, but as wet and cold as I was, you cannot imagine the pleasure I felt, seeing two stunning, fully scaled carp in the bottom of my nets. Steve Mogford was over the way, baiting up on his way to work, so I gave him a quick call, and he said he would be round as soon as he was done. As I waited, the remaining rod ripped into life and I slipped the net under a 26lb common, which made a nice addition to my already impressive collection of carp. We weighed the two mirrors at 33.12 and

The snow greeted me on my next session

25.08, and I remarked that I would probably never again have the pleasure of catching such a good looking brace. I made us a brew with some difficulty, because I couldn't stop laughing...Hell, I love carp fishing!

The snow greeted me on my next session, and I concentrated on staring at the rods. It may surprise you, having fished through more winters than I care to mention, that I have never caught a carp when there has been snow on the ground, so I really wanted a run. As the day went on, it started to melt, and as the last vestiges turned to liquid, one of my rods was away. I had just got control, when one of the other rods started screaming too - now I was in a bit of a pickle, so, as quickly as possible, and whilst trying to slow the second fish down with one hand

This 29.02 common made me smile

on the other spool, I got the first one in the net. With no time to dwell, I played the other but, unfortunately, just as I was getting the upper hand, the bloody hook pulled. Aaaargh!! Although the snow had gone, and I had lost a fish, the 29.02 common made me smile. I fished on until the following morning, but got no more action.

I had to laugh

Over the next couple of days I again baited up, and although the action wasn't frantic, I was still getting bites when most of the other hardy souls were blanking. I really didn't believe I could do more, so, as February began, I was as determined as ever to get that big old common in the bottom of my net. It was at this point, and I know my wife will pay testament to this fact, that I gave up on everything, nothing else mattered, and I would let nothing get in the way of things. It was shit or bust time!

As serious as I was, there were moments that brought a smile to my face, like when I was doing a feature with Mat Woods for instance. We were going to talk about climatic conditions, and the effects they have on carp, but that is something that is very hard to take pictures of. Mat had come up with this marvellous idea of drawing pictures on a white board, it was one of those things that made him so good at his job. As he was about to leave, he left me a little present on that very board. It was a picture of a big common, and at the top he had written, "Dream on". I had to laugh, but it made me more determined than ever.

As February unfolded, so the weather improved, and it was almost spring like. At first the carp responded to it with gusto, and the baited areas continued to produce the goods, but more and more I was wondering where the bigger fish were, and most importantly, Charlie's Mate. Most of the fish I was catching were twenty pounders, which for February isn't really a bad thing, it's just that the lake has so many big fish in it; I couldn't believe I wasn't catching any of them. I was now at the lake every day, if I wasn't fishing, I was baiting up after dark, spending as long as I could there in the hope of uncovering a clue or two.

Midway through the month, I thought things were improving when I hooked

A long torpedo shaped common

an absolute animal. I have no idea how long we battled away, but it seemed an age before I had a long torpedo shaped common in the bottom of my net and, at 32.15, it was a fish that I had not seen before. With the old confidence sacks overflowing once again, the next trip started out full of hope, but finished with me ripping my hair out! For a couple of months, the fish had refused to show, so I was very surprised on my arrival one morning to see carp leaping everywhere. I couldn't help thinking that at long last they had all woken up, and were on the lookout for some food. I had plenty of that with me, and spent the next couple of hours sorting out a feast for them; I was rubbing my hands together in anticipation. For the next forty eight hours I sat there and didn't receive so much as a liner, I had tried just about everything I knew, but all to no avail. For twelve days the lake didn't produce a single fish, and although we all worked so hard, nothing happened. I spent the majority of my time up in the trees, watching what was going on, and I could always see carp, because they weren't spending any of their time on the bottom of the lake. But as March began, my wheel of fortune started to slow.

The wheel of fortune started to slow

I continued baiting the spots throughout that period, still confident it would work, but it was the next visit when I first clapped my eyes on Charlie's Mate, that year. I was keen to get aloft again, and once up the tree, the first thing I saw was her gliding along the margins, right under my feet. Just along the way there were a couple of carp, one common and a mirror, both about 30lb, and they appeared to be feeding. She approached, but on nearing them, she turned away sharply, going out to the middle of the bay. She repeated this a few times, before travelling straight out into the lake, and came to a halt over one of my baited areas when, all of a sudden, she disappeared and sent up a couple of patches of bubbles. I watched for a while longer, but didn't see her again. You will understand, then, the utter panic I was in when the rod on that very spot burst into life. I really took my time playing that fish, all the while expecting a bloody great common to break the surface, but as it did so, I was sure I saw some mirror carp scales. And so it proved to be, but being so highly prized, I could hardly be disappointed, now could I? A couple of hours later, and I was once again playing a fish with my heart in my mouth, it was a common, but wasn't as big as expected. I got a couple of shots, and gently sent the twenty four pounder on his way.

Whatever I did here, I couldn't for the life of me fathom out what to do to get the one bite I desperately

The scales read 34.04

wanted. So, in time honoured tradition, I let them have another few kilos of boillies. I had to endure a Pike sexual marathon from mid-night until first light, and many was the time I had to reposition the hookbaits, so violent was their courtship. Just as I was answering a call of nature, one of the rods hollered for my attention, and as soon as I had the rod in my hand, I knew it was a good fish. Most of the fight took place under the rod tip, but with some relief, I got it into the net. Rather pleasingly, the scales read 34.04, and as I knew Steve Mogford would be down to bait up shortly, I sent him a text asking him to call round, but I hadn't even put the phone down before one of the remaining rods was ripping off. At 29lb, this fish deserved a picture too, so I secured him in the other net along side his friend. After suffering some verbal abuse from Mogford, I was once again on my own, but he couldn't have reached his van before the remaining rod joined in the party. Eventually, a rather chunky, and very familiar common lay in my net. I was so pleased with the action, but this particular capture made me feel a little sad. This

was the very first carp I ever landed from Pit 3, so I had come full circle, right back to where I started, and for a moment I felt as far away from catching Charlie's Mate as it was possible to get. At 28lb, the fish had obviously grown a tad, but I slipped him home with a message for his big sister. If she would just pay me a visit, then I would leave them all alone forever! Two twenty pound

A rather familiar common

commons rounded off the session, but my head was still in a spin. I needed a little Divine intervention, and I remembered where I may have just the place to find it. Two days later, Lynn and I were heading off to the Five Lakes carp show in Essex. I was determined to put Frimley to the back of my mind, it was our wedding anniversary, and I didn't want anything to spoil it. That said, I did have a plan.

You see, the last time the show was held at this venue, Chris Ball was compering a panel, and asked us what the immediate future had in store for us. I told him that I was going to catch Shoulders that week, and blow me down, I did just that. All that was needed, by my reckoning, was for Tim Paisley to do the same and it would be all over bar the hangover. Just by way of insurance, I tracked down Chris Ball and demanded he ask me as well! It didn't work out quite that way, but unbeknown to me, my time was fast approaching.

I was back on Pit 3 as soon as the show was over, but one thing was troubling me greatly. In a couple of weeks time, the spring tickets for the lake would go on sale, and as much as I was sure where the big girl was spending much of her time, I couldn't help wondering what the extra pressure would do to her routine. To that end, for about three weeks I had been baiting a spot that was a bit off the beaten track, I never put that much bait on it, but everyday it had received about four pouchfuls of boillies. It would soon be time to fish it, but not just yet. The next trip, an over-nighter, brought me two fish, a long 27lb common and a real bruiser of a fish at 32lb. There is a two day rule at Frimley, so the next visit would start on a Saturday, which also happened to be the first day of the spring ticket. It was bound to be busy, so I wasn't sure if I would be able to get back into the swim and, at this

A real bruiser

point, I was probably at my most unbearable. I have no idea what it must have been like for Lynn, but I had totally lost the ability to think of anything else.

I baited the spots heavily on the Thursday night, and made my way back shortly after dark on the Friday. Thankfully, Steve Mogford was set up in the Fallen Tree, next door to the Double Boards and was able to tell me when the day angler had left. I couldn't stay long so got on with the job in hand, making sure to put a few boillies on the new spot. Tomorrow I would fish it for the first time. Whether or not I was having a premonition about the next day or so, I have no idea, but I found it almost impossible to sleep that night. The alarm clock barely made a bleep before I had dispatched it across the bedroom. Under normal circumstances, I have a quick brew before I leave, but today was different; I had to get to the lake in double quick time. Just a few minutes later I pulled up, for the thousandth time, at the Hatches and quickly loaded my barrow. My phone was silent, so I guessed Steve had had a quiet night; there was also the fact that there were no more cars parked in the area, and it was a good bet that the swim was free, so, I was off like a steam

The rods were first, as always

train towards the lake. I normally stop at swim three, because it gives a good view of the whole lake, but this time, however, it was occupied and anyway, I had absolutely no intention of stopping until I reached my destination. There was only one place on the whole planet that I wanted to be, and as I belted through the trees, I could see that the Double Boards was empty.

With a huge sigh of relief I dumped my barrow down, now I needed a cup of tea! I didn't have to wake Steve, and we shared a couple of brews, he had had a 21lb common in the night, but other than that, all was quiet. I left him to catch up on some beauty sleep and started to sort my gear out. The rods were first, as always;

there was no need for a bivvy as the day looked like being a nice one. Two rods were cast to the baited areas, with a small PVA bag on each, and once that was done, I let them have a few pouchfuls of boillies. Now I could concentrate on the new spot, I hadn't cast a lead at it in ages, so as much as I didn't want to, I had a feel with the marker float. Three casts later and the float was above the spot where the gravel began, a cast a couple of yards beyond it, would put me into the silt, just where I wanted it to be. With the traps set I could fire up the kettle and have a nerve settling brew, I needed it!!

Dawn on the fateful day

I went into action

Spring is a great time at Frimley for Zigs and I could just make out Steve, through the trees, getting his rods sorted out. While I was sure that this tactic would catch me more carp, I was working to a plan and I wanted to see it through. I sat by my rods and watched as more and more anglers turned up, it was now the busiest I had ever seen it. I couldn't resist reaching down and stroking the rod that was on the new spot, hoping it was the ace up my sleeve that I was looking for. Around nine thirty I lost interest in counting the amount of people turning up, and decided to have a bite to eat, but with so many anglers on the lake, I was starting to get very anxious indeed. One thing for sure, I had never worked so hard for a fish, and neither had I become quite so obsessed with one either. I was asking her to put me out of my misery for the hundredth time, when the rod fished to the new spot hooped round, and the buzzer howled. It took me by surprise, and on auto pilot, I went into action. Because my alarms are always turned right down, and I have the trot box in my bivvy, no one was aware of the bite, which meant that I could just concentrate on getting control of an obviously big fish. On and on it raced, and there was very little I could do at first, but the pressure eventually told and I turned it; at least it was a bit more normal now, although its deep heavy lunges did nothing to settle my nerves. For now, I was in control, and a few minutes later I had the fish twenty yards out and boiling just below the surface. But when that big back broke the surface for the first time, all I could see was the indentation where the dorsal fin starts, and then I knew.

I was now playing my obsession, all the hopes and dreams of a young boy rested on the next few minutes of my life. Even my heart joined in the action, and was thumping just as rapidly as the ticking of the clutch. With her staying deep, I concentrated on getting her into netting range. I have no idea how many times I pleaded for her not to fall off, but it must have been a lot, and inch by painful inch, I drew her over the net. At full stretch, I lifted the mesh and she was mine! Steve was out of his bivvy by now, and quickly realised that something was going on.

Light My Fire!

Oh, it was going on fella, so much so, that I thought my head was going to explode. I really didn't know what to say, so asked him if he would look in the net, and tell me what was in there. Up he strolled, and quickly turned.

"That will be Charlie's Mate then, fella".

With apologies to everyone on the lake, I let out the loudest, "Light My Fire" ever!! At which point, I was torn by a hundred different emotions, I really didn't know whether to laugh or cry. The most important thing to do was to ring Lynn, and much as I expected, she promptly burst into tears, although I wasn't too sure if it was about the capture, or the fact that she may just get her husband back! One thing I do know, she had played as much a part in all of this, as I had. Steve, thankfully, brought some order to the mayhem, and eventually we were ready to weigh her.

44.04... well bloody done son!

She looked absolutely enormous, and there was a long moment of silence as I lay her on the mat. The scales were zeroed, but I could not bring myself to read them, so Steve looked over the top of them and smiled,

"44.04, well bloody done, son!"

I was speechless, and as the image of Clarissa and Richard Walker flashed into my mind, I was, once again, that little boy.

This was everything I had ever wanted from my fishing, it had taken a while, that was for sure, but all good things come to he who waits. The next person to ring was Mick Barnes, and he kindly gave me permission to sack her for a few minutes, but the call was far more than that. Long before he had become the boss at CEMEX Angling, Barney had been around to help, and I will never be able to thank him enough. And so, with a battery of photographers, I held my obsession aloft in the early spring sunshine, and sooner than I wanted, I released her back to her home. At which point, I quickly packed everything away, which was entirely the right thing to do. To put myself in front of that magnificent carp again would be so wrong. A line had been drawn in the sand, another chapter in my life had come to an end. Good bye Frimley, I shall miss you.

Frimley, I shall miss you

Light My Fire!!

Never Ending Story

Now you are nearly at the end of this tome, you may well have noticed that there is one glaring omission, and that is ECHO. Having set out to tell you how carp fishing has changed my life, and changed me as a person, I didn't want to cloud that picture with what many will perceive as a political agenda. It never started out that way, all Keith and I ever wanted to do was raise awareness about the dangers that our carp and carp fishing were facing. And for the record, because some people think they know what they are talking about, it was never about the size of the fish or 'my fish are better than yours'. It was purely about protecting that which so many of us proclaim to love. For four years, from 2000, I was swamped with all the work, but as much as it affected my life, I will always believe it was the right and proper thing to do. You may well remember when I was talking about Pit 5 at Farnborough, when all those marvellous old Leney's died because of some ones blissful ignorance, well it was then that I wanted to do something, but who would take any notice of me? It wasn't until I had been writing in the magazines for some time, that I felt I could do something about it. However, after kicking numerous doors down at Government level, it became very obvious that I was not the person to walk through them, and talk to those on the other side. It was at this point, that Ruth Lockwood entered the arena. She could see

Ruth and Mike have taken angling further than anyone believed possible

that I was struggling, and talked me into letting her get involved. I may well have started this thing off, but it is Ruth that has taken it to where we are today. She, along with Mike Heylin, have voluntarily taken angling further than anyone ever imagined possible. I, for one, shall be eternally grateful to them, as should the rest of the angling community. Carp fishing is now an infinitely safer place, not only for the carp, but for the carp anglers of the future.

After the capture of Charlie's Mate, I really didn't know what to do with myself. Having thrown everything at the quest, it left me wondering what I wanted from my fishing. After all,

Time for some social fishing

that one capture was the culmination of a lifetimes dream. I thought hard for a while, and as always, I came to the same conclusion...Fun, and lots of it! With nothing to go at for the immediate future, I spent some time at the North Lake at Yateley, just getting my head back into gear. Not only was the fishing fantastic, there was also plenty of time to do some social fishing. Being in the company of Mick Barnes, Ian Russel and Barry Hearn (yes, he is Terry's daddy) was always guaranteed to get my feet firmly back on the ground. Then, of course, there was Keith. He even managed to change jobs whilst I was spending time at Yateley, which meant that the weekend warrior could do a little angling in the week. The world had got itself in an awful mess, because we had had so little time to put things straight. A few glasses of wine and once again all was well, we even managed to catch some carp. Eventually, I decided that I wanted to fish the syndicate lake that I had fished with Shorty, on a full ticket for the summer. Much as I loved the place and most of the anglers there, I personally found the fishing was rather boring. Basically, the further

you cast and the more bait you put in, the more you caught. There was little chance of varying my tactics. That said, I did catch some huge fish up to 41.10, but once again I started to double up on the fish, I don't believe there are the numbers of fish in the lake that people think there are. To that end, I have now decided that I won't be fishing there again. Although the following year, I did have one final fling for the TV cameras, but we will get to that in a while. The Estate Lake in

My greatest friend

Northampton was high on my list of waters to visit. Having fished it a couple of years before, I was keen to see if I could catch a couple of the bigger fish that I had spotted. Unbelievably, on the first night, I landed probably the biggest in the lake; at 37.02, and totally unknown, she represented all that is good in carp fishing. It was great to be catching the odd bigger fish, but even the smaller ones gave me so much satisfaction. Landing carp that have never seen the bank before, gives me such a massive high. It is somewhere I will return, but I don't wish to achieve all I want from there too soon, it is far too special a place to turn my back on it just yet! I returned to Sandhurst in the winter, and enjoyed fishing the place immensely; it was great to see how the carp in there had thrived. The maggot fishing 'thing' was all a bit fiddly and smelly for my liking, but it was good to revisit the place that reinvigorated my carp fishing so many years before. And then of course, as it always does, my life took another new direction.

I was approached by Oval Films to do some carp fishing programmes that would be aired on the internet, Onlinefishing.tv to be exact. And yet again, I threw myself at that with all the enthusiasm I could muster. The pressure a camera puts you under is quite frightening, to be honest, but David Hatter and John Dunford have hopefully got the best out of me. They have been great fun to work with, and I can only hope that you enjoy the end result. My return to Shorty's syndicate lake provided the most amazing action I had ever experienced. The plan was to cover short session angling, and to that end, I fished three consecutive days, from five in the morning until midday. In all, I landed ten carp, with the biggest two being over forty pounds. With every take on film, it really is a unique bit of footage. It is so

The unknown... The biggest buzz of all!

much better to be lucky than good! There was also the small matter of writing this book which, at times, has nearly driven me to tears. Not so much out of frustration, but of having to recount some dire times. It is those incredible lows that have made the good times so good. I have always striven to ensure that carp fishing is just part of my life, but there can be little doubt that, at times, it has all but taken over it. I also work within the carp fishing industry, and much of what I do

The TV work has been great fun

revolves around writing. I have recently returned to where that all started for me, Catchmore Carp was the title of the DHP publication then, but now I am writing for both their titles on a monthly basis. I actually enjoy that side of things, and get a tremendous satisfaction from doing it. I also consult for Mainline, the bait company that I have been using exclusively for fifteen years now, and for Fox. The latter being the place I always wanted to be. There is a tremendous sense of achievement when you see products that you have had a big hand in developing, then being used to such great success by anglers on the bank. All in all, I couldn't be happier with life at the moment, and I still have to pinch myself on a daily basis when I think of what I do.

But what of the future? As much as I have spoken about Lynn, you have only read a tiny part of her battle, and unfortunately, that still continues. Indeed, unbeknown to me, she had delayed an operation so that I could complete this book. My wife has given me more strength than she will ever know, and without her, none of the things I have achieved would have been so special. When it comes to the fishing, I have never been too bothered about catching the biggest fish, as long as my chosen targets are something that I want to catch, then I am happy. In saying that though, next year I will be fishing for a carp that will, if I am lucky enough to catch it, be a

personal best. I suspect that the main thing about chasing it, will be the fun I will have along the way. That will always be my primary motivation to go fishing, because I cannot for the life of me, think of any other reason to go. For now, I am just content with coming to the end of this book, I can only hope that you have enjoyed reading about my crazy life, and the role carp fishing has played in it. At which point, I am now going to reach for a fine glass of Nuits St George, dim the lights and put my feet up, until it is time to start all over again...and I just can't wait!